The French Encounter with Africans

THE
French Encounter with Africans

White Response to Blacks, 1530–1880

William B. Cohen

Foreword by James D. Le Sueur

INDIANA
University Press
Bloomington and Indianapolis

This book is a publication of

Indiana University Press
601 North Morton Street
Bloomington, Indiana 47404-3797 USA

http://iupress.indiana.edu

Telephone orders 800-842-6796
Fax orders 812-855-7931
Orders by e-mail iuporder@indiana.edu

First paperback edition 2003
© 1980 by William B. Cohen
Foreword by James D. Le Sueur © 2003
by Indiana University Press
All rights reserved

The paper used in this publication meets the minimum
requirements of American National Standard for Information
Sciences—Permanence of Paper for Printed Library Materials,
ANSI Z39.48-1984.

Manufactured in the United States of America

Library of Congress Cataloging-in-Publication Data

Cohen, William B. 1941–
The French encounter with Africans.
Includes bibliographical references and index.
1. France—Colonies—Africa—History. 2. Africa—Colonization.
3. Africa—History—To 1844. 4. Africa—Race relations.
5. France—Race relations. I. Title.
DT 33.3.C63   325'.334'096   79-84260
ISBN 0-253-34922-2
ISBN 0-253-21650-8 (pbk.)

2 3 4 5 6 08 07 06 05 04 03

For Leslie and Natalie

Les peuples sont inintelligibles les uns pour les autres.

STENDHAL,
Promenades dans Rome

CONTENTS

Foreword

William B. Cohen was thirty-nine years old and in his thirteenth year of teaching French history at Indiana University–Bloomington when he published his groundbreaking, now classic book, *The French Encounter with Africans: White Response to Blacks, 1530–1880* (Indiana University Press, 1980). Along with his first book, *Rulers of Empire: The French Colonial Service in Africa* (1971), *The French Encounter with Africans* clearly established Cohen's reputation as one of the world's leading historians of modern France and European colonialism. However, his prescient understanding of intricate historical connections and his ability to call into question a fundamental assumption about France remained so far ahead of its day that it took nearly two decades for the fields of French and European colonial history to catch up to him. Published at a time when few American historians invested their time in colonial history because it seemed to be relegated to the very margins of history itself, *The French Encounter with Africans* represented a solid break from the then dominant themes of French history and offered a serious and sustained critique of one of the biggest myths about modern France—that it was innocent of racism, unlike many of its European counterparts and unlike the United States, with its long and established tradition of racist ideology. The fact that Cohen took to task the notion of French exceptionalism with regard to the race (and even the slave) question already placed him at odds with many of his colleagues in the United States and France, who tended to embrace (if not find cause for celebration in) the claim that France

had *not* been deformed by the unsightly history of racism and
slavery with which other nations were all too familiar. In addition,
Cohen pulled his seemingly irreverent critique of modern France
from the deepest sources of intellectual history and made few
attempts to soften his scrutiny. As a result, Cohen called into question keepers of the Enlightenment, favored actors and historical
personae of the Revolution, and even celebrated liberals such as
Alexis de Tocqueville—not to mention intellectuals such as the
Marquis de Condorcet, Abbé Henri Grégoire, and, of course,
Arthur de Gobineau.

In many regards, therefore, *The French Encounter with Africans*—
published here in paperback for the first time—helped usher in a
new generation of researchers and with them new lines of inquiry.
Given its importance and the questions about France and empire
that it generated, it is hardly surprising that Cohen's iconoclastic
book would draw the attention of French observers—especially
those who resisted its principal thesis about racism in France. In
fact, the book's immediate publication in French by Gallimard as
Français et africains: les noirs dans le regard des blancs, 1530–1880
(1981), a rare feat for an American historian, caused an unprecedented storm when it was reviewed in *Le Monde* by the well-known
French historian and public intellectual Emmanuel Todd. Todd
offered such an offensive and violent attack against the book that it
would later be presented as evidence of the derisiveness of the
French–American divide and the French reluctance to engage fully
with the race question.[1] According to Todd, Cohen's obsession with
historical muckraking knew no historical or intellectual bounds
and was so filled with contempt toward anything French as to be
useless to readers. What the book represented, in Todd's words, was
"flagrant historical delirium, suffering simultaneously from a con-
ceptual simplicity and a factual amnesia."[2] Of course, the book is
anything but that, and I also take Todd's reaction to it as evidence
of how deeply Cohen's book cut into the myth of the anti-racist
nation.

But we must remember that Cohen's book appeared in the early
1980s when historians of France were only beginning to confront
the colonial question, just as another dominant myth about France
was falling apart. Robert O. Paxton and others focused on the
French government's actions during the German Occupation, and

examinations of the Vichy regime revealed that the myth of Marshal Philippe Pétain as a shield from Nazi abuses could not be sustained; in fact, archival evidence showed that the Vichy government had used the Occupation to further its agenda of national renewal. I mention the effect that Paxton and his colleagues had on the field of French history in the 1970s and 1980s because I believe that there is a remarkable similarity of intent between Paxton's central theme, as presented in his important book *Vichy France: Old Guard and New Order, 1940–1944* (1972), and Cohen's, as articulated in *The French Encounter with Africans.* Both books, classics in their own right, upset cherished and well-protected myths about France. Just as Paxton insisted that the Vichy government's actions were often not imposed from without by the Nazis but came from within the deeply conservative regime out of a desire to counter the reforms and the secularism of French republicanism, so, too, did Cohen insist that the race question and then later the civilizing mission in France were conditioned by a fundamental and internal "impulse to inequality," an impulse that was eventually embraced by the Third Republic during the so-called scramble for Africa at the end of the nineteenth century. In other words, what I find so appealing about Cohen's work, and why I believe that this new edition is especially timely, is that it helps readers understand that France, like other nations, has a deeply troubled past, especially when it comes to the history of racism and slavery.

There are other reasons why this book resonates so well today. Cohen clearly anticipated the field, and he used France's rich intellectual and cultural history to tell his story from within the French intellectual world itself. As a result, Cohen traced the history of the "impulse to inequality" to the earlier representations of Africans from ancient times to the Third Republic. He linked this theme to the establishment of slave societies in the Antilles and elsewhere in the sixteenth and seventeenth centuries. He presented evidence taken from the writings and letters of even the most revered philosophes of the Enlightenment as proof of the disdain that French writers held toward African blacks. He explained how race relations varied in separate cultural contexts—metropolitan France, the West Indies, and Senegal—in order to illustrate variations in the white–black dynamics. He linked the French slavery debates to the issues of labor and colonialism and insisted that the debate over the abolition of slavery was rarely considered without other motives such as competition and wider imperial concerns. He connected the issue of race to the rise of European imperialism broadly conceived and also made efforts to separate discussions of racism and slavery in his reconsideration of the anti-slavery movement of the nineteenth century. He offered one of the best and earliest analyses of the history of scientific racism in France and its links to the growth of the biological sciences.[3] He followed several aspects of the nineteenth-century race toward empire, and he closed the book with a brief analysis of the way in which the impulse toward inequality and specifically the notions of black inferiority established patterns for prejudice and discrimination that continue to weigh heavily on contemporary France. In short, what Cohen concluded, and where his research continued to point up to his untimely death in November 2002, was that the "criteria by which blacks were averred to be inferior" changed from century to century and from context to context and that racism itself "was not a constant in French reactions to the African, but prejudice was. Racism was but a variant of the essential traditional French consensus on black inferiority" (292).

To be sure, many of the themes Cohen addressed in *The French Encounter with Africans* have continued to resurface in the writings of other prominent historians. One of those closest to Cohen's thinking is Tzvetan Todorov, especially Todorov's *On Human Diversity: Nationalism, Racism, and Exoticism in French Thought* (1993; *Nous et les autres: la réflexion française sur la diversité humaine,* 1989). In this book, Todorov advances many of the questions written about at length by Cohen. Today, there is intense interest in the issues raised by Cohen, and many of our most prominent historians continue to share his curiosity about the intersections of the questions of race and colonialism sounded out in this monumental work. There is no question that readers interested in the issues of race and colonialism (many of whom may be discovering the work of William Cohen here for the first time), as well as the history of slavery in Africa, the Caribbean, and America, will be amazed by the breadth, passion, and depth of the humanitarian mind at work here. It is certain that Cohen believed, and I say this as a friend and colleague, that his writing could help illuminate the dominant features of race relations and therefore encourage a broader and more humane discussion of racism in modern France. However, it is also clear that Cohen was intent on improving race relations and believed that only by acquiring the knowledge and arguments necessary to help put myths to rest could France move on to solve the nagging and crucial issues left to it in the postcolonial metropolitan world.

JAMES D. LE SUEUR
UNIVERSITY OF NEBRASKA–LINCOLN

Notes

1. See Nancy L. Green, "*Le Melting-Pot:* Made in America, Produced in France," *Journal of American History* 86, no. 3: 1205.
2. Emmanuel Todd, "Les Français sont-ils racistes?" *Le Monde* (February 19, 1982): 16.
3. See also George W. Stocking's powerful analysis of the history of scientific racism in *Race, Culture, and Evolution: Essays in the History of Anthropology* (New York: Free Press, 1968).

Preface

France was a major participant in the European expansion overseas. Frenchmen's experiences and conceptions of black peoples helped form the image of the African in Western culture. This study of the French response to Africans in the three-and-a-half centuries following earliest contact in the 1530s seeks to describe and explain the origin and development of the image.

Many of the French experiences paralleled those of other nations that also encountered foreign peoples during the course of empire-building and enslavement. While this is the history of the French record, it is also intended as a contribution to the broader literature on race relations. A number of assumptions presented in that literature are tested for France.

A general feeling of despair among white American intellectuals about the history of white-black relations in the United States led to a widespread consensus about the uniqueness of Anglo-Saxon behavior toward blacks. True, a growing scholarship, most of it dealing with Iberian interaction with blacks, discounted that view, but that work tended to be oriented to specific regions and periods, and might still be dismissed as unrepresentative or exceptional.

Frenchmen have traditionally asserted that their countrymen, unlike their neighbors and the white inhabitants of the United States, have upheld the principles of racial equality overseas and at home. This view is given voice in the standard three-volume history of French colonialism that declares,

"Frenchmen have never adopted the racial doctrines affirming the superiority of whites over men of color."[1] Official spokesmen for the French government have also pointed with great pride to what they perceive as a record of unparalleled racial egalitarianism. At the significant conference of French colonial officials held at Brazzaville in 1944, the commissioner of colonies, surveying the French overseas experience, declared, "By instinct as well as reason Frenchmen shun racial discrimination." Twenty years later the French representative in the United Nations Security Council made a similar claim: "There are few traditions which are so much a part of the history of my country as the concept of equality between the races."[2]

American observers have usually accepted this view. Black G.I.s stationed in France after both world wars were met with far greater acceptance than prevailed at home. Seen as further evidence of color blindness was the warm welcome the French reserved for black entertainers and intellectuals—many of them American—in the 1920s and 1930s. Such experiences seemed to confirm the French view of themselves as a people imbued historically with a strong sense of racial justice, and to whom the doctrines of racial inequality were unknown.

The present work reveals, however, that these instances of racial egalitarianism were exceptional, explainable by particular circumstances. To my surprise, in examining the historical record I found that in regard to blacks the tradition of racial inequality was dominant in French history. While claiming that their race relations have been unique, Frenchmen, in their encounters with blacks, have conformed to patterns similar to those common among Iberians and Anglo-Saxons. On second thought, of course, that should not have been so surprising. By the sixteenth century, when contacts with Africa first occurred, French civilization shared many traits with the cultures of England and the Iberian peninsula. Their populations were Christians who lived in centralizing political states and had similar material cultures. Those shared characteristics contrasted sharply with the traditions of the non-European world; hence, the ways of the Africans struck Europeans as particularly unusual.

Not all European powers developed exactly the same image, but on the whole one is struck by the similarities, rather than the differences, that marked white-black relations. Within each nation there has also been considerable continuity. Images often persist and do not readily accommodate to change. The continuity in the French response makes a study of the sources a relatively discouraging experience for the historian.

This study traces the varying reactions that Frenchmen at different times had toward Africans and considers the persistence of images and stereotypes imbedded in French culture and institutions. Both chronological and topical approaches are used. An historical approach best allows individuals, thoughts, and actions to be examined within the context of their time. Other insights borrowed from psychology, anthropology, and sociology have also proved useful. But this is primarily an historical work, asking historical questions, about the origins, development, and persistence of the tradition of inequality that the French developed toward Africans in their home continent, on the slave plantations in the West Indies and Indian Ocean, and in France proper.

While Frenchmen traveled in several parts of Africa, it was West Africa that helped shape the French reactions to the inhabitants of the continent. This was the area where France had the longest and most important relations. Later, when conquest began, West Africa played the most important role in French colonial policy toward sub-Saharan Africa.

In their contact with Africa, even with only the western part, Frenchmen encountered a variety of peoples differing in their physical appearances and in religious, social, and political mores. While at times the French speculated about ethnic differences among Africans, most Frenchmen were struck by Africans' black skin color, by their heathenism, and by their social mores and institutions, which the French perceived as very different from those of Europe. All blacks were seen as having more in common than separating them. Europeans created the image of the "black man," who was thought to have certain inherent characteristics. In this book, when reference is made to the "African" or to the "black man," the term is employed in the context in which it was used. I do not believe that there was such a man; he was an abstraction, a part of the mythology surrounding the peoples of the African continent.

The study ends in 1880. The date is chosen deliberately to

coincide with the eve of French expansion in black Africa, and thus to clarify the extent to which the image developed independently of the conquest itself. As two recent books on the image of Africa in French fiction testify, however, that image continued relatively unchanged through the colonial era.[3]

This examination of the French image investigates only the written record of French reactions to Africa. It should be pointed out that until the nineteenth century the majority of Frenchmen were illiterate. Maybe there was an unwritten subculture at variance with the written tradition. That is possible, but seems unlikely. The written records reveal such a consensus of views about Africans that it would be surprising to discover a subculture that had had no effects on the written tradition. In fact, investigations of popular culture, as expressed in ballads and folklore, have revealed a general agreement with the written culture.

The written sources examined were generally limited to those expressive of high culture. Thus, for the nineteenth century, a notable lacuna has been the daily and popular press. A recent study of this medium, however, shows that, with some delays, the popular press picked up the themes elaborated by scientific groups, social theorists, or public officials.[4]

While this study is devoted to the interaction of Frenchmen and blacks, it is conceptually dependent upon the vast literature that has appeared in the last few years on white-black interaction. Not all the books can be acknowledged here, but the ones that have played a seminal role in this work need to be mentioned.

The Anglo-Saxon image of blacks has been masterfully developed in three books: Philip Curtin's study of the British view of Africa, *The Image of Africa: British Ideas and Action, 1780–1850* (Madison, Wisconsin, 1964) and, on the American view, the definitive works by Winthrop D. Jordan, *White Over Black: American Attitudes Toward the Negro, 1550–1812* (Baltimore, 1969), and George M. Fredrickson, *The Black Image in the White Mind: The Debate on Afro-American Character and Destiny, 1817–1914* (New York, 1971). Slavery has played an important role in the Euro-African relationship, and no one can afford to ignore the magisterial volumes by David Brion Davis, *The Problem of Slavery in Western Culture* (Ithaca, N.Y.,

1966), and *The Problem of Slavery in the Age of Revolution, 1770–1823* (Ithaca, N.Y., 1975).

Specific to the French experience, a number of works on the image of Africans in literature were helpful: Roger Mercier, *L'Afrique noire dans la littérature française* (Dakar, 1961); Léon Fanoudh-Siefer, *Le mythe du nègre et de l'Afrique noire dans la littérature française (de 1800 à la 2ᵉ guerre mondiale)* (Paris, 1968); and Léon-François Hoffmann, *Le nègre romantique* (Paris, 1973). The eighteenth-century French attitude toward blacks is critically examined in the general work that Michèle Duchet devotes to the Enlightenment and non-European man in her important *Anthropologie et histoire au siècle des lumières* (Paris, 1971). My chapters dealing with the eighteenth century owe much to this work. Gabriel Debien has published important works that were crucial in my examination of French slavery in the West Indies, among them, *La société coloniale au XVIIᵉ et XVIIIᵉ siècles* (Paris, 1953) and *Les esclaves aux antilles françaises (XVIIᵉ-XVIIIᵉ siècles)* (Basse Terre, Guadeloupe, 1974). Many other works were, of course, also important, and my dependence upon them is acknowledged in the text.

In the writing of this book, I incurred a debt of gratitude to many institutions and people. Grants from the following allowed time for research and writing. The National Endowment for Humanities bestowed a Younger Humanist Fellowship for the academic year 1971–72. Summer grants were provided by the Cross-Cultural Studies Committee, the West European Studies Program, and the Office of Research and Graduate Development of Indiana University. My sabbatical year 1975–76 was spent as a visiting scholar at the Hoover Institution, Stanford, California. I am grateful for the hospitality extended to me by the curators of the African Collections at Hoover, Peter Duignan and Lewis Gann.

Many individuals shared their ideas with me over the years and gave useful advice for improving the manuscript. I should like to thank my colleagues at Indiana University: Michael Berkvam, George E. Brooks, Jr., William Harris, George Juergens, and John Lombardi. Equally helpful were colleagues at other institutions: Raymond F. Betts, Kim Munholland, Thomas Cassilly, and Paule Brasseur.

I should also like to thank Thomas Grabau and Stephen

Morrison, research assistants who were particularly engaged in this project. Susan Wladaver gave the manuscript a careful reading and suggested many improvements in style and expression. Debbie Chase and Mollie Duckett typed several drafts of the manuscript with accuracy and cheer.

Finally, I want to thank my family. Habiba S. Cohen continuously offered valuable suggestions and was supportive during the many stages through which a work like this inevitably progresses. Our daughters, Natalie and Leslie, were encouraging, although they expressed the hope that their father would choose a "happier" subject the next time. This book is dedicated to them with the hope that they will reach adulthood in a world where the concerns discussed here will no longer be of burning relevance.

Introduction

In the fifteenth century, Europeans set out on an expansionist course, stretching their trade, their political power, and
even their ideas across the seas. The process generated a culture clash between European and non-European peoples. The
images formed in the course of that contact helped shape
whites' reactions to non-Europeans. Combined with a pre-
eminence of technological and, hence, military power, those
images allowed Europeans to play a significant role in shaping
the destiny of the non-European world.

France was one of the main expansionist powers. Its overseas adventures influenced the actions of other European
states, while its mental image of the encounter with non-
European peoples became an important part of the manner in
which Western culture was to regard those peoples. This was
true of the French image of blacks.

Beginning in the sixteenth century, French traders plied the
coast of West Africa, trading for ivory, gum, gold, and—to
begin with—a few slaves. When a group of Rouen merchants
founded a fort in the 1630s at the mouth of the Senegal River,
near which the town of Saint-Louis was later built, they
created the base for what was to become a more active French
involvement in West Africa. From there French traders and
administrators were later to attempt to establish a network of
trade and eventually even political control both inland and
down the coast.

Sporadic contact with Africans in the sixteenth century and

Reflect on Hull's representation of difference to understand

more continuous contact in the following century led Frenchmen to reflect on the nature of blacks. Those early observers
were struck by the Africans' physique, manners, and customs.
The differences, apparent and real, put in question the European concept of man and society, and led to formulations
about the place of the Africans in creation. Merchants, travelers, officials, and others visiting Africa tried to understand the
strange new world with which they had come into contact.
Their accounts often lacked originality: writers borrowed from
each other or fell back on classical and medieval lore about
Africa. But the images created in the first couple of centuries
were crucial to the French-black experience: they became
deeply implanted in French culture and exercised a pervasive
influence over later generations of Frenchmen.

Compared with the societies of the west coast of Africa, the
European powers enjoyed a military and economic superiority
that permitted them, from the early sixteenth century, to
enslave Africans for use in plantation colonies in the Americas.
For Europeans the slave experience paralleled early experiences in Africa and seemed to reinforce negative stereotypes
of blacks.

For the French the most significant contact between whites
and blacks occurred in the plantation colonies in the West Indies, established in the 1620s and 1630s. In 1625 a buccaneer,
Pierre Belain, sieur d'Esnambouc, captured the islet of Saint-
Christophe. He enlisted the interest of the French government
in the neighboring islands, and a decade later Guadeloupe and
Martinique became French. Inhabited by French pirates, buc-
caneers, and various other adventurers, Saint-Domingue came
under French government in 1655. These islands were initially
discovered to be valuable places for breeding cattle, then for
growing tobacco and, finally, sugar. Even before the islands
had fallen under official governmental control, French settlers
had introduced black slaves. By the 1660s it was clear that
slavery would become the dominant form of labor and the
basis for French wealth in the Caribbean. The institutions, customs, and laws that developed around black slavery in the
French West Indies confirmed the inequality between the races
that travelers to Africa and writers in France had already
proclaimed.

The eighteenth century marked a potential transitional era in the French response to Africans. The philosophes upheld the need for dispassionate observation and proclaimed the equality of man. Their doctrines of environmentalism implied cultural relativism. But the reliance of the philosophes on earlier sources and their view of Africa as a harsh and hostile environment led them to a negative appraisal of blacks. The premium on materialism that developed in the second half of the eighteenth century resulted in an emphasis on human biology as an explanation for the perceived differences in social structures and customs of various peoples. Biological racism thus developed. That view may have been stressed more strongly in France than elsewhere because of the philosophes' anticlericalism, which led them to combat some of the religious doctrines on the unity of man and the assertion of a common descent of all people from Adam and Eve. The French philosophes also addressed themselves to the issue of slavery. While opening a new chapter in the history of abolitionism, they nevertheless fell short of unambiguously advocating emancipation. Their position on abolition revealed that they shared their contemporaries' views of blacks as inferior, not quite worthy of the rights they had proclaimed as the birthright of every Frenchman.

The intellectual attitudes of an age are in part shaped by social forces, and such forces, in turn, are apt to vary from region to region. Comparative study of white-black interaction in different conditions reveals that, while prejudices were the same, the nature of race relations varied, depending on the demographic and political setting. Despite the deeply entrenched French belief in black inequality in the eighteenth century, blacks were treated better in Africa, where whites were keen to make political and commercial inroads, than in the racially rigid plantation societies of the West Indies and the Indian Ocean. As for France proper, there Frenchmen, fully dominant, neither desiring advantages from black hosts nor fearing what was regarded as a dangerous black population, revealed their feelings unbeset by social constraints. Those feelings paralleled closely the belief system underlying the doctrine of black inequality.

From Saint-Louis, French trade penetrated inland. Com-

merce in gum was particularly profitable on the right bank of
the Senegal River. In search of customers, the French followed
the river and in 1687 reached the Félu Falls, 1,000 kilometers
upstream. Down the coast, a trader, Villault de Bellefond,
reached the Gold Coast in 1666. Chartered companies such as
the Senegal Company (1634–58) and its several successors
were given a monopoly of trade in those areas. Searching for
wealth, they underwrote French expansionism. Members of
these companies took seriously the promise of wealth in the
interior spun by officials, traders, and writers. Conquest of
Africa was actively advocated by these men, who saw blacks as
fit only for domination, not as having an intrinsic right to the
land. Since Africans were viewed as lazy and inept in developing their land, their rights were declared to have passed to the
more hardy and ambitious Europeans.

Frenchmen in the nineteenth century were the heirs to
three centuries of speculation about black inequality, which by
then had become firmly crystallized. Biologists and members
of the nascent profession of anthropology gave racist ideas
seemingly greater credibility by lending them a scientific aura.
Neither travelers, missionaries, nor other Frenchmen in prolonged contact with Africans, although presenting much empirical evidence that should have shaken the claims of the scientists, were able to undermine the attraction of scientific
racism. Nineteenth-century abolitionists continued trends
begun by their predecessors; like them, they were weak in
number and divided in their convictions on the wisdon of immediate emancipation. When freedom came it was less the result of abolitionist effort than of economic developments in
France and in the West Indies that undermined the slave system. Abolitionists were seldom racists, but they did little to
rectify the tradition of inequality that had become deeply
entrenched in the French attitude toward blacks.

The expansionist ethos of the nineteenth century furthered
older ambitions for African conquest. Frenchmen viewed
black men and their continent as needing a white master to
make of Africa the rich and prosperous region that, by the
calculations of traders, officials, and publicists, it could and
should become. The imperialist dream thus coincided with and

reinforced the tradition of racial inequality. The tradition was advanced and institutionalized in scientific groups such as geographical or anthropological societies, in school texts and encyclopedias of the day, in the press, and in fiction. Such media became the channels through which opinion on blacks spread to the larger population. A consensus existed in French thought, which relegated the black to a position of inferiority.

Throughout the white-black encounter, French attitudes toward Africans were dictated not only by direct perceptions or misperceptions of blacks, but also by general attitudes toward the nature of man and society. The economic, political, and social contexts of an era and of the regions where encounters occurred established the intellectual constraints within which these ideas developed. What made the tradition of black inequality so pervasive and persistent was that it was anchored firmly within the general sociopolitical context.

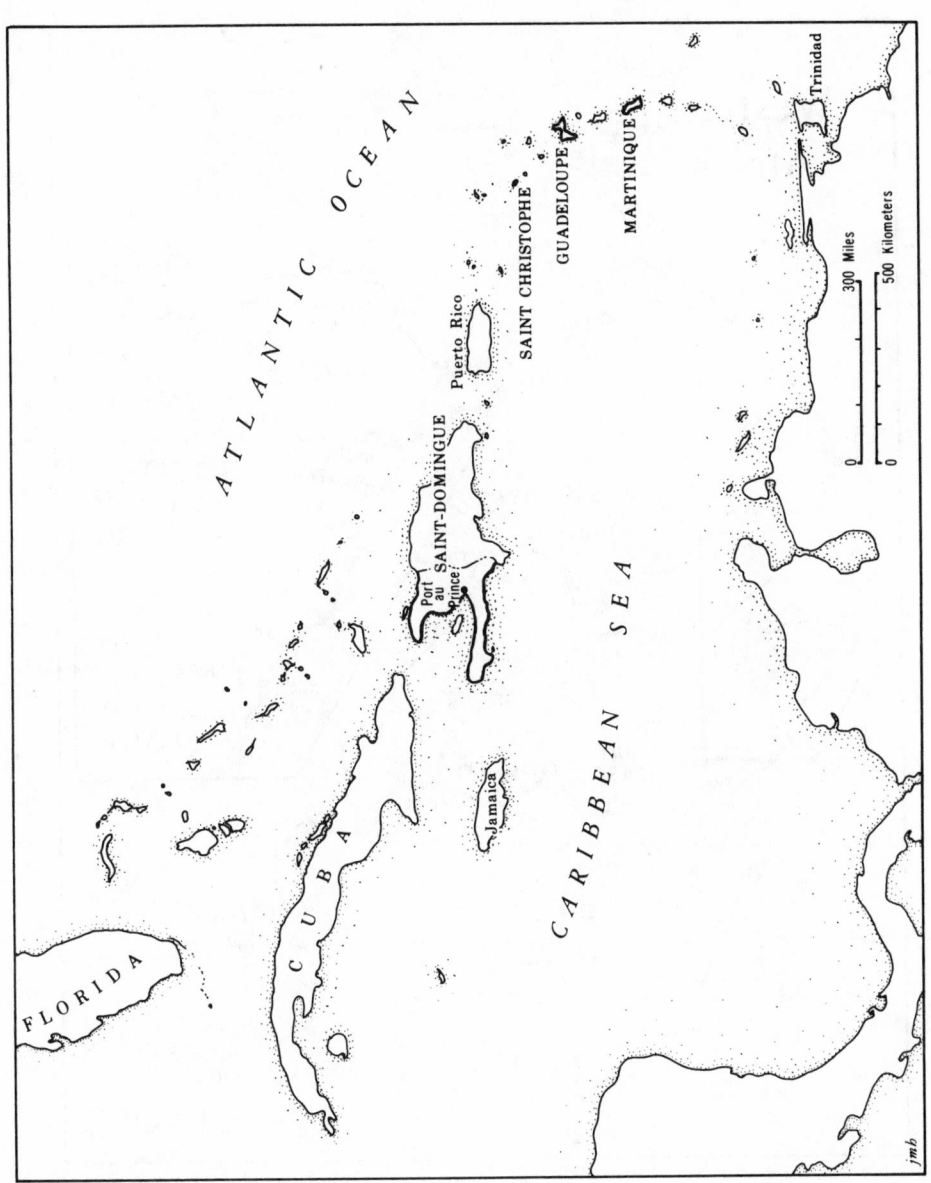

ATLANTIC OCEAN

CARIBBEAN SEA

FLORIDA

CUBA

Jamaica

SAINT-DOMINGUE

Port
au
Prince

Puerto Rico

SAINT CHRISTOPHE

GUADELOUPE

MARTINIQUE

Trinidad

300 Miles

500 Kilometers

jmb

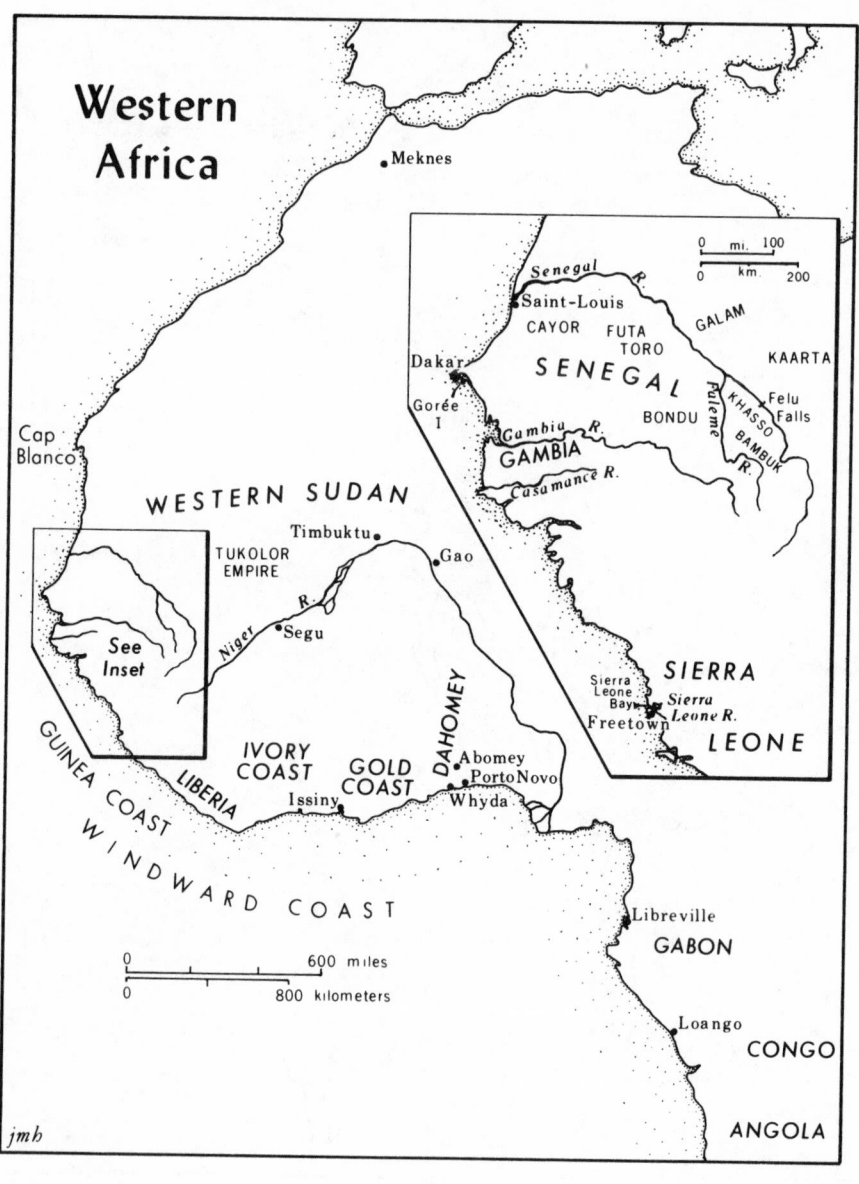

Western Africa

Meknes

Cap Blanco

WESTERN SUDAN

TUKOLOR EMPIRE

Timbuktu

Gao

See Inset

Niger R.

Segu

GUINEA COAST

LIBERIA

IVORY COAST

GOLD COAST

DAHOMEY

Abomey

Porto Novo

Whyda

Issiny

WINDWARD COAST

0   600 miles
0   800 kilometers

Libreville

GABON

Loango

CONGO

ANGOLA

jmb

Inset

0   mi.   100
0   km.   200

Senegal R.

Saint-Louis

CAYOR

FUTA TORO

GALAM

KAARTA

Dakar

SENEGAL

KHASSO

Felu Falls

Gorée I

BONDU

Pulème R.

BAMBUK

Gambia R.

GAMBIA

Casamance R.

SIERRA

Sierra Leone Bay

Sierra Leone R.

Freetown

LEONE

The French Encounter with Africans

I

The Impulse to Inequality

Africa Through the Eyes of Others

The French developed initial negative reactions toward Africa and its inhabitants long before setting foot on the continent. Their early impressions were based largely on ideas received from other cultures already in contact with blacks. First, ideas were inherited from the classical world. Although the ancient Greeks and Romans may not have revealed race prejudice in their social relations with blacks,[1] in their geographic descriptions of Africa, they developed a number of negative stereotypes about the inhabitants of what was commonly called either Libya or Ethiopia. The Greeks and Romans, who were in contact mainly with Northern Africa, may well have been affected by the tales told there of the monstrous habits of peoples further south. The ancients' climatic theories also emphasized that extreme temperatures made people act in extreme, savage ways, whereas temperate climates were a prerequisite for civilization. All of these influences, added to a vivid imagination, help explain Herodotus' description of Africans who eat locusts and snakes, share wives, and speak no human language, but rather "screech like bats." Africa, wrote Herodotus, was inhabited by wild animals and by men with "dogs' heads and those with no heads whose eyes are in their chests."[2] These fantastic descriptions were taken over uncritically by the Roman compiler Pliny.[3]

The third-century geographer Solinus was the medium through which these views of Africa were passed on to the Middle Ages. The Garamantes, Solinus wrote, "use their women in common." As described by Solinus, the Cynamolgies resembled dogs and had "long snouts," whereas others had no noses, no mouths, and still others, no tongues.[4] While Herodotus and Pliny were not known to the Middle Ages,

1

Solinus was read and copied for over a thousand years, providing the basis for most geographical compilations. Although no French translations of Solinus have survived, we know they existed in the fifteenth century.[5]

As he had corrupted Pliny, Solinus in turn was bowdlerized by medieval writers. Some of the classics had, of course, been rather well informed on Africa; thus the Ptolemaic maps indicate that the ancients had at least a knowledge of East and Central Africa as far west as the Niger River. But Ptolemaic knowledge was lost to the Middle Ages, and myths, such as those of Pliny, of a fiery area inhabited by monstrous men, were perpetuated.[6]

In the Renaissance those myths were strengthened, thanks to the revival of the classics. Pliny was rediscovered; between 1450 and 1550 forty-six editions of his *Natural History* were issued.[7] One can sense his influence on Rabelais, who declared, "Africa always produces new and monstrous things."[8]

Besides the Greek and Roman worlds, Islamic culture had an effect on early French images of blacks. Although the Koran preached racial equality, it seems to have been practiced only in the lifetime of the Prophet. The beginning of Islamic conquest and the enslavement of blacks by Moslems gave the light-skinned Arabs a sense of superiority over blacks, even if the latter were converted to Islam.[9] The Islamic image of blacks may also have been influenced by the classics, which Islam had preserved far better than had the West. An echo of classical views appears in passages such as the following: "There is no marriage among them; the child does not know his father, and they eat people. . . . As for the Zanj, they are people of black color, flat noses, kinky hair, and little understanding or intelligence."[10]

Some of the most important accounts by Arab travelers to the African interior were not known in Europe. Neither the twelfth-century accounts of El Idrissi nor those of the fourteenth-century Ibn Battutah were known in the West until several centuries later. If the Islamic image of blacks had any direct effect on the views of the French, it came probably through an early sixteenth-century Moslem traveler who won large renown. He had accompanied a mission sent by the

Moroccan sultan to Timbuktu, and, while on another mission to the Orient, he was captured by a Sicilian pirate, enslaved, and given as a present to Pope Leo X. He was converted to Christianity and in Rome was baptized Johannis Leo de Médici; posterity was to call him Leo Africanus. While in Rome he wrote his travel descriptions of Africa.

Leo's account contains detailed information about the institutions and customs of several African states. While his description of the peoples of the Sudan revealed the refinement of their manners and the sophistication of their economic and political institutions, his conclusions expressed some of the negative stereotypes then common in Islamic society in regard to blacks. Contradicting his text, he concluded, for example: "The Negroes are brutes without reason, without intelligence or knowledge. They have no notion of anything. They live like animals, without rules or laws."[11] Leo's account was widely translated and read; in 1556 it appeared in a French edition. Jean Bodin, the political theorist, was to greet this work as "pre-eminent" and as an "accurate description of all the regions and peoples of Africa."[12]

The third source of information available to the French was the travel accounts of other Europeans who had preceded them to the continent, notably the Portuguese. Beginning in the mid-fifteenth century, the Portuguese started to send ships to the African coast; before the end of that century, they had reached the Cape of Good Hope, the east coast of Africa, and India. A number of travel accounts by persons accompanying the Portuguese expeditions appeared. Some accounts matter-of-factly described the habits and material cultures of the people encountered; others were imbued with a hostility that reflected the frustration of the writers, Europeans unable to understand the people with whom they had come into contact. In general, the accounts of those who had actually been to Africa reinforced the classical and medieval images of Africa as inhabited by monsters and beastly people.

One of the earliest travelers to West Africa was the Venetian Alvise Cadamosto, serving Henry the Navigator, who in 1455 went as far south as the Casamance River, south of the Gambia. Cadamosto's account was first published in Italian in

1507; Latin and German editions appeared in 1508, and a French edition, in 1515.[13] The book became truly influential in France only after its republication in 1556 by the editor who brought the Leo Africanus account to France.[14] Cadamosto gave a generally sympathetic and fair rendering of the people he met. Shocked by some customs, he seems to have been appreciative of others. But, like so many European travelers after him, he was prone to generalize from an unhappy encounter. Finding the Serers unwilling to trade with him, he denounced them: "They are exceedingly idolatrous, have no laws, and are the cruelest of men."[15] Further south in the Gambia, he observed, "The people of the coast were so rude and savage that we were unable to have speech with them on land or to treat about anything."[16]

The French should also have been able to cull some information from their compatriots who had begun to ply the trade off the West African coast. Although the claim of some that Frenchmen had gone to Guinea in the fourteenth century seems erroneous, they certainly had reached there by the 1520s,[17] thus defying the trade monopoly that the Portuguese had attempted to establish. It appears that none of the French sea captains or traders was either sufficiently excited by the new geographic contact or sufficiently literate to give an account of his impressions. At least, no accounts have survived.

There were some blacks living in France as early as the thirteenth century, and they might have been a useful source of information. A black woman from the Sudan, Ismeria, married a man of royal lineage, Robert d'Eppes. When she died, sometime in the mid-thirteenth century, she was enshrined as a black Madonna.[18] A contemporary chronicle told of the Toulousain, Anselme d'Ysalguier, who lived on the Niger River in the city of Gao for eight years. In 1413 Anselme returned to his native city with an African wife and a beautiful and well-proportioned daughter named Martha. Martha's only white coloring—according to the chronicle—was "a small white line on her forehead and two fingers on the left hand."[19] Anselme wrote an account of his stay in Gao, which included a description of the Sudan and its inhabitants and a dictionary of their languages. Unfortunately Anselme's account was lost and thus, except for word of mouth, his experience was to have no effect on his contemporaries.[20] It is known that Francis I had among his mistresses a young black woman,[21] and that Africans were brought to France in large numbers later in the sixteenth century. In 1571 a shipowner placed some blacks on sale in Bordeaux, but they were ordered released by the Parlement, on the grounds that slavery did not exist in France.[22] Those blacks and others who had served as sailors lived in France for varying periods before returning to Africa. The Portuguese Alvarez d'Almada, visiting Senegal in 1594, noted that many "Negroes speak French well and have even been to France."[23]

None of these contacts, though, seems to have led to any particular knowledge about Africa and its people. In fact there was, as Geoffroy Atkinson has noted, a remarkable lack of interest in exotic countries during the Renaissance.[24] There was not the thirst for knowledge about non-European peoples that would, for instance, characterize the eighteenth century. Thus, despite opportunities for developing some knowledge about Africa, the medieval lore was allowed to stand. The *Cosmographie,* published by Alphonse de Saintonge in 1544, described the interior of Africa in terms echoing Pliny and Solinus:

> And inland there are people who have no heads and whose heads are in their chests while the rest is formed like a man. And further east there are those who have only one eye in the forehead. And south of the Mountains of the Moon there are others who have feet like goats' and still others with the face of a dog.[25]

Francis I's geographer, the monk André Thévet, in his *Cosmographie universelle,* published in 1575, even obliged the reader with an illustration of this creature.[26]

The tradition of classical lore did not dissipate even in the face of increasing contact with Africans in the seventeenth century. In 1648 Pierre Bergeron published what was purported to be the *Voyages fameux de Vincent Le Blanc*; this popular work had appeared in three editions by 1658 and was translated into Dutch and English. It portrayed the inhabitants of interior Africa as "peoples who are so savage that they hardly know how to speak, so dirty that they eat the intestines of animals full with manure without washing them, and so brutal that they resemble more hungry dogs than men who use reason."[27]

Africa and the Non-European World

Africa was, of course, not the only part of the world with which France came into contact in the sixteenth century. Beginning in the 1520s, Francis I sent explorers to North America; the mores of the American Indians were observed with great interest and, generally, with sympathy. Through the Portuguese, information about Asia was also available to the French. Both these areas were important sources of trade in Western Europe, and they therefore received far more attention than did Africa. Atkinson has calculated that of roughly 250 geographic works published in France between 1480 and 1609, only 5 dealt with sub-Saharan Africa.[28] In the first half of the seventeenth century, of 341 books devoted to extra-European areas, only 16 were devoted to the coast and interior of black Africa; after 1650, 22 books out of 334 were on that subject.[29] Of the 1,704 books in the library of Guy Allard, a provincial man of learning, in 1676, 121, or 7 percent, dealt with geography; among these 89 dealt with Islam, 17 with the New World, 11 with Asia, and only 4 with the coast of Africa.[30] This proportion reflected rather well the share that Africa was to occupy in the publishing industry from the sixteenth through the eighteenth centuries. (Books on geography published in France during that period are divided, by region, as indicated in Table 1.) The French lack of interest in Africa, in contrast to other "exotic" areas, is striking. Envoys from African royalty to Paris were rarely mentioned in contemporary chronicles. If some publicity was given to the arrival in France and the conversion to Catholicism in 1688 of Aniaba (a young man from Issiny in the Ivory Coast who pretended to be an African prince), it pales in comparison with the enthusiastic French reception of the Siamese ambassador three years earlier.[31] In general, other exotic areas were treated with greater interest and sympathy than was Africa.

TABLE 1

Books on Geography Published in France, 1500–1800

Continent	16th Century Number	%	17th Century Number	%	18th Century Number	%	Total Number	%
America	119	26	218	14	458	13	795	14
Africa	37	8	127	8	241	6	405	7
Asia	107	23	428	27	457	13	992	18
Europe	120	28	554	35	1884	53	2558	46
Pacific	—	—	32	2	76	2	108	2
General	73	16	207	13	424	12	704	13
Total	456	100	1,566	100	3,540	100	5,562	100

SOURCE: Jean Meyer, *Les Européens et les autres de Cortès à Washington* (Paris, 1975), p. 6.

An investigation of sixteenth- and seventeenth-century French writings on North Africa found at least three hundred geography and history books, travel accounts, and novels. The proximity of the area, the close trade and political relations—sometimes punctuated by wars—explain the high French interest in the region. The image was ambiguous. North Africans were seen as having refined manners and sophisticated learning, living in a zone depicted by some as paradisaical. At the same time, however, and often by the same author, they would be castigated as uncommonly cruel, treacherous, and sexually depraved. The hostility that did exist was tempered by doses of enthusiasm arising from the French alliance with the Turks and their economic interests in the area.[32] No such influences tempered French attitudes toward black Africa.

With regard to North American Indians, French opinion seems to have been informed by contemporary travel accounts. Indians were examined with curiosity as peoples who had been unknown to the ancients. They came from a new world, which perhaps had not known original sin. But Africa had been the subject of the writings of the ancients and of some medieval texts. In the sixteenth century, thinkers still relied on authority and tried to understand the world, not so much by observation as by an assiduous study of the knowledge imparted by the ancients. Although neither Africans nor American Indians were Christians, their paganism was viewed differently. American Indians lived across the seas, in a world unknown to Europe, a world that had not had the opportunity of receiving the gospel. The Indians were, like the ancients who lived before the birth of Christ, capable of wisdom and virtue; their paganism was no fault of their own. Indeed, it was quite common for missionaries in North America to associate Indians with the ancients.[33]

Additionally, an even older tradition was used in projecting the European imagination onto the Americas, especially with regard to Brazil. The New World was thought to be the location of either the Elysian Fields, described by Homer, or the Fortunate Isles of Hesiod. There people still lived in the innocence that Adam and Eve had known before the fall.[34]

Although, in the eyes of the French, non-European peoples shared several attributes, especially lack of the Christian faith, they were not seen as co-equal. Symbolic of this view is a sixteenth-century painting in the Church of Saint-Jacques in Dieppe that depicts Indians from Asia and North America and blacks from Africa. The first two peoples are shown fully dressed; the Africans are represented as naked. In the background behind the Africans appears a snake curled around a tree. Africans were thus perceived as closer to a life of lust and to Satan.[35]

Although Asians, Indians, and black Africans shared a non-white skin, the French preferred certain races over others. American Indians had bronze skin that appealed to French aesthetic tastes; in 1615, for instance, the missionary Father Yves d'Evreau compared them to Greek gods.[36] Often the coloring of the Indian was not even noted, and the same was true of the Chinese. Only after the mid-eighteenth century do travel accounts indicate the supposed yellow coloring of the Chinese. In the seventeenth century a Frenchwoman in Paris was able to pass herself off as Chinese; no one remarked on her lack of Chinese racial features. But the blacks' physiognomy struck the French immediately. In 1684, when François Bernier published the earliest racial classification, he included the American Indian in the same group as whites, but he classified blacks as clearly distinct.[37]

The Causes of Blackness

The Africans' skin color struck Europeans as unusual, and they tried to explain how they had become black. The royal geographer Thévet thought that Africans owed their color to the heat that had dissipated "the most subtle elements," leaving only "the earthly parts that retain the color and consistency of the earth."[38] In Neoplatonic thought, which was still influential in the sixteenth century, identity with the earth and distance from the heavens were signs of remoteness from God and perfection, and were therefore confirmation of baseness and depravity.

The classics had ascribed the Africans' color to the heat of the sun. The sun's ability to darken was seen as immediate. Thus in the Middle Ages one reason seamen purportedly were hard to recruit for voyages southward toward the Equator was fear that they might turn black under the sun's rays.[39] Differences in skin colors were attributed to differences in climate.[40] If the sun were the cause of the Africans' color, why was it that not all peoples living at the Equator—for instance, those in South America—were black? The color difference thus was further attributed to the soil[41] and to other influences unique to Africa: "They go naked and are involved in hard work during the greatest heat; they eat coarse food that makes their skin rough. . . . Apparently the air they breathe and the water they drink contains iron and acid particles."[42]

More intricate explanations were also presented. The Jesuit missionary Lafitau argued in the eighteenth century that African women painted their bodies with black paint and thus exerted a prenatal influence on the color of their offspring.[43] While the Africans' black color immediately stirred the interest of French observers, their body shapes and physical features remained for the most part unobserved. When those features were mentioned, Africans were perceived to have flat noses and wide lips, even though, of course, many of the Africans whom Frenchmen encountered did not have such physical features. To explain the causes for the distinctly "negroid" features of Africans, Europeans usually pointed to direct environmental forces. Some of the missionaries who met blacks in the Antilles, where enslavement had just begun, maintained that African children were born with neither flattened noses nor wide lips; these were produced, they asserted, by parents who, thinking such forms shapely, kneaded them with their hands. Another common explanation was that Africans had flat noses because as children, tied to their mothers' backs, they were bounced against the women who were beating the millet in a movement that "breaks the children's noses and makes all their noses flat and enlarges their nostrils."[44]

All this interest in the causes of the blacks' physique reveals a strong ethnocentric conviction that blackness indicated an anomaly of man, nature, or God that needed explanation. As Léon Hoffmann remarked, Europeans were never concerned about their own skin color, which they presumably accepted as the norm.[45]

Environmental explanations, especially in regard to color, left a number of questions unanswered. Father Labat, a missionary in the West Indies in the late seventeenth century and compiler of accounts of travel to West Africa, put it best when he denied that the Africans' color was caused by climate, for

> if that were so, all the people who would live with them or at least their children who were born there would get the same color; and equally as a result the Negroes who were transported to the countries furthest away from the sun, more temperate or colder, should change color. But no such thing occurs, the experience of several centuries shows that.[46]

An alternative explanation that took care of this objection claimed that some inherent force created the physical differences between Europeans and Africans. The Hamitic myth that had developed among the Hebrews was readily adopted as an explanation for the blackness of Africans.[47] Writing in the 1670s, the Frenchman Chambonneau, who had served in Senegal as a company official for many years, disparaged the climatic explanation for the differences between the races. Sharing the same climate, the peoples living on either side of the Senegal River nevertheless had different skin colors; those on the right bank, the Maures, were white, while those on the

left bank were black. Chambonneau wrote that the cause for
the Africans' blackness was an inherent force, for they were
descended "from the line of Ham, cursed by his father [and
so] they have been distinguished from other men in eternity as
a sign of the curse."[48] The Hamitic myth relegated blacks to
the lowest order of humanity. The three main social orders of
medieval society and their permanence had also been justified
by an attribution to Noah's sons; thus Japheth was seen as the
father of the nobles, Shem as that of the clerks, and Ham as
that of the serfs.[49] It is worth wondering whether the ready
attribution of the epithet "Sons of Ham" to blacks did not
reflect the notion that it was proper for blacks to serve—to be
to the white man what the serf had been to the other medieval
social orders.[50] Some also thought that Africans were descended from Cain, another cursed biblical figure; God's dis-
pleasure with Cain was manifested by the black coloring of all
his descendants and by their being deprived of the true religion.[51] Both these religious myths were rejected by Father
Labat. He thought of the Canaanites as Ham's descendants and
correctly pointed out that the Bible had nowhere mentioned
them as black. Moreover, the Cain myth raised serious
theological issues, for had not all mankind except Noah and
his family been obliterated by the flood?[52]

There developed a more secular explanation, which took
into account the arguments advanced by those who saw either
environment or some inherent force as determining the Africans' physique. A paper given at the French Royal Academy of
Sciences in 1702 suggested that Africans acquired their color
as a result of exposure to the sun's rays, but that, at the same
time, they had a propensity to change color. Africans had a
special skin layer receptive to sun; they were born white with
the exception of black spots on the tip of the penis and the
fingernails, spots that spread as a result of exposure to the
heat.[53] A traveler to the west coast of Africa agreed that African children were born white; they turned black, not as a result of the sun, he argued, but because of internal "tempera-
ment."[54]

On a theoretical level, the environmental explanation
affirmed the intrinsic equality of all races, presenting physical

differences only as evidence of accidental environmental factors. But from the view that some inherent force made Africans black, it was only a step to attributing their coloring to a separate creation. The idea that all races were descended from the same original pair and that differences were due to environmental forces (such as the sun or knocking against a mother's back) is known as monogenism; the belief in the separate origin of races and their lack of affinity to each other is known as polygenism. Though not influential until the nineteenth century, polygenism had a number of supporters well before then.

Braving the resolutely monogenist position of the Church, based on the Genesis account of human creation, were such intellects as William of Conches, Leonardo da Vinci, and Giordano Bruno.[55] One of the earliest French thinkers to have embraced polygenism was Isaac La Peyrère, who in 1655 published *Prae-Adamitae*. La Peyrère saw the differences between whites and blacks as so fundamental that he could not think of them as descended from the same original pair of humans. Rather, he believed that whites were descended from Adam but that the other races had a separate, pre-Adamic origin. La Peyrère was imprisoned for his heretical views; in the end he recanted and presumably died a good Christian, having declared, "A Catholic who understands the need to follow the common opinion held by the holy fathers avoids the peril of straying."[56]

Despite La Peyrère's unhappy experience with ecclesiastical authorities, others continued to advance similar speculations. François Bernier anonymously published an article in the *Journal des savans* in 1684 in which he proclaimed his conviction that Africans belonged to a separate species because of the following considerations:

> If a black African pair be transported to a cold country, their children are just as black, and so are all descendants until they come to marry with white women. The cause must be sought for in the peculiar texture of their bodies, or in the seed, or in the blood.[57]

A few years later, the hero of a novel claimed to have dissected a black and found under the epidermis "a very thin delicate membrane," which presumably was the cause for the darker coloring. As the author slyly put it, he

> was going to draw consequences that would have tended to no less than the intire [*sic*] subversion of the system of the sacred author. . . . But I was silenced by being told that there were many things, which it was the will of Heaven we should admire, but we are forbid to delve into.[58]

The influential *Journal des savans* concluded in 1725 that examinations of the texture of the blacks' skin by the Dutchman Leeuwenhoek and the Italian Malpighi might mean "that the blacks are men essentially different"; it added cautiously, "at least in skin."[59]

The myths regarding descent from Ham and Cain and the doctrine of polygenism established for blacks a separate destiny from whites—an innate inequality. On a theoretical level, environmental theories, which were the dominant modes of explanation, were egalitarian; in practice they were not. Being black was definitely less desirable than being white. The climatic theory posited people who were originally white and who turned black only as a result of exposure to extreme forms of temperature; in varying degrees it was thought that this transformation was a form of degeneration, implying a departure from the norm.

All theories thus shared the assumption that there was something special in the creation of Africans that set them apart from white people. This special, separate creation denoted some form of disadvantage to Africans, a trait of inferiority.

The Meaning of Blackness

The Africans' color drew much attention because of the shock that Europeans experienced in seeing people of dark skin. In Europe the color black denoted evil and depravity and, in an age that believed in symbols, some meaning was attached to the fact that some humans were black. It has been argued that negative feelings for the color black are a primeval human impulse, created by the aversion that every child is taught toward its bowel movements and its fears of the dark at night.[60] But Western cultures have been particularly rich in assigning negative values to the color black.

In Indo-European languages black seems to have had consistently negative connotations. Thus in Sanskrit, white symbolizes Brahmans, the highest class, and black typifies outcasts.[61] In Greek black is associated with dirt in both the physical and the moral sense; it also connotes sinister intent.[62] The Romans did not add any special significance to the Greek formulation; black symbolized death and filth in contrast to white, which epitomized life and purity.[63] Seeking clues to and symbols of the deeper meanings of nature, churchmen saw in the color black a symbol of sinfulness and divine curse. One of the oldest and most widespread manuscript accounts of the early church fathers was written by a fifth-century monk, John Cassian. Dealing with the problem of temptation, the account depicted a hermit being tormented by the devil in the guise of "a Negro woman ill-smelling and ugly."[64] In the Christian tradition blackness has been considered ugly and revolting; the story is told of Saint Benedict of Palermo, who, afraid of temptation by women, prayed to God that he might be made ugly. God obliged and turned him black, thus transforming him into Saint Benedict the Moor.[65] The identification of blackness with evil and danger was reflected in the twelfth-century *Chanson de Roland,* which spoke of the king of Ethiopia's leading 50,000 warriors: "cursed race that is blacker than ink and that has nothing white except its teeth."[66]

Frenchmen saw the blackness of Africans as symbolic of some inner depravity, since they thought the color aesthetically unappealing. They followed a tradition rooted in the classical doctrine of *physiognomos,* which held that what was not beautiful was somehow depraved. Prolonged contacts with Africa began for the French only after the mid-seventeenth century. And it was exactly at this point that the negative image of blackness reached a climax in French literature, as a symbol for wickedness and treachery. Corneille spoke of "black actions," Racine of "black malice" and of crimes of "full blackness." Molière wrote of "black intentions" and "black character" when depicting personages as absolutely depraved and evil.[67] Blacks were depicted as the ultimate symbol of evil:

the devil. Thus, within the medieval tradition, the devil was often referred to as the "black horseman," the "great Negro."[68] Blackness was portrayed as an embodiment of evil and of the devil, as in the following travel description of Africa: "The inhabitants have nearly as black a soul as body and their bodies are as black as the color we paint our demons."[69] Black color was not only a symbol of depraved character; it was also sometimes seen as its cause. Labat, for instance, declared that, if Africans "are rogues, that is caused by their black color."[70]

The sentiments of fear and horror which Europeans felt toward blacks could sometimes be used to political advantage. When the French ambassador went to Munster in 1644 for peace negotiations, he was accompanied by 140 black servants; involved in a "protocol war" with the Spanish, the French won, for the Spanish emissaries, upon seeing the French ambassador approaching with his troop of blacks, "were horrified" and fled.[71]

Religion

If in their physical shape Africans had struck Frenchmen as being different, their religion also drew much attention. Europeans came into contact with Africans at a time when religious feeling ran especially high as a result of the controversies caused by the advent of the Reformation and the Counter-Reformation of the Catholic Church. If there was one aspect of African life that struck Europeans, it was African religion. In his guide for authors, Jules La Mesnardière, physician and court writer, reminded his readers that, when depicting different peoples, it was essential to take into account their proper characteristics, for otherwise they would not be credible; thus, Africans could not be described as "believers."[72] They were quite the opposite.

The Africans' animism piqued Europeans' interest, as perhaps their most prominent feature, next to coloring. Thévet condemned African animism in words that were to be echoed in later accounts:

> If there ever was abominable idolatry, brutish superstition and ignorance in the world, you will find it among these poor

people. . . . This people is so stupid, bestial, and blinded by folly that it accepts as divinity the first thing it encounters in the morning when it wakes up.[73]

Some failed to see that Africans had a religion. Froger, who, as a ship engineer, had visited the coast in the mid-1690s, wrote, "Most of the Negroes are without religion."[74]

The Africans' lack of the Christian faith was at first seen as due mainly to external influences. Father Alexis Saint-Lo went to West Africa in the 1630s and ascribed the Islamization of the people of Cap Vert to their victimization by "an accumulation of stories which the poor stupid Negroes take for revelation."[75] The devil was also blamed.[76]

The earliest missionaries had been generous in their assessment of Africans. Saint-Lo objected to the negative image that his contemporaries had of Africa, proclaiming in the beginning of his account, "You will see that the air is good and the Negroes are human."[77] But as missionaries continued coming to Africa and still met with no success, their impatience turned into antagonism. They became convinced that the Africans' failure to embrace Christianity reflected the Africans' sinfulness and perversity.

In the second half of the seventeenth century, while missionary activity in Africa was an obvious failure, the Jesuit order was making important headway in China. The Jesuits converted the emperor and chose to see in Confucianism a form of Christian morality. To bolster their position at home, the Jesuits tended to exaggerate the extent to which they had been successful in missionizing China. And they attributed their success to the wisdom and nobility of the Chinese people. The attributes of China were advertised in the Jesuits' *Lettres édifiantes et curieuses,* published in thirty-four volumes between 1702 and 1776, and reissued in a twenty-four-volume edition in 1789. This influential collection helped shape the positive French attitudes toward China for a century.[78]

In Africa there were many hindrances to successful missionizing that the French did not recognize. The climate, which decimated the missionaries, made any sustained activity difficult. The European practice of slaving alienated the

peoples of the African coast and must have hindered pros-
elytizing. And, of course, there was no particular reason why a
people already possessing a religion should embrace another
one. But Europeans, believing that they were in possession of
the single true religion, found African resistance to Christianity irritating.

The relative success in China led to a generally sympathetic
press by missionaries, but failure in Africa led to condemnation. If French missionaries used China as a model of Christian
virtues and piety, the missionaries to Africa used the Africans
as a symbol of what deprivation of the gospel would mean:
barbarism and savagery. Father Loyer, frustrated by his inability to make many converts, in the end blamed his failure on his
hosts. Africans, instead of restraining their passions, he declared in his account of 1714, would "foment and cultivate"
them "and thus make themselves unworthy of the sentiments
that the knowledge of the true God and of their conversion
would give them." A note of personal bitterness is revealed in
the following definitive judgment on all Africans: "Thus I can
say without exaggeration that of all the countries of the earth,
the most deceitful and the most ungrateful one is that of the
Negroes, who the more good you do for them, the less liking
and gratitude do they show."[79] Loyer was to be an important
source of information on Africa; he had liberally plagiarized
from earlier writers and, with some poetic justice, was to be
dealt with similarly by subsequent writers on Africa.

If the early missionaries had viewed the Africans as innocent
victims of Satan, after 1700 Africans were depicted as responsible for their lack of Christianity, a condition due, it was said,
to their moral failings and to their bestiality. Dralsé de
Grandpierre, a naval officer who visited the west coast of Africa, cited sympathetically a comment by a traveling companion who, on seeing fetishism, had exclaimed that peoples who
transformed "such ridiculous objects into gods . . . give us the
right to consider them less as men than as animals."[80]

Father Labat, who had served as a priest in the West Indies,
gave a similar interpretation. Labat's personal knowledge of
blacks was based on his stay in the Antilles from 1693 to
1705; in 1722 he published his six-volume *Nouveau voyage aux*

îles de l'Amérique. He never visited Africa (unlike some of his contemporaries, he did not pretend he had), but published two accounts of Africa based on the notes of officials who had served there. The first work, *Nouvelle relation de l'Afrique occidentale,* appeared, in five volumes, in 1728. It claimed to be an account of the stay in Senegal of André Brüe, who had been an official there from 1697 to 1702, from 1714 to 1720, and again in 1723. Drawn from Brüe's writings, the account was also, without acknowledgment, based on a manuscript (which remained unpublished until 1913) by Michel de La Courbe, director of the Senegal Company from 1688 to 1690 and again from 1709 to 1710. Either out of friendship for Brüe and a desire to give him added importance or as a result of careless notetaking, Labat attributed to Brüe many of the activities and opinions of La Courbe.[81] In addition, Labat plagiarized from older published accounts, such as those by Loyer and Villault de Bellefond.[82] But such points are of interest only for an understanding of the origins of the work; what is far more important is that Labat's work presents "an exact image of the eighteenth-century knowledge of Africa."[83] A third source, which was less widely read, was Labat's *Voyage du Chevalier Des Marchais,* published in 1730, the account of a traveler who went as far south as Dahomey. Labat's writings reflect the ever-increasing bitterness among missionaries who had failed to convert Africans.[84] Africans were no longer the innocent victims of Satan; rather, their lack of Christianity was due, Labat wrote, to a basic flaw in their natures:

> Their hot temperament, their fickle and licentious personalities, the ease and impunity with which they commit crimes don't prepare them adequately for a religion in which justice, . . . humility, continence, abstention from pleasures, love of one's enemies, contempt for riches are so fundamental.[85]

Labat recognized a number of social factors that also helped explain African resistance to Christian proselytism. For instance, he pointed out that Africans who practiced polygamy would hesitate to adhere to a religion that denounced it.[86] Africans also had to take into account social pressures; when some notables in Whyda who were supposedly sympathetic to Christianity were asked why they had not converted, they answered that, if they did so, their people would "beat them to death and burn their houses." Labat concluded that "one can see thereby how impossible it is for missionaries to make any converts."[87] Overall, however, Labat suggested that the failure of Christianity in Africa was due to the moral perversion of Africans. In the passage on the moral failings of Africans, he concluded that blacks could be converted and preserved in their faith only as slaves in the West Indies. Only in the presence of Europeans, who could serve as constant examples, would blacks remain Christian.[88]

The argument that Africans could be converted by being enslaved was one of the most common apologies made for the slavery that Frenchmen had begun to establish in the West Indies in the mid-seventeenth century. Louis XIII was frequently quoted as having permitted the enslavement of blacks because he had been told that it was the only way of saving their souls.[89] The stress on the barbarity and infidelity of Africans could justify slavery. The horror Frenchmen felt toward a people whose religion they abhorred seems to have been genuine enough. That their feeling of horror was conveniently combined with an apology for slavery cannot be denied, but it does not seem to have been developed solely as a rationalization.

Sin and Immorality

If for Labat the lack of religion was caused by the Africans' immorality, the connection was seen the other way around by many other observers. Because they lacked the true faith, Africans were prone to sin. The depravity of the Africans was seen as manifesting itself in several ways. Ever since classical times, people living in hot climates had been thought of as hot-blooded and deranged in their passions. It was in the context of climate that Thévet had described African women as "incontinent."[90] His contemporary, Jean Bodin, introduced into French political thought the claim of the classics that excessive departures from temperate climes deranged man and his institutions.[91] He saw the tropical sun as making Africans inordinately lusty and prone to bestiality:

They can only restrain themselves with great difficulty, and once launched on debauchery, they maintain the most execrable voluptuousness. Hence the intimate [sexual] relations between men and beasts that still give birth to monsters in Africa.[92]

Relative nakedness was a striking attribute of Africans. Thévet wrote of the people of the Guinea coast that "these rogues walk around mostly naked."[93] Travelers to Africa also noted the Africans' lack of clothing. [Nakedness was usually viewed as a sign of shamelessness and licentiousness. Unmarried European males, most of them young and away from home for long stretches of time, may have projected their own sexual fantasies onto the Africans, especially the women.[94] Father Loyer complained that Africans were "much given to wine and to women who are very immodest." The black women, the good father claimed, "love wantonly the whites which often causes the perdition of the gentlemen of the Royal Company, the women are not ashamed when someone lands to run after him and to solicit him to commit sin." François de Paris, probably a naval officer who had visited the Senegambia in 1682, wrote that Africans spent their days drinking, getting drunk, and fornicating.[95]

The sexuality of Africans was seen as so excessive as to shorten their life.[96] Polygamy demonstrated their licentiousness; the geographic compiler La Croix wrote in 1688, "These Negroes are given to voluptuousness, they take a large number of wives." The practice even proved the Africans' bestiality: "They live nearly like animals, their wives being in common."[97] Curiously, Father Labat was one of the few writers on Africa who did not see in polygamy some sign of African licentiousness; rather, he explained that the African habit of nursing children for several years forced women to abstain from sex, and thus their husbands found it necessary to have additional wives.[98] While showing understanding toward polygamy, Labat nevertheless concurred in the general description of Africans as sexually depraved.[99]

The probability that missionaries would judge the customs of non-European peoples in a Eurocentric fashion had been foreseen by the Propoganda Apostolica, a missionary arm of

the papacy. In directions issued in 1659, it warned missionaries not to try to change any of the customs of the
peoples they were trying to convert, nor to compare them
with Europe—unless, of course, the customs were contrary to
the precepts of Christianity.[100] These wise instructions, however, had little chance of affecting the missionaries, who were
too startled by the differences they found between the habits,
customs, and material conditions of Africans and of Europeans
not to condemn the former. In any case, in the seventeenth
and even in the eighteenth century, the religious view of life
was so inclusive that any aspect, from the way one dressed to
the manner in which one buried one's dead, was considered to
be a question of religion.

Social and Political Institutions

Traders also gave voice to the image of Africans as miscreants. These Europeans were men of action, anxious to
perform the duties they had been assigned. Resentful of hindrances to their plans, they were apt to blame their failures not
on their own or their superiors' unrealistic expectations or er-
rors, but instead on basic shortcomings in the peoples with
whom they had contact. Africans were used to trading with
Europeans and had carried on commerce with the Portuguese
for over a century prior to the establishment of regular French
trading relations in West Africa. Africans knew how to size up
a European customer and were astute at making bargains.
French traders, accustomed to cheating both their masters at
home and the Africans with whom they traded, were surprised
to meet their match in Africa. Du Casse, on a voyage in 1687,
complained that Africans mixed gold dust with impurities,
"and if by chance one is not knowledgeable, they make you
pay double its worth."[101] Father Labat complained that Africans who brought gold to ships or trading forts mixed as many
impurities into the gold as they could, impurities such as "cop-
per filings and those large yellow pins that we sell them from
Europe."[102]

In dealing with each other, African traders commonly gave

presents to their African hosts. The stranger was given protection and access to the host's clients; a gift confirmed the relationship of dependency between the stranger and his host and was also a reward for the latter's services. Since these gifts were a common practice among Africans, they were naturally expected by the African hosts of the white strangers who came to trade in their country.[103] Demands for presents, however, were resented by many Frenchmen, who, unaware of the practice, denounced it as an unfair exaction. Du Casse denounced Africans as "great thieves and great liars, they pester one more than one can believe. The ministers and great lords never come and see anyone without asking for presents."[104] Mostly, French traders found their contacts with Africans frustrating and difficult and, hence, imputed bad will to Africans, branding them as thieves, liars, and cheats.[105] But when trading was unhindered and conducted to the satisfaction of a European, he was more willing to give a favorable account.[106]

Exposed to African society in a limited way and not having a full opportunity to understand these people, so different from Europeans, French travelers, like other Europeans, were wont to misconstrue much of what they saw, for instance, of African work habits. First, some of the observed African societies had specialized work routines according to sex; in those societies, men did not perform agricultural chores. Second, as a result of the heat, people had to work intensively for a few hours and then rest. During the few hours they worked, they might well put in as much energy as Europeans did in a day. Contemporary studies show that the energy costs of agricultural work are severe in West Africa, and often half a day is needed for recuperation. If the effects of disease and malnutrition are added, one can understand why European travelers often saw Africans seemingly at rest and not working. A third reason for the Europeans' distinct image of Africans as lazy was the Africans' failure to carry on intensive agriculture. In areas lacking sufficient manure and human labor, the slash-burning techniques of agriculture made sense. But to Europeans, coming from a society with a large population, available manure, and limited land, one sign of dedication to work was the willingness and ability to carry on intensive agriculture. Since Africans did not do so, they were presumed lazy.[107] Chambonneau, an explorer and one of the earliest administrators in Senegal, wrote in 1677, "The men mostly do nothing, are very lazy and lascivious; as long as they sit in the sun and have something to smoke, some millet and water, they are happier than the princes of France." African property concepts in regard to land were not understood either, although the persistence of communal land ownership in much of seventeenth-century France might have served as a helpful analogy. The acquisitive Frenchmen found in the Africans' property concepts evidence that "they have no ambition for riches, everything is held in common among them; they neither buy nor sell the land. They cultivate wherever they desire."[108]

The lush, wild vegetation of much of the African coast induced Frenchmen to believe that the region was fertile and that the absence of extensive cultivation was due to lack of effort by the local inhabitants.[109] Many of the early officials in Senegal tried to interest the French government in plantation schemes in West Africa. They made exaggerated claims for the fertility of the land and, in trying to explain why such promising terrain had not already been cultivated, they resorted to arguments about African laziness.

The claims regarding African laziness thus had many motives and was repeated an infinite number of times, finally becoming a basic European belief.[110] The charge of laziness was transmitted to later generations by Labat, who wrote, "At an early age they are vicious and only love their pleasures. They are excessively lazy, flee work as if it were the worst thing in the world; if hunger did not force them, they would never cultivate their land. . . . They love to dance."[111]

The Europe that came into contact with Africa in the seventeenth century had been affected by the increasing rationalization of life. The commercial revolution put a premium on the development of a time consciousness based on the calendar, rather than on the seasons, and led also to an appreciation of precision in measuring size, volume, weight, and amount, or in calculating numbers. For trading purposes Africans had developed complex measures and means of arriving at the price of a good, which long-term European residents in Africa had no trouble understanding; they were readily able to trade with Africans.[112] But, to the uninitiated visitor, the lack of any uniformity in measures and prices, which fluctuated according to circumstances, seemed to reveal an African failure to possess any intellectual appreciation for quantity.[113]

France came into contact with Africa at a time when the French monarchy was consolidating its political authority. The diffusion of power that had marked the feudal age was replaced by the establishment of a powerful crown, which increasingly attempted to bring France under uniform law and a central bureaucracy. The African societies that Frenchmen encountered varied a great deal, but all of them were smaller in size, with far less extensive bureaucracies, and had royal courts lacking the material splendor that characterized seventeenth-century European royalty and achieved its apogee with Louis XIV. At the same time that Europeans experienced the growth of royal absolutism, however, they maintained a strong body of law limiting royal power and upholding the rights of private property and (to a limited extent in France) individual freedom.

By contrast, the rather humble surroundings of many African political authorities struck European travelers. Chambonneau wrote, "When one says that one would like to be king, one should qualify it, because instead of being king in these countries, I would rather maintain the condition I am in."[114] Likewise, differences in administrative structure and legal norms between African societies and those of Europe were so great that Frenchmen came to believe that Africans lacked both. Repeating the phrase used by the classics to describe Africans, La Croix referred to Africans as living "without laws."[115]

According to Walter Rodney, African political authority underwent important transformations under the impact of the slave trade and became increasingly arbitrary and tyrannical.[116] From nearly the beginning of their contact with the Africans, the French observed a society affected by the slave trade; the Portuguese and the English had already been slaving on the coast. Although the French had inherited from the classics a negative image of African political institutions, it may well be that they were, in fact, witnessing a political system that, as Rodney has suggested, had become seriously distorted as a result of the slave trade. Furthermore, of course, the traders were in contact with very specific political systems, nearly exclusively those located on the coast, not necessarily representative of Africa as a whole.

In France, while the power of the sovereign grew, personal rights also developed and some limits on royal power were recognized. Slavery had long since ended in France, and even serfdom was in decline. The authority and power of African kings shocked some French observers. Father Loyer described the manner in which the king of Cayor went on slaving expeditions against his own subjects and in which the king of Issiny was able to confiscate his subjects' goods. Loyer condemned the first for "barbarous conduct"; of the second he wrote, "He commits other villainous acts which would be intolerable to all other nations except those of the Negroes." François de Paris, on the basis of a visit to the Senegambia, concluded that African royalty was so absolute that a king at his whim could pass a sword through one of his subjects or enslave him.[117] Slave raids and slavery itself were African institutions indigenous to that continent.[118] But when Europeans wrote of the slave trade, they seemed unaware of their own contribution in making it possible. They reserved their criticism for the African intermediaries. Lemaire wrote that the inhabitants of Senegal were "so perfidious that they sell each other even when related." "The man, his wife; the wife, her husband; the father, his child; the child, his father," wrote François de Paris.[119]

That the European contact with Africa occurred simultaneously with the development of the slave trade may have had a double impact on the French image of Africans. European observers failed to understand the distortions that the trade had brought to various African institutions and instead saw the institutions as always having been in the state in which they found them. Second, and more important, Europeans involved in the slave trade may have depicted Africans in an especially negative light in order to rationalize the trade. But this possibility should not be exaggerated, for at least in the beginning of Franco-African contacts, it was by no means clear that black slavery would be the main means of plantation labor in the French West Indies.[120] Once the slave trade developed, however, its practitioners denied the humanity of their cargo and viewed them as animals nearly as a matter of course.[121] The nature of the triangular trade, from France, to Africa, then to the West Indies and back to France[122]—even when it involved only legitimate trade and not slaves—meant that French traders came into contact with the plantation societies developing in the Antilles and assimilated the planters' attitudes toward blacks.[123] Writers on Africans seldom kept their views of blacks in the Antilles and of those in Africa apart; by the late seventeenth century it had become rather common to interweave accounts of blacks living in both Africa and the Antilles. For purposes of analysis attitudes toward blacks in Africa and in the West Indies have been kept separate in this study; nevertheless, it is clear that there existed a nearly inseparable web of connections.[124]

From the Particular to the General: The Formulation of an Image

It was nearly the end of the nineteenth century before Europeans had completely explored Africa and come to know all the peoples of the continent. In the first two centuries of their contact with Africa, they generally became acquainted only with peoples on the coast. Their experience and knowledge of Africa were fragmentary. They had met with Moslems and animists, with people living in well-organized, extensive states, small city-states, and states that may have been acephalous. At times French writers recognized that Africans did not form a single category of humans about whom one could generalize.[125]

In the West Indies the French developed a fine sense of differentiation between African groups. Many of the proclaimed differences were based on myths among the planters, but they reveal at least a willingness to think about Africans as not forming a single category. Labat, echoing planter sentiment, saw different African peoples as endowed with varying abilities. The Bambaras were best suited for labor; "they are robust, gentle, don't lack wit . . . they love their masters, are obedient, and don't run away." The cleanest blacks, Labat claimed, were the cattle-herding peoples of the Senegambia. The blacks of Guinea were better fit for heavy labor than were those of Senegal, who instead made good household slaves and craftsmen. Many of these judgments must have been mere stereotypes, but Labat presented others as the logical outcome of the slaves' previous experience in Africa. The Aradas made the best slaves: "Enslavement disturbs them little because they are born as slaves." The men from the Mine "are not qualified to work the land because they don't do so in their own country."[126] Despite warnings by some writers on Africa that it was dangerous to generalize about the continent and its people, and despite the habit developed among planters in the West Indies to differentiate among African ethnic groups, the idea that Africans formed a homogeneous group developed and became widespread. La Croix had been one of the earliest to note that it was difficult to generalize about Africans "because they were made up of too many nations," yet he argued that most areas shared the common characteristics of having fertile land and being inhabited by peoples who "all have black skins, white teeth, . . . who are strong and vigorous and yet don't live long because they frequent women too much."[127] The differences that African peoples might reveal notwithstanding, the characteristics that seemed to put them so dramatically apart from Europeans—their color, their lack of Christian faith, and their social customs—led to the formation of the concept of a single black people.

Bewildered by their contact with foreign peoples, early travelers often relied on stereotypes already existing in France or on facile generalizations to formulate their own opinions. They shared a fault common to many travelers: every act they observed became typical of a whole society; every individual, a prototype of all his fellow inhabitants. With rare exceptions the peculiarities noted among one people were assumed to be characteristics of all others. This assumption helped build the myth of the "black man."

The human image of reality rarely works with the precision of a computer or a mathematical formula. The latter are sensitive to every new input of information, and the outcome is affected by the slightest bit of information either added or taken away. Once having drawn a generalization, humans frequently hold onto it, even though additional information is in a contrary vein and tends to discredit their preconceptions.[128] Thus, many of the writings on Africa in this early period contained, in addition to negative comments on the Africans, much evidence that either put these judgments into question or else contradicted them outright.

One of the sea captains visiting West Africa described in 1719 how he had told an African that "Negroes were thieves." The African, who had been to France, retorted that, judging by the number of punishments meted out in Europe, it was obvious that Europeans were just as dishonest. The captain commented, "I changed the conversation and was angry at myself for having spoken to him in the way I had."[129] Yet the wise perspective that the African offered was not allowed to disturb one of the basic themes of the book, monotonously repeated throughout: Africans were prone to lie and to steal.

If Africa was generally depicted in a negative light, still, a number of virtues specific to Africans were seen. One was hospitality. Another, Labat noted, was the Africans' respect for the aged, their affection for each other and especially for their children.[130] A misogynist who held French women in special contempt, Labat presented the African woman as a model. The women of Gold Coast, he wrote, gave birth without complaint, not because of lack of pain, but rather through "greatness of spirit."[131] Even if Father Labat condemned African religions, he found the Africans' devotion admirable. In Whyda the inhabitants "carry out the duties of their religion with a conscientiousness which should shame those who have been enlightened by the Gospel and knowing the only and true God live as if there was not any, or as if he did not deserve any worship."[132] If positive traits were thus ascribed to the African, they were still attributed far more sparingly, compared with contemporary French appreciation of the North American Indians or of the Chinese.

The formation of a specific image in the early phase of French contact with Africa was particularly important because it became the source for later images. Rarely did French travelers look at Africa with completely fresh eyes. They were men of their times, sharing certain predispositions of their culture. Perhaps they had even read previous travel accounts prior to embarking for Africa. What is certain is that, when they described their own experiences, they often copied shamelessly from earlier accounts. The priest Godefroy Loyer began his *Relation* with the boast, "I have not written this on the witness of others but that of my eyes" and assured his readers that they would find a "sincere account."[133] Yet much of his book is plagiarized from Villault de Bellefond and from Lemaire. Villault, in turn, had copied lengthy passages (some acknowledged, others not) from Dutch travelers who had preceded him to West Africa.[134] The painstaking work of comparing texts has by no means been completed, but we know, for instance, that the most famous of all these writers—Labat—resorted to the same stratagem. Not only did Labat assign to Brüe the work of La Courbe, but he also liberally plagiarized from Villault de Bellefond and from Loyer.[135] Thus, new contacts and experiences often were not allowed to change the essential image that had evolved.

Certainly the contacts developed in the seventeenth century did dispel much of the medieval lore about Africa and its inhabitants. Some of the myths were weakened also by the growth of a critical spirit that placed greater emphasis on empirical experience.[136] Thus the king's cartographer wrote in 1666:

> Every day reveals to us what the ancients did not know, it shows us that the greatest heat of Africa is also accompanied by some cool weather . . . that the animals are not so dangerous that the men cannot defend themselves, that the men are not so faithless that there is no trade or human relations between them and foreigners; that their dragons, their serpents, their griffins etc. are mostly imaginary ones.[137]

At the same time, new myths were born from the shock of early culture contacts. An essentially negative perception of the African developed as a result of misunderstandings based on lack of knowledge and insufficient time to observe, frustra-

Illustration, 1660. The image of Africans is strongly influenced by the "turqueries" of the era. *Hennin Collection, Photo Bibliothèque nationale, Paris.*

Idealized image representing Africa as a personage, 1695.
Hennin Collection. Photo Bibliothèque nationale, Paris.

tions in trade and missionary work, and, finally, a basically ethnocentric view of African institutions and mores. Culture contact was not made under ideal conditions. Life was often grim for Europeans in Africa; climate and disease took their toll. Nerves were on edge as Europeans contended with the heat, mosquitoes, malaria, and dysentery. Many of the Frenchmen in Africa lacked education and represented the rough elements of European society, exiled to an inhospitable continent. Their cumulative frustrations were evidenced by what was, even for that time, excessive alcohol consumption. They projected their frustrations and their own depravity onto the African and may have blamed him for their unhappy exile. Such conditions did not allow for serene observation of a foreign and strange society.

While contact increased toward the end of the seventeenth century, during the period between 1530 and 1720 relatively few Frenchmen had come to know Africa. The most common Euro-African encounter was slaving, and even in that field France had not made many inroads. Frenchmen, for lack of many new experiences, drew on earlier ones, and, in the written culture, considerable reliance on the authority of the classics continued. Thus, the French image was remarkably stable for nearly two centuries. It is possible that individual sea captains, as a result of personal relations established in Africa, possessed different views from those preserved in the literary culture, but no traces of them have been found, even in the remaining log books.

The French view did not differ significantly from that of the Iberians or the English who came into contact with Africans. All were struck by the physique, social systems, and material culture of the Africans. This common view is, of course, not surprising; Western Europe shared a common outlook and had similar experiences with other cultures. Prior to contact with Africa, Europeans had already been in contact with other non-European peoples such as the various Islamic societies and Asians. But these peoples were not so radically different in appearance, and they possessed institutions more easily appreciated by Europeans. While Africa also had complex state structures, those of Asia were more apparent because of the splendor and material wealth of the courts that Europeans visited. Besides, Asians had religions with written traditions and literary cultures. As a result, Asians did not shock Europeans in the same way as Africans did. In Africa, travelers did not find institutions with European parallels so readily. With no easy analogies to use, most Europeans fell back on classical lore, or on their own imaginations, which sometimes were fired by the disappointments that resulted from early contacts.

These common experiences suggest why there were no significant national variations in European reactions to Africa. That England was an island or Protestant did not particularly explain its reactions to Africans. The French, continental and Catholic, shared the same response. Even the Iberians, who had been ruled by the darker Moors, were shocked when they encountered African society.[138]

Moreover, Africa served Europeans as a convenient mirror, or as a screen onto which they projected their own fears about themselves and their world. The encounter with Africa in the seventeenth century occurred in an era that emphasized order, self-discipline, self-abnegation, sexual restraint, and Christianity. These were difficult ideals. The Europeans' failure to realize these lofty goals, or even their temptations to deny them, created serious inner tensions to which the contact with Africa gave an emotional release. Following the Renaissance, Europeans became obsessed with their own animality; they sought to flee the lowly condition imposed upon them by careful cultivation of soul and body. While sexual promiscuity was rampant, the ideal was disciplined sexual conduct within marriage. Though Christian unity had faltered in the mid-fifteenth century, its faltering culminating in the Reformation, both Protestants and Catholics upheld the principles of religious conformity. The harsh economic conditions of the seventeenth century necessitated a work ethic, which was strengthened by the values of the nascent commercial bourgeoisie and by religious notions of work as the necessary condition of man after the Fall. Leisure was viewed as a rebellion against divine plan.

Naturally, Europeans' behavior fell short of their goals. When Frenchmen came into contact with Africa, they readily projected onto the continent their fears about what they themselves would be like, without the fetters of European institutions and conventions.[139] They were constrained by law and convention to act in a certain manner, but their fantasies tempted them to doubt their civilized humanity and revealed instead their own animality. Christianity enforced the line between man and animal, but ancient myths of man as half-animal, of animal as man, haunted the European imagination. The myth could permissibly be revived by projecting it onto other peoples.[140] The African could thus be depicted as animalistic, sexually lustful, lazy, and religiously unregenerate.

2

The Establishment of Slave Societies

Most Frenchmen came to know blacks in the context of slavery, and the French view of the African was strongly affected by the slave experience. In fact, until slavery was abolished in the mid-nineteenth century, it was not in Africa, but rather in the Antilles, that the most extensive interaction between Frenchmen and blacks occurred. The social context of slavery dictated to an important degree how Frenchmen viewed blacks; slavery further debased the image of blacks. The interconnection between the image of blacks and slavery is, however, complex.

The Unthinking Decision

The French reliance on Africans as slaves evolved over a long period of trial and error. As in the case of the British, the French enslavement of blacks was less the result of a conscious decision than of an unconscious process, an "unthinking decision."[1]

Although the exact date is unknown, the first use of black slaves by the French occurred sometime before 1625, when the French officially colonized part of the West Indies. Before that, French settlers there possessed African slaves purchased from passing Spanish slavers and from French ships sent out by the Compagnie de Rouen. But only at the end of the seventeenth century, after long experimentation with various modes of labor, did the French settle on black labor as the principal means of cultivating their West Indian empire.

One means by which the early French settlers in the New World secured labor was to enslave the original inhabitants:

the Caribs in the Antilles and the North American Indians in
Canada. Although the French regarded them sympathetically,
both groups were enslaved.[2] And when their enslavement
ended, it did so for reasons extraneous to the French perceptions of them. That the French could have a positive image of
the Caribs and Indians and yet enslave them suggests that
there was not necessarily a relationship between the negative
appreciation of blacks and the decision to reduce them into
chattel slavery.

Caribs and American Indians were made slaves because
their French captors needed labor, but the arrangement
proved to be impractical. Father Bouton, one of the earliest
observers in the West Indies, noted that the disadvantage of
having Carib slaves was that, even after they had lived in captivity for long periods of time, "among the French and being
comfortable, at the first opportunity, [they] fled and returned
to the other savages." Similarly in Canada the French found
that Indian slaves could escape with ease. Moreover, enslaving
Indians caused hostility on the part of the local populations,
and even continuous wars; such occurrences disrupted the valuable fur trade.[3]

The truly decisive reason for not relying on Caribs for labor
was that, upon contact with Europeans, many died, probably
because they lacked immunity to European diseases. The
Caribs' high mortality made their bondage impractical, and a
decree of 1640 forbade their further enslavement. This decree
was not implemented, however, and the extermination of the
Caribs continued.[4]

A second source of labor was French indentured servants.
Indentured servants were used in France to clear uncultivated
land, and the institution was now transferred to the West Indies. Under the French system young men committed themselves to work in the Antilles for thirty-six months, in
exchange for payment of their passage and a certain remunera-
tion; after completion of their service these benefits theoretically provided them with the means to become small landown-
ers in the colony. The French government viewed this system
as necessary for the continued well-being of the colonies and
therefore regulated the number of indentured servants that

every sea captain trading with the Antilles had to have on board ship.

The engagés, as the indentured servants were called, were supposed to enter into their three-year commitments freely, but many of them were forced by economic necessity at home to embark overseas, and still others were victimized by sea captains avid for the high prices that West Indian planters paid for them. Once in the islands, the indentured servants were often treated very badly. Knowing that they could use this labor for only three years, planters tended to work the engagés extremely hard.

While serving, the engagé was in bondage, deprived of all legal rights; he had the status of a minor. He had no right to make contracts, to vote in parochial elections, or to marry without his owner's permission.[5] No matter how poorly treated, he was not allowed to leave his master. After the indentured-servant system was extended to Guiana, an elaborate system of punishments for escaping was established: those who fled their masters for the first time had their ears cut and were branded with a fleur de lys on one shoulder; a second desertion meant branding on the other shoulder and amputation of a leg; a third desertion meant death.[6]

African slaves constituted a third, but much smaller, source of labor. Slaves were not seen as forming a special category; rather, in the manner in which they were regarded by contemporaries and by law, they were included with indentured servants. Except for the duration of service, no special legal regulations were established for them; when in 1619 the Compagnie de Rouen was formed to buy Africans for the purpose of transporting and selling them to the Antilles, the government issued rules for their treatment. The rules declared: "The treatment of Negroes is not to differ from that of French indentured servants except that they will serve perpetually."[7] In fact, the harsh disciplinary means of social control imposed on the indentured servants were carried over to the slaves.

Little difference was seen between the status of indentured servants and that of slaves. A travel account of the West Indies in 1640 (probably the earliest one written) explained that French planters, short of labor, would buy from passing English and Dutch ships "Negro and More slaves." They were, the writer declared, "no different from the French [indentured] servants, except that they are servitors for life whereas the French serve only for three years."[8] Once they landed, any difference in treatment seems to have been to the disadvantage of the engagé. Intendant Robert of Martinique wrote to the minister of the navy in 1698 that the planters constantly mistreated their engagés, "caring much less for an engagé than a black slave and having far less concern for the death of an engagé than a slave because they lose more at the death of the latter."[9] Since a slave represented lifetime service, he was far more expensive to buy than the service of an engagé.

Only at the end of the seventeenth century did it become clear that slave labor would be the predominant mode of production. In 1664 there was an equal number of whites and blacks in Martinique; shortly thereafter, the balance tipped entirely in the direction of the latter. By the 1670s the number of indentured servants going overseas began to decrease, probably as a result of word reaching France of the miserable lot of the engagés.

Until the 1690s the economy of the French islands was based mainly on the breeding of cattle and the raising of cocoa, indigo, and tobacco. After 1690 these industries became less important, compared with the growing and more profitable sugar industry,[10] which required large supplies of workers. Since the indentured-servant system no longer supplied a sufficient number of workers, the dependency upon slave labor increased. A slave cost the equivalent of 9,000 pounds of sugar; the service of an indentured servant, only 1,200 pounds of sugar.[11] Although the slave was a better buy in the long run, few settlers dependent upon cattle and cocoa could probably afford the capital outlay. Toward the end of the seventeenth century, the transformation of the islands from a ranch economy to a plantation economy based on sugar created the need for a large-scale labor force and at the same time generated the economic means for the capital outlays that slave purchases required. The critical labor needs of the growing sugar industry and the drop in the availability of indentured servants made it necessary to depend on slaves for labor;

thus, by the end of the seventeenth century, slavery, rather than the indentured-servant system, became the hallmark of production in the French Antilles.[12] Only gradually, as black slaves continued to be brought into the colonies, was a definite advantage perceived in using them rather than the other forms of labor. This idea seems to have dawned on contemporaries only gradually; it may have been first articulated by Father Bouton:

> A black slave is much more useful than a French servant who serves only for three years, needs clothing, asks for wages, is not as used to the heat; the blacks on the other hand serve for their whole lives, need only some cloth to cover their privates . . . , content themselves with just some cassava and peas, they are made for the air and heat.[13]

C. de Rochefort, writing in 1658, noted an additional advantage of slaves: since their service was "perpetual, their numbers increase from time to time by having children, who inherit the yoke of their parents."[14]

The advantages of slave labor seemed demonstrated in neighboring Barbados. By the 1640s its economy had already become predominantly based on sugar and slaves. Seeing the success of their English competitors the French settlers now favored blacks over engagés as a source of labor.[15] Besides the increasingly apparent economic advantages of having slaves instead of engagés, there was a social component to the planters' preference. The colonists saw the indentured servants as potential rivals, because once freed of their contract, former servants could compete economically and make claims to social and political prominence. But slaves were never such a danger, for they were bonded for life.[16]

Considering the success of the slave plantation colonies of rival states, France could not sit idly by. In 1670 Colbert had the Council of State exempt the French slave trade of its 5 percent tariff, in order to encourage its growth, for "there is nothing which contributes more to the development of colonies and their soil than the hard working toil of Negroes."[17] In spite of these encouragements, however, the French slave trade was still unable to supply the ever-increasing demand of the colonists for black labor.[18]

That the decision to depend mainly on black slaves for plantation labor was made gradually can be seen in the fact that a legal code regulating them was not adopted until 1685. At first slaves were seen as forming a special category of indentured servants, and therefore the laws regulating indentured servants were extended to them. The promulgation of the slave code, the *code noir,* in 1685 signified a recognition by the state that black slavery was in the colonies to stay.

Motives for Black Enslavement

While the slave had been subject to the same laws and generally treated in the same way as the engagé, the black man, because of his African origin, was made a slave for life. Why? Why was it seen as unnatural to retain the service of white men for longer than a certain time while making bondage perpetual for Africans? This is a difficult question to answer.[19]

Clearly race prejudice and slavery were interconnected, but which was cause and which was effect is hard to ascertain; it is best to emphasize instead the manner in which they reinforced each other—acted on each other, as M. I. Finley has written, in a "dialectical" manner.[20] Winthrop Jordan, who had far richer documentation for the English colonies, finds this problem nearly intractable and offers a number of hypotheses that will be examined here in regard to the French experience[21] since they also seem to explain the French motivation for enslaving blacks.

Slavery was not a moral problem for Frenchmen in the sixteenth and seventeenth centuries. The ancient world had essentially accepted slavery as part of the natural order of things: the result of the inequality of humans—a natural law, whereby stronger and more capable humans controlled those less well endowed. Some Christians had seen slavery as contradictory to the order of nature, but had argued that as a result of human sin it had perhaps become necessary to keep certain individuals in check. In any case, Christians affirmed that, no matter what human bondage was imposed, there really was only one true form of enslavement—enslavement to the devil. To be freed from the latter was the only freedom of consequence.[22] In comparison with the human drama of sin and salvation, the problem of slavery dimmed in importance. The enslavement of the African may not have created a crisis of conscience also because no particular change was seen in his status as he crossed the Atlantic; it was widely assumed that he had already been a slave in Africa. While slavery did exist in many societies in West Africa, it was mostly a form of domestic servitude and was seldom comparable to the plantation slave system of the European colonies. Moreover, domestic slaves were rarely sold into the transatlantic trade. Contemporary observers had little appreciation of these nuances and instead viewed the slave trade as bringing people who were already slaves across the ocean.[23]

The Indians in the Americas were considered to live normally in freedom. Colonial officials in Guiana were instructed to take care that they employed as slaves only Indians who were already slaves, but they were forbidden to enslave free Indians. Such instructions may well reflect problems of conscience, or else may have been the result of practical considerations. Enslaving free Indians would have created hostility among the surrounding peoples and would have endangered the French position in Guiana.[24]

Because the process of enslavement was so gradual, there was no real pressure to examine whether it was right or wrong to enslave Africans. There was also the Iberian example. The Portuguese and Spanish had used black slaves in the Americas since the early sixteenth century.[25] In competing with their Iberian neighbors for wealth overseas, the French copied them, not only to the extent of establishing tropical plantation colonies, but also in introducing black slavery. In the competition for power, European states put great emphasis on mercantilist policies that assured them of the most bullion while depriving their rivals of gold. Colbert was irked that French settlers were buying slaves from the Spanish, thus enriching the coffers of Spain. To put an end to such a situation, he encouraged French entry into the slave trade and even hoped that the French would become suppliers of slaves to the

Spanish.[26] He was overambitious, for the French, unable to meet their own limited demand for slaves, continued through the seventeenth century to purchase slaves from Spanish and Dutch ships.[27]

The benefit the slave trade would bring to France in its political and economic rivalry with other European states was outlined in detail in a memoir by a certain De Gallitzer. This memoir explained the mercantilist rationale for preferring slaves over engagés: engagés brought to the Antilles would signify the loss to metropolitan France of a labor force needed at home, whereas slaves taken there would not constitute any loss to the state and would mean rather the addition of "new subjects who form new provinces." The wealth the slaves produced would belong not to them but to France. The slave trade employed French sailors and encouraged the growth of French naval power; as a result, "the king and the state would acquire immense riches and a prodigious navy." Further, in the European power struggle,

> the multitude of Negroes is necessary to compete successfully with the English, the Dutch and the Portuguese in the production of plantation staples and in navigation; furthermore one must try to trade as many slaves as possible so that these nations will find that many fewer slaves for themselves.

A final appeal pointed out that enslaved Africans represented "that many more people won over to [our] religion."[28]

It was natural for Frenchmen to view their actions in religious terms. Following the French wars of religion and the Counter-Reformation, religious sentiments intensified. Colonial expansion was seen not only as the expansion of the king's domain and of the state's wealth, but also as part of a missionary effort. In 1603 the French king declared that his main aim in supporting expansion in the New World was the conversion of the Indians in America; such views reflected a real concern for the souls of the heathen, but were also occasioned by the need to win papal support for France. It had been a common belief that the Pope had the right to divide the earth, and he had indeed partitioned the Americas between Spain and Portugal. France had acted as an interloper in America, ignoring papal bulls, but, by showing missionary zeal, it wished to convince the papacy that it was a dependable instrument for spreading the Catholic faith and papal authority. Thus, for political reasons, religious feeling was further intensified in French colonial enterprise. Overseas, Frenchmen had a sense of creating new societies, without the failings of the old. If a certain heterogeneity was permitted in France, in the colonies neither Protestants nor Jews were legally allowed admission.[29]

Religious intolerance was especially strong against heathenism, which had to be stamped out. Black slaves brought to the West Indies had to be made Christian, and their enslavement was justified because it was seen—as was the rest of the French colonial venture—as the means by which Christianity could be spread. Enslavement as a means of Christianizing had been given papal sanction by Nicholas V in a papal bull of 1454.[30] French divines similarly justified the practice. Father Bouton wrote in 1640, only a few years after the importation of the first black slaves: "It is good fortune for them [the Negroes] to be with the French, who treat them gently enough and among whom they will learn that which will be their salvation and they will persevere in the faith as long as they remain [in slavery]." Another missionary declared that, while slaves of man, blacks, by being brought to the Christian faith, "enjoy the liberty of the children of God."[31]

The decisive role of religion in resolving who should be enslaved may be seen in the French government policies of recruiting galley slaves for its ships. While the state condemned to galley service various Christians considered to be deviants, it did not make them slaves; rather, they were prisoners serving terms of a sentence (which sometimes was arbitrarily prolonged to fill the need for oarsmen). Huguenots, after 1685, when the toleration of Protestants was revoked, were condemend to galley service, but were not enslaved because, even though heretics, they were still considered Christian. As Paul Bamford points out, "This distinction, though it was no advantage to the Huguenots, does underscore the recognition given to religion as a basis for distinguishing between non-slaves and slaves."[32] Most of the galley slaves were

Moslems, taken in warfare with the Barbary states, in fighting with corsairs, by purchase in the slave markets on the southern and eastern Mediterranean coast, and even in occasional slave raids on the North African coast.[33] The use of Moslems as slaves was approved by the Pope and by all of Christian Europe as a just form of punishment for the infidels, and was thought to ensure their conversion. The impressment of Moslems into galley slavery was a legacy from the Crusades and tended to strengthen the emphasis on religion as the factor that decided who would be enslaved.

The colonial enterprise was, however, rent by contradictions; when ideals clashed with the interests of the colonists or of the state, the latter did not always yield. Thus, the charter establishing the French trading company in Canada had provided that "savages who are baptized as Catholics are counted and considered as natural Frenchmen." Yet baptism did not safeguard all Indians; some were enslaved.[34] An equal disregard for religion seems to have been shown when Louis XIV ordered the enslavement of Iroquois for his galleys; even though they belonged to a friendly group, among whom the Recollet Fathers and other religious orders were carrying on active missionary work, they were sent to France in chains.[35] The number of Christian Indians injured in this manner was small; nevertheless, the action revealed a willingness to compromise an important principle—that Christians could not be enslaved.

The French carried out this policy also against Christian Europeans. At various times, when the number of galley slaves was in short supply, French royal officials, including Colbert, were willing to enslave Greeks, Russians, and various Balkan peoples for ship service; while none of these peoples was Catholic, all were Christian. There was some soul-searching over these policies, however, and when it was shown that some galley slaves labeled as Russians were actually Poles (and therefore probably Catholic), this source of recruitment was stopped.[36]

It is unlikely—one wishes one could say impossible—that if Africans had been Christian they would have been enslaved in such large numbers without causing a considerable strain of conscience for their French captors. In any case, the initial French image of the black as pagan was so strong that even after conversion his retention in slavery was not seen as a violation of precepts against enslaving co-religionists. When the African slave was converted to Christianity, the cause of his enslavement should have ended; by the logic of the argument justifying slavery as the instrument of African conversion, the black slave, having become a Christian, should have been freed. In his opinion on slavery in 1698, for instance, Fromageau, the Sorbonne theologian, declared that slaves could be bought in good conscience "if it was to convert them and give them back their freedom."[37] In part, it seems to have been this doctrine that Fathers Bouton and Labat were combatting when they claimed that the slave could preserve his faith only if he were retained in bondage.[38] Freedom would lead to religious backsliding.

While the Church showed interest in participating in the conversion of African slaves both in the galleys and in the colonies, it did not agitate for their freedom after conversion. The official opinion of the Church was articulated by Bossuet, famed theologian and Louis XIV's personal chaplain, who declared that slavery not only was commensurate with natural law but followed the orders of Scriptures. "The Holy Ghost," declared Bossuet, in citing what became a favorite passage of many apologists for slavery, "through the mouth of Saint Paul has ordered the slaves to remain in their condition, and does not obligate the masters to free them."[39]

There was a legal aspect, however, at variance with the attitudes favoring slavery. Slavery had long since been abolished in France and was illegal. When, in 1571, a shipowner placed slaves on sale in Bordeaux, the Parlement ordered them released, declaring that slavery did not exist in the French realm. This was still the policy over a hundred years later; in 1691, a slave ship had to free all of its human cargo when it sailed into a French port.[40] But the law contained strange contradictions. Legally, the colonies overseas were considered part of France; unless specifically exempt, the colonies were ruled by the same laws as those of France. The administration was identical, and there was no reason to assume that the settlement colonies,

inhabited by Frenchmen, should be governed by rules different from those of France. Yet slavery was permitted in the
colonies although it was declared illegal in France. The dis-
junction between colony and mother country was so great
that, even though it was legal to own a slave in the Antilles,
when this same slave was brought to France—as sometimes
was done when planters returned with a black domestic—he
had to be freed. Only in 1716 was this principle altered so that
slaves could be brought into France.[41] And there was another
strange anomaly: galley slaves of the French state were permitted on metropolitan soil, although privately owned slaves were
not. This last contradiction seems not to have been tested in
the courts, but probably could have been handled by the tradition of Roman law, which permitted the state a latitude of
powers denied to individuals.

The failure of French legal institutions to face the problem
of slavery in the colonies (and on the galleys) might perhaps be
explained by the fact that slavery was considered a temporary
aberration, not an institution that would last.

The gradual, trial-and-error methods by which the French
embarked on black enslavement suggest that it was not immediately considered natural to enslave blacks. At times, however, existing prejudice against blacks or acquaintance with
Spanish practices brought the possibility to mind. This occurred when the French established Fort Dauphin on the
southeastern tip of Madagascar in 1642. While the Malagasy
were not Negroid, they were considered such by the colonists
and officials. The leader of the expedition, Jacques Pronis,
hoping to curry favor with the Malagasy, married the daughter
of a local chief; this marriage with a "black" woman was deplored by his men. The addition of another hundred Frenchmen to the fort created food shortages and general discontent.
Forced to plant food and to work on fortifications, the men
began to grumble. According to an account of the period, they
"found it very strange to be carriers and do the work of slaves
when they saw Negroes in the fort [Pronis's friends and in-
laws] who were not being forced to work."[42]

Whites and Blacks in the West Indies

While colonists' demands and mercantilist concerns prompted the French government to encourage the slave trade, it was by no means a development that the government totally favored. It had promoted the colonization of the Caribbean primarily as a base from which to conquer the Spanish colonies. At least the French made several forays against them.[43] To make such an attempt, the French needed a large white population in the West Indies and thus, for military reasons, favored an increase in the number of engagés.[44] As late as 1699, while the islands were developing their plantation economies, the governor of Saint-Domingue, Du Casse, declared that it was not the staple products of the island, but its strategic position, which made it valuable, for it could serve as a military staging area from which "to unite to the French monarchy, Mexico, Peru, and the Kingdom of Santa Fé."[45] A larger number of engagés was also favored because authorities feared that the growing number of slaves would become increasingly hard to control. For purposes of slave control a royal decree of 1686 required that there be the same number of indentured servants as slaves in Saint-Domingue.[46] Colonists ignored the law, and it was unenforceable; the number of engagés arriving had diminished, while the demand for and supply of black slaves were increasing.

Although the engagé system had become moribund by the end of the seventeenth century, it was officially discontinued by royal edict only in 1774. The ordinance explained that the engagés had stopped coming and were no longer necessary because a sufficient supply of labor had been assured by the importation of slaves and because the white population had grown.[47]

The authorities' concern about the racial composition of the colonies was prompted by fear of slave revolts. In 1656 the first one occurred in Guadeloupe; in 1671 there was an attempt in Saint-Domingue, repeated in 1691 and 1697, and Martinique saw its first large slave conspiracy in 1699.[48] Despite the similar treatment to which engagés and slaves were subjected, it was assumed that engagés would side with the slaveowners. This was not true in all instances. In the "slave conspiracy" of Port-de-Paix in Saint-Domingue in 1691, one of the three leaders had been an engagé.[49] On the whole, however, it seems to have been correct to assume that the engagé would not see his interests as identical with those of black slaves. From very early, there seems to have been hostility between the two groups. Although subject to the same treatment as slaves, engagés seemed to have felt humiliation at being assimilated to them. Father Dutertre, who served in the Antilles in the early years of colonization, claimed that, of all the abuses to which engagés were subjected, "to have to work in the company of slaves afflicts these poor people more than all the excessive maltreatment to which they are subject."[50]

Knowing that he would become free after three years of service, the engagé did not view with equanimity the possibility of black emancipation. He did not desire competition from freed blacks for the positions in the colonial economy that were open to former engagés, such as skilled crafts and the farming of food crops. In fact, former engagés and poor whites in general tended to oppose emancipation of slaves and to favor laws strongly discriminatory against freedmen.[51] By the end of the seventeenth century they formed a group strongly hostile to blacks and to "people of color" (the West Indian term for persons of white and black parentage and their descendants), although they themselves had little political power and were therefore unable actually to influence the course of legislation. It is possible, though, to view legislation favorable to poor whites as having been fostered by the large planter class and the government, as a device to preserve poor-white loyalty and to mitigate what otherwise could have been severe class tensions within the white community, between the wealthy, landowning planter class and the landless, powerless whites. For a long time the existence of a large black population prevented class conflict within white society.

Intermarriage

One measure of the level of interethnic acceptance or rejection is the rate of intermarriage between two groups. The early years in the plantation colonies were marked by serious imbalance between the sexes; most of the colonists, the indentured servants, and the slaves were male. Authorities tried to help the situation by transporting white women to the colonies. These women, usually orphans, vagabonds, prostitutes, or other undesirables, were eagerly picked as mates by the white men, who themselves often had similar backgrounds.[52] The continuous lack of white women contributed to the tendency of white males to have sexual relations with black women. In 1681 a government official in Saint-Domingue reported that the colony had 4,000 white males but only 435 white women. Governor Blénac reported in 1713 that "the number of young [white] men is much larger than that of girls, which throws the young men into the disorder of living in nearly public concubinage with Negro and Mulatto women."[53] The willingness of Frenchmen to have sexual contact with women of another race does not, of course, connote any real acceptance of racial equality and reflects instead physical needs and opportunities in a society in which whites possessed a disproportionate share of money and power.

Marriage with women of another race could be seen as a greater sign of acceptance, and it did occur to a limited extent. A visitor to the West Indies in 1640 noted that black women, if they converted to Catholicism or married white men, were freed "and esteemed to be members of honest society." But the measure was clearly an expediency, for the writer explained that because of the "lack of French women one accommodates oneself to this necessity."[54] In 1688 it was reported that there had been twenty marriages that year between whites and negresses or women of color.[55] In Bourbon in the Indian Ocean, where a slave plantation society had similarly evolved, a ship's officer reported of the settlers in 1674 that "the unfortunates asked for wives, most of them having had to marry Negresses, their slaves."[56] But even dire necessity could not maintain this custom for long. The authorities in Bourbon wished to make clear that the right of white rule imposed a caste system and forbade intermarriage between whites and blacks, since allowing intermarriages "would discourage the blacks from serving, and it is forbidden for blacks to marry white women; it is a confusion to be avoided."[57]

The slave code for the Antilles, the *code noir* of 1685, based on Roman law, declared all free men equal, regardless of previous status; it permitted marriage between a slaveowner and his slave, provided that she and her children were freed, and it attempted to discourage sexual exploitation of female slaves by fining the owner and by confiscating the slaves and any children born of an illicit union. The code, however, was more a legal ideal than a social reality. The mores of the settlers and government regulations in both Versailles and the colonies eroded many of its provisions. Slave women were not protected from sexual exploitation, and the provisions for confiscation of concubines and illegitimate offspring were not enforced. The code allowed marriage between free blacks (slaves who became free at the time of their marriage to whites) and whites, but these provisions were also quickly eroded. Before the promulgation of the code, as early as 1667, there had been attempts in Guadeloupe to discourage marriage between whites and blacks, and in 1711 Guadeloupe became the first French colony in the Americas to forbid it. The 1724 code for Louisiana followed suit.[58] These laws reflected local prejudice. Even the colonial clergy, which should have insisted on the equality of all before the marriage sacrament, denounced miscegenation; the superior of missions called it "a criminal coupling of men and women of different species, whence comes a fruit which is one of Nature's monsters."[59]

If in the 1660s some settlers had taken black wives, the tradition had quickly waned in the face of local prejudice. Father Labat, who had served in the West Indies in the 1690s, observed that he had met only "two whites who had married Negresses."[60]

The legal obstacle to intermarriage sought to prevent any confusion between the status of free men and slaves, thus keeping intact the master-slave relationship; but these provisions also included a racial component. Whites were forbidden from marrying not only their slaves but also free black women; yet the law did not forbid all free men from marrying black women. Thus, the Louisiana slave code of 1724 reiterated the 1685 provision forbidding slaveowners from keeping their slaves as concubines and threatened owners with heavy fines. A separate provision regarding colored or black freedmen also forbade them from sexually exploiting their female slaves, but allowed them to escape the punishment of the law by marrying them.[61]

That laws against miscegenation were not motivated solely by the desire to prevent a breach in the slave system may also be seen in attitudes toward marriages of white men with free colored women. Father Dutertre found it to be a "disorder" and lamented that it was "terrible and almost without remedy."[62] Later in the seventeenth century, marriage with women of color was denounced in terms that bordered on biological determinism; echoing the opinion held by planters, the Church, and his peers in the administration, a government official wrote in 1681:

> I am only too well convinced of the bad results of such marriages which have caused much scandal and disorder. It is true that the debauchery of the Spanish and Portuguese has brought them to alliances with such an impure stock; but I can also say that their colonies are abodes of abomination, vice, and filth, and that from these unions, there has sprung a people so wretched and so weak that a hundred of our buccaneers can put to rout a thousand of that *canaille*.[63]

While some lower-class whites did marry women of color, a stigma was attached to interracial unions, and such marriages were forbidden for the higher classes. Louis XIV revoked the titles of several noblemen who had married women of color.[64] The choice of marriage partners and the laws regarding marriage are not necessarily proof of racialism, however. After all, it is rather common among ethnic, social, and religious groups to choose marriage partners from within the group. And even laws restricting intermarriage can be seen in a different light. It was possible during the Ancien Régime to dissolve marriages that were viewed as improper or degrading to one of the members, because of either the chasm in social position between the partners or the personal life of one of them.[65] But if one looks at the laws and customs regarding interracial marriage as part of a larger social matrix, then indeed their racial nature becomes more apparent. For it was not only in regard to marriage that custom and law imprinted inequality among the races.

The Freedmen

The slave code of 1685, which outwardly had the appearance of promoting racial equality,[66] contained contradictions between egalitarian pretensions and the determination never to forget the slave origin of the freedmen. Thus the *code noir* in its article 59 assured the equality of all men, regardless of their previous servitude: "We desire that they have the same rights for their persons and their property as our other subjects enjoying natural liberty." Yet there was a difference; the previous article, number 58, commanded the freed slaves to "special respect" for their former masters; if they injured their masters, they were to be more harshly punished.[67] Freedmen giving asylum to runaway slaves were given far stiffer sentences than were the other subjects of the king.[68] The mores of the settlers and government regulations both in the islands and in Versailles further eroded the equality granted freedmen. The willingness of whites to arm freedmen has been seen as denoting a certain egalitarian attitude,[69] but even slaves were armed. Such policies were motivated by desperation and by the lack of sufficient white men for militia service, and do not really say very much about the attitudes of one group toward another.[70]

It is easy to explain the increasingly discriminatory policies of the late eighteenth century, when the colonies contained large populations of free colored peoples whom the colonists distrusted and felt the need to control. But the early legislation against freedmen reveals a sensitivity to race that cannot be explained totally in terms of social control; after all, in 1700 there were only 500 free coloreds in Saint-Domingue. Many of them were slaveowners themselves; thus, in the eyes of whites, there should not have been any necessity for suspecting that the freedmen would throw in their lot with the slaves.

Racial attitudes, especially those of whites toward freedmen, it has been argued, were often influenced by demographic factors. Thus, it is pointed out that in England's North American colonies the number of white settlers was so large that the slaveholding society did not have to be accommodating toward the free coloreds, since whites provided sufficient military and free-labor forces. In the Iberian colonies, however, it is averred that the shortage of whites made the society far more dependent on freedmen and therefore more accommodating toward them.[71] The French colonies should fit into the pattern posited for the Iberian colonies, for they were characterized by slave societies containing very few whites, constantly short of skilled labor and dependent for the artisan work force, as well as for the military, on the freedmen. The need of white society to secure the aid of the free colored should have led to a moderate policy toward them. But it seldom did.

The curtailment of full equality for freedmen already inherent in the *code noir* was increased as the years passed. As early as 1705, a government ordinance provided re-enslavement for any freedmen and their families who helped runaway slaves.[72] The 1724 code of Louisiana seemed to assimilate freedmen to slaves when, in the same article, it threatened with physical punishment "thefts committed . . . by slave or by freedmen."[73] In that same decade, freedmen in the Antilles were forbidden to dress as whites.[74] As early as the 1680s, freedmen were subject to poll taxes; by 1724 the few loopholes that had existed for a few of them were abolished, and all freedmen had to pay these discriminatory taxes.[75] These laws also reflected the increasingly pronounced attitude that the colored were more akin to blacks than to whites. In the seventeenth century, most officials seem to have assimilated them with Europeans, but after only a few decades they began to refer to them as "Negroes." A royal ordinance of 1713, for instance, did so.[76]

By custom in the early years, colored slaves were manumitted upon reaching a certain age; with time this age was periodically raised, and, by the 1670s and 1680s, it was no longer automatic for slaveowners to free these slaves, often their own progeny. The code of 1685, by proclaiming the Roman law of "partus sequitur ventrem" (a principle that seems to have been adopted in custom after 1674), reinforced the resistance to liberating colored slaves. If it could be proved that the slaveowner had sired the child, he legally had to free him, but this provision seems to have been rarely enforced. In the face of a growing number of freedmen, legal restrictions on manumitting slaves were adopted in 1711; henceforth, slaves could be freed only with government authorization.[77] Later, prohibitive fees were imposed upon slaveowners wanting to free their slaves. This was quite different from the policy of the Spanish government, which interfered (after the 1789 code) only when manumission was obviously a way of ridding oneself of an overaged or sick dependent.

Although not all people of color were free, nearly all freedmen were colored; few were black.[78] After the 1680s emancipation depended upon the individual whim of owners, who were more likely to free illegitimate offspring than to free anyone else on the plantation. Regardless of who had sired the colored slaves, it seems to have been their occupations that brought them their freedom. By custom they were not field workers. The planters had developed notions about which "nations" were suitable for various kinds of work around the plantation, based on what they imagined to be the "nature of each nation," their physical or intellectual ability to carry out certain kinds of work, or their previous experiences in Africa. The colored were seen as having certain innate capacities that qualified them for skilled artisan work. While the service of fieldhands would be lost if they were liberated, this was not necessarily true of artisans. Slaveowners could free their colored slaves without fearing the loss of their services. In addition to manumissions, the growth in number of the freedmen was due to biological reproduction. Unlike the white and black populations, which constantly needed replenishing by imports of new manpower, the colored population, which was indigenous to the Antilles (as large proportions of the other two groups were not), seems to have gained considerable immunity to the various diseases that ravaged the colonies.

The impression that the French were relatively generous in their manumission policies comes from the fact that the ratio of freedmen to the total free population was allowed to grow. From having constituted 13.6 percent of the free population in Martinique in 1764, for instance, this group grew to 50 percent by the end of the century; by 1786 a similar trend in Saint-Domingue led to freedmen's constituting nearly 40 per-

cent of the free population. Such figures compare favorably
with the emancipation policy of Barbados, which, throughout
the eighteenth century, did not permit free colored people to
constitute even so much as 5 percent of the free population.
(But, lest one generalize hastily about national traditions, it
should be noted that in 1775 British Jamaica had a free
colored population constituting as large a proportion of the
free population as that of Martinique—25 percent.)

These proportions, of course, not only are a function of the
number of freedmen but also depend upon the number of
whites in the colony; if the number of whites drops or stays
stable while the number of freedmen grows, the ratio of free
men of color to free population seems to rise disproportionately. For example, in Martinique in 1726 the white population was 10,959; after subsequent fluctuations, in 1789 it was
10,636. In the meantime, the number of freedmen had increased from 1,304 to 5,235. (It is worth repeating that,
though some of this increase was undoubtedly due to emancipation, how much of it was due to natural increase is not
known.) In proportion to the total free population, the freedmen had gained substantially—from 13 percent to 50
percent—but in part this larger proportion was due to the
failure of the white population to increase. Had the white
population increased between 1726 and 1789 at the same
yearly rate as it had in the thirty years prior to 1726, the proportion of free men of color to free population would have
been only 25 percent.[79] Thus the significance of the proportion of freedmen in the free class should not be exaggerated.

A better index of the willingness of slave societies to grant
freedom to ex-slaves would be the ratio of freedmen to slaves,
for, except through natural increase (admittedly, an important
exception), it was from the slave group that freedmen
emerged. The ratio of freedmen to the total population of African descent (colored freedmen plus slaves) shows far less variation among slave societies than one might have suspected.
Thus, in the 1780s, free colored people provided 4.2 and 4.3
percent of the total population of African descent in Martinique and Saint-Domingue, respectively. The proportion in
Barbados was 1.3 percent (in 1786); in Jamaica, 2.3 percent (in

1775); in the Upper South of the United States (in 1790), 5.5 percent, and in the Deep South, 1.6 percent. Brazil had a truly liberal policy of manumitting slaves; in the 1780s over 40 percent of the total population of African descent was freed. In the face of Brazilian conditions, the variance of the French West Indies from other Caribbean colonies (1 to 3 percent), loses significance.

The Treatment of Slaves

The treatment of slaves in the French West Indies reveals no particular sensitivity to the personality of the slave, as Tannenbaum allegedly found in the Spanish slave system. It was a highly exploitative system that put a premium on production. Even though the French colonies were behind many of their neighbors in adopting the use of animals and mechanical devices in agriculture, they had higher rates of production. The Englishman Bryan Edwards observed in the late eighteenth century that Saint-Domingue yielded 25 percent more sugar per acre than did Jamaica. And generally French slaveowners had the reputation of being the most efficient in the West Indies.[80] They enforced harsh discipline, which demanded long hours of hard work from the slaves.

Punishments of extreme severity were meted out without the local authorities' taking much interest in the way slaves were treated. True, the code of 1685 had set certain limits. For instance, killing a slave was a crime. But penalties were light: banishment from the colony was a common way of punishing a white man who had killed a slave, and sometimes only a fine was imposed.[81] The nineteenth-century historian Peytraud revealed a scale of punishments for slaveowners who abused their slaves: thus, the fine for having cut off a slave's hands was two livres; for having burnt a slave alive, sixty livres; for having cut out a slave's tongue, six livres.[82] These relatively small fines were hardly an important deterrent. To use a contemporary yardstick, the price of a slave was between 600 and 1,000 livres. Standards of justice differed for whites and blacks; on the same day in 1670 that a court in Martinique demoted a white militia lieutenant for "aggravating his wife and mutilating his Negroes," a slave was condemned to have his leg cut off and be hung from the gallows because he had killed an ass.[83] Any concern that the state did show for slaves was occasioned partly by the knowledge that extreme mistreatment might cause slave disorders and the breakdown of an efficient, disciplined, slave-labor force. One could not really say that either the planters or the government authorities had an overriding concern for the welfare of the slaves.

The harsh discipline of the slave system was seen as essential for its preservation. Father Dutertre explained that it was necessary to treat the slaves with "disdain, not to pardon them any faults . . . because if these slaves thought one feared them, they would become more insolent and defiant and form conspiracies to free themselves from captivity."[84] This was a point of view that became ever stronger with the passage of years, as the slaves began to outnumber whites, and as the problem of slave discipline became increasingly intractable. Father Labat explained that it was necessary to intimidate the slaves, since they outnumbered their masters ten to one.[85] In French Canada slavery was far milder and the slave had a legal identity: he could serve as a witness at marriages and testify against free persons. His status there has been seen as proof of French sensitivity to the humanity of blacks, and the result of a paternalistic policy by both Church and state.[86] The situation in the French West Indies seems to reveal, however, that the treatment of slaves in Canada was due not to specific cultural traits of the French but, rather, to demographic factors. From 1630 to 1759, French Canada had a total of only 3,604 slaves, of whom 1,132 were blacks.[87] No complex system of discrimination was necessary to keep this small number under control; in proportion to the white population, they represented a fraction of one percent.[88]

The severity of the French slave system in the Antilles was dictated by what was seen as the necessity to dominate a hard-to-control, difficult population. Father Labat spoke of the slaves as "ready to revolt, to do anything and commit the most horrible crimes to win their freedom."[89]

Slaves sometimes did revolt. They did murder their owners and engage in various conspiracies, thus justifying their masters' fears. But there also seems to have been a certain projection of guilt by the colonists. By attributing a constant criminal tendency to the slave population, they justified the harsh method of control exercised. Assumptions about the danger that the black population posed and the consequent need to deal with blacks harshly pervaded the thinking of white planter society. If these attitudes were not shared by Frenchmen in Europe, once they crossed the ocean they too became afflicted by fear of the black population, and also convinced of the rightness of the harsh discipline that negated the slave's humanity. Father Labat told of the shock that French visitors experienced upon first seeing the slaves' naked shoulders scarred by the whip; he added that such a view "excited the compassion of those who were not accustomed, but soon one is."[90] Legally, the slaves were not fully human beings; the *code noir* had declared them to be property. And, as Father Dutertre noted, they were treated "like animals."[91]

The French slaving experience paralleled that of the other European powers: England, Holland, Spain, and Portugal. They too had ruthlessly exploited black labor and established racial legislation. While the modes varied, all plantation colonies were characterized by racial barriers erected by law and social custom. Europeans, regardless of national tradition, reacted in the same ways and attempted to regulate and control slaves and their offspring. The dominant white minorities in all these societies reacted similarly because they faced similar problems: they were minorities, confronted by growing black-slave and colored-free populations. By insisting on racial categories, whites could exclude freedmen and preserve their own power. Fear and the desire for domination helped reinforce existing negative attitudes toward blacks. Doctrines upholding racial domination served to justify slavery, and, it was hoped, would help preserve it. The similarities among Europeans in their reactions toward blacks in the plantation colonies are far more striking than the apparent national differences.

The Image of Blacks in Slavery

As a result of observing blacks in slavery, the whites in the Antilles formed an essentially negative view of the African race. Such an image was nearly inevitable, since slaveowners have always assumed that their right to domination was based on physical and moral superiority. Observing Africans in captivity, Europeans felt that they had empirical evidence that proved blacks to be particularly depraved. The colonists were usually insufficiently aware of the extent to which slavery as an institution had led to the blacks' condition. Whites deplored that the Africans were shiftless and unwilling to stay in the plantation at night, roaming the countryside instead.[92] They did not understand that it was because they were often insufficiently fed, and because the sex ratios of the plantation made it necessary for males to search for sexual companionship elsewhere. Likewise, if blacks were prone to steal, it was for good reason, for they had to supplement the meager diet provided. If they seemed less than eager to work, that was the natural condition of their involuntary employment, further aggravated by malnutrition and various diseases. And, of course, feigning certain behavior patterns was a means of protection against further exactions from their masters.[93] It is certainly ironic that whites, who considered plantation work far too tiring, denounced their slaves' lack of enthusiasm for working in the fields.

Slave resistance to the masters' attempted controls frustrated white society. Baffled in their efforts, plantation owners and missionaries complained of black perfidy, stupidity, and laziness.[94] This litany was monotonously repeated in most descriptions of blacks. Before the French seriously began to engage in the slave trade, they had developed hostile attitudes toward blacks in the sporadic contacts that they had had with Africa. The slave trade, however, seems on the whole to have come about independently of the negative image that the black occupied in French thought. But once the slave enterprise began, this experience further injured the French view of blacks; in law and in reality, slavery confirmed the proclaimed inequality of blacks.

3

The Philosophes and Africa

The French philosophes' approach to the African was affected by a total view of man and society. The image of the black man was a by-product of eighteenth-century thought about the impact of nature on man and about the structure and destiny of human societies. In the process of creating a general science of man, eighteenth-century thinkers also helped develop and strengthen an earlier era's image of black people.

Despite a belief in human equality, eighteenth-century thinkers, in their very eagerness to understand and classify people, developed a concept of human inequality based on climatic, cultural, and racial criteria. By the end of the century, a systematic body of thought, which claimed to see a coincidence between the physical and the cultural person, and even to see the latter as shaped by biology, had developed. The Enlightenment thus has served not only as a source of inspiration to the cultural relativism of the waning twentieth century but also as an origin of the biological racism so prevalent in the nineteenth century.[1]

The Search for a Science of Man

Filled with curiosity about the world around them and convinced that all knowledge was within their reach, the philosophes had a voracious appetite for the intellectual conquest of the new world revealed through European expansion overseas. This expansion had taken the forms of missionizing, trade, exploration, and conquest. Sometimes all four occurred in a region simultaneously, as was the case with the Spanish in South America and with the French in Canada, but at other times the four elements were not necessarily interconnected.

The information about distant and strange lands did not rep-

60

resent merely a collection of curiosities, as it had earlier, but rather it provided material from which to fashion an understanding of man. The eighteenth century marked the development of a truly comparative method of studying cultures.

In many ways, the eighteenth-century approach to the study of man was closer to the anthropology of our day than, for instance, the nineteenth-century view would be. In its universalism, in its concept of man as a function of his total environment, both natural and human, the program for the science of man established by eighteenth-century thinkers still inspires the modern anthropologist.[2] Twentieth-century Europeans, used to thinking of their own culture as brittle and of the world as a small, insignificant globe lost in the cosmos, can identify easily with the universalist aspirations of the philosophes.

The Enlightenment contributed to the development of what was later to become ethnology by stressing the need for exact observation and for the objective reporting of actions in terms of the values and assumptions of the foreign society, rather than as projections of Eurocentric values.[3] Frenchmen's voyages around the world created a heightened interest in geography; in 1785 it was suggested that a geographical society be founded in Paris, for the purpose of collating information and producing more exact maps.[4] A little more than a decade later, the Society for the Observation of Man was founded to chart, not the earth itself, but the different peoples who lived on it. Writing for the Society, Joseph Marie Dégérando, in the essay *The Observation of Savage Peoples,* established a program for the fledgling scientific group. Explorers were often mistaken, Dégérando wrote, because "they habitually judge the customs of savages by analogies drawn from our own customs, when in fact they are so little related to each other." Prejudice clouded the vision of travelers, and "they have inferred too lightly from the circumstances of their reception, conclusions about the absolute and ordinary character of the men among whom they have penetrated." Anticipating twentieth-century notions of the role of the anthropologist as observer-participant, Dégérando wrote, "The first means to the proper knowledge of the Savages is to become after a fashion like one of them."

Dégérando pushed furthest a long line of criticisms of past travelers and presented new criteria for observation.[5]

In the same vein, J. A. Perreau, an international legal authority and judge, wrote in 1802 his *Considérations physiques et morales sur la nature de l'homme et ses facultés*. He blamed travelers for their superficial reporting about foreign peoples. He argued for a functional approach to all societies. All acts of every people were essentially rational; thus, if a people were found putting grease on themselves, it was probably because originally the climate had necessitated it, and then it had become a tradition. Religious customs, too, were fulfillments of some kind of social need.[6] Perreau's ideas were nearly a century ahead in social thought, but they were to have no immediate echo.

Impediments to Knowing Africa

In spite of the developing sensitivity to the need for exact and empathetic observation, there was relatively little exploration of Africa. The difficulties of knowing the continent were real enough; the physical terrain and the disease-laden environment effectively blocked Europeans from successfully penetrating inland. The most frequent European visitors to Africa were the slave crews, and their mortality rate was a frightful indicator of what might await other Europeans.[7]

The myths of African savagery that had existed for so long also created some trepidation of penetrating the interior. Pruneau de Pommegorge, who had been a merchant in the Upper Senegal, declared, "It is impossible to have knowledge of the far interior of the country, because to reach it one has to cross so many nations which are often barbaric, that the white who would be brave enough to attempt such a voyage would have his neck chopped off before he reached it."[8] Quick and safe means of exploration such as following the rivers that flowed out to the coast of West Africa were preferred. As a result, by the late seventeenth century, the French had already been up the Senegal River to its sources, but relatively little overland exploration had been undertaken. Abbé Prévost remarked that European knowledge of Africa is limited nearly to the coast and some of the rivers such as the Senegal and the Gambia. We know the interior sites so little that we cannot with certitude speak of their location, their extensions and limits. ... Africa is nearly unknown as compared to Asia and America, although it hardly is inferior in the variety and value of its products.[9]

Although the difficulties of knowing Africa were real enough, it should be noted that there was also a general lack of interest in the continent. Exploration overland in South America was virtually as forbidding, yet that had not stopped the intrepid expeditions of La Condamine in 1733 and 1743.

Africa just was not the object of as much intellectual curiosity as were the Americas or Asia. Montesquieu's library included forty-five books that contained geographic and topographic descriptions, but none was specifically on Africa. Only one book concerned itself at any length with blacks, and that was on the Antilles—Father Labat's *Nouveau voyage aux îles de l'Amérique*.[10] Voltaire, who had written a successful play using China as a backdrop, was told he should write a play with Africa as a setting, but, significantly, he never did. His library reflected his interests; among the 3,867 titles that Voltaire owned, 133 dealt with the non-European world, and of these seventy dealt with Asia, twenty-six with the West Indies, and only four with Africa.[11]

The small interest also meant a dismal lack of knowledge. In literature Africa was often assimilated to the other non-European areas of the world, without any recognizable characteristics of its own. Typical was the anonymous publication in 1740 of *Histoire de Louis Anniaba, roi d'Essénie en Afrique sur la côte de Guinée,* the story of an African who had pretended to be a prince and who had been received at Louis XIV's court. Anniaba is not described as black, for the fictional account included many comedies of error involving mistaken identity, implying that the author must have thought of Anniaba as being at most no darker than a North African. The novel seems heavily affected by the "turqueries" so popular at the time. Thus Anniaba's father's favorite wife is called "Sultan" and so is his aunt.[12]

Local color was never well depicted in novels that claimed to have Africa as a scene. The young Anne-Louis de Staël made no particular distinction in depicting Indians of America and blacks of Africa; they were even given the same names. Another author also writing at the end of the eighteenth century, Marie Gouze, writing under the pseudonym Olympe de Gouges, seems to have had the same problem, and in fact she referred interchangeably to her heroes, Zamor and Mirza, as Indians and blacks.[13]

Some geographic knowledge was available from the travel literature, but there was a disconcerting lack of interest in using it. For instance, Father Loyer's travel account about the Ivory Coast, which contained rather precise information on that region, was reprinted in 1740, but there is no clue of its having been used by the anonymous author of the Prince Anniaba history, nor may one even surmise that the author ever looked at any of the maps of Africa then available. Anniaba is described as docking his ship at Meknès, although it is located eighty miles inland, and he is said to have arrived in Issiny after disembarking at the mouth of the Senegal River, although that river is some 1,500 miles north of Issiny.[14]

Thus, as a result of the European powers' rather modest attention to Africa, few new ideas and attitudes toward the continent developed; instead, many of the issues first broached in the seventeenth century were further elucidated. Some issues were, of course, transformed, but many vague ideas crystallized and helped form even the nineteenth-century image of Africa. These attitudes, it should be made clear, were shaped by the educated class that was exposed to the travel literature and to various other treatises of the day. As for the rest of the populace—if the literature that was aimed at them is any indication—they remained totally ignorant of Africa.[15]

Popular experience with or knowledge of Africans was limited to contact with the 5,000 or so blacks who resided in France. Mostly abandoned or freed slaves and stranded seamen, blacks occupied marginal positions in French society. They were jugglers, boxers, servants, and sometimes, in port cities, were connected with the underworld of crime and prostitution. Few in number but visible by their color, blacks were held in low esteem, ridicule, and fear. Popular opinion thus joined with the written culture in creating images of the African.

Perpetuation of Old Images

Few eighteenth-century French travelers to Africa published descriptions of their experiences and so the image of the African held during the Enlightenment was essentially based on works published in the seventeenth century or in the first quarter of the eighteenth. These views were easily available and became pervasive through the eighteenth century as a result of their appearance in a number of collective works. The general interest in travel literature of the eighteenth-century reading public led to such successes as the *New General Collection of Voyages and Travels,* published from 1745 to 1747 in London by John Green; one volume of this four-volume work concerned Africa.

Abbé Prévost, who had lived in England and who was one of the leading French Anglophiles, was attracted by the format of the Green volumes and by their commercial success. Constantly in debt, he was on the lookout for means of rehabilitating his financial situation, the result of a life-style quite at variance with that expected of a man of the cloth.[16] Prévost translated Green in seven volumes and then added a considerable number of new accounts; Prévost's work was published in fifteen volumes from 1746 to 1759, as *Histoire générale des voyages.* Like Green, Prévost organized his volumes by regions and included a survey of what various travelers had said of them. Prévost's work was an immediate publishing success. After his death five more volumes were edited under his name, so that the whole *Histoire générale,* including the index, ran to twenty-one volumes. The first edition was sumptuously edited and became a collector's item. A copy of the quarto edition appeared in a much cheaper, eighty-volume version, published between 1746 and 1789.[17] It was handy enough so that voyagers such as Montcalm and Bougainville carried this popular edition with them overseas. Prévost was read throughout the eighteenth century, and his ideas had considerable influence in shaping the philosophes' attitudes toward non-Europeans. Buffon, the *Encyclopédie,* and Rousseau gleaned most of their information from Prévost and often even plagiarized the *Histoire.*[18]

The information on Africa that Prévost disseminated was a compilation of the rather contradictory and mostly negative material from seventeenth- and early-eighteenth-century travel accounts. A hastily compiled work, the *Histoire générale* lacks a consistent view. Of the peoples of West Africa, Prévost wrote as follows:

> Since they are naturally sly and violent they cannot live in peace with each other. The Europeans who are not safe from their insults can find no better vengeance than to burn their huts and ruin their plantations. On the other hand the Negroes of Sierra Leone are sober. . . . They have more feeling and intelligence than the Negroes in the other parts of the Guinea Coast.

Prévost generalized:

> The Negroes in general are given over to incontinence. Their women, who are no less stirred by the pleasure of the senses, employ herbs and barks to excite their husbands. These vicious customs reign here. . . . But the inhabitants (of the Guinea coast) are more moderate, more gentle more sociable, than the other Negroes. They do not like to shed blood, and don't think of war unless they are forced to by the need to defend themselves.

Prévost further found blacks to be friendly, generous, and hospitable, and commented that "theft is very rare among them."[19] While giving a balance sheet of both virtues and vices ascribed to Africans, Prévost on the whole left a negative impression with his reader. He would admit that a particular ethnic group had some positive qualities and then would add that these were exceptions to the rule of African behavior.

A second eighteenth-century collection of writings that informed the French public about the non-European world was Count Buffon's *L'histoire naturelle.* While not pretending to deal with geography or travels, Buffon's work contained much information on the various populations of the world. Like Prévost before him and the *Encyclopédie* afterward, Buffon summarized and crystallized the ideas of his era. Buffon's writings had great importance because of their wide dissemination; in his investigation of 500 eighteenth-century private libraries, the historian Daniel Mornet discovered Buffon's works to be the third most commonly owned.[20] The beautifully bound volumes with the name of France's foremost naturalist on them gave the volumes and the ideas contained in them an aura of authority. With no particular experience of Africa, Buffon, pen in hand, used his literary gifts to paint a dramatic picture of the African. The passages on the African's character were spicy and—as Buffon intended his whole work to be— entertaining. He described the blacks of Guinea as idle and inactive, having passion only for women. Lacking any sense of imagination or innovation, Africans trudged old pathways, rather than cutting new and shorter ones. "Deficient in genius," they lived in rich agricultural areas but did not cultivate them. Africans became debauched at an early age and also died young, having exhausted themselves by too frequent sexual intercourse since youth.[21]

A negative opinion of Africans was common among thinkers of the Enlightenment. Montesquieu declared that most of the people "of the coasts of Africa are savage and barbarian"; they were bereft "of industry and have no arts." Voltaire said of blacks that "they are incapable of great attention, they reason little, and do not seem made to enjoy the advantages nor the disadvantages of our philosophy." The worst condition of human barbarism that Voltaire could imagine was that of the Africans. In order to emphasize the immorality of allowing people to live in such unhealthy conditions as the Parisian slums, Voltaire exclaimed that the housing tenements were "a witness of the barbarism which puts us much lower than the Hottentots or the Negroes." Similarly, Diderot, in an article contributed to the *Encyclopédie,* described the people of the Ivory Coast as debauched, without church, religion, or belief in life after death. Drawing from Labat, the *Encyclopédie* described a king in Senegal to be a "wretch who most often does not have enough millet to eat and who pillages neighboring villages. . . . They steal from each other and sell each other to the European." The supplement to the *Encyclopédie* published in 1780 summarized the prevailing attitude toward African institutions and peoples:

> The government is nearly everywhere bizarre, despotic, and totally dependent on the passions and whims of the sovereign. These peoples have, so to speak, only ideas from one day to the next, their laws have no principles . . . no consistency other than that of a lazy and blind habit. They are blamed for ferociousness, cruelty, perfidy, cowardice, laziness. This accusation is but too true.[22]

A notable exception, based both on personal observation and on accounts of fellow missionaries in the Congo (but by no means free of "borrowings" from other writers), was Father Proyart's *Histoire de Loango, Kakongo et autres royaumes,* published in 1776. Proyart denounced Abbé Prévost's *Histoire des voyages* for misleading the public by giving such a negative image of Africans. Misunderstandings about Africa had occurred as a result of credence in accounts by traders and slave-dealers who did not dwell in Africa for any length of time. Cheating the coast dwellers with whom they came into contact, Europeans quickly discovered that Africans also cheated in commercial transactions and from this experience drew the conclusion that all Africans were unreliable.

Proyart tried to lay to rest most of the prevailing myths about Africans. Africans were not lazy: those who found it profitable to work did so. Women always worked, and, besides, the climate was so hot that no one could work regularly. The inhabitants were gentle, hospitable, just, and polite. Unlike most of the missionaries preceding and succeeding him, Father Proyart was not shocked by African nudity. He explained that it was perfectly natural to be scantily clad in warm weather and suggested instead that the demi-nudity of French women at court, intended purely to be suggestive, was scandalous. Both men and women in Africa were chaste. Unlike so many other missionaries, Proyart was a realist; he understood the difficulties inherent in the missionary effort and made clear that the slow progress of Christianity was not the fault of the

Africans. The cause was rather the inability of missionaries to adjust to the climate, the ravages of tropical diseases, and the difficulty of the local languages. Proyart complained that prejudiced views of the Africans were based on insufficient observation and wild speculation and did not belong to a "century which preaches reason and humanity."[23] Proyart's account bears witness to his intellectual integrity, but did little to reverse the existing modes of thought.

Few Frenchmen who had had firsthand experience of Africa resisted the general eighteenth-century attitude toward the continent; rather, they tended to reinforce it. Demanet, who served as a priest in Senegal and who was more interested in a good phrase than in accuracy, penned a clever aphorism about Africans. Wrote Demanet, "They pass their youth in debauchery, their middle age in laziness, their old age without remorse."[24]

In writing of Africa, those who had been there often integrated personal observations, current prejudice, and older travel reports. In 1802 Golberry, who had served in Senegal in the 1780s, published *Fragmens d'un voyage,* which contains all three elements. The personal observations tend to be inconsistent. Many of the notes may have been written in the 1780s, when a certain Negrophilia existed in France; some other passages were probably added just before publication, in the atmosphere of Negrophobia caused by the Saint-Domingue uprisings. As a result, the *Fragmens* does not show a coherent attitude toward blacks. At times blacks are shown as noble, at other times as savage, and slavery is depicted as a beneficent institution.

Lamiral, a former official who proclaimed himself deputy for Senegal in the Revolutionary Assembly, made positive assessments of the peoples of Senegal; he was impressed by the tender care that mothers gave their children and by the lack of hypocrisy in the relations between sexes. But at the same time he described all blacks as deprived by nature "of all moral character; they only have instincts. . . . Indulgence leads them to laziness, laziness to crime."[25]

The Noble Savage

The negative attitudes toward Africans were modified slightly by the existence of the Noble Savage myth. The myth was voiced particularly strongly by opponents of slavery, who wished to point out how unsuitable it was to enslave a people of so much virtue. Given the proslavery argument, which had rationalized black servitude in terms of African baseness, it became nearly inevitable that abolitionists would develop at great length a counter-myth of African nobility.[26]

Well developed in regard to the American Indian since the sixteenth century, the Noble Savage myth was extended with great ease to the "wise Chinese." The deist philosophes saw a desirable model in China, a society where mandarins (intellectuals) ruled and where Confucianism (a secular religion) predominated. It was inevitable that the general cult of the Noble Savage would also affect to some degree the French attitude toward other non-European peoples, including Africans. Rousseau and Raynal, using selective examples from Abbé Prévost's *Histoire des voyages,* wrote with admiration of the simple pastoral Hottentots who shared their belongings, of the blacks on the coast of Guinea who were hospitable to strangers, tender to their children, and respectful to their elders.[27]

Not only theorizers sitting at home but also men who had been to Africa added to the literature about the Noble Savage. Michel Adanson, the government botanist in Senegal, romanticized as he gazed from afar at an African village:

> Which way so ever I turned my eyes on this pleasant spot, I beheld a perfect image of pure nature. . . . The ease and indolence of the Negroes, reclined under the shade of their spreading foliage, the simplicity of their dress and manners, the whole revived in my mind the idea of our first parents, and I seemed to contemplate the world in its primeval state.[28]

To Golberry, nature in Africa seemed to provide a paradisiacal existence. Entering the bay of Sierra Leone, he admired the untouched forest filled with trees, which, instead of being hewn down, were admired and even regarded as "so to speak the object of a cult" by the peoples living there. Such lyricism was perhaps not an altogether personal reaction; though he had actually seen these landscapes, Golberry described them in phrases borrowed from that well-known painter of the romantic landscape, Chateaubriand.[29] The visual artistic iconography of the period often assimilated Africans to figures of the classical age or to American Indians.[30]

To members of an increasingly complex society, the presumed simplicity of the African was a virtue. What earlier had been pointed to as a sign of abasement was now singled out for praise; thus, a member of the abolitionist Société des amis des noirs was to praise Africans as having "few laws, few judges, few taxes."[31]

The Noble Savage myth was created to remind Europeans of the virtuous existence that was thought to be possible in a simpler, more natural environment. The African was upheld as noble in illustration of this thesis. In a letter to Pierre Hennin, his fellow philosophe Claude Rigobert Lefebvre de Beauvray wrote of the nobility of the Serrer peoples of the lower Senegambia. Their nobility was shown by their natural goodness even in the absence of religion and government. They did not need the strict dogmas of Christianity, Judaism, or Islam, or the control of government. Rather, from nature itself, they drew wise laws for human interaction.[32]

When the African was depicted as a Noble Savage, he was not always given the attributes with which Lefebvre endowed him. At times, the African's presumed savagery and barbarity were accentuated, the better to point out that if even such peoples could be generous and hospitable, take care of their children and the aged, respect authority and share property in common—then Europeans should be still more virtuous. Holbach used such an argument to vaunt the advantages of natural religion. Even though Africans idolized anything, "These gross superstitions do not prevent the Negroes from having correct ideas of a Supreme Being whom they regard as the ruler of heaven and earth." Diderot wrote that the Hottentots were a physically repugnant people who had neither churches, idols, nor cults, yet they lived under a prudent and wise government. He was implying that European peoples who believed themselves more brilliant still suffered under tyranny. Under the heading "Negroes, character of Negroes in general," the *Encyclopédie* described "the large number" as "always vicious . . . mostly inclined to lasciviousness, vengeance, theft, and lies." But they were also "all generally brave, courageous, charitable, obedient to their parents, especially their godfathers and mothers."[33]

The very authors who described Africans as noble also had strong reservations about them. Raynal in his antislavery polemics glowingly reported the virtues of the African, but he was repelled by the Hottentot, whom he described as a man who "always sat in the doorway of his hut, touched more by the past than the future, who slept a lot and got drunk." And, like the cattle they cared for, the Hottentots were dirty and stupid. Abbé Grégoire, for all his efforts to point out the nobility of blacks, cautioned that defense of the black's humanity should not lead to an exaggeration of his qualities. If the official Adanson had been reminded of a golden age when gazing upon a Senegalese village, he had also concluded from the lack of a regular road in the village that there could be no "stronger proof of the laziness and indolence of the Negroes." And Golberry, Boufflers' romantic aide, favored the continuation of black enslavement.[34]

The literary convention of the Noble Savage at times affected the manner in which Frenchmen viewed the African, but such an image was never consistent; the same author might be torn between conflicting views of the African as a noble savage and as a debased savage. Significantly, none of the eighteenth-century utopian writers who constructed imaginary societies for Europeans to emulate located them in Africa. While there was a vogue for setting utopias among the noble Chinese, American Indians, Persians, or Tahitians, Africans as a whole were not deemed worthy of such honors.[35]

Whereas the Noble Savage enjoyed a literary vogue, he never really conquered eighteenth-century French thought. After all, the philosophes wished to see their own society emerge from what was considered a dark age, a primitive stage of humanity, a level of life often thought to be similar to that of the various peoples living overseas in the Americas, Asia, or Africa. For Voltaire, there was nothing attractive in the life of the peoples whom Europeans, by common consent, called "savage." The whole purpose of humanity's struggles was to escape the "savage" state and ascend toward civilization, for savagery was a deformation of man and his purposes.[36] If the Enlightenment admired the laws of nature and therefore found reason to praise the Noble Savage, who presumably lived by nature's precepts, followed its laws, and shunned all artifice and hypocrisy, then the philosophes also were proud of man's triumph in taming nature, which allowed him to escape its worst elements.[37]

The Noble Savage theme was persistent in the eighteenth century, but it never was sufficiently dominant to color the way in which all non-European peoples were to be viewed. The literary convention of using "primitive" societies as foils for European shortcomings or as rival paradigms led to the inclusion of the African in the Noble Savage concept. While blacks were used in this manner, they appeared less often than other non-European peoples and never securely enough to avoid being condemned as savages and brutes.

The Force of Environment

The Noble Savage myth heightened European curiosity about the world overseas. This interest, in turn, led to the massive collection of data about various societies and to the first attempt at organizing a systematic science of man. Who man is, and why and how he is different in the various latitudes of the earth were some of the questions posed in the eighteenth century. To an age that had increasingly freed itself from the authority of revealed religion, an understanding of human variety was detectable not in some divine plan, but rather in the study of natural forces.

In its universalism, the Enlightenment declared all men to be equal; in the words of the philosophe Helvétius, "When born, men have no qualities, no tendencies for the good or the bad. They are then but the product of their education. If the Persian has no idea of liberty, the savage none of slavery, that is due to differences in education."[38] Helvétius was here articulating the Lockean notion of man's nature as a *tabula rasa,* subsequently formed by his environment. The development of individuals or groups was the result of climate, social arrangements, political institutions, and formal education.

European thinkers frequently pointed to climate as a crucial formative factor. Developed as early as Hippocrates and given much attention by the sixteenth-century political theorist Jean Bodin, the climatic theory flowered fully in the eighteenth century.[39] The extent to which climate was seen as crucial is shown in a claim in the memoirs of the French Academy of Sciences in 1705: that a child who had learned the rudiments of Latin forgot it all during the hot season, but regained the knowledge during the winter. This naive environmentalism is also reflected in the assertion of the *Journal des savans* that Newton could work more easily and successfully during the winter than during the summer.[40] Such statements reinforced the prevailing notions that men were more reasonable in temperate zones and more prone to violence and passion in hot climes. Montesquieu claimed that despotism flourished in hot countries, whereas constitutional systems were to be found in and were best fit for more temperate zones. Raynal saw climate imposing challenges to which societies had to respond: cold climate necessitated a struggle for subsistence and made members of societies in such a climate stronger, more hardworking, and active. But warmth created an abundance of vegetation and fruits, and thus, presumably, people did not have to labor for their existence; they became slothful, concerned only with satisfying their pleasures.[41] In theory all men were thus equal, but they did not all live under the same intensity of heat, so that there were gradations among men. As Montesquieu put it:

> You will find in the climates of the north peoples with few vices, many virtues, sincerity and truthfulness. Approach the south, you will think you are leaving morality itself, the passions become more vivacious and multiply crimes. . . . The heat can be so excessive that the body is totally without force. The resignation passes to the spirit and leads people to be without curiosity, nor desire for noble enterprise.[42]

Social forces were likewise seen as formative. Aristotle had already posited a link between types of government and mores. The Enlightenment, in upholding the need for governments to follow the laws of nature, had argued that, if governments departed from these natural laws, the result would be the perversion of the citizens. That, in part, had been the message of Montesquieu. In the same vein, Helvétius declared:

> Experience proves that the character and spirit of peoples change with the form of their government; that changes in government produce in the same nation a high or low, serious or flighty, courageous or timid character. Men are then nothing else but the product of their education.[43]

From seventeenth-century sources, the philosophes had gleaned information about African governments that gave the impression that there were either no governments or else very despotic ones. Either situation could be interpreted as leading to African depravity. The *Encyclopédie* supplement explained in its article on Africa, "The government is nearly everywhere bizarre, despotic, and totally dependent on the passions and whims of the sovereign." And it was as a result of these institutions that Africans were prone to vice.[44]

The *tabula rasa* concept emphasized education as a formative force. The *Encyclopédie* supplement explained the immorality and brutality ascribed to Africans as due to "the profound ignorance in which most are held, the barbarous and martial education which they nearly all have received, these [experiences] are enough to stifle or to prevent them from having the least ideas of natural law." Abbé Grégoire's essay, *An Enquiry,* which was meant to rehabilitate blacks, accepted the negative image of the Africans that his contemporaries had propagated. Grégoire wished to show that these shortcomings were not biological but, rather, were formed by the environment:

> What likeness can be found between whites, enlightened by the truths of Christianity (which leads to almost all others), enriched by the discoveries and information of all ages, and

stimulated by every species of encouragement, and blacks
deprived of all these advantages and devoted to oppression
and misery?[45]

In stressing the impact of climate, political institutions, and
education in the formation of group character, the Enlightenment was saying that men everywhere were the same; Buffon
declared Africans to "have the seeds of every virtue."[46] The
differences were due to external accident. But whatever the
reasons for these differences, they had occurred. Extreme
heat, despotic government (or anarchy), and lack of the
philosophes' ideas (or of Christianity) were deviations from
the European norm, inevitably leading to a degeneration of
man. Africans, subject to all these "abnormal forces," had in
fact become debased. If at a primary theoretical level all men
were equal, in real life their subjection to different environ-
ments had led to inequality.

The gradation of men according to environment gave rise to
the concept of a hierarchy of human races, with Europeans at
the top, subject, presumably, to the most benign environment,
and Africans at the bottom, subject to the worst.

Social Evolution

Eighteenth-century thinkers were fascinated by the study of
history and contributed to the development of history as a science. This interest was imbued with the conviction that history
was the story of human progress. The evolutionary view saw
modern European man as the accomplished result of centuries
of struggle against barbarism and ignorance. If in the seventeenth century there could still be a debate between the ancients and the moderns, one side vying for the superiority of
the classical age, the other optimistically insisting that there
had been considerable human progress since then, in the
eighteenth century the latter view was hardly open to debate.
It represented *grosso modo,* the general conviction of the age.

This evolutionary, historicist view had considerable impact
on the French image of non-Europeans. Frenchmen resorted
to a temporal historic paradigm to order and understand the

differences in material culture, social institutions, and mores that they observed overseas. As early as the sixteenth and seventeenth centuries, Frenchmen, when observing Indians or Caribs, had ascribed to them characteristics that they claimed reminded them of ancient Greece or Rome. It was, of course, an old classical tradition to ascribe to people with a less developed material culture virtues akin to those of mankind in some primeval era.[47] This tradition was further developed in the eighteenth century. The classical view of geographically distant peoples as representing a much earlier stage of human development also occurred, as early as the sixteenth century. The Jesuit fathers saw the Indians in Canada as latter-day Greeks or Romans. René Descartes declared that "traveling is nearly the same thing as talking with men of past centuries."[48]

Various non-European peoples were referred to as "savages" until the eighteenth century, but then they were increasingly called "primitive." "Primitive," originally meaning the initial, primary level, in the eighteenth century came to be used for contemporary men and societies that were believed to live at stages comparable to those of Europe in earlier eras.[49] The influential jurist Charles De Brosses asserted that some peoples were still living in "childhood," at a stage similar to the past of other peoples who by now had been able to raise themselves to higher levels. The possible identity of Africans with Europeans of the classical age was suggested by the missionary Father Proyart, who claimed that the peoples of Loango in Angola spoke a language related to both Hebrew and ancient Greek.[50] Just as Europe itself seemed "primitive" as one went further back in time, so places geographically distant from Europe became "primitive" as well. Space had assumed the same function as time.

This line of reasoning led to the assumption that peoples were more nearly perfect the closer they were to Europe. Thus one of the men accompanying Bougainville was startled by his experience in the South Seas: "How is it possible that a people so charming could be so far from Europe?" he wondered.[51] Implicit in the theory that proximity to Europe brought perfection was the ethnocentric belief that the "development" of a people could be measured in terms of how closely its agricultural, religious, political, and economic organization approached that of Europe. De Brosses concluded that there was a law of nature by which the more civilized a people was, the more it had a "religion which was truly pure and intelligent, as with us." Technical achievements and knowledge were another measure. When Poivre, the enlightened administrator of Ile-de-France, visited West Africa, he concluded that the lack of agricultural methods comparable to those in Europe meant that the inhabitants were "stupid men." Moreau de Saint-Méry even suggested that the manner in which a people danced might "serve as a way of creating a scale to know the varying degree of civilization of different peoples." His thesis was that savages had simple dance steps, whereas civilized Europeans had complex ones. Lamiral spelled out the implicit assumption of his age when he declared, "If nature had given all peoples the same amount of intelligence and the same genius, would they not all have made the same progress in the sciences, in the arts and civilization?"[52]

If human history made any sense—and the Enlightenment ardently held that it did—then the passage of time must have helped to perfect humanity as it passed through various stages. Condorcet sketched out the process by which humanity went from the credulous, pastoral stage to the scientific, urban stage. On the whole, eighteenth-century thinkers were optimistic and foresaw all societies eventually reaching perfection; by becoming enlightened, peoples could free themselves of the fetters that held them back. Holbach put it well when he wrote, "A chain of experiences leads the savage to the stage of a civilized society in which he concerns himself with the most sublime of sciences and the most complicated knowledge."[53]

"Primitive society" would, with the passage of time, reach levels of development akin to those of European society. The abolitionist Pétion de Villeneuve saw Africans through the evolutionist prism: "Certainly the African race has not brought its civilization, its industry, its development to the level of Europe." But his assumption was that it eventually would. Condorcet answered in the affirmative his own rhetorical question: "Will all the nations one day reach the level of civilization which the most enlightened, the freest, the least ignorant peoples such as the French and the Anglo-Americans have reached?"[54] Eighteenth-century thinkers saw African societies as being at the level of development where Europe had been not just a hundred, but maybe a thousand, years earlier. It seemed logical to believe that Africans might take a similar amount of time before they would reach European levels of "development." Most of the evolutionists had a rather static conception of their own society. They rather smugly felt that it had reached the pinnacle, the height of perfection that was possible for any society ever to attain. Typically, Condorcet thought of contemporary Europe as having reached the tenth and final stage. All of human history had a goal, which had been reached in eighteenth-century European society, or, at least, in the society about to be born through the efforts of the philosophes. All men had an equal potential for development; in this sense, the Enlightenment was egalitarian.

The Enlightenment recognized the humanity of peoples whose stage of development was as yet "primitive." The philosophes recognized the impact of climatic and other environmental forces in shaping human societies. And yet they clearly believed that Europe was the scale by which other societies were to be measured. Compared with Europe, Africa was "behind," "primitive," "savage."

The evolutionary view of history proclaimed each age as a stage in the improvement of man; the eighteenth century was superior to the seventeenth and considerably advanced over the Middle Ages. Since the philosophes had drawn an analogy between non-European cultures and Europe itself at earlier stages of history, it was quite natural that they would see "primitive" man at an inferior stage of development, far below Europe in the evolution of humanity.

The Debate on African Origins

Eighteenth-century thinkers, in their attempt to understand the variety in the physical makeup of man, tried to go beyond making singular statements about individual groups of men, but wished rather to understand where they all fitted into the great scheme of nature. By so doing they developed a hierarchical notion of human races and, by the later part of the century, had come to the conclusion that race was the determinant of human culture.

The most striking quality about Africans (although the *History of Anniaba,* for instance, revealed some obtuseness on even this point) continued to be their color. Seventeenth-century thinkers, in attempts to explain the Africans' blackness, had indirectly implied only that color gave a clue to the natural link between Africans and other men. Eighteenth-century thinkers were fully aware of the implications of the idea and were in fact interested in the question of the Africans' somatic features as explanations of their link with other men.

The most common explanation for the Africans' physique and color was environmental; the philosophes in their universalism believed that variations could be explained by accidental, environmental factors. Typical was Abbé Prévost, who collected all the evidence he could find in his successful periodical publication, *Pour et contre*; on balance, he favored an environmental explanation. Africans were black because they were exposed to the sun, he wrote. On the other hand, Prévost recognized problems with this explanation. The peoples of Brazil, it was true, were not so dark as Africans, even though that part of South America was also in the tropics. Prévost's explanation was somewhat tortured; Africa was larger than Brazil; therefore the sun dwelled longer on the continent, heated it up more, and darkened its people further. While Brazil had rivers, Africa was supposedly bereft of them, and hence was hotter.

Buffon added authority to the environmental explanation. Climate had such a pervasive effect on color, he wrote, that if a Senegalese were transplanted to Denmark, over the centuries his descendants would turn white. Conversely, if whites were transported to the Equator, the rays of the sun and the food available in hot regions would over a long period of time darken them and finally transform them into blacks. Unlike some other, more extreme seventeenth-century interpreters of the climatic explanation, Buffon did not believe that black children were born white and that their dark complexions

were due to sun exposure; rather, he recognized that "blackness is hereditary."[55] Only after long exposures to environmental forces could these hereditary traits be transformed.
That, of course, was not completely wrong, but still transformations in races require, as we now know, spans of time never
suspected by Buffon.

Daubenton, a scientist in his own right and Buffon's assis-
tant, believed so strongly in the effects of environment that he
maintained not only that the color of Africans was formed by
the rays of the sun, but also that Africans were not born with
"noses that flat, and lips that thick." Repeating earlier theories,
he asserted that Africans who did not find their children attractive enough would "crush their noses and squeeze their
lips so that they swell and thus believe they have beautified
nature while disfiguring it." Volney had a different explanation
for the supposed features of blacks; their physiognomy came
from squinting at the sun:

> The countenance of the Negroes represents precisely that
> stage of contraction that our faces assume when strongly af-
> fected by heat. The eyebrows are knit, the cheeks rise, the
> eyelids are contracted and the mouth distorted. This state of
> contraction, to which the features are perpetually exposed in
> the hot climates of the Negroes, has become the peculiar
> characteristic of their countenance.[56]

Environment seemed such an influence on physique that such
a popularizer as Abbé Delaporte wrote that, if an African were
transported to Europe, his descendants would turn white by
the second generation.[57]

The suggestion that Africans had become black as a result of
the tropical environment meant that nearly everyone thought
of humans as originally having been white; the blackness of
Africans was a degeneration caused by what were regarded as
unnatural ecological conditions. An anonymous article in the
Jesuit review *Mémoires de Trévoux* ascribed the Africans' blackness to climate; the article saw the transformation of white into
black as occurring rather naturally, since colors usually have a
propensity to turn into darker shades. The transformation was
seen as a degeneration; if climate changed colors, it took a

shorter time to go from white to black than the reverse. Whereas one could in "two centuries or six generations *descend* from white to black, it would take six times longer to *rise* again from black to white" (my italics). Buffon also saw the black man as a degeneration from the white, as the inevitable result of being exposed to extreme climate.[58] This theory was due mainly to Buffon's ethnocentrism, for it did not fit into his general theories about the interrelationship of climate and creation. On the contrary, it contradicted it. Buffon had posited that plants and animals had been created in hot areas and then spread to the rest of the globe. Man, curiously, was an exception to this principle. It was unthinkable for Buffon and most of his contemporaries that their race did not represent the pinnacle of creation, the first man.

First created white, man had been able to preserve his perfection in the climate in which he was created, but elsewhere the variations in temperature had led not only to a change in color but also to a "degeneration" of the whole body: hence the Africans' baseness. Cornelius de Pauw, building on climatic theories, declared Africans to be victims of the sun, leading to their dark color, a physiognomy that was "disfigured." Worse still: "The most delicate and subtle organs of the brain have been destroyed or obliterated by the fire of their native land, and their intellectual faculties have been weakened."[59] These climatic theories upheld the theory of a common descent of all human races, but such a doctrine was by no means egalitarian. Rather, it pointed to a definite belief in a hierarchy of races. Monogenist theories asserted the unity of man, but the obvious diversity that existed could best be explained by theories of degeneration. Thus, in origin the same, and maybe through evolution destined to the same end, human races, according to the philosophes, were unequal.

Beside environment, eighteenth-century thinkers pointed to other factors to explain physical differences, especially to hereditary biological forces. Doctor Barrère from the University of Perpignan, who had been in French Guiana, applied a classical notion in arguing that Africans' bile was black as ink and colored their skins. Le Cat, a medical doctor who had written a treatise on color, argued that a special liquid within the nervous system—*aethiops melanium,* he called it—colored Africans' skin. He thought he had corroborative evidence, for, in dissecting a black's brain, he found it to be darker than that of a white man. The presence of this liquid created a hereditary predilection among Africans to become black, but whites, if sufficiently upset, could also turn black. And Le Cat cited the case of a Miss Yeury, who in 1749, upon being rudely insulted in the street, developed a black skin.[60] Cases of whites becoming black, as Le Cat made clear, were abnormalities. Between the points of view of the environmentalists and those who saw an inherent biological force as shaping the Africans' color, a moderate position, which attempted to synthesize the two, evolved.

In the biological literature of the seventeenth century the process by which parents passed on their traits to their descendants was a major intellectual problem; the only theories that seemed to solve the problem satisfactorily were those positing that all creatures at their creation contained the seeds of their progeny, or had their descendants encased in them. These theories would explain how children could resemble their parents, but not how varieties of races could exist if all men had descended from one original pair. Maupertuis came up with an ingenious explanation that foreshadowed later theories of mutation. He used the theory of *emboîtement* (the encasement of descendants in the seed of their parents) as an explanation for the differences in color of blacks and Europeans. Original man, Maupertuis wrote, had in him the seed that could potentially lead to the development of all races of man. Through an accident of nature, some people turned black. They were driven away to Africa by the whites, and there they continued the color of their first black ancestor. Although their color had become hereditary, Maupertuis thought Africans could become white again. That they still possessed a white strain, Maupertuis considered proved by the existence of albinism in Africa.[61] Maupertuis' notion that every man possessed all racial characteristics was taken over by the *Encyclopédie,* which claimed that the sperm of the original man contained matter that could color people either black or white.[62] Environment had brought out the blackness in Africans; by environment the *Encyclopédie* meant not just climate, but also food, mores, and customs.[63] The mixture of belief in simple environmentalism and heredity can be seen in the *Encyclopédie*'s attempt to explain the facial traits of Africans. While it was possible that in Senegal blacks were born with straight noses and thin lips and that these were deformed by parents' crushing them, other Africans, the *Encyclopédie* asserted, had "traits given by nature."[64]

Monogenism and Polygenism

The environmental explanation for the existence of various races affirmed the unity of man, since it saw the races as caused by accidental, external means. The in-between explanation that saw races as formed initially by an environmental force and then passed on hereditarily was similarly monogenistic. The validity of monogenism seemed assured by Buffon's observation that, despite differences in appearance, all the races of man could mate with each other, thus clearly belonging to the same species. (Later he was to admit that cross-speciation was also possible, especially among plants.)[65]

Monogenism was thus given some scientific basis apart from the authority of the Scriptures. But it is possible that the espousal of monogenism by eighteenth-century thinkers was in part grudging, based less on personal conviction than on concern about royal censorship. Maupertuis and the *Encyclopédie* declared that Africans "appear to constitute a new species of man," but their response to the question of whether "so many different men have . . . come from the same mother" was "Il ne nous est pas permis d'en douter."[66] This sentence means both "We cannot doubt it" and "We are not allowed to doubt it."

That monogenism was officially supported by the Church caused some of the philosophes to support polygenism, the doctrine of separate origins of human groups, which declared races to be separate species. Voltaire in particular seems to have taken great delight in denying the Genesis account of creation. If climate affected the color and physical form of Africans, why did Africans retain their physical characteristics when transported "to the coldest of countries"? The blackness of the Africans' skin was due to a colored mucous membrane, which was not created by climate, but rather was passed on to their offspring, Voltaire wrote. Differences in color, as well as in physical form and even intelligence, distinguished blacks from other peoples: "Their round eyes, their flat nose, their lips which are always thick, their differently shaped ears, the wool on their head, the measure even of their intelligence establishes between them and other species of men prodigious differences." While the intelligence of blacks may "not be of another kind than ours, it is far inferior. They are not capable of great attention, they reason little, and do not seem made for either the advantages or disadvantages of our philosophy."[67]

It should be noted that eighteenth-century thinkers had rather vague notions about species, often confusing them with or ascribing to them attributes of varieties.[68] On the one hand, Voltaire said that blacks differed from people of other colors in the same manner that plant species differed. On the other hand, he proclaimed blacks and whites to be different "species of man," just as there are different "species of dogs." In spite of such inconsistencies, Voltaire should on balance be described as a polygenist.[69]

Like Voltaire before him, Abbé Raynal, in his influential *Histoire philosophique et politique des deux Indes,* one of the most widely read books of the century, claimed in the 1770 and 1774 editions that the differences between whites and blacks were so great that it was clear they constituted separate kinds of men. In the 1770 edition, Raynal ascribed to "Negro blood" the power to "corrupt and destroy our people." The dominant Enlightenment thought on the unity of man asserted itself in the 1780 edition. The different sperm from which whites and blacks were conceived, the Abbé repeated, might prove "that the Negroes are a particular species of men." Then he added, "But with more attention one has recognized this as an error."[70] Raynal seems to have retracted his stand on polygenism because it better suited his antislavery argument to show that blacks were directly related to whites. And he bowed to what was the overwhelming scientific opinion of the day. Buffon, Linnaeus, and Blumenbach were monogenists.

The polygenist-monogenist argument was not based on any a priori commitment to black enslavement; for instance, both Voltaire and, until 1780, Raynal were opposed to slavery and yet were polygenists. Monogenists such as Buffon were also opposed to slavery, but there were many monogenists, such as members of the West Indian planter class, who favored slavery.[71] If monogenist opinion in the eighteenth century averred that all men were descended from an original pair, this opinion by no means suggested that the common descent signified equality between the races. Monogenism explained the variety in races as a degeneration from the original pair, due to extreme conditions of environment. Potentially the polygenistic position was more egalitarian. It was rarely interpreted in this way, however. More commonly, polygenists argued, as did Voltaire, that blacks, because they were separately created, did not fully share in the common humanity of whites. It could also be argued that the physical differences of blacks were not due to some deviation from whites, but rather reflected a separate creation, equal to that of the whites. This position was taken by Peyroux de la Coudrenière in the influential *Journal de Monsieur*: "If God could put white men in Europe and Asia, then he could put black men in Africa."[72] Created separately, blacks and whites were nevertheless equal. The egalitarian possibilities of polygenism were left undeveloped, however. Rather, supporters of polygenism stressed a separate and inferior destiny for the black race.

The Chain of Being

Since Aristotle, Western thinkers had commonly asserted that nature formed a chain of being. Every creation existed for a purpose, linked to every other creation, in a progression from an inanimate object, to a humble worm, to higher animals, then to man, and finally to God.[73] This idea was particularly popular in the eighteenth century, and it was only natural to place the black man within this chain. Naturalists and men of letters in the eighteenth century had a mania for categorization—it was, indeed, a near necessity, in view of the enormous growth of knowledge about nature. This categorization was applied in part to building up the chain of being, filling in all the existing gaps.

Not only was man considered one link in creation, but the various races were themselves seen as forming a chain of being. The Swedish naturalist Carol von Linnaeus listed five human races: white, American, Asian, African, and, just after African, a race he called monstrous, consisting of Troglodytes of ancient classical mythology and orangutans.[74] The list implied a descending order within the chain of being, from the highest creature, the white, to the lowest, the orangutan. Rousseau and Bonnet in France and Monboddo in England[75] also believed that the orangutan was a variant of the human species, but that opinion was exceptional.

That blacks formed the lowest rung among humans on the chain of being and were thus a link between the lower primates and white men was thought self-evident. The similarity in the dark color of blacks and of many monkeys and the fact that primates—orangutans, chimpanzees, and gorillas—had been found in Africa underscored the imagined link between blacks and primates. In this vein, J. D. Robinet, an important French writer, pointed out that orangutans lived in Angola, where "the ugliest and stupidest" Africans also resided.[76] To Robinet the geographical proximity implied a biological affinity, making blacks a link between the orangutans and non-African races. In his multivolume collection of interesting and curious phenomena, Rousselot de Surgy denounced the Africans' intelligence and mores as animalistic. In the chain of being, Africans were located between "animals" and "men." "Nature," Rousselot concluded, "seems to mount from orangutans to Pongos [a Congolese ethnic group] to man."[77]

Confirmation of such theories seemed to come from Frenchmen who had been to Africa. Lamiral, a former official in Senegal, claimed that the peoples south of the Gambia River physically resembled primates in their appearance, their social relations, their lack of "proper" language, and their nudity; he concluded that there was "no intermediary species between this race of men and the men of the woods [orangutans]." Lamiral directly and unequivocally advanced an underlying belief in the chain of being:

> There is a chain which unites all beings. . . . Depending on
> the place he occupies in the chain, each being is endowed
> with more or less intelligence. From the man of the woods
> down to the germ, he degenerates, and in rising from him to
> the civilized man he perfects himself. . . .[78]

While Voltaire did not put black men into the chain of being
between Europeans and primates (since he did not believe in
the chain), he did subscribe to the notion that Africans had
simian qualities. Drolly, Voltaire wrote:

> It is a serious question among them whether they are de-
> scended from monkeys or whether the monkeys come from
> them. Our wise men have said that man was created in the
> image of God. Now here is a lovely image of the Divine
> Maker—a flat and black nose with little or hardly any intelli-
> gence. A time will doubtless come when these animals will
> know how to cultivate the land well, beautify their houses
> and gardens, and know the paths of the stars: one needs time
> for everything.

While intended to ridicule the Genesis account, this passage is
not at variance with other utterances by Voltaire on blacks.
Elsewhere Voltaire wrote that Africans had only "a few more
ideas than animals and [only] more facility to express them."[79]
He seemed to suggest that the similarities were more important than the differences.

Buffon believed that there was an important gap between
men and animals; he did not accept the idea that blacks were a
link between primates and white men, for Africans, just like
other men, had the facility for speech and thought, and also
had a soul. If Buffon subscribed to the theory of the chain of
being, he did not want humans to participate in it fully, lest
they be deprived of their status as special creations, elevated
above animals. He would not accept too close an affinity between blacks and primates. Mused Buffon, "The interval
which separates the monkey from the Negro is hard to
understand."[80]

But this interval was usually seen as close. If interbreeding
was characteristic of a species, eighteenth-century observers
pointed to the alleged possibility of Africans and primates mating as "evidence" of their being of the same species. Travelers

to Africa observed orangutans in the vicinity of Africans and—carried away by vivid imaginations, memories of classical myths about women having intercourse with animals, and perhaps local folklore—concluded that black women had sexual contact with primates. While not fully certain, Voltaire also seemed to place credence in such theories; in hot climes, he wrote, "it is not improbable that the monkeys have subjugated girls." The possibility of blacks and primates mating was pointed to as a sign of the blacks' animality. Blacks' sex organs (both male and female) were averred to be unusually large, a condition that was taken as confirmation of blacks' animality. With some literary circumlocution, Lamiral wrote, "We are dwarfs in comparison with those men who are really children of nature."[81]

Seeing humans increasingly as biological beings, the philosophes found it difficult to draw an intelligent distinction between men and animals. The relationship of humans and animals is now understood in an evolutionary manner, but, by and large, eighteenth-century thinkers did not subscribe to the theory of a several-million-year evolution of species. Having observed obvious anatomical similarities between humans and animals, they attributed them to some immediate contemporaneous link. The link between humans and animals fascinated Europeans, and in the eighteenth century the concept contributed to the Noble Savage myth. It was believed that animals lived free in nature, communing in harmony with it. Thus, ironically, the supposed animality of the black did not totally contradict the claim that he was a Noble Savage.[82] Yet Europeans were unwilling to accept animality as one of their own qualities; they reserved this trait for the group alleged to be the lowest rank of men—the African.

Physiognomics and the Chain of Being

In physiognomy eighteenth-century thinkers claimed to see the closest proof for the affinity between the African and the primate, an affinity that indicated the African's alleged baseness.

The doctrine of physiognomics was an ancient part of the Western intellectual tradition. Aristotle had stated that "when men have large foreheads, they are slow to move; when they have small ones, they are fickle; when they have broad ones, they are apt to be distraught; when they have foreheads rounded or bulging out, they are quick-tempered." Galen, basing himself on Hippocrates, Aristotle, and others, wrote what became the handbook of physiognomy in the ancient world: "that the faculties of the mind follow the mixtures or temperaments of the body."[83] Renaissance interest in the classical world led to a revival of physiognomics. These ideas were summarized by the Neapolitan J. B. Porta in 1588, in a book translated into French in 1655. Inspired by the Neoplatonic belief that nature was filled with symbolic meanings, Porta posited the thesis that "the mores and nature of men" could be discovered "by the outer signs of their bodies."[84] Cureau de la Chambre, personal physician to the chancellor of the realm and the first to teach anatomy at the Jardin royal des plantes, published a multivolume but unfinished work, "Character of the Passions." He posited the doctrine of an existing relationship between facial expressions and human passions. Those people who resembled animals, for instance, were bestial in their behavior; thus one could predict how individuals—or a whole people—would act, based on their outward appearances.[85] That physiognomics was especially popular in France explains the enthusiastic reception given in the 1780s to Caspar Lavater, the Swiss popularizer of the physiognomic school. The first edition of his work, published in 1780, was followed by eight more editions in the next half-century.[86]

Although physiognomics held that one could judge individuals by their appearance, with time it evolved to include the belief that the character of whole peoples could be told by appearance. In looking at groupings of human beings, the first difference that always impressed Europeans abroad was the difference in skin color. Skin color was seen as indicative of inner character. Darkness of skin was viewed as a sign of depravity, while lightness suggested a noble personality. The English author Aphra Behn made her black hero, Oronoko, rather light-skinned; only in this way, it appears, could his nobility be accepted. But the Laplace translation of Behn's play in 1745 went much further; thus, while Behn made clear that the heroine was black, Laplace described her as white and suppressed passages mentioning the color of various protagonists. It was as if a play peopled by noble characters would not be credible if the characters were known to be black. Shakespeare had dared to have a noble hero in *Othello,* but, when interpreted in France, Othello was considerably "whitened."[87] The actor Talma did not blacken his face in playing the role, but made his skin appear only copper-colored, for it was explained that such a color "had the advantage of not revolting the eye of the public, especially that of the women." J. F. Butini, in presenting *Othello,* explained that certain changes were "indispensable": "One can feel the necessity of taking away from Othello his dark face." It seems that the French theatre had a greater sensitivity to such issues than its English counterpart. In the 1760s, for example, Oronoko was played in London for a time by a former black slave, Ignatius Sancho.[88]

The French aesthetic dislike for the black physiognomy was reflected by the *Encyclopédie* and by Maupertuis, who declared blacks to be ugly. Daubenton, quite unaware of the ethnocentrism of his judgment, declared that the European was "the model for beauty."[89] Bougainville, who by both learning and lust for adventure seemed the answer to Rousseau's call for the traveling philosophe, saw in the color of human races a revelation of their levels of civilization. In his *Voyage autour du monde,* he claimed that "blacks were much more savage than the Indians, whose color approached that of whites." Throughout his voyage he seemed to equate darker color with savagery. Although most of the peoples he visited in the South Pacific had similar skin hues, invariably those who received him in a friendly manner were described as light in skin color, whereas those hostile to the expedition were noted as dark. The ornithologist and traveler in South Africa, Levaillant, protested against the prevalence of such ideas, exclaiming, "We are no longer living in the centuries of ignorance where everything which was black was considered cannibalistic. Travelers and even more enlightened philosophy teach us that an ugly envelope can cover a precious diamond." If Levaillant shared the aesthetic values of Maupertuis, the *Encyclopédie,* and Bougainville, he at least did not draw the same conclusions they did about the relationship between physical appearance and social institutions. But Levaillant's attack on the theory of physiognomics did not prevail.[90]

In the early formulation of physiognomics, as early as Aristotle, the shape of the human face had been seen as an indicator of character. In looking at human races, travelers had noticed the difference in the physical shapes of faces. Fourteenth- and fifteenth-century painters had been aware of this in painting Africans, and Leonardo da Vinci had written on the question. Cureau de la Chambre had made plaster casts of heads of men of different races and, by various measurements, had tried to clarify the physical differences between races.[91]

Having become aware of the differences in face shapes, Frenchmen, following the doctrine of physiognomics, saw not only in color but also, more importantly, in facial shape the real essence of the doctrine—an indicator of internal character. One traveler to the Gold Coast in the mid-seventeenth century found the trade there more profitable than elsewhere and seemed to think that the reason was that the peoples there were superior—a superiority proved by their having few Negroid features. He described the inhabitant of the Gold Coast as "big and well proportioned . . . he does not have an ugly flat nose, nor that large mouth which other blacks have."[92]

The more the African in his facial traits and skin color departed from the Negroid (as a type) and the more closely he resembled a European, the more noble he appeared. In fiction this view often recurred. Saint-Lambert's black hero in the play *Ziméo* was compared to Apollo, with "regular traits and the most beautiful proportion." In Staël's youthful novel, the hero, also called Ximeo, was described as so "perfect" that he did not possess "the faults of men his color."[93] French officials who had served in Senegal in the late eighteenth century had similar views. They depicted lighter colored peoples, such as the Fulani, as more able and virtuous than their darker neighbors. Equally, peoples excelling in trade and statecraft, such as the Manding, or peoples with whom the French hoped to establish ever closer contacts, such as the Wolofs in the Senegambia, were averred to be light-skinned and to have non-Negroid facial structures.[94]

Men of learning shared the belief in physiognomics and helped popularize it. Linnaeus clearly believed in the coincidence of facial traits and social and intellectual capacities. In defining the African, he had joined to the physical portrait a presumed description of mores and institutions:

> Afer: black, phlegmatic, relaxed
> Hair, black, frizzled. Skin silky. Nose flat. Lips tumid.
> Women without shame. Mammae lactate profusely, crafty, indolent, negligent
> Anoints himself with grease
> Governed by caprice.

And the much-read Cornelius de Pauw posited that blacks "differ as much from white peoples by their lack of memory and weakness of intellect as they differ in the color of their bodies and the appearance of their physiognomy."[95]

The belief in physiognomics seemed to be scientifically grounded in the differing skull measurements that were found for various races. To help fellow painters depict Africans, the Dutch painter Peter Camper explained how the skull of the African differed in shape from that of the European. The German scientist Blumenbach at the University of Göttingen attempted to classify races by skull shapes; he claimed that the most perfect skull came from the white man, as epitomized in a Caucasian skull he owned. In unpublished notes Camper pointed out indications of racial differentiation in the proportions of a skull.[96] Camper's and Blumenbach's notions about facial and skull shapes in relationship to racial categories were essentially aesthetic perceptions, and yet they were to have an important impact on French scientific thought. The shape of the skull was henceforth considered an important indication of race and of a hierarchy of races.

Camper maintained that the salient difference in drawing the white and the black was depicting the prognathism, the prominence of the lower part of the face, in the latter. This prognathism, Camper wrote, brought the black race close to animality: "If I make the facial line lean forward, I have an antique head; if backward, the head of a Negro. If I still more incline it, I have the head of an ape; and if more still, that of a dog, and then that of an idiot." Camper's system, difficult to measure, was severely criticized by Blumenbach and by nineteenth-century English naturalists such as Lawrence and Prichard, but in France it was uncritically adopted and became the basis for nineteenth-century French racist thought.[97]

Racism

Physiognomics had suggested a coincidence between physical appearance and intellectual and moral predilections; by the end of the eighteenth century, the physiognomic theory had been transformed to suggest not a coincidence but rather a cause-and-effect relationship. Ever since François Bernier's essay of 1684, races of man had been defined in terms of specific physical differences. The physiognomicists had pointed to these physical differences as indicating intellectual and moral differences, and eventually physical variations were seen as not only *indicating* but also *causing* these differences. Georges Cuvier, writing at the end of the eighteenth century, proclaimed the relationship of race and society: "The white race, with oval face, straight hair and nose, to which the civilized peoples of Europe belong and which appears to us the most beautiful of all, is also superior to others by its genius, courage, and activity." Borrowing from Camper, Cuvier not only announced an aesthetic dislike for the black but also declared that there was a "cruel law which seems to have condemned to an eternal inferiority the races of depressed and compressed skulls." Certain races were impeded from progressing even "under the most favorable of circumstances." Blacks had never progressed beyond barbarism. Races were clearly differentiated by the physical proportions of the face, "and experience seems to confirm the theory that there is a relationship between the perfection of the spirit and the beauty of the face."[98] J. J. Virey, a medical doctor, wrote, "All the ugly peoples are more or less barbarians, beauty is the inseparable companion of the most civilized nations." Drawing on the aesthetic ideas of Lavater and of the German art historian Johann Winckelmann, he declared that "our capacity to think is normally analogous to the shape of our body." The European body was an expression of an inner intelligence and of a universal mission: "The European, called by destiny to run the empire of the globe which he knows how to enlighten by his intelligence, tame by his abilities, is man par excellence, the others are nothing but hordes of barbarians. . . ."[99] This was not just an assertion of an accidental coincidence between race and civilization. Rather, this was the racist interpretation of world history to which the late eighteenth century had come.

It may have been inevitable that the clash between white and nonwhite cultures, dating from European expansion in the fifteenth century, the mutual misunderstandings, and the natural tendency of every society toward ethnocentrism would lead Frenchmen to have certain amounts of prejudice toward Africans. In the seventeenth century this prejudice had been expressed by emphasizing the different religion and morals of the African and, in most of the eighteenth century, by stressing the malignant environmental forces that had shaped the African. By the end of the eighteenth century, under the influence of materialism, an increasing interest in biology developed, and it was in biology that the key to African behavior was now seen. It was the black's different biological makeup that seemed to mark him off from the European.

In France, by the end of the eighteenth century, racism had gained the upper hand. Racism, in its simplest and most obvious form, is here defined as the belief that groups of human beings differ in their values and social accomplishments solely as a result of the impact of biological heredity. (Using any other concept of racism, the historian risks falling victim to misleading vagueness.) An American sociologist has suggested a strict definition of racism that is used in this work:

> Racism is any set of beliefs that organic, genetically transmitted differences (whether real or imagined) between human groups are intrinsically associated with the presence or the absence of certain socially relevant abilities or characteristics, hence that such differences are a legitimate basis of invidious distinctions between groups socially defined as races.[100]

Racism took on a powerful influence in France because it had become a common method of thought. It had originated not as a means to distinguish differences between Europeans and non-Europeans, but rather as a concept in the internal dispute over social class in France. Beginning in the 1560s, the French nobility faced a double attack from both kings and commoners; in order to uphold its prerogatives, the nobility created the myth of a common racial origin. Citing the blood that had been shed on behalf of France and king by the ancestors of the embattled nobility, polemicists argued that the blood of nobles had certain virtues, hereditary in nature, passed on from one generation of the aristocracy to the next. By the late sixteenth century the aristocracy claimed that it was superior to the other orders of society because it was descended from the Germanic conquerors of France.[101] This idea developed in the seventeenth century and became best known through the pen of Count Henri de Boulainvilliers, who wished to reassert the power of the nobility that had been diminished by the absolutist reign of Louis XIV.

The idea that nobility of character was conferred by birth was very common in the Ancien Régime. Richelieu seemed to be alluding less to social milieu than to biological determinism when he declared that "the virtue of a well-born person has something nobler in it than that found in a man of lesser extraction."[102] In legal cases it was common to refer to the birth of the parties involved as proof of guilt or innocence. Arguing against his client's opponent, a Toulouse lawyer wrote that, though the opponent was a military officer, "he offers on all sides of his genealogy nothing but vile artisans, village tailors, butchers, and a domestic for a paternal grandfather."[103] The extent to which the racial idea had permeated French society may be seen in the fact that Abbé Sieyès, who wrote an apology for the third estate and an attack on the nobility on the very eve of the French Revolution, did not deny the idea that the different estates were descended from different racial groups. Sieyès accepted Boulainvilliers' theory and chose rather to draw the opposite conclusion: the nobles were traitors to the national cause because they were descended from and identified with the foreign Franks, whereas the third estate was descended from the "true" native elements of France, the Gallo-Romans; therefore it was the third estate who should rule.[104] In the midst of the Revolution, Rouget de Lisle penned "The Marseillaise," making in the refrain a charge similar to that of Sieyès—that the king and the aristocracy had "impure blood." The enmity between the forces of privilege and democracy was portrayed as based upon their different biological makeup, and the struggle was considered a racial one.

The Ancien Régime was a highly structured society, in which a person's rank at birth usually marked him or her for life. True, these values had come under attack; and the system was fluid enough that men of relatively humble birth could by merit rise from the estate into which they were born and become nobles. But neither caprice nor exceptions to the system could eradicate the fact that birth was the single most important factor affecting a person's power, wealth, and life-style. It therefore came rather naturally to men of the Ancien Régime to assert the importance of biological heredity.

Having become accustomed to ascribing social and political differences to race, it was only natural that Frenchmen would extend this approach to explain the great differences they found among peoples of other climes. Not only France, but the world itself, they believed, consisted of a hierarchy of races. Racism is possible only when a systematized body of scientific knowledge is available to justify assumptions of the superiority of one human group over another. Such a systematic underpinning of racism was fully developed in eighteenth-century France. The nineteenth century did not invent scientific racism, but only further developed ideas that had been formulated in this earlier era.

The belief that developed in the eighteenth century—that inherited biological characteristics determined the superiority of one people over another—was racist, but this mode of thought differed from nineteenth-century racism in that it also relied on environmental explanations for human differentiation. Even so pronounced a racist as Virey, after stating that human races were all constituted physically different from each other, was also to affirm climatic impact on human behavior. Regardless of his race, a man, by protecting himself from exposure to the hardships of the weather, could retain a greater ability to maintain his balance. And although Virey primarily saw the development of civilization as the function of race, he also, in the tradition of the Enlightenment, at times maintained the opposite: "The more a people is advanced in its social institutions, in its morality, the more beauty, nobility, elegance and grace does it possess. ... The ugliness with which a people may have been born diminishes under the impact of a less harsh soil."[105] Thus, the most ardent developer of eighteenth-century racism seemed to believe that human nature was not immutable. The shape of someone's body determined his social accomplishments and even his morality, held the eighteenth-century racists, but it was assumed that under the influence of environment the body could change, as could characteristics of behavior.[106] If they believed in the inequality of races, eighteenth-century thinkers also posited that at some distant point in the future this inequality would cease. Thus, while helping to shape racist ideology, the eighteenth-century view nevertheless differed from the racism of the nineteenth century, which was to see race as immutable, and social and intellectual differences of human groups as resistant to any and all experiences.

The Enlightenment had developed ideas that led to racism. It had posited a chain of being that placed races in a hierarchy, with whites far superior to blacks. Notwithstanding some of the literary conventions of the day and occasional references to blacks as Noble Savages, the overall impression had been created, however, that Africans were unusually bereft of intelligence, living in squalor, subject to whimsical tyrants, and without religion or morals. As the Enlightenment had attempted to characterize the physical differences between population groups, it had simultaneously attempted to characterize people's social and political institutions and even their personal qualities. And, finally, not only were parallels perceived between physical characteristics, social development, and character, but the latter two were considered dependent upon the former. Cuvier and Virey carried this notion furthest, introducing racial determinism. While it is true that, until the mid-nineteenth century, biologists were somewhat confused in defining the exact nature of race, racism did not have to wait until then to emerge full-blown. Strong notions of cultural, religious, and national prejudice had already existed in the sixteenth and seventeenth centuries in the very first contacts between whites and blacks. In the eighteenth century a strong interest developed in the physical characteristics of blacks, at the same time as information was collected on African institutions and mores. Building on Camper's notions about aesthetics and Lavater's about physiognomy, some of the later eighteenth-century writers expressed the theory that culture and character were formed by race. Admittedly, they were not so clear in defining race as were the mid-nineteenth-century biologists, but racism had come of age.

4

Three Patterns of Interaction: West Indies, France, and Senegal

Although ideas played their role in forming race relations, the actual interaction of whites and blacks needs to be examined. There were three main scenes of contact in the eighteenth century: the West Indies, France itself, and Senegal on the coast of West Africa. In the West Indies, relationships were dictated by the slave system; the policy of racial exclusivism practiced by whites was a function of slavery. In the Metropole the perceived needs of the white planter class overseas partially shaped governmental policy toward blacks residing in France; essentially, however, the policy was influenced by the fear and hostility that a foreign population, easily identifiable by color, created in the white host group. In Senegal the desire of the small number of white officials and traders for political and commercial expansion inland led to more liberal race relations. Rather than practicing racial exclusivism, as in the West Indies, whites in Senegal proved to be accommodating and tended to include blacks and men of color in their circle.

The different patterns that evolved in these three regions demonstrate that, despite very well developed attitudes toward blacks, the French varied their reactions, depending on how they assessed their own status. Race relations were formed not only by ideas but also by the social situation in which race contact occurred.

The West Indies

By the 1720s most of the features of race relations that characterized the slave system had developed. During the rest

100

of the century, as the problems of social control became more serious with the growing slave population, these features were further intensified. The increasingly rigid approach to the treatment of slaves and of free colored people after the mid-eighteenth century or the 1770s is sometimes viewed as the result of a sudden development of racism in the French colonies.[1] But racism had existed earlier and had just manifested itself more strongly with the passage of time. The foundations for this harsh system had already been laid in the period before 1720. The system's development during the rest of the eighteenth century indicates the manner in which Frenchmen in the century of Enlightenment treated blacks and men of color in their most valuable overseas possessions.

The Freedmen

With the advance of the century, it became increasingly hard for slaves to escape their condition legally, by manumission. Although in 1721 the law had put limits on the right of an owner to free his slaves, later high fees were levied for the right to emancipate a slave.[2] While these fees brought in revenue, they were intended mainly to discourage manumission; the fee equaled the price of a slave. To avoid paying, slaveowners resorted to many subterfuges, but the most common one was to free the slave from his duties and allow him to move around at will. The slave would not then be free *de jure,* only *de facto;* men belonging to this category were known as *soi-disant libres* or *libres de savane.* Fouchard in his *Marrons de la liberté* has argued that there were many more *libres de savane* than there were legally freed ex-slaves. Since they were not a legally recognized group, it is impossible to estimate their number; Fouchard might well be correct. Thus when one looks at manumissions as a measure of the flexibility of the slave system, one might have to include not only those legally freed but also the *libres de savane.* Since they did not possess their patents of liberty, the *libres de savane* always lived in some fear that they might be re-enslaved.

The growth in the ratio of freedmen to the total free population (white plus freedmen) during the century had serious repercussions on the whites' reaction to what they viewed as the rising tide of the free colored. Thus, in Martinique in

1764, the free colored group represented 13.6 percent of the total free population and by 1789 33.3 percent. By the latter date, they amounted to 40 percent in Saint-Domingue and 18 percent in Guadeloupe. The growth in the absolute number of freed coloreds was seen as even larger than it really was because of the proportionate increase vis-à-vis whites.[3]

The slave system had attempted to preserve a situation in which everyone who was black (including colored) would be a slave and everyone who was white would be free. But exceptions to the system had been allowed over the years; in particular, the offspring of the slaveowner and his black or colored slaves were emancipated throughout the period. While the slaveowners fulminated against the large number of freedmen allowed in the colony, they themselves contributed to the number by their sexual activities. The best way to stop the growth of the colored class would have been for the white planters to cease sexual exploitation of their slaves, but the planters did not do so and thus endangered their own security. Comments Fouchard, "The planters, without being aware of it, dug their graves with their penises."[4]

The growth in the number of freedmen led to ever more stringent legislation aimed against the free colored, depriving them of the legal near-equality that the code of 1685 had attempted to grant them. It was early felt that the slave system could best be preserved if a mark of inferiority were associated with the black color. In 1734 the minister of the navy forbade intermarriage of white men with free colored women, on the ground that such unions "would augment the insolence and insubordination" of the slaves.[5]

It has often been argued that the growth in the number of free coloreds and the whites' perceived need for social control after the mid-eighteenth century led to racially segregationist patterns. The assumption is that prior to this date such attitudes did not exist. Yet, as we have already seen, there had been such policies by the 1720s, long before the free colored numbered more than a few hundred and while they were still an infinitesimal proportion of the total free population. A second factor that tends to disprove the demographic interpretation is a comparison of the experiences of the plantation islands. For instance, Guadeloupe, which had far fewer free colored in number and in proportion to the total free population than Martinique or Saint-Domingue (and thus, presumably, had less reason to establish racial legislation), often preceded the other two with harsh discriminatory measures against the free colored.[6] Thus the theory that either the presence of large numbers of free colored or the growth in their numbers helped form racist policies in the colonies needs to be taken with some reservation. Development of racist policies and demographic changes may have coincided, but interaction between them is still to be demonstrated convincingly.

It would be hard to express quantitatively the extent to which the white population felt more insecure in the eighteenth century than it had in the seventeenth. At all times the white, slaveowning population seems to have felt the precariousness of its position, and, by the end of the seventeenth century, had developed a clear hostility against the free colored.

Perhaps as a result of the growing number of free colored or perhaps because of the natural development of bureaucracies, which, with the years, tend to adopt ever more detailed legislation, legal restrictions against the free colored increased. And the racial fears and hostility already felt in the seventeenth century may also, with the passage of time, have become more ornate and detailed. Whites living in a society in which they were outnumbered by more than ten to one lived in mortal fear of a slave uprising; rebellion did not always take overt form, but insubordination and running away were frequent forms of slave protest. Any misfortune hitting a plantation was blamed on a slave conspiracy. Little was known about tropical diseases and the patterns of epidemics; when disease broke out on a plantation, the slaves were often suspected of having poisoned fellow slaves, owners, and animals. In 1757 in Saint-Domingue, a fear of poisoning swept the island; white families ate and drank only with trepidation. Thereafter, even into the nineteenth century in Martinique, where slavery lasted until 1848, great fear at times spread throughout that island. By the end of the eighteenth century, Debbash writes, the plantation owners in Saint-Domingue believed that all chronic diseases were the result of poisoning. The dread of poisoning reflected the apprehensions of a small, beleaguered, white minority fearing its black slaves. The black man had become an object of fear—a threat to white security.[7]

The paranoia in the islands was so pervasive that even a liberal official such as Governor Fénélon could not resist it. In 1764, in a letter to the minister of the navy, the new governor wrote, "I arrived in Martinique with all the prejudices of Europe against the harshness with which the Negroes are treated." But, after a short stay, he was certain that "the safety of the whites requires that the Negroes be treated like animals."[8]

Together with the harsh treatment of slaves went an obdurate policy of discrimination against men of color. They were feared lest they join with the slaves in a common conspiracy. The interlocking bonds of color and family between the two groups created insecurity and fear of both blacks and colored in the planter community. Free men of color were treated with contempt, retained in a lowly, separate condition, and subjected to legal discrimination. An edict of 1733 prohibited free men of color from serving in the judiciary, in the militia, or in any other government post. Ordinances of 1764 forbade descendants of blacks to practice medicine and surgery—the result of the perennial fear of poisoning plots. But other professions were forbidden for the mere purpose of depriving freedmen of gainful employment and of reserving these positions instead to the poor whites. Ultimately, the administration wanted to limit the professions open to free men of color, and an edict of 1788 provided that freedmen would need a license for any trade except farming.[9]

Legislation and social custom further ostracized the freedmen from white society. Government ordinances prescribed special clothing, jewelry, and hairdos for freemen of color so that they would not be confused with whites.[10] To call a white person "colored" was considered the worst form of slander; two men convicted of having committed this "atrocious injure" were condemned to make public penance.[11] The fear of being classed with coloreds was so great among whites that they passed legislation establishing the principle that certain names belonged exclusively to white families. Even the titles by which people were addressed were to be restricted by race; people of color were to be addressed as neither "sieur" nor "dame." Free men of color and free blacks were not allowed to congregate in the same social gatherings as whites.

While, in Barbados, a man of color four generations removed from black ancestry (in Jamaica, three) was regarded as legally white, this was not the case in the French plantation colonies. The governor in Cayenne asked the minister of the navy in 1766 at what generation of descent from black parentage a man of color could be considered in the "white class" and consequently freed from the discriminatory poll tax. The minister's answer was categorical: "Those who descend [from blacks] can never enter the class of whites. For if there were a time when that could happen, they would then enjoy all the privileges of whites which would be against the constitution of the colonies."[12] This system of rigorous separation was at times breached, but conventions had to be preserved. A newly arrived director of a hospital, on discovering that one of the doctors under his authority was unusually dark in complexion, wanted to dismiss him, since men of color were not allowed to practice medicine. The doctor in question was indeed a man of color, but he claimed to be of Brazilian Indian extraction. His fictive genealogy was accepted as true by the Superior Council of the colony, and he was allowed to keep his job. It seems that the Council was willing to circumvent the law, because the doctor was a descendant of one of the early members of the Council.[13] Such exceptions reveal that there was room in some cases for flexibility in the racial system. But exceptions were infrequent, and the very pliability of the system allowed its preservation. The lifting of the rules in individual cases did nothing to remedy the general situation of inferiority to which all the men of color were relegated. On the contrary, it emphasized their dependence on the white community.

Kept apart, not enjoying the same rights as other free men, those of slave descent lived in some insecurity because the law did not extend to them the same protection as it did to the white community. In 1767 a free man of color was sentenced to be flogged, branded, and sold into slavery for assaulting a white. The principle that whites were inviolate and should not be struck—even in cases of self-defense—was considered essential for the security of the colony.[14]

In the second half of the eighteenth century increasingly large numbers of freedmen acquired plantations and slaves. If the concern of the white planters or the authorities had been the preservation of the slave system, then racism was no longer an appropriate method of social control, for it excluded the freedmen from making common cause with the planter class—a group with which many of the freedmen would have liked to mingle. By the 1760s, in the face of the growing number of black slaves, it was often proposed that whites integrate the free men of color among themselves, thus creating a larger bulwark for the slave system. The liberal planter Hilliard d'Auberteuil suggested that a man of color removed from his black ancestry by six generations should be considered white. His somatic features would be virtually indistinguishable from whites' and thus there would be no reason to keep him apart: "There is a point at which one should not research [a person's ancestry], where it even becomes useless."[15]

The practical needs for the security of the colony seemed to make it imperative to enlarge the freed class as much as possible. Thus in 1734 the minister of the navy suggested a more lenient policy of emancipation of colored slaves, since they "were enemies of the Negroes."[16] Provisions that kept the free colored separate from the slave population were encouraged in order to help retain them in the ranks with the white population in defense of the slave system. Attempts at strengthening the bonds between the whites and free men of color were often advocated by Paris, especially in the 1780s, in the face of the prodigious growth of the slave population. The white class, many colonial reformers felt, had to be enlarged by joining to it the colored group.[17]

Measures attempting the rapprochement of the two groups were often promoted by metropolitan France. But it would be an error to believe that invariably the Metropole was an advocate of toleration in the face of the obdurate racism of the settlers.[18] At times the Metropole found it in its interest to sow discord between the two groups. The settlers on occasion showed a strong strain of independence, exacerbated by their frustrations with France's mercantilist control of the economy of the Antilles, which prohibited trading with the nearby British West Indies and especially with the mainland American colonies on terms far more advantageous than those with France. The settlers might have opted for autonomy, but they knew they had to continue depending on France because of their precarious situation—outnumbered by their slaves ten to one and nearly equalled in number by a hostile, free-colored population. As such threats prevented movements favoring autonomy from developing fully, the French government at times fanned intergroup hostilities overseas. Paris instructed the governor of Saint-Domingue in 1776 that he should not encourage a rapprochement between whites and freedmen, for if that happened "the colony would be able to free itself easily from the authority of the king."[19] The Metropole, then, was not always the voice of reason attempting to liberalize race relations and was itself beset by its own racial phobias.

Whatever the forces for rapprochement between white and colored were, in either the Metropole or the colonies, planter society in general was adamantly set on continuing to view as inferior anyone with the least amount of African ancestry. The security of the colony demanded, as a memoir of 1777 stated, that, at whatever distance men of color were from their black origin,

> they will always retain the stain of their enslavement and are ineligible for all public service; even the men of gentle birth who descend in any manner whatsoever from a woman of color cannot enjoy the prerogatives of nobility. This law is harsh but necessary in a country where there are fifteen slaves for each white person; one cannot establish sufficient distance between the two species; one cannot instill enough respect in the Negroes for those they serve. This distinction [between black and white] is the principal foundation of the subordination of the slave, namely, that his color has made him into a slave and that nothing can make him the equal of his master. The administration must be careful in severely maintaining his distance and respect.[20]

Comparison with Iberian Attitudes

In the Spanish colonies, prejudice against blacks and people of color as a group existed. But the Spanish reacted differently to individual people of color than did the French or, for that matter, the English. Whites in Iberian America felt less hostility toward and a closer affinity with people of color, especially if they were light-skinned, than did the French or the Anglo-Saxons. Many reasons have been advanced for this difference. The first one, which can be immediately dismissed, is the Catholicism of the Iberians; in the French case, this did not help create racial harmony.[21] A second argument is that the capitalist exploitation of the plantation system in North America created a harsher slave system and therefore a more hostile attitude toward blacks and their descendants.[22] But this typology is unconvincing; many regions and plantations in the southern North American colonies exhibited noncapitalist attitudes, while in Brazil, for instance, advanced capitalist features existed.

A third argument is based on the demographic situation. According to this line of reasoning, in North America there was no need for accommodation to either blacks or men of color, since there was a large white population. In Iberian America, however, the settler population was small; there was a greater dependence upon free blacks and men of color, and, therefore, both a willingness and a need to integrate them into white society.[23] The example of the French West Indies reveals the limited applicability of this explanation, for the French Antilles were just as short of white settlers as the Iberian colonies had been, yet were not so accommodating toward men of color.

A fourth explanation sees differences in race relations as having been shaped by the earliest Euro-African contacts. For the Iberians, the first contact was conquest by Moors, who had greater military power and a more developed culture than their own. The Moors were dark and slightly Negroid. Since dark skin and Negroid features could thus be identified with the superior Moors, the Iberians, it has been averred by

Gilberto Freyre among others, were less likely to consider these attributes repulsive. The other European states, the argument continues, did not have such an experience; rather, they came into contact with Africans much later, when Europe had developed military prowess and a material culture superior to those of the West African coast. But this argument wrongly assumes a high opinion of blacks in Iberian thought; in fact, Iberians also found Africans in the fifteenth and sixteenth centuries, and for that matter thereafter, to be a repulsive, deformed, and inferior people.[24]

One remaining explanation in the general literature on race relations, examined in the light of the French experience, might still be plausible. As presented by the Dutch sociologist Herman Hoetink, this line of reasoning suggests that the Iberians, as a result of commingling with the Moors in earlier periods, had acquired the darkest skin color of all Europeans involved in colonial ventures. Thus, unlike the Anglo-Saxons and even the French, who were relatively light, the Spanish found themselves less at variance physically from people of color. Their somatic norm image is different from that of the Anglo-Saxons and the French; the Spanish consider a slight darkness in skin color to be beautiful.[25] That the somatic norm image of the Iberians seems to be the only variant mentioned in the literature on race not replicated in the Anglo-Saxon and French experiences does not mean, of course, that it is the only possible explanation for the Iberian attitude.

Too much is probably made of the uniqueness of Iberian race relations. The Spanish and the Portuguese had slave plantations for a longer period than other Europeans; they had the opportunity to experience more varied economic fluctuations than other nations. Some of the colonies were enormous in size, such as Brazil, which varies dramatically in economic potential from region to region. That slavery varied according to period and region gives an impression of more flexibility in the treatment of blacks and freedmen than was the case with the French. The very brevity of the French slave system and the small size of the plantation colonies probably create an undue impression of rigid racial control. The Iberian, British, and French mindsets originally may not have been that different from one another, but the varying experiences of white-black interaction overseas crystallized differing attitudes toward race.

Blacks and Coloreds in France

Racism in the colonies is thought to have developed separately from metropolitan France, and even to have been deplored by the French in France. But even in metropolitan France, strong racial policies aimed against blacks prevailed. Black slaves were not allowed into France as slaves, on the principle that presence on French soil brought with it freedom. This rule was broken in 1716 when slaveowners from the Antilles, who had brought their slaves to France, were allowed to retain them. The authorities, however, became concerned lest there come to be too many blacks in France, and in 1738 they limited the duration of a slave's stay to three years and only for the purpose of learning a trade. Masters breaking the law were liable to heavy fines. The French government wanted to limit the stay of slaves because, while they were in France, slaves could be freed without receiving the necessary authorization from the administration in the colonies. Racial fears were actually responsible for the law of 1738. The entry of slaves into France should be discouraged, wrote the king, "for they give the occasion . . . of the mixing of black blood in the kingdom."[26] Hoping to prevent such a development, the government introduced specific laws against miscegenation; no slave was allowed to marry in France, even with the permission of his master.[27]

The presence of blacks and coloreds in France was a cause for great worry among the settlers in the Antilles. They felt that in France the slaves or freedmen would be exposed to egalitarian ideas and that they would become unruly upon their return to the colonies. The raising of a colored military company in France by the Maréchal de Saxe in the 1740s created considerable opposition in the West Indies. Reluctantly, the French government allowed the Maréchal to proceed, but, when he died in 1750, the colored troops were immediately disbanded and then very carefully supervised.[28]

The number of people of color residing in France is unknown, but the figures cited for the eighteenth century vary between a high of 5,000 and a low of 1,000 at any given moment.[29] Despite their small number, they were of great concern to French authorities in Paris and in the colonies, planters in the Antilles, and their sympathizers in the port cities. Metropolitan opposition to the entry of more black slaves was in part due to the fear that slavery as an institution would again win a legal recognition in the Metropole.[30] But the racist fears of being "contaminated" by blacks also played a role. For it was not just the entry of slaves but of any person of color that the metropolitan authorities opposed.

The colonial plea that the Metropole retain slaves and freedmen and not send them back to the Antilles was heeded for a while; thus, at colonial insistence, the minister of the navy in 1753 decided not to deport them.[31] But by 1764 the colonial concern for safety was ignored, giving precedence to the metropolitan fear of miscegenation, and the slaves were sent back to the colonies. No further slaves or freedmen were allowed to enter the territory of France because, in the words of the intendant general of Guadeloupe, the introduction of these groups "results in a mixture of blood that increases daily in France."[32]

The measures prohibiting men of color from entry into France were apparently enforced, and a new measure introduced in 1777 repeated earlier provisions, but allowed colonists crossing the seas to take with them a slave. Slaves could not land in France, however, and a special depot was built to house slaves until it was time for the colonists to return.

The motives for the decree of 1777 reveal a concern for the security of the colonies, but equally important were the racial fears. It declared:

> The Negroes are multiplying every day in France. They marry Europeans, the houses of prostitution are infected by them; the colors mix, the blood is changing . . . these slaves, if they return to America, bring with them the spirit of freedom, independence, and equality, which they communicate to others.[33]

By the royal order of 1778 the slaves in France were all sent back to the colonies or kept apart in stockades. Free men of color were not allowed to enter the country, and those who legally resided in France because they had arrived before the promulgation of the decree were forced to register with the authorities and were forbidden to marry whites.[34] It should be noted that no legal restraints were placed on free men of color or blacks in England, even though they constituted a ten-times-larger proportion of the population. The possible 5,000 blacks in France were part of a nation of 20 million inhabitants, whereas in England blacks represented 20,000 out of 8 million inhabitants.[35] Free blacks in England did suffer from serious discrimination; the plan to establish the Sierra Leone colony in 1787 was enthusiastically embraced by the government and by many individuals simply because it would provide a dumping ground for a population that was seen as dangerous and undesirable in England.[36] But the lack of legal restrictions seems to reveal a less profound level of hostility than was the case in France. Added to the weight of the law in France was social ostracism and prejudice.

If French officials thought that a racially defined society had to be maintained to preserve slavery, some of them also took the view that slavery should be preserved to maintain a racially separate society. A legal commentator in 1776 explained his opposition to freeing slaves: "The freedmen might in great numbers come to live in the kingdom, mix with French blood by marriage and pass on to their children their vicious tendencies, the traces of which will continue until a distant posterity."[37] Malouet, a colonial administrator and planter, argued that legal equality of the races could not be granted, for,

> if the black man is assimilated to whites, it is more than probable that we shall shortly see noble mulattoes, financiers, and traders whose wealth would procure them wives and mothers from all estates. . . . It is thus that individuals, families, nations become altered, degraded, and dissolve.[38]

The fear of miscegenation was great enough that proslavery thinkers evidently felt that they had a promising argument in favor of their position when they maintained that slavery ought to be preserved in order to avert miscegenation in France. Racism had served as a mechanism of social control in the West Indies, upholding the slave system, but racism had also become, in and of itself, sufficiently valued as a means of preventing racial equality and race mixing.

In France racial intermarriage was generally regarded with horror. Novelists and playwrights usually avoided it as a theme. And when playwrights did treat the subject, it was at their own peril. A play produced in 1787 that showed intermarriage between white and black was met by rioting.[39] Like the poor whites in the Antilles, the lower classes in France, finding little that could distinguish them from men of color of equal or higher professional skills and wealth, stressed race instead. In the 1780s there was an ugly race riot in Bordeaux. In August 1789, as various groups met to present protests to the government, a meeting of porters, footmen, headwaiters, and maids gathered at the Belleville theatre in Paris to petition the Estates-General. They asked for twice as much pay, an end to wearing livery, and the dismissal of black servants, "who annoyed white servants." It was not their antiblack sentiment but rather their agitation against their masters that led the government to call out the cavalry and to arrest fifty-two of the assembled servants as rioters.[40]

When a few years later the Revolutionary Assembly abolished slavery, public reaction varied. Police spies reported a rather mixed popular attitude. Some people, apparently moved by the plight of the slaves, favored the emancipation, but women in the marketplace were heard to say of the governmental decree, "My God, they are giving us black sisters, we shall never be able to live with women like that."[41]

Race and Slavery: From the Revolution to Napoleon

The extension of civic rights to free men of color and the freeing of slaves during the Revolution were not due to a fundamental reappraisal of the black man, but were rather the result of political and strategic exigencies.

The granting of full rights to persons of color had been considered by the Ancien Régime as an expedient way to strengthen colonial whites in the face of the ever-increasing slave populations and to safeguard the colonies against foreign attacks. These plans had not come to anything, nor did the Revolutionary Assemblies rush to grant equality to men of color. At the meeting of the Estates-General in 1789, delegates representing the colored population of the Antilles petitioned the Revolutionary Assembly for full citizenship. By all logic an assembly that had declared the Rights of Man should have been receptive to such an appeal, but it was not. Fearing to offend the planters, who declared that the adoption of such legislation would spell the ruin of the colonies, the Assembly turned down the petitions of the men of color.

Strongly seconded in the Assembly by representatives from the port cities, the planters were able to stop legislation giving the freedmen legal and political equality. When the legislature passed a law on March 28, 1790, giving the vote to "toutes les personnes" in the colonies, its failure—on the insistence of the planters and their sympathizers—to emphasize that persons of color were included in this category meant that the colored would in practice continue to be disfranchised. The Société des amis des noirs, which had initially opposed slavery, now, under the influence of Abbé Grégoire, began to concentrate instead on the question of the rights of the free colored.[42] (There is something unseemly about Grégoire, the abolitionist, arguing that the colored should be given rights as good loyal slaveowners, on whom the whites could depend against the slaves.)

The colored, heartened by the egalitarian slogans of the Revolution in France and by their understanding of the law of March 28, now more than ever agitated for their rights. An alleged plot by the colored was discovered in Martinique in June 1790, and whites massacred over 200 colored people. Ogé, a man of color who in Paris had been spokesman for the rights of the colored, landed in Saint-Domingue that October; he started an uprising to try and force the whites to grant the colored their rights, which in principle had already been declared in Paris. The colored were defeated, and their leaders, among them Ogé, were tortured to death. His demise was pictured as a form of martyrdom by the Amis, and the despair of the freed colored, as revealed in the Ogé uprising, was a powerful argument in helping to pass a law on May 15, 1791, which gave full political rights to freedmen born of free fathers and mothers.[43] This law applied to only a small group, numbering in Saint-Domingue, for instance, only 400 out of a total population of 25,000 freedmen.[44] And yet it created deep bitterness among the settlers; the colonial deputies stormed out of the National Assembly. Planters' feelings were well summed up by one of them:

> Do you think we will take the law from the grandson of one of our slaves? No! Rather die than assent to this infamy! That is the cry of all. If France sends troops for the execution of this decree, it is likely that we will decide to abandon France.[45]

The whites in the colonies, despite the serious cleavage that was developing between the rich plantation owners and the poor whites, closed ranks, determined to deny the free coloreds their rights. But circumstances changed their resolve. On the night of August 22, 1791, a slave revolt broke out. The planters had no time now to fight the freedmen; confronted by immediate danger, they joined forces with them. This alliance was advantageous for the planters, who were facing not only the slaves in rebellion but also the poor whites. Racial solidarity had begun to break down, once the spirit of the Revolution had infected the poor whites, who were now intent on possessing political power themselves. The freedmen-planters alliance went through many vicissitudes and was repeatedly dissolved and restored in the autumn of 1791 and the spring of 1792. In Paris the colonial need for colored support against the slaves was understood, and in March 1792 the Assembly gave full political rights to all freedmen.[46]

The alliance of the free colored with the whites often fell apart because the whites in Saint-Domingue found it repugnant to grant the colored full rights. The latter—in spite of repeated disappointments—joined with the whites when offered the opportunity. In the face of the slave uprising, the free colored, many of whom were large slaveholders, felt a natural affinity with the whites. The free colored, possessing "white blood," proclaimed themselves superior to the blacks, who in turn were hostile toward them.[47]

In the face of white intransigence, the colored-black hostility was at times overcome, and the two groups joined forces. But within that alliance, as the struggle against the French continued, definite groups based on color continued to exist. Toussaint L'ouverture was the leader of the blacks, while Rigaud represented the colored. In 1799 the two groups went to war against each other. Defeated, Rigaud fled to France, since he could not reconcile himself to subordinating colored interests to those of the blacks. In 1802 he sailed with the French in the Leclerc expedition, which attempted to reconquer Saint-Domingue and to re-establish slavery there. The ambiguous position that the colored took toward emancipation in the Revolution helped worsen relations between black and colored in the independent state of Haiti. Tensions between the two groups was so significant that from 1807 to 1820 there was a black kingdom in the north and a colored republic in the west and south. When the two sections were joined, hostility continued between the colored elite and the black lower classes. In the nineteenth century, several massacres of the minority colored population occurred, and, in the twentieth century, dictatorships flourished on the promise of holding the colored in check. Thus the pathological heights to which racial feeling had been raised by white society in seventeenth- and eighteenth-century Saint-Domingue hampered the development of independent Haiti.

In Martinique and Guadeloupe, which have remained French territories, metropolitan authority prevented racial conflicts from developing into mutual massacres. But this does not mean that racial feelings abated; sociological studies in the second half of the twentieth century reveal considerable racial consciousness in Martinique and Guadeloupe. Intermarriage between whites and blacks or colored is rare, and, while the races commingle in official public meetings, they tend to exercise segregation in their private social affairs.[48]

Emancipation

In the face of the slave revolts, the French military forces that were rushed to Saint-Domingue in 1792 encountered opposition from an unexpected quarter—the planters. After the deposition of the king in August 1792 and especially after the outbreak of war in the spring of 1793, the Revolution in France became increasingly radical; the planters were out of sympathy with the new egalitarian Republic that was emerging. The new government would no longer allow the distinction between the planters and the poor whites that had existed under the Ancien Régime, and the government was suspected (wrongly) of favoring slave emancipation.

While there had been, throughout the eighteenth century, some desire for autonomy in Saint-Domingue, the tendency was held in check by the willingness of the Metropole to maintain the power of the large plantation owners and to uphold slavery. With both these advantages now seemingly gone from the colonial relationship, the planters took arms against the French forces. The French authorities had to fight not only the planters but also the Spanish and later the British, who had decided to take advantage of the turmoil to attempt to wrest away France's richest colony. To protect French sovereignty in Saint-Domingue, the commissioner, Sonthonax, decided to rally the black population. On August 29, 1793, he decreed the emancipation of the slaves.[49] In Martinique the planters also joined the opposition to France and delivered the island to Britain. To restore French rule, general emancipation of the slaves seemed a worthwhile gambit. On February 4, 1794, the National Convention abolished slavery in all of France's colonies. Not the principles of humanity, but rather the practical exigencies of attempting to save the empire motivated the French National Convention to abolish slavery. Now the blacks would rally to France against the British, and the example of French emancipation would undermine British authority in its own domain. As Danton exclaimed when the bill was passed, "Citizens, today England is dead! Pitt and his plots have been unravelled. The Englishman will see his commerce destroyed!"[50]

In addition to its strategic advantages, however, abolition was, of course, little more than a confirmation of what had already happened. Just as the peasants by their uprising in the summer of 1789 had destroyed feudalism before the Assembly abolished it in August, so the slaves by their uprising and

Sonthonax by his decree had already destroyed slavery. Still, the orators of the Revolution proclaimed abolition as a great act of generosity by the Republic, and emancipation was accompanied by an outpouring of egalitarian rhetoric.

The Revolution, while tardy in ensuring the rights of freedmen in the colonies, forbade all slavery and the introduction of slaves into France, both of which had been allowed under certain circumstances under the Ancien Régime. In a decree of September 1791, the colored in France were given all the rights of citizenship.[51] The rights of freedmen in the colonies had been defended with varying degrees of ardor by Paris, but, once slavery was abolished, these rights could be upheld unequivocally. The extent to which discrimination against the colored had been seen as a necessary concomitant of slavery was revealed in the resolution of the National Convention that abolished slavery: "The National Convention declares slavery abolished in all the colonies; *in consequence* [my italics] it decrees that all men without distinction of color living in the colonies are French citizens."[52] If the decree had some impact on the treatment of the colored in France, it had none in the colonies. Saint-Domingue was in the midst of a full-scale revolution, and the French could not reimpose their rule there; Guadeloupe and Martinique were under British control.

As soon as peace was made with England in 1802, France regained control of Guadeloupe and Martinique and had a free hand in trying to reconquer Saint-Domingue. But the France of 1802 had different plans for the colonies than did the France of 1794. Napoleon decided to reimpose slavery. A practical man who did not set much store by ideals, Napoleon thought slave production the best means of ensuring the wealth of France's restored Caribbean empire. Moreover, in the minds of most Frenchmen, the massacres in Saint-Domingue were due to the failure to control the blacks and to keep them in subjugation. Whereas the slave uprisings had finally led to emancipation, it was generally thought that emancipation had led to the slaughter in the colonies. The bloodshed seemingly confirmed the belief in black savagery, which had been so prevalent among the proponents of slavery. Freedom for blacks was unthinkable to Napoleon, who asked,

"How could I grant freedom to Africans, to utterly uncivilized men who did not even know what a colony was, what France was?"[53]

With the reintroduction of slavery, Napoleon also brought back the racial legislation of the Ancien Régime. In Guadeloupe and Martinique the freedmen were discriminated against and were refused entry into France as they had been before; miscegenation was strictly forbidden.[54] Haiti remained unconquerable and was able to preserve its independence despite a French invasion led by General Leclerc, Napoleon's brother-in-law.

The racial legislation that Napoleon reintroduced does not seem to have been due solely to what were seen as the exigencies of the slave system. Rather, Napoleon appears to have suffered from a genuine racial phobia, perhaps abetted in part by Josephine, who came from a settler family in Martinique. Thus Napoleon ordered Leclerc to deport from Saint-Domingue any white women who had had sexual contact with blacks.[55]

Later in life, at Saint Helena, when Napoleon was building his legend as an enlightened liberal ruler, he maintained that he had considered means of creating racial equality in the plantation colonies. He had supposedly held discussions with theologians to find out whether whites in the Caribbean could be allowed to have two wives, one white and one black. Having the same father, the descendants of these marriages would feel close to each other. Thus, Napoleon asserted, he had planned to abolish racial antagonisms.[56] Given the thoroughness with which racial legislation was enforced during Napoleon's rule, however, there is little reason to believe that he attempted to attenuate racism. Instead, he shared the fears of miscegenation expressed by former plantation owners, who again warned of the dangers of race mixing. One of them, Deslozières, wrote that since the Revolution African blood had been allowed to run in the veins of Parisian women; if race mixing were allowed further, "it will attack the heart of the nation by deforming its traits and darkening it. Morality will, like the color of the body, be blackened, and in no time the degeneration of the entire French people will occur."[57] Napoleon forbade blacks and coloreds not only from the Antilles but also from Senegal to enter France. (This decree was in effect until 1818.)[58] His failures in Haiti furthered his Negrophobia; for instance, he ordered the Ecole polytechnique in Paris to dismiss its black and colored students.[59]

Race Relations in Senegal

In the Antilles the largest number of Frenchmen came into contact with the most blacks and coloreds, and there, in the seventeenth and eighteenth centuries, they showed themselves prone to racial exclusivism and developed racist theories. By the 1770s such ideologies were also familiar to many living in France, and racial legislation was enforced in the kingdom. There were some exceptions to this situation, however, and these reveal that, though color prejudice is important in determining how one group will treat another, such a sentiment can to a certain degree be held in check when it is counterproductive. Such was the case in Senegal. Unlike the other French possessions, Senegal was characterized by the lack of rigid racial categories; the groups intermingled with ease. Colored persons were given the status of honored citizens, rather than being reduced to a marginal existence, as had been the case of the freedmen in the Antilles.

The historic demographic and economic development of Senegal dictated race relations there. The French had established themselves in the 1630s and maintained a precarious hold on the trading fort of Saint-Louis on the Senegal River. When they arrived they were faced by a continent inhabited by black people, upon whom they depended to ensure a steady supply of trade goods—gold, gum, and slaves. The latter were exported to the West Indies and were not part of society in Saint-Louis, the capital of Senegal. The only slaves in the city were domestics.[60] Their treatment was mild and they were in no way so necessary to the economic production of the colony as were slaves in the Caribbean. Since most of the slaveowners were Africans, the institution could not be strengthened by the development of racial legislation and ideology, as happened in the American colonies. In any case, the issue of slavery was unimportant in Saint-Louis.

In the Antilles a policy of racial exclusivism had been useful as a way of preserving white power and influence; in Senegal the opposite policy was preferable. Contrasting Senegal with the Antilles, the minister of the navy noted in 1823 that, in his African possession, "the prejudice of color hardly exists, the European allies himself with the native of color without contravening any deep-seated prejudices; the native of color enjoys the same rights as the European and even occupies public office."[61] Such a policy ensured the spread of French influence into the continent. The white population was small, approximately 10 percent of the population of Saint-Louis; in the 1780s Golberry estimated the city to be inhabited by "2,400 free native Negroes and Mulattoes," 2,400 slaves, and 660 whites. Of the latter, 600 were trading agents, soldiers, and administrators; only 60 whites were permanently established. Golberry described them as "established merchants, retired soldiers married to Mulattoes, or laborers." Gorée had fewer people, but the population had a similar distribution; there were 1,840 inhabitants, of whom 638 were free blacks and Eurafricans, 1,044 were domestic slaves, about 200 were slaves held for shipment, and 70 to 80 were Europeans, mostly soldiers, government administrators, and employees of trading houses.[62] Probably less than a dozen whites were permanent residents. The demographic balance between the races in these two African enclaves was quite different from that in the Antilles, where the permanently residing white population approximated 10 percent; in Saint-Louis and Gorée it was one percent or less. Adding even further to their sense of numerical inferiority was the deep awareness of whites (both permanent residents and the temporarily assigned officials, soldiers, and tradesmen) that they lived on a continent inhabited by black peoples. They were an insignificant minority that had to accommodate the African environment and that could not impose itself. Governor Roger wrote in 1824, "We are establishing ourselves in a country that is already inhabited, we are coming into their midst."[63]

Politically and militarily, the French position was weak. The populations up the river from time to time threatened war, and the British, established in nearby forts, tried to evict the French and establish hegemony over the Senegambia. The

French were dependent on the black and colored populations in Saint-Louis. The goodwill of the nonwhite population had to be enlisted by carrying out liberal race policies. Harsh treatment of the indigenous groups would have led only to their abandoning Saint-Louis and weakening the already precarious white position, whereas close relations allowed French influence to spread inland. Traders and administrators wanted to extend their influence up the river, but the disease pattern of the Upper Senegal discouraged most whites from venturing forth. Blacks and coloreds, more immune to disease, went up river, ensuring French commercial and political penetration. Their cooperation benefited France. As the minister of the navy noted in 1817, it was the easy, relaxed nature of race relations in Saint-Louis that won over the population and that "singularly facilitated our relations with the interior."[64]

In contrast to the Antilles, where the black and colored populations were kept at a distance and excluded from the political and social life of the colony, in Senegal they were included. France practiced a policy of assimilation, extending French culture to the populations of Saint-Louis and Gorée. Schooling was provided, in order, it was hoped, to create a young elite "with the taste for our goods and industry,"[65] who would be faithful to France and who would spread European civilization. Furthermore, there were practical aspects to this education: it would produce clerks for French commerce and administration. The rights of the civil code were extended to all free men in 1830. A local representative body, the *conseil général,* was created for Senegal; coloreds and blacks voted for its members and participated in it. In 1848 Senegal was given a parliamentary seat in the National Assembly in Paris; the first deputy elected was a prosperous Saint-Louis trader, a man of color, Durand Valantin.[66] The mayor of Saint-Louis had since the eighteenth century been a man of color.[67]

Theoretically, no post in the colony was closed because of race. While it was rather easy for the colored children to assimilate the culture of their white fathers, who ensured that they were brought up as Catholics, saw to it that they received the available local education, and sometimes even sent them to Europe for an education, some of the black population also assimilated French values. Although most remained Moslems, some converted to Christianity. Religious assimilation was sometimes incomplete, leading to syncretic forms of worship. Lamiral wrote in 1789:

> All the people of color and a few Negroes profess the Catholic religion but with a singular admixture of Mohamedanism and idolatry; they celebrate both Christian and Moslem feasts. . . . There are those who, after having been to mass, say their prayers in the direction of Mecca, and they pray with the same fervor to Jesus Christ and Mohamed.[68]

Some blacks attended French schools and like the Eurafricans found careers as scribes, accountants, or agents of the local French traders.[69]

French assimilationist policies in Senegal had created by the end of the eighteenth century a population closely identifying with France and relatively free of racial cleavages. The patriotism and cohesiveness of the Saint-Louis population was manifest in the petition Lamiral penned on its behalf to the Revolutionary Assembly in 1789: "Negroes or mulattoes, we are all French, since it is the blood of Frenchmen that flows in our veins, or in those of our nephews. This origin fills us with pride and lifts up our souls!"[70] Inhabitants of Saint-Louis named their children after revolutionary leaders or classical heroes popular in France at that time: "The son of Mamadu was given the name of Robespierre and that of Ma Semba was naturally transformed into an African Scipio."[71] Enthusiasm for the Revolution led to voluntary gifts of money to the Republic raised by the citizenry of Saint-Louis, who, "if they cannot yet show the Republic their wounds and blood shed on its behalf, . . . can at least pay it homage, and reveal the feelings which they all share regardless of estate, fortune, and color."[72] In other ways the population identified itself with the cause of France; to the sound of drums, the community of Saint-Louis celebrated the news of Napoleon's crowning as emperor, or the victory at Austerlitz.[73]

There was assimilation with respect to language and clothing. Father Boilat, one of the first Eurafrican priests, overstated the totality of assimilation in these areas; nevertheless, considerable inroads must have been made for him to write of the Goréens in 1853, "Today the men are wholly dressed in the French fashion and all speak French without a trace of accent. . . . The young people of both sexes are wholly dressed in the French manner and in the latest mode."[74] Boilat, like many other men of color, felt that he lived in a society where "the prejudice of color is unknown" and in which careers were in no way racially restricted, but rather were open to talent. Founding the first secondary school in Saint-Louis, Boilat told his students' parents in 1843, "The children graduating from our college can aspire to all honorable positions that a young man may desire." Turning to his students, he assured them "all the positions of the colony will be open to you: medicine, pharmacy, the judiciary, all will depend on your will and vocation."[75] The Frenchified colored population enthusiastically backed the French presence and desired its expansion to the rest of Africa. Running for deputy in 1849, another priest, also a Eurafrican, Abbé Fridoil, adopted as his motto "Colonization and civilization through religion, education, and commerce."[76]

Only after the mid-nineteenth century, when French expansion started in earnest and when the French had acquired a preponderance of power in their relationship with Africans, did this racially relatively egalitarian society dissolve. The French, becoming wary of the rising colored elite, restricted education and employment opportunities and tried to take away political rights that previously had been extended. With the advance of French imperialism, especially after the 1880s, French dependence on the assimilated populations of Saint-Louis ceased, and a new relationship between white and black, which was more rigid and racially exclusive, was established in West Africa. True, in Saint-Louis, Gorée, and two more communes added in the nineteenth century (Dakar and Rufisque), some of the old patterns of assimilation continued into the twentieth century, but they were now vestiges of a bygone era.

The liberal attitude toward blacks and coloreds that existed until the mid-nineteenth century was revealed in the willingness of whites in Senegal to intermarry. In the 1720s the director of the Senegal Company suggested that his employees be allowed to marry local black and colored women; his plan was countermanded, however, by Paris, already beset by fears of miscegenation.[77] Whites did marry blacks and coloreds, nevertheless; there was no local prejudice or legislation against it as there was in the Antilles, although the most common relationship was marriage *à la mode du pays,* a stylized, contractual relationship that was binding only as long as the European remained in Africa. Governor Blanchot, already married in France, contracted such a marriage during his second term of office between 1802 and 1807; the last governor to do so was Faidherbe in the mid-nineteenth century. Regular Catholic marriages performed according to French law were extremely rare; Abbé Boilat recorded for the years 1819–1840 nine in Gorée and forty-four in Saint-Louis.[78] If European types of marriages were uncommon and thought by the good priest to be the only ones worthy of moral persons, the marriage *à la mode du pays,* in establishing the mutual responsibilities of the spouses and their duties to any children born of the relationship, nevertheless represented a serious public commitment. What marked it apart from a civil-code marriage was that it was not for life but for the duration of the European's stay in Senegal.

Many of the unions were between European traders or officials and African or Eurafrican women known as *signares*; these women were wealthy or had extensive trade and commercial relations, which they made available to their white mates.[79] Children born of interracial unions, unlike those in the Antilles, took on their fathers' names. Records for Saint-Louis and the island of Gorée show that most children who were baptized, even when illegitimate, had been legally recognized by their fathers.[80] Such recognitions created less embarrassment than in the Antilles, where white fathers, whose white families were with them, did not want to recognize publicly the offspring of an illegitimate connection. Of course, whites hardly ever brought their French families to Senegal.

The prejudice against coloreds in the Antilles was based in part on the presumption that any child born of the union of white and black was of slave descent. But in Saint-Louis most Africans were free and the whole African continent consisted mostly of free people. Colored persons thus could not be presumed to be of slave descent; nor did they suffer from the onus of ancestral servitude, as was the case in the New World.

In the Antilles most wealth was in the hands of the small white elite, but in Senegal the colored population possessed the most important property in individual hands (the Senegal Company and its successors—among them the East India Company—as chartered companies were the largest corporate owners). In Gorée in 1749, ten of thirteen large residences qualified as *propriétés* belonged to colored women. In 1767 a *signare* named Caty Louette possessed twenty-five slaves and forty-three house slaves, making her the richest person on the island.[81]

The easy relationship between the races in Saint-Louis and on the island of Gorée has often been pointed to as an indication of the lack of French race consciousness. But the situation in West Africa was highly exceptional. In terms of both the numbers involved and the impact in France, the experience in the Antilles was far more telling.

The situation in the West Indies even had an impact on the way in which the inhabitants of Senegal were legally classified. Until the nineteenth century, the French, used to the social divisions of the Antilles, classified the people of Saint-Louis and Gorée in categories such as "white," "mulatto and free Negroes," and "captives" (or variants thereof). Thus, as in the Antilles, the colored and the free blacks were thought of as a group separate from the whites.[82] Although it was more rare, some whites living in Senegal even applied the infinite gradations dependent on the degree of white ancestry to persons of color, as was the custom in the Antilles.[83]

Racial legislation adopted in France and aimed against the blacks and freedmen of the Antilles also had its impact on the nonwhite community of Saint-Louis. Even though he was mayor of Saint-Louis, Charles Cornier was refused permission to enter France in April 1789 because he was colored.[84] Such legislation was nullified after 1794 when slavery was abolished, but when Napoleon reinstated slavery, the concomitant racial laws were again introduced. Napoleon, for instance, ordered that the militia in Senegal no longer have racially integrated companies "in order always to maintain distance between the races."[85]

The operation of the legal system in Senegal reveals that, despite the fluid nature of race relations, coloreds and blacks were not fully assimilated with whites. Cases involving the former were always placed last on the court calendar, and the judgments were made public. Most of the blacks and coloreds found guilty of serious crimes were sent to America as slaves, whereas whites found guilty of the same crimes were sent to France and retried. In commercial disputes the governor was the first arbiter, and an appeal could be made to an appointed group of arbiters. Whites served as arbiters for whites, and blacks for blacks. In a dispute involving both a white and a black, each would choose three arbiters of his race. For minor offenses the mayor, a man of color, could send a black or colored inhabitant of Saint-Louis to jail or order him whipped, but he could not so punish a white.[86] Although the social system was rather open, the legal system enforced a color barrier.

The small white community considered it essential to give enough rights and privileges to nonwhites to ensure their loyalty to the French regime. Still, it was felt that a certain amount of white superiority should be asserted, in order to retain some control over the nonwhite population. Such an attitude had been expressed by the enlightened young botanist Michel Adanson, who had lived in Senegal in the 1750s. Adanson was a humane person, sympathetic to blacks, yet when he met an African he would not take off his hat. He explained why he and his fellow Europeans did not do so: "I followed the French custom, which is never to take off our hats to people of his complexion . . . submission ought to be encouraged as much as possible."[87] A generation later the self-proclaimed Senegalese representative to the Revolutionary Assembly, Lamiral, quite at variance with his official petition, extolled the "wise rules that fix the distance that must exist between the two species [white and colored]. . . . We must always establish a profound respect for our blood."[88] Whereas it would be a mistake to think that perfect racial equality was practiced in Senegal, admittedly, when compared with the West Indies, the situation was remarkably fluid and liberal.

Conclusion

If anything can be learned by comparing race relations in the Antilles and Senegal in the eighteenth century, it seems that the inherent prejudices of a culture do not necessarily predetermine how one race will behave toward another. Thus the Frenchmen who came to Senegal probably entertained no fewer negative stereotypes about Africans than other Frenchmen did, yet in West Africa the survival of the white community depended on maintaining an open and relaxed attitude toward race. Although such a policy was implemented, it was not perfect. At least the legal provisions and some comments by officials give the impression that the general prejudice against blacks and the methods acquired in the Antilles to some degree also manifested themselves in Senegal. As a whole, however, the French experience in Senegal reveals the lack of influence of the antiblack ideas then prevalent in France.

In the Antilles French policy coincided with the general hostility and prejudice that Frenchmen revealed toward blacks. But here again ideas seem to have been less important in dictating French policy toward blacks than were the perceived needs of preserving a slave society. It was thought that the best way to safeguard white control over a large, black, slave population was to uphold the values of racial exclusivism. In France the treatment of blacks coincided with the generally hostile attitudes toward them. Ideas, however, were never so powerful that they were allowed to dictate actions that would have hurt what were seen as essential interests of the white communities in Senegal and the Antilles.

The French experience in the eighteenth century suggests that the demographic interpretation of race relations has some applicability. It is not, however, so deterministic as Marvin Harris and Carl Degler have suggested and does not readily explain national differences. In the French West Indies, the small white population was not so accommodating as it proved to be in Latin America. But the demographic situation seems to have been an important variable, explaining differences in white-black interaction within the French world. Thus, in France, where the population was white, with the exception of a handful of blacks, racist policies could be practiced and were not particularly counterproductive. In the West Indies, the white minority was small enough to live in fear, but large enough and strong enough to practice a policy of racial domination. In Senegal, where the population was exclusively black and where there was an infinitesimal number of whites, it was necessary for the latter to practice accommodation.

The policies carried out in these three societies were viewed as being in the interest of the whites. People act not always according to their actual interests but according to how they perceive them. The white slaveowning class in the West Indies grievously miscalculated. It refused to enlarge the class of freedmen or to attempt to win the latter's loyalty. Given the weakness of the Metropole as a result of the Revolution of 1789, a policy of rigid racial exclusivism led to the extermination of whites in Saint-Domingue and to France's loss of the "pearl of the Antilles." Racism in the West Indies was not the result of exceptional behavior by Frenchmen in a faraway region; rather, it reflected closely the cultural values of the era.

5

The Issue of Slavery

The Slave as Man

The French had only gradually adopted slavery as the main means of production in their Caribbean empire. Thus, slavery was not an issue that stirred up much debate in the seventeenth century. Social, political, and legal inequalities were seen as the norm. In France severe maltreatment of the human body was publicly acceptable; men found guilty of crimes were condemned to galley slavery or to death by disembowelment or fire. At a time when such actions were considered normal and rarely received reproof, enslaving Africans in distant lands seemed even less objectionable. As David Brion Davis has pointed out, none of the major seventeenth-century authorities such as Descartes, Malebranche, or Pascal, for instance, condemned the abominable trade in which France had become fully involved.[1]

Slavery, even when Frenchmen were the victims, was not condemned as an institution. Countless Frenchmen were taken prisoner and enslaved by the North African states. A whole literature developed around the theme of the Christian slave in Barbary, detailing his suffering and sometimes exotic adventures. While the writers often showed the horrors of white slavery, they did not attack the institution of slavery. Since the French enslaved North Africans for their galley ships, white slavery was seen as but the reverse side of French practices.

There were some exceptions. From time to time, French writers in the sixteenth century, in their attack against the Spanish, inveighed against their cruel slavery in the Americas. Montaigne, for instance, did so in the chapter "Des coches," where he complained of how the Spanish treated the Indians "like savage animals." In the seventeenth century, French pamphleteers listed the horrors of black slavery, but also in

130

the context of attacks against France's secular enemy, Spain.[2] Otherwise, slavery did not gain much attention, and no systematic antislavery literature developed prior to the eighteenth century.

The eighteenth-century philosophes addressed the question of slavery in a way that had never been done before in French society. In part, this new ethos was due to the emergence of a different attitude toward authority. Within limits the philosophes questioned the order of society as it existed under the Ancien Régime. They were by no means democratic thinkers suggesting the leveling of a hierarchical society, but they saw human merit (and they thought of their own intellectual activities as particularly meritorious) as the basis for rank in society. They adopted the principle that not the age but rather the reasonableness of an institution ought to be the mark by which to judge it. These new attitudes allowed for a critical examination of slavery as an institution.

What made slavery a relevant issue was, of course, the growth of the institution. Until the end of the seventeenth century, it was not yet clear that slave labor would become the major means of production in either the French or the British colonies. But, as slavery became firmly established, French participation in the slave trade grew considerably, and French colonies were peopled by an ever-increasing slave-labor force. While the French experience helped shape the philosophes' attitude, there was also considerable awareness of the practices of other European states. In Voltaire's *Candide,* the hero encounters slavery in the Dutch colony of Surinam. The reaction among various groups in England and its colonies against slavery (for instance, the campaign of the Quakers) was known early in France. Many of the eighteenth-century French writers who were to address themselves to the slavery issue were Anglophiles; sympathetic to reform movements in England, they were not unaffected by the attacks against slavery that had been going on there.

What marked the Enlightenment's attack on slavery and in the end helped to abolish the institution was the insistence that slaves were men and, therefore, had full rights to humane treatment. Sentiments, including pity, were cultivated in the eighteenth century. A more delicate appreciation for human suffering developed. The slave became an object of sentimental concern; for a long time, however, this feeling represented a minority view.

The more common attitudes are detectable in the dictionaries, which, in a sense, are a synthesis of the knowledge, or prejudices, of an age. Two French scholars who scrutinized the entries in seventeenth- and eighteenth-century dictionaries found that a large number of dictionaries had no entry for "nègres," while others systematically avoided the issue of the blacks' humanity.[3] The official Académie française, which formally defines the French language, had the following entry for "Nègre": "It is the name that one generally gives all black slaves working in the colonies."[4] The term "nègre" was equated with "slave," but the slaves' humanity was left obscure.

With the Enlightenment, however, came the increasing use of the term "nègre" instead of "esclave" in speaking of labor in the Antilles. Furthermore, even the term "nègre," which, in its close association with slavery, had a pejorative connotation, was in part supplanted by "noir." It was no accident that, at its founding in 1788, the abolitionist society took on the title Société des amis des noirs.[5]

The eighteenth century was not so uncompromising in its condemnation of slavery as some were later to claim, yet there developed a discussion of slavery that clearly addressed the question of how enslavement could be justified, given the humanity of the slave. By the second half of the eighteenth century, Poivre, an enlightened colonial official in Ile-de-France, would declare that slaveowners must not forget that their slaves were "men like them," and the governor of Guadeloupe (brother of Mirabeau, the future revolutionary) would write, "The slave, although he is a slave, must be considered as a man and I think he has to be thought of as a brother." The impossible situation created by recognizing the slave as a brother was announced by Marmontel: "*My brother you are my slave,* is an absurdity in the mouth of a man, it is perjury and blasphemy in the mouth of a Christian."[6]

The philosophes' attack on slavery began early. Montesquieu bitterly attacked slavery, sarcastically suggesting that it would have to be just, for "otherwise we cannot be called Christians." In the *Encyclopédie* it was stated that slavery "violates religion, morality, natural law, and all the rights of human nature"; then, in a burst of anger anticipating Abbé Raynal and Robespierre, the writer expostulated, "It would be better if the European colonies were destroyed than that so many men be made unfortunate."[7]

The Ambivalence of Antislavery

Attacks on slavery, however, were not totally straightforward; a number of intellectual inconsistencies about slavery as an institution also were expressed at the same time. Montesquieu declared that "slavery is against nature," but then, resorting to his climatic theories, he added, "Though in certain countries it is founded on natural reason. . . . One must then limit slavery to certain particular countries of the earth." Presumably, Montesquieu accepted slavery in the Caribbean. And also while opposing slavery, he recognized its economic value: "Sugar would be too expensive if the cane were not harvested by slaves." While Montesquieu's overall thought was antislavery, he showed enough ambiguity toward the institution of slavery that he could be usefully cited by those favoring slavery; in fact, he was.[8]

Voltaire, who accepted Aristotle's notion that slavery was based on the inequality of various groups, saw blacks as definitely inferior: "As a result of a hierarchy of nations, Negroes are thus slaves of other men." He seems to have believed that the supposed African acquiescence to enslavement justified considering the African a lesser being: ". . . a people that sells its own children is more condemnable than the buyer; this commerce demonstrates our superiority; he who gives himself a master was born to have one."[9]

If the *Encyclopédie* opposed slavery in a most uncompromising tone, as Davis has written,[10] it still shared in the general ambivalence of the era toward slavery. While it protested against the injustices of slavery in one place, in another article, "Negroes considered as slaves in the American colonies," it uncritically accepted the slavers' reasoning: the Antilles could be developed only with black labor (this was a general belief), and black servitude was in no sense a despotic imposition, for

> these black men, born vigorous and accustomed to coarse food, find in America amenities that make their physical existence much more agreeable than in their own country. This improvement makes it possible for them to resist work and to multiply in large numbers.

Abbé Grégoire, in *An Enquiry Concerning the Intellectual and Moral Faculties and Literature of Negroes,* presented a determined attack on slavery and a defense of the blacks' status in European thought. Yet he too was not immune to the environmental theory. Since excessive heat "inclines to indolence" and creates an "abundance of consumable commodities," productive labor could be ensured only through a slave system, he noted. Grégoire wanted to limit slavery to the tropical areas, but that, of course, did not differentiate him radically from the slavers. Thus, while the total thrust of Abbé Grégoire's life and work favored abolition, his acceptance of climatic theory—like Montesquieu's—created a certain tension in his thought.[11]

The ambiguities and blatant contradictions in the philosophes' attitudes toward slavery are difficult to explain. In part, they were due, as Davis has argued, to the philosophes' belief, despite their criticism of much of the Ancien Régime, that society had to be arranged in some kind of rational, hierachical order and that the existing system had some kind of basis in either the laws of nature or economic necessity (for example, the need for manpower in the Antilles).

Slavery was not so integral a part of the social and economic fabric of France as it was of the colonies; nevertheless, the colonies, dependent on slave labor, were a significant factor in France. They helped provide the wealth that contributed to the development of the polished salon society of the philosophes that, in turn, allowed the philosophes to enjoy the pensions that so many of them received.[12]

The plantation colonies were of paramount commercial interest to France in the eighteenth century. The wealth of maritime cities such as Nantes and Bordeaux was derived from the plantation colonies. One third of Bordeaux's trade was based on contact with the colonies. The wealth of the large ports had a ripple effect; a whole hinterland was supported, for instance, by shipbuilding and sugar refining. One quarter of all French foreign trade derived from the colonies, and it was universally agreed that the West Indies were by far the most profitable part of the empire. The Antilles trade was so much the more valued because it was an area of foreign commerce that had grown twice as fast as the rest of French trade in the eighteenth century.[13]

Trade with the Antilles helped fuel France's commerce in the Mediterranean and in Northern Europe. The French economic historian, Louis-Philippe May, has suggested that trade with those regions (except Spain and the Levant) depended almost totally upon goods from the French Caribbean, or goods which had to be supplied to it. Most of the staple goods from the plantation colonies were not consumed by Frenchmen, but rather, after having been refined, were exported to the rest of Europe and thus benefited France's foreign trade balance. In comparison with its most formidable trade rival, England, France had a greater share of the European market for exotic products. May goes so far as to suggest that France's "industrial revolution" was supported by the Caribbean.[14] While it is hard to see that such a revolution occurred in the eighteenth century (some historians even argue whether it occurred in the nineteenth), there can be no doubt of the importance of France's commerce with the colonies. Contemporaries recognized it as a significant element in the well-being of the nation and seem even to have exaggerated its importance.[15]

As Frenchmen eager to see their country prosper, the philosophes shared a certain anguish at the thought of what would happen were France deprived of the wealth of its plantation colonies. Many had an interest in colonial questions, as well as close relations with the Ministry of Marine, having access to the latest reports circulating in the Ministry. Much of the antislavery thought of the philosophes, Michèle Duchet has argued, was not a brave assault on the plantation system, but rather an echo of the concerns of the colonial officials themselves.[16]

By the mid-eighteenth century, the French colonial bureau-cracy was well aware of the precarious nature of plantation colonies dependent upon slave labor for their productivity. French officials wished to have strong, internally cohesive societies in the Caribbean that would be able to withstand suc-cessfully possible military attacks from Dutch and, later, British rivals; therefore, they tried to discourage the increasing divisions along racial lines. The failure of the planters to rec-ognize the need to be both conciliatory toward the growing free colored population and temperate in their treatment of their slaves was condemned by the more enlightened members of the French colonial bureaucracy. The problems of neighbor-ing colonies further stressed the instability of slave societies. Particularly instructive was Dutch Guiana, which experienced large-scale revolts. Fugitive slaves formed such powerful groups of resistance that they were able to force the Dutch to negotiate treaties with them and to recognize their indepen-dence. Even those concessions did not ensure peace, however, and massive slave revolts in Dutch Guiana continued to break out between 1764 and 1776.[17]

Some officials had their doubts about continuing to rely on slave labor and on a rigid racial system overseas, but they were cautious reformers, concerned lest too rapid changes upset the delicate balance in the colonies. In advancing proposals for change, they had to take into account the objections of those who ardently supported the *status quo*. Thus the colonial re-formers in the bureaucracy were not outright abolitionists or egalitarians. Their caution, expressed in their memoirs and in various government reports, was also assumed by philosophes such as Diderot and Raynal, not only because they reflect-ed the ambivalence of their age, as Davis argued, but also because they adopted as their own various proposals of reform bureaucrats.

Some of the philosophes had personal interests in the French colonies. Diderot had close relatives serving overseas and good friends at the Ministry of Marine; he identified closely with the bourgeois class, whose wealth, in many parts of France, was based on the colonies.[18] Voltaire, who was maliciously accused of having dabbled in the slave trade, owned stock in the Compagnie des Indes, the fortunes of which were partly based on the slave trade and labor.[19] Whatever influence his economic involvements may have had, the personal correspondence he carried on with colonial officials probably had greater direct impact. In his contacts with them, Voltaire seems to have taken on some of their attitudes.[20] Raynal maintained direct contact with his friends who served in the Ministry of Marine, and he also received subsidies from the Ministry. At its behest he was sometimes willing to delete embarrassing material from his *Histoire des deux Indes.*[21] Some of the ambiguity of Raynal's work may be due to the conflict between his ideals and the exigencies of the Ministry. A more charitable interpretation would be that he was supported by the Ministry because of the views he held.

The ambiguity and internal inconsistencies of Raynal's massive *Histoire des deux Indes* can be attributed also to the disorganized manner in which the multivolume work was put together.[22] That it was a collaborative effort, financed by imperial interests and written by many authors under rather loose editorial supervision, in part explains the conflicting attitudes toward slavery. However, the work mirrors rather well the ambivalence of the era toward black enslavement.

If Raynal forcefully condemned slavery, he was also sympathetic to the growth of plantation colonies and made clear, for instance, his belief that the original interdiction of slavery in the American colony of Georgia was a mistake.[23] In the 1781 edition of the *Histoire,* he modified his view somewhat; still recognizing the colonies' need of slave labor in order to develop, he embroidered on a thought already expressed in the *Encyclopédie,* namely, that abandonment of the colonies was preferable to dependence on human enslavement: "Well then, let them lie fallow, if it means that, to make these lands productive, man must be reduced to brutishness, whether he be the man who buys, or he who sells, or he who is sold."[24] What has rarely been noted is that, although Raynal suggested this policy of abnegation for the English colonies, he did not specifically advocate it for the French colonial system. A posthumous edition claimed that France could abolish neither slavery nor the slave trade, for to do so would "ruin the colonies

and the Metropole."[25] In writing on colonial questions, Raynal
was not free of patriotic sentiment. If he denounced the European slave trade as a whole, he liked to point out national
differences. He maintained that the French treated the slaves
brought across the Atlantic more "liberally" than the British
did, and he implied that, unlike the British, the French did not
sexually abuse the women on the slave ships.[26]

The ambiguity and contradictions of Raynal, attached to the
Ministry by personal friendships and pecuniary rewards, were
also to be found in other prominent writers of the day who
have generally been regarded as abolitionists. Bernardin de
Saint-Pierre wrote movingly of black slavery in his romantic
novel *Paul et Virginie* and attacked slavery and prejudice
against blacks in his *Voyage à l'Ile de France,* but, while serving
as an official at Ile-de-France, he put down his innermost feelings (now preserved in manuscript). Of all the peoples he had
ever seen, Bernardin confided, he had never seen a people
more vicious than blacks; perhaps, he speculated, it was part of
the order of nature that men who were superior should dominate blacks. Moreover, Bernardin, who in France passionately
denounced slavery, had been a slaveowner at Ile-de-France.
When invited to join the Société des amis des noirs, he refused, claiming ill health.[27] The gap between ideals and self-
interest is not unique to the Enlightenment, but it created
added tension in the Enlightenment's attitude toward slavery.

The abolitionists were usually practical men who were not
willing to sacrifice national advantage to humanity. If at times
the rhetoric of Diderot and Raynal[28] indicated a willingness to
see the colonies perish if they had to depend on slavery, the
general approach was far more cautious. It was clear to
abolitionists that the country that prohibited slavery would be
at an economic disadvantage compared with its rivals. France
alone could not abolish slavery without similar British action.
Necker, Louis XVI's enlightened minister, opposed slavery
but favored its continuation until an international agreement
could regulate it. The Société des amis des noirs also demanded an international agreement to abolish slavery.[29] Thus
the ideals of humanity could be served without unduly damaging the national interests of France. Of course, a fundamental

belief of the Enlightenment was that the interests of humanity and personal or national interests were not incompatible. It was left to later generations to learn that humanitarianism sometimes requires self-sacrifice.

The tensions and contradictions in the French abolitionists' attitudes toward slavery might have contributed to the failure of the Société des amis des noirs to become an effective organization. But the same ambivalence was also part of the British abolitionist tradition. It was probably not intellectual attitudes so much as a number of other factors that account for the failure of the Société. It had high dues and concentrated on having important, well-connected members, rather than large numbers.[30] Founded the year after the Society for Effecting the Abolition of the Slave Trade was established in London, the Société consciously copied the English program; it therefore was open to the charge that it was inspired by (and even in the pay of) London and English interests. Maybe the English colonies could survive without slaves, but the French, it was thought, could not. It was predicted that, in the absence of the French slave system, the English would gain not only a commercial but also, it being the era of mercantilism, a political advantage.[31] Advocates of slavery tried to pin the charge of treason on the Société.

In response to these charges, to which it was very sensitive, the Société trod carefully and hesitated to mount a full-scale campaign against slavery. The members, drawn from the French social elite, tended toward a natural conservatism. They found slavery to be abhorrent, a violation of "the rights of man," but they were also men of property, who respected the values of hierarchy and order. The belief that human bondage violated the natural order led many of them to oppose slavery; they were not imbued with the basically egalitarian evangelical fervor that was such an important ingredient in British and American abolitionism. The religious element in Anglo-American abolitionism drew a great mass following, but the French organization slumbered, making little impact on French society in general. As Gaston Martin so aptly put it, the Société des amis des noirs represented hardly more than a "société de pensée," or a debating club.[32] It was but a pale imitation of its British counterpart. Significantly, the Société gave the French National Assembly a collection of books and pamphlets on the slavery question, most of which had been written across the Channel. The antislavery literature penned by members of the Société tended to lack originality, at best repeating arguments borrowed from English abolitionists.

Abolitionist thought did not penetrate very deeply into French society. Despite the writings of the philosophes and a number of emotional plays denouncing slavery, the institution was secure. The slave trade reached its apogee on the very eve of the Revolution. The period from 1783 to 1791 surpassed the "golden era" of French slaving, from 1748 to 1754. Nantes, the main city from which the slave trade was directed, underwent a renaissance of wealth and architecture. Between 1749 and 1755, the number of ships equipped for the slave trade in Nantes averaged 21 per year; the average number fell to 16 per year from 1763 to 1777, but more than doubled in the decade from 1783 to 1792, rising to 35 per year.[33] Curtin has estimated that the French bought 72,500 slaves in the decade 1751 to 1760, 115,400 from 1761 to 1770, 98,800 for the decade of the 1770s, and 271,500 for the years 1780 to 1790.[34]

The large increase in the number of slaves imported into the French Antilles in the 1780s was due in part to an attempt to make up for the decline during the American Revolution, when British seapower had prevented French trade. Yet, whatever the cause, the flourishing of the trade was proof of its imperviousness to the play of ideas in France.[35]

The extent to which popular sentiment was affected by the "campaign for humanity" (Roger Mercier's phrase) can be gauged for 1789, the year after the founding of the Société des amis des noirs, when, in electing representatives to the Estates-General, the French population was also invited to draw up petitions. The port cities, which depended so heavily on the plantation economies of the Antilles, systematically omitted any mention of slavery.[36] The other electoral units barely raised the issue. Out of a possible two thousand *cahiers* from representatives of the three estates in French towns, only twenty-one favored abolition of slavery while an additional twenty-eight petitioned for the abolition of the slave trade.[37] The latter was in some ways a more emotional issue, which in the long run could have resulted in the abolition of slavery; with the high death rate in the Antilles, the lack of new slave imports would have meant the eventual disappearance of the institution.

The formulas adopted by the *cahiers* pleading for abolition of the slave trade seemed to reveal a knowledge of the arguments made by the Société des amis des noirs; the clergy of Péronne, in asking for an end to slavery, referred to blacks as their "unfortunate brothers."[38] One electoral district, the Senéchaussée of Mont-de-Marsan, asked that "the most prompt means be found to give them [the slaves] liberty, to which they have as much right as we, since they are our equals."[39] The ambivalence of French abolitionist thought also came to the fore; the *cahier* of the third estate of another district, the bailliage of Amiens, proclaimed that "a man can under no circumstances become the property of another," but then added, "The assembly is at the same time convinced that justice is not the work of a day and that it must not lose sight of the agriculture of the colonies and the plantation owners' property, which it does not desire to destroy. . . ."[40] From the Franche-Comté came a *cahier* that made a less calculated and more emotional appeal:

> The inhabitants and the community of Champagney cannot think of the sufferings of the Negroes in the colonies without being deeply pained in considering that their fellow human beings united to them too by the bonds of religion are more harshly treated than pack animals.
>
> We cannot believe that people would be willing to use colonial products if they considered that such products had been fertilized by the blood of our fellow human beings; we fear that future, more enlightened generations will accuse Frenchmen of this century of having been cannibals, which denies us the quality of Frenchmen and Christians.

This *cahier* was written by a local nobleman with liberal pretensions, a certain Antoine Priquelet.[41] Such authorship is probably typical of many of the *cahiers*; they were not the result of being hammered out spontaneously in popular session. Rather, specific points were written by local notables, who then presented them for acceptance to mass meetings that with little debate approved them. Thus the presence in the *cahiers* of some sentiments echoing the Enlightenment's and the Société des amis des noirs' critique of slavery should be taken more as an indication that such ideas had become familiar to small-town lawyers, notaries, "men of letters," and other notables than as evidence that they had become the concern of a broad mass of the French population.

The success of abolitionism in 1794 was due in part to the coincidence of its ideology with the generally egalitarian aspirations of the age. In writing the anthem of the Revolution, "The Marseillaise," Rouget de Lisle cried out against the forces of the king and the aristocracy: "C'est nous qu'on ose méditer/ De rendre à l'antique esclavage." The concept of slavery had become widely hated—not slavery in the Antilles, but rather the subservience that the Ancien Régime had demanded of its subjects. But this general opposition to human repression benefited the abolitionist movement, even though its ultimate success was due to specific political and strategic conditions. Once emancipation had been proclaimed, however, it was absorbed in the general egalitarian euphoria. After the emancipation an illustration showed Reason, dressed as a woman, measuring two men of equal height, one black and one white, and declaring, "All mortals are equal. It is not birth but only virtue that makes the difference." And a song composed at the time, "La Liberté des nègres," declared, "Equality now proclaims you brothers. . . . The color disappears and man remains."[42] Such feelings were part of the cult of equality that had led to the uprising of 1789 and then was cultivated by the revolutionary leaders. The claims of "fraternité" created a fount of ideas from which reformers could later draw. Their effusions were part of the enthusiasms of the moment, but did not signal a transformation in the general assessment of the black man.

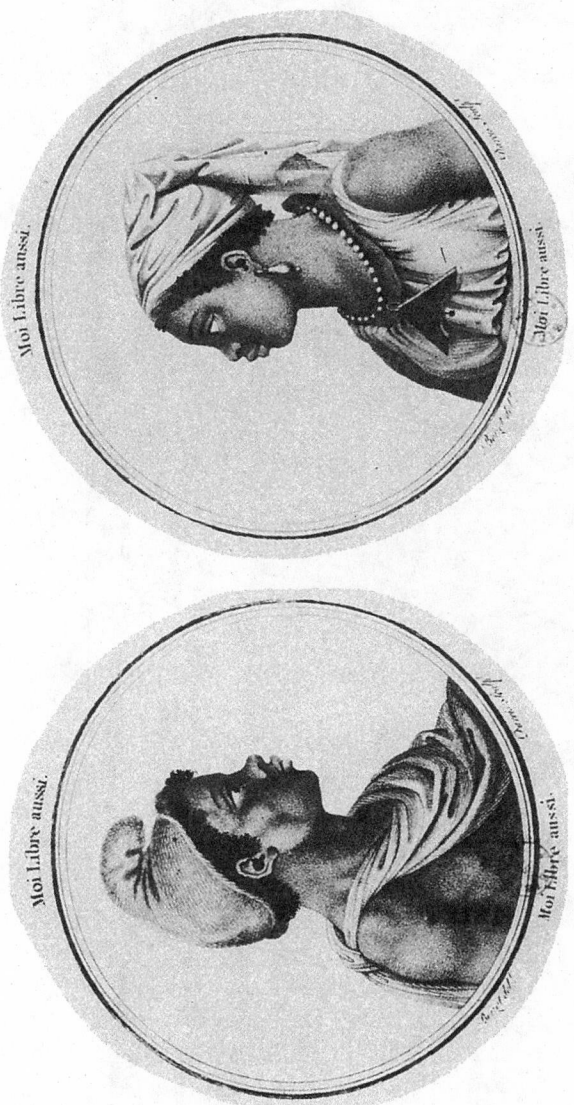

Freed black man and woman proclaiming their emancipation in *petit nègre* phrase.
De Vinck Collection. Photo Bibliothèque nationale, Paris.

Illustration after emancipation in 1794 proclaiming racial equality: "All mortals are equal. It is not birth, but virtue that makes the difference." *Hennin Collection. Photo Bibliotheque nationale, Paris.*

Proslavery Opinion

The lack of strong popular feeling about slavery during the entire eighteenth century meant that there was little consciousness of French responsibility for the slave trade. Guilt, if it existed, was either projected onto the African or neatly side-stepped. Dictionaries commonly defined "Negroes" as the "slaves which are extracted from the African coast";[43] who did the extraction was not mentioned. Montesquieu, who condemned slavery in the European plantation colonies, but seemed to make African rulers the authors of the slave trade, declared that "the minor kings or village chiefs keep selling their subjects to European princes to be carried off to their colonies in America."[44] Voltaire blamed the trade on the Africans who sold themselves and each other to the Europeans. The Trévoux *Dictionnaire* stated, "The Negroes sell to the Spanish, the Portuguese, and the Dutch not only the neighbors they can catch, but sometimes their own wives and children."[45] The implied nonexistence of French slavers was significant.

The attribution of slavery to African causes helped present a negative image of the blacks and their homeland. Savary's *Dictionnaire universel de commerce,* a commercial compendium and a widely read and copied work, explained how blacks were enslaved:

> These slaves are brought into bondage in several ways; some in order to avoid starving sell themselves, their children, and wives to their kings and those more powerful among them who can feed them. . . . The others are prisoners of war, the result of the fighting which these kinglets carry on against their neighbors, often for no other reason than to enslave them, catching young as well as old, women, girls and even children still at their mother's breast.
>
> There are Negroes who capture each other, while the ships from Europe are at anchor; they bring those they have caught to the ships and sell them; it is not unusual to see sons selling their unfortunate fathers, fathers their own children, and even more often those to whom they are not related for the price of a few bottles of brandy or for a bar of iron.[46]

Africans were seen as having a chronic penchant for enslaving each other. Parents were depicted as having children only in order to sell them as slaves; in his old age a father "most often has no children, he has sold them when death puts an end to his career."[47] Europeans were not seen as responsible for the enslavement of Africans; rather, they were perceived only as transporting across the seas people who were already slaves in their homeland.[48]

Many eighteenth-century thinkers depicted despotism as a form of government in which all the subjects lived in "political slavery"; hence they saw "civil slavery" as akin to political subjugation, but more tolerable because the people were already used to living without freedom. This was the view of Montesquieu and, later, of Rousseau. Since Africa was often described as having political despotism, it was thought that Africans were predisposed to be slaves. The *Encyclopédie* states of the Gold Coast that "there, free men, too weak to struggle against the government, want to become the slaves of those who are tyrants, the government. Notice that in despotic states, where people already live under political slavery, civil slavery is more tolerable than elsewhere." Not only political despotism but also other influences were seen as reducing blacks in Africa to slavery. Abbé Roubaud, who wrote a general compendium on the non-European world, listed the reasons he and his contemporaries believed African slavery to be rampant:

> In general they are all slaves, because the heat and the climate make them cowardly; or because religion has put them under the chains of despotism, or their barbarism makes them incapable of establishing a moderate system of government. . . .[49]

A French official in Senegal resorted to casuistry to erase any doubts about the previous status of Africans acquired by European slave traders: " . . . slavery is their proper condition. In effect from the moment that they are bought by a white man, even if they had been free previously, they blindly obey him and recognize his absolute authority over them. . . ."[50]

Not only did enslavement by Europeans not change the Africans' legal condition, but, the proponents of slavery argued, it helped Africans become civilized.[51] Malouet, an enlightened official and West Indian planter, had only praise for slavery as an educational institution that helped blacks survive, for they "are incapable . . . by nature to be self-sufficient and free." Thanks to the slave trade, blacks "leave a despot who has the right to strangle them for a master who has the right to make them work." Brought across the seas by Europeans, Africans, "in becoming our laborers, have approached the condition of being reasonable men instead of remaining in their country, victims of all the excesses of brigandage and ferocity."[52]

Moreau de Saint-Méry, deputy for Martinique in the National Assembly, also favored the slave trade as a civilizing mission, which "has saved the lives of thousands of men." In their homeland Africans were prone to human sacrifice, polygamy, and cannibalism, but arrival in European colonies, insisted Moreau, marked a definite improvement in the Africans' lot.[53] The proslavers presented an image of contented slaves, who, they insisted, were better off than the workers or peasants in France. The planters, in the face of abolitionist criticism, depicted the slave trader as a philanthropist who did a "great service to humanity" in saving the Africans from their homeland, which was "infertile, without industry, the arts, laws or civilization."[54]

Abolitionism and the general enlightenment of the period left their marks even on the proslavery group, which rhetorically embraced the notion that it too belonged to the party of humanity. There were, however, some "unreconstructed" proslavers who did not make any concessions to the intellectual mode of the day and probably revealed the underlying conviction of most proslavers. Slavery could neither improve nor worsen the condition of the blacks, wrote one pamphleteer, for they were incapable of any improvement: "Most of the Negroes are innately unjust, cruel, barbarous, cannibalistic, treasonous, cheats, liars, drunks, . . . vain, lazy, dirty, shameless, uncontrollably jealous and cowardly."[55]

The Abolitionist Attack:
Slavery, the Scourge of Africa

If the proslavery lobby argued that black enslavement was a positive force, an aid to the African, the abolitionists depicted the savagery of the trade, which encouraged African warfare and brought ruin and desolation to the continent. Doumet, an official in Senegal who favored slavery, was one of the few to agree with the abolitionists about the destructive effects of the trade; he presented a kind of law of the trade:

> If the kingdom is governed by a peaceful and gentle king, the slave trade will be very limited; but if it is ruled by a despotic and war-like master nearly always campaigning, heading a small army of three to four thousand chosen and devoted men, then the most numerous villages will be looted.[56]

Although Voltaire did not discuss the devastating effect of the slave trade on African society in any of his essays, he approached the issue at least twice in his correspondence. In a letter to his friend Charles De Brosses, he wrote that it was the slave traders who had desolated Africa and "made it so barbarous." But this does not necessarily seem to have been his prevailing conviction; four years later he stated that the slave trade transported 40,000 Africans to the Americas annually (a figure representing 75 percent of what current scholarship believes to have been the number).[57] Yet, despite the loss of 40,000 people, Africa, Voltaire wrote, "does not seem exhausted. It seems that nature has favored the blacks with a fertility other nations have been denied."[58] Here Voltaire revealed an unwillingness to see the trade as in any way having a negative impact on African society; but Voltaire's opposition to slavery had never been very intense. Those who sympathized with the slave trade also ignored its devastating impact.

If abolitionists were ambivalent toward slavery, the trade itself did raise their ire, and they painted in vivid detail the destruction it had wrought. Pruneau de Pommegorge, who himself had been a slave trader in the 1760s and who twenty years later regretted it, indicted the trade for depopulating Africa; not only did it take Africans away from their homelands, but it also encouraged warfare, the "destruction of men, women, children and the aged." According to Pommegorge, Africa prior to the trade had been a place where lived "happy peoples under the laws of nature"; the trade had transformed Africans into "ferocious beasts."[59] In trying to assess the impact of the slave trade, abolitionists put forth various figures on the number of Africans enslaved. Raynal estimated that eight to nine million Africans had been brought to the Americas.[60] This informed estimate is among the lowest advanced by abolitionists, but still considerably higher than that advanced by Philip Curtin, who has suggested that approximately five million Africans were involved in the transatlantic slave trade prior to 1770. Abolitionists' estimates were often influenced by the passions of the day and by a projection of the volume of the trade in the 1780s back over the entire period of contact—some three hundred years. Many abolitionists seemed to ignore how exceptional the 1780s were in the history of the trade and, consequently, how unrealistic figures such as sixty million were. Africans perished while both resisting and carrying on slave raids in Africa; their number can never be known, but the abolitionists presented varying figures, some going as high as three hundred million.[61] These were very high figures for the desolation wrought by the trade, but even lower ones advanced by other abolitionists prompted Abbé Sibire, who in the 1760s had served as a missionary in the Congo, to ask, "How has Africa been able to endure these incredible losses? At such a rate, I should think that it would long since have been reduced to a desert."[62] It was considered a miracle that any kind of human society did exist in Africa, and Sibire, while accepting the image of a savage Africa, pointed to the slave trade as its cause. Frossard suggested that, if the slave trade had not occurred in Africa, "we would maybe see not only peace but the flourishing of individual liberty, the sciences, the fine arts, in a word, all that which constitutes the splendor of a state."[63]

The Abolitionist Image

The abolitionists generally had a more positive image of Africa than did other Europeans. Such an image was, in a sense, necessary in order to combat the slavers, who had proclaimed the African a beast, fit only for enslavement. In upholding the Africans' humanity, the abolitionists painted a positive picture of the blacks in their homeland. The Société des amis des noirs agreed that the freedom of the slaves required a rehabilitation of the Africans' tarnished image; in fact, the first point in its published program was to give a "correct impression of Africa."[64]

Raynal spoke of noble Africans, living in harmony with each other, loving their kin, and enjoying a simple, pastoral existence. To counter the slavers' assertions that Africans sold each other, he spoke of Africans who, realizing the horrors of slavery, offered themselves as slaves to ransom their unfortunate fathers, brothers, sons, lovers, and so on. This was a popular theme among abolitionists, and it even became the plot for a play in 1795.[65]

If at times some abolitionists upheld the black as a superior form of man, most tended to agree with their era's prejudicial view that African societies were inferior to those of Europe. In time, however, the abolitionists insisted, Africans would be capable of improvement. Lecointe-Marsillac described the Africans as "civilized peoples, hardworking, cultivators and merchants in all products of their countries, they are intelligent men capable of European knowledge." What they lacked in material wealth or technical knowledge, he pointed out, they made up in other virtues, and, if given the chance, they "are disposed to learn from us." Pétion de Villeneuve wrote, "Certainly the African race has not brought its civilization, industry, and development to the levels we have accomplished in Europe; but although far behind us, it is not stupid."[66]

To buttress the argument that Africans had the potential for development, various writers cited examples of individual black achievement. Lecointe-Marsillac described Ben Solomon, a black slave who when freed wrote his memoirs in

England. Brissot de Warville, a founder of the Société des amis des noirs, cited the example of Jack Denham, a black who could carry out complicated mathematical calculations in his head. To prove black humanity, Abbé Grégoire compiled a long list of blacks who were men of genius.[67]

Slavery seemed a violation of natural law, because as humans, Africans were the equals of Europeans, in the sense that they had, the abolitionists declared, the same rights. The Société des amis des noirs, in a question emblazoned in the seal of its organization (which depicts an enchained black man) asked, "Am I not your brother?" It was necessary to establish this basic equality to prove that slavery was unjust. Most abolitionists shared with the proslavers the Aristotelian notion that slavery could be defensible on the grounds of human inequality. Since the slavers said blacks were unequal, the abolitionists, if they were to ground their theories in natural law, had to affirm the equality of black and white.

However, abolitionists tended to share the slaveowners' views of those blacks who were already in slavery. Raynal described black slaves as ignorant and brutal, not because of any innate defects, but rather because of having been degraded by slavery. Abbé Sibire, staunch opponent of slavery, had harsh words to say about the condition of the blacks in the colonies: they were "physical brutes, not only with an underdeveloped moral sense, but lacking one completely"; if freed, the slaves would make up for the excessive work they had performed and lean in the other direction, becoming too lazy.[68] Whatever the causes of his degradation, the black's condition was thought to be so low that abolitionists could not recommend immediate emancipation. The abolitionists also seemed unable to free themselves from the sense that slaves were property and that some fair and equitable means had to be found to compensate the owners for their loss if the slaves were freed. Raynal, while suggesting that the slaves themselves would arise, or should, in order to free themselves, also presented a gradual program, the effect of which would eventually eliminate the slave system.[69] In the 1774 edition of his *Histoire,* Raynal favored freeing slave women who had had several children; in the 1780 edition, he suggested that slaves should belong to their masters for the first twenty years of their lives to reimburse the masters for future emancipation and, upon being "freed," should serve another five years as paid laborers.[70] In the face of the failure of gradual reform, Raynal in each edition strengthened his call for slave uprisings in order to show the planter class the danger of not bringing gradual reforms to the slave system.[71] Various methods of freeing the slaves were contemplated, but most included compensating the planters.[72]

The fear that precipitate emancipation would bring death and mayhem to the colonies exercised the imagination of the abolitionists. The abolitionist Lecointe-Marsillac warned that "a too sudden emancipation would throw the Negroes into a state of inebriation and fury that perhaps would lead them into the worst excesses." Benézet, an American Quaker of French origin who was closely read in France, wrote that, if suddenly freed, slaves would resort to savagery and would menace the safety of their former owners. According to Benézet, the slaves should rather be kept in bondage until they were ready for freedom and could be counted on to become trustworthy citizens. One of the abolitionists, Jean-Baptiste Sanchamau, wrote that, "in a country in which the number of slaves surpasses heavily the number of masters, a quick passage of the Negroes to liberty would give society dangerous and violent commotions." The Société des amis des noirs emphasized the need to present the best methods of "bringing gradually and fruitfully the abolition of slavery." In an appeal to the National Assembly, the Société wrote that sudden emancipation would harm the blacks themselves; they would need time to be ready.[73] Condorcet found the slaves to be stupid and to have a penchant for vagabondage and violence. He blamed these vices on slavery, but concluded that the slaves' baseness was such that they could not be freed immediately; he proposed an apprenticeship period of up to seventy years. Hardly any of the slaves living when Condorcet wrote would have seen their day of emancipation, had his plan been followed. Condorcet's pessimism on the blacks' condition was reflected also in his idea that the differences in status between white and black, which had developed as a result of slavery, could be erased only by the sexual mingling of the two races. That blacks could be treated as equal was considered impossible by Condorcet.[74] Abbé Grégoire, an ardent abolitionist, also trod warily. He warned that "the rights of man suddenly granted to those who don't know their obligations could become a harmful gift." Privately he expressed the idea that immediate emancipation would be like "kicking a pregnant woman to make her give birth sooner."[75]

The very day that the Revolutionary Assembly finally voted for emancipation, Danton, usually quick to be swept by enthusiasm, cautioned the legislature that "we must be useful to humanity without imperiling it."[76] And when the legislature had voted in favor of emancipation, the measure struck Grégoire and all his friends from the Société des amis des noirs as "a disastrous measure."[77]

The gradualist approach of the abolitionists revealed an unwillingness to attack slavery directly. There lingered the feeling that, even if slaves were humans, they were also legitimate forms of property. Gradualism revealed also a persistent suspicion of the Africans' ability to sustain freedom. Although the abolitionists blamed slavery for the Africans' condition, their hesitations about emancipation paralleled the slavers' argument that blacks were debased and unsuited for freedom. Until a Montesquieu arose among Africans, Raynal observed, enslavement would be beneficial, bringing them "closer to the conditions of reasonable men than [would] remaining in their countries open to the excesses of brigandage and of ferocity."[78]

Thus the hard struggle against the traditional acceptance of slavery as a normal human institution and the age-old images of black depravity was not unequivocal. The philosophes and their heirs opposed slavery and upheld the humanity of black slaves, but they operated within certain confines: even though enslaving blacks was wrong, immediate emancipation was not the remedy; if blacks were humans and theoretically equal to whites, their condition both in Africa and in the Antilles had rendered them inferior. The abolitionists created an intellectual climate that forced the government and even the slave interests to address the question of slavery. But in discussing the condition of the Africans, both in their homeland and in the Antilles, the abolitionists reinforced contemporary opinion. Even as they attributed their condition to causes beyond the Africans' control, they nevertheless depicted them as degraded and diminished in their humanity.

6

The Rise of Imperialism

In the three centuries preceding the Revolution, French power expanded overseas. While a large empire was created in North America, only small territorial enclaves were established on the coast of West Africa. Nevertheless, influential groups of opinion and policy makers considered expanding France's possessions in Africa. Among them, the most important were traders and administrators in Africa, officials in Paris, and abolitionists trying to find an alternative for the slave plantation colonies of the West Indies. The abolitionists, in fact, became the most important propagandizers for expansion. To a large extent, imperialist ambitions were focused on the Senegambia, an area seen as valuable in itself and also as a base for further penetration inland, especially to the Western Sudan, reputed to be rich beyond imagination.

Many of those advocating expansion were divided about whether it should include the acquisition of territory or be limited to commercial and intellectual influence. All agreed on the desirability of establishing French preeminence in most of the western part of the African continent. By the end of the eighteenth century, actual French advances into Africa were still modest, but ideas for a full-scale conquest already had been formulated.

Metropolitan Theories

During the Ancien Régime, the principles of overseas expansionism derived from two schools of thought: population theory and mercantilist theory. In the face of demographic pressures in France, the most populous state in Europe, several writers expressed concern about how the growing population could make a living on the available land. Jean Bodin, at the end of the sixteenth century, had already pointed out the advantages of colonies as outlets for surplus (or undesired) populations. The eighteenth-century publicist De la Morandière also suggested the colonies as good places in which to settle "the beggars, the vagabonds, the professional gamblers, the intriguers, the prostitutes, the unemployed servants."[1]

When considering colonization as a solution to the population problem, some thinkers looked to Africa as a possible place of settlement. For instance, in 1737 d'Argenson, secretary of state for foreign affairs, proposed establishing an association of all Christian princes, who would colonize Asia and Africa and settle Europe's excess population there.[2] These ideas had no direct impact, nor did they reflect actual French emigration policies. Between the sixteenth and eighteenth centuries, Spain sent 2 million emigrants overseas; England, 1.75 million; Portugal, 1.5 million; and Central Europe, between 300,000 and 500,000. France, the most populous of all these regions, nevertheless sent fewer than 200,000 emigrants.[3] While not affecting actual emigration, however, the population theorists implanted in French thought the importance of overseas expansion.

A second source for expansionist thought was mercantilist theory, developed in the seventeenth century. The advantage of colonies, it was pointed out, was that they could be a valuable source of trade, providing the mother country with goods for which it would not have to pay gold to foreigners and thus safeguarding the French supply of bullion. According to mercantilist theory, bullion was the source of national well-being and strength; in the competition for power among states, it was important for each state to amass as much bullion as possible. One of the early theorists of mercantilism, the merchant and publicist Antoine de Montchrétien, suggested that establishing colonies in America and in Africa would give France wealth comparable to Spain's.[4] Mercantilist doctrines, in stressing the strength of the individual state, sometimes conflicted with population theory. Mercantilists feared that colonies would drain France of the manpower necessary for her economic and political strength. So thought Montesquieu,

who in the *Persian Letters* noted, "The normal effect of colonies is to weaken the countries from which they [the col-
onists] are drawn without populating those to which they are
sent."

In the eighteenth century, however, the dominant thought
in regard to colonial expansion was probably represented by
the physiocrats. They answered Montesquieu's complaint and
posited that, if wisely administered, both the kingdom and its
colonies could have flourishing populations. They argued that,
because France could not grow certain exotic plants because of
its climate, it had to acquire new provinces or colonies. They
pointed out that overseas possessions had the advantage also
of providing those unable to make a living at home with new
sources of livelihood.[5] As free traders the physiocrats opposed
mercantilistic control over the colonies, and Turgot foresaw
independence for all colonies. Nevertheless, even he saw a
role for the colonies to play; they were necessary for any state
that wanted to rid itself of its poor and needy.[6] The
Encyclopédie reflected the opinion of the period, when it
endorsed colonies also for their commercial value: "Intelligent
people who have not found the goods they need . . . establish
colonies."[7] This narrow commercial advantage was of course
stressed by the merchants. In 1765 the Bordeaux Chamber of
Commerce described colonies as "establishments founded
to consume and to be an outlet for the products of the
Metropole."[8]

Traders and Administrators
as Imperialists

In these general theories about France's need to acquire
colonies, Africa played a minor role. Following the example of
the Spanish, the Portuguese, and the English, the French
thought mostly in terms of colonizing the New World, where
land could be used both for settlement and for acquisition of
mineral wealth such as gold and silver or of exotic staples such
as sugar and coffee. Most of the interest in Africa was stimulated by merchants and officials already serving in Africa, who
called for an active French political role on the continent.

Despite the low opinion of Africans, their land was thought

to be rich, particularly in gold. Leo Africanus, whose account had created such interest in sixteenth-century France, had spoken of the gold trade of Timbuktu. In 1687 the French government sent an expedition to the Ivory Coast for the purpose of securing slaves and gold, which was believed to be abundant there.[9] Reports of such expeditions seemed to confirm the highest expectations; going to Issiny in the Ivory Coast some eleven years later, the chevalier Damon reported that the area was so rich in gold mines that "in one day 200 men could fill six chests with gold."[10]

West Africa had many sources of wealth, French officials reported. Chambonneau, serving in Senegal, wrote in 1677 that Senegal not only was rich in gold, but also had the capacity for growing large amounts of tobacco, indigo, and sugar cane. These crops grew wild; Chambonneau reasoned that the local peoples could be encouraged to cultivate them and sell them to the French. Sugar cane was especially promising and probably could "grow as well as in the islands of America, this country being at the same latitude."[11] That vademecum of French traders, Savary's *Parfait négociant,* echoed travelers' descriptions of Africa as a source of wealth, not only in slaves, but also in "gold, amber, pepper . . . wax, ivory, hides, and gum."[12]

Like other European powers, France established in Africa coastal trading forts from which they engaged in commerce and, especially, in the slave trade. These forts comprised but a tenuous foothold on the mainland, and some thought that it would be better to dismantle them and limit trade to French ships.[13] But forts had the advantage of creating a steady African clientele; moreover, in the European competition for trade, it was thought that forts discouraged rival European powers. Chevalier Damon suggested that the French build a chain of forts along the Gold Coast and "by this means become master of the best sixty leagues of the Gold Coast and we thus can prevent the interloping commerce of the Dutch and the English."[14] Du Casse and Labat also advocated destroying the Dutch and British forts on the West Coast.[15] While they fell short of openly advocating conquest of the region, such plans for exclusive French control of the coast came close to an imperialist position.

In 1687 Chambonneau, the administrator of Senegal, became the first Frenchman to go to Galam, up to the Félu Falls, where he heard about the gold of the Bondu region. He wrote that the Senegal Company, which was then controlling the colony, should

> seize such land, as one would desire on the [Senegal] River in the name of the king, to send there men and women and give them land to cultivate (as was done in America [Antilles]) to plant tobacco, indigo, cotton, sugar cane . . . [to] raise silk worms, [to mine] iron and gold.

According to Chambonneau, twelve hundred Frenchmen should be sent to Senegal; in the beginning, there might be some conflict between them and the local peoples, but the latter, seeing that the new arrivals were peaceable, would accept them. Like so many Europeans after him, Chambonneau misunderstood the nature of the land-tenure system when he explained to Paris that there would be no trouble in seizing the land for purposes of cultivation. He reported that the land "is not property among them, changing hands every year, without the need to ask permission of anyone."[16]

In the late seventeenth century, the most ambitious and comprehensive imperialist program for West Africa was articulated by André Brüe, director of the Senegal Company in the years 1697 to 1702 and then again from 1714 to 1720. His plans were the most far-reaching of any that French officials proposed for Africa until the nineteenth century. Brüe dreamed of placing under his authority all the territory watered by the Senegal River, as well as the coastal area from the Cap Blanc to the Sierra Leone River. If ill health had not forced him to return to France in 1720, Brüe might have been able to realize his dream.[17] He was particularly interested in establishing French domination from the fort of Saint-Louis (which the French already possessed) all the way up the Senegal River valley; he wished to see a territorially compact colony as far as Galam.

The general European intention to dominate West Africa is even more remarkable when one recognizes the weakness of the French position there. Europeans were tributaries, dependent upon the goodwill of the local African population. On the Ivory Coast, French traders were unable to buy slaves at prices other than those dictated by the local ruler; despite heated protest the French accepted the royal decision. Even in the fort of Issiny, the French were vulnerable to local pressure; when the local population refused to supply them with more food, they ignominiously evacuated.[18] Of the seventeen directors of trade who served between 1712 and 1789 on the Dahomey Coast at the fort of Whyda, four were forced by the Dahomeans to evacuate and one was killed.[19]

In the largest French establishment in West Africa, the situation was potentially just as precarious; Saint-Louis would not have been able to withstand an African assault. Until the mid-nineteenth century, the French were paying "coutumes," or taxes, for their right to be established there. The island of Gorée, lacking in fresh water, wood, and food, was always dependent upon the goodwill of the inhabitants on the mainland on Cap Vert. And the few forts down the coast and up the Senegal River were in similar situations of dependency.

That was the reality of the French position: they were present at the sufferance of Africans. As an official memoir of 1773 noted, "We pay the kings of the lands in which we have trading posts 'coutumes'; nevertheless, we often have difficulties with their people. . . . We also fear that they will fall upon the garrison [of Gorée] and murder [the inhabitants] so they can steal the merchandise."[20] Such possibilities may in fact explain why French officials so anxiously advocated absolute dominance over the Africans. The desire for expansion also may have been a reaction to the narrow confines of barracks life in the forts. Wars of conquest would give some activity, a change from the dull routine, and would assure some glory and promotions.

Officials on the spot, in their attempts to win the attention of Paris for their projects, tended to disregard matters of power and health and to make extreme claims about the potential wealth of the regions they wanted annexed. Filled with racial pride, French officials asserted their claims to superiority. Ignoring real power relationships, Europeans continued to weave intricate plans for ensuring French domination in Africa. They seldom paid attention to the difficulty of maintaining a persistent expansionist policy in the face of continuous assaults of tropical disease. Each year, Du Casse noted, a third of the Europeans in the forts died; nevertheless, he persisted in advocating a greater French presence in West Africa.[21] Assessments of the wealth of the region equally lacked realism. The optimistic reports of the gold of the Upper Senegal in Bambuk, for instance, had little basis; there was an ongoing local gold-mining operation in the region, but it was modest and valued only as a seasonal occupation by the local inhabitants. (Even the modern mining techniques put into use there in the twentieth century have not led to much gold extraction.)[22] The Senegal Company in Paris retained a healthy skepticism, however, and announced that the real mine of wealth remained the slave trade.[23] Not discouraged by the company's position, Pierre David, who was director in Senegal from 1738 to 1746, gave enthusiastic reports of the gold mines of the Upper Senegal; having explored the region, he attempted to interest Paris in its acquisition.[24]

The French lost Senegal in 1758 and regained it only in 1778. The recovery of Senegal, David thought, opened new opportunities for France in West Africa; back in France, he bombarded the ministries with at least two dozen proposals. He declared that the mines of the Upper Senegal would produce an income of 104 million livres a year. This was a fabulous sum, representing nine times the average amount of gold made into coin annually.[25] An official in the Ministry of Foreign Affairs, impressed by the exaggerated claims of officials on the spot, described the Upper Senegal as having the "richest gold mines on earth"; if Europeans were installed there, they could extract "a thousand times" more gold than the Africans were capable of.[26] Any information on the low production actually occurring was considered not a true measure of the potential of the area but rather proof of African indolence. The Ministry of Marine in 1781 described the Bambuk region as consisting of "countries in which can be found the richest minerals and mines of gold. The Negroes who live there are lazy, indolent, without ambition, and don't even give themselves the bother to pick up the riches that they brush against every day."[27]

Mercantilist theories on colonization stressed that expansionism benefited the state, making it relatively stronger than its rivals. During the naval war with England in the war of American independence, Africa was thought of as a suitable place where the French could limit English power by cutting off their slave supply, conquering their colonies, and achieving comparatively greater wealth by founding tropical plantations on the African coast.[28]

The Search for an Alternative to the West Indies

By the mid-eighteenth century, the overall attitude toward colonies was favorable. They were seen as economically advantageous, providing France with products not available in Europe and giving the kingdom an outlet for what was feared to be an excessive population. Although such ideas were common, the French had not succeeded in creating colonies with French populations. Few were the French who settled in Canada and in the Antilles. Yet the West Indies were the most important possessions in the empire, providing France with tropical staple products that in turn made up a large proportion of France's foreign trade. The Antilles formed the hub around which French colonial thought developed. Given the extent to which the West Indies were the source of French wealth, it was not surprising that, after the Seven Years War (1756–1763) France was willing to give Canada to the British in exchange for regaining its West Indian empire. At the time, Voltaire was correct in describing Canada as nothing "but a few acres of snow." That was all that it represented compared with the wealth of the Antilles.[29]

Essentially, impetus for French policy in West Africa derived from French interest in the West Indies. In the seventeenth and eighteenth centuries, West Africa was viewed mainly as a source of slaves. The weakness of the French position in the Caribbean, revealed by the Seven Years War, created a new and ardent official interest in expanding French influence in West Africa. Even while the war was raging, it was thought that in West Africa France might make up for the precarious situation of the rest of its empire. India was clearly lost; in Canada the French forces were not faring well; the islands of Martinique and Guadeloupe were occupied by the English; and in West Africa Senegal also had been lost. French officials advocated the reconquest of West Africa, seeing the area, if developed, as ample compensation for any losses elsewhere. One official wrote to the French foreign minister that Senegal should be reconquered because it provided an important source of slaves for the French Antilles and Louisiana. But its main value, he insisted, was that it contained rich gold mines, "without number, the richest which have ever been discovered by the Europeans anywhere in the world." The colony grew indigo, and cocoa could be planted, as well as tobacco, coffee, sugar, and cotton. The country was populated by free blacks who, it was felt, could easily be encouraged to harvest the crops without slavery. In time whites could settle there. Thus the development of Senegal could indemnify the losses that France might suffer elsewhere.[30]

The foreign minister, Choiseul, seems to have adopted some of these plans; in 1758 he considered reconquering Senegal. Even though he did not embrace plans for developing the colony, he thought it might serve as a bargaining chip for losses certain to occur in the Antilles. In the end he did not order the reconquest of Senegal, for the commercial interests in France did not deem it valuable; the part of West Africa they were interested in was the Windward Coast (which they called Guinea), which provided most of the slaves.[31] If individual officials waxed eloquent about Senegal, Choiseul's view of Senegal as a mere bargaining chip indicated the real degree of consideration that French authorities gave the possibility of colonizing West Africa. Nevertheless, one underlying principle was revealed even in Choiseul's thought: Africa might provide some compensation for French weakness or defeat in the Caribbean.

Alternatives to the dependence upon the Antilles had been explored at an early stage. In the 1740s attempts were made to cultivate tropical goods in France, and in 1763 an expedition of 10,000 colonists was sent to develop a plantation system at Kourou in Guiana. The crops in France failed; 90 percent of the colonists in Guiana died within two years, victims of climate and disease.[32] These failures seemed to suggest one alternative to the West Indies—Africa. Officials as well as abolitionists ardently supported such a plan.

Abolitionists and the
Colonial Program

French abolitionists, who had close ties to official circles, echoed the theme of Africa as an alternative source of tropical staples. For the abolitionists such a plan had the attraction of sparing Africans from enslavement while ensuring France's economic well-being. By establishing plantation colonies based upon free labor in West Africa, France would be both fulfilling the laws of humanity and enriching its exchequer.

The earliest published suggestion that Africa was a promising alternative to the slave colonies as a source for tropical staples was made by Abbé Roubaud, who in 1762 suggested that, if Africans had never been enslaved, but had remained free in their own home, they would have cultivated "a greater quantity of sugar cane, thicker, and more succulent, more delicious than that we get" in the West Indies. He pointed out that not only sugar but also indigo, cotton, and tobacco could be cultivated in Africa.[33]

That free labor could grow sugar cane had been demonstrated by Pierre Poivre, intendant in the Ile-de-France and Bourbon, who had been in Cochin-China.[34] That it could be done in Africa was the message of Roubaud and then of Du Pont de Nemours, leader of the physiocratic school, who, in his journal, *Ephémérides du citoyen*, repeatedly tried to show the advantages of establishing plantation colonies in Africa based upon free black labor. He assured his readers that it would be easy to do, that France would find "some peaceful establishments on the coast" of Africa and tell the inhabitants: "friends, cut this cane, boil the juice, and we shall pay you well." By so doing, "we shall have perfected their ways of life and ours, we shall have made them into industrious farmers, and we will not be oppressors." The first sovereign who established such a colony would "be the benefactor of Europe and Africa—his virtue and wisdom will bring him the reward of heaven and the products of nature on his states and that of his neighbors." Abbé Raynal also pointed to the possibility of cultivating sugar cane and other tropical staples in Africa with free labor, thus precluding cruel slavery.[35]

In the mid-eighteenth century, a few thoughtful men had considered the possibility of colonies based on free labor in West Africa, but it was the example of Sierra Leone that later stimulated a lively pamphlet literature describing the riches of Africa and the commercial advantages of desisting from slavery. The Société des amis des noirs proclaimed in 1788 that, once the slave trade was abolished, the wars in Africa would come to an end, and "then would become opened with greater ease the countries until now closed to commerce; then will the domain of European activity spread—to ensure for its industry raw materials and markets."[36] Abbé Sibire subscribed to the very popular notion that self-interest and humanity were mutually reinforcing; that is, if Europe ended the slave trade, it would benefit financially:

> Let us cease to be ferocious and we shall become richer. America gives us only samples; it is in Guinea where there is abundance. Cotton, rice, tobacco, sugar, cloves, all spices grow wild; ivory, copper, silver, quicksilver, even gold are known in these fertile areas.

In his abolitionist tract, Frossard did not declare that Africa was richer than the West Indies, but he pointed out that it was closer and therefore more convenient. As free men Africans would be happy to work on European plantations in Africa, and "these countries until now the theatre of our barbarity could become the source of considerable wealth for Europe."[37] Condorcet wrote that, if sugar were planted in Africa, slavery would disappear and Europeans would set up trading posts in Africa and spread "the principles and the example of liberty, the light and reason of Europe." Africans were waiting "to be civilized, to receive from us the means, and to find in the Europeans, brothers, in order to become their friends and disciples."[38]

In 1796 Abbé Grégoire and his abolitionist friends founded a new abolitionist society, the Amis des noirs et des colonies,

to replace the Société des amis des noirs, which had disbanded
four years earlier. The new society had among its members
Jean-Baptiste Say, the economist; Sonthonax, the emancipator
in Saint-Domingue; and Granet, the director of the colonial
office. By 1798 it had sixty members; one of its most active
was the Swede, Wadström. Ideas similar to his were entertained, namely, that the establishment of colonies in Louisiana,
India, and Africa would make it possible for France to ensure
itself a steady supply of tropical staples cultivated by free
labor. As France had freed its slaves in 1794, the society
hoped that finding alternatives to the system in the Antilles
would lead other nations to emulate France and to free their
slaves.[39]

The abolitionists, by presenting an alternative to slavery,
depicted a rosy picture of the economic potential of Africa and
encouraged the idea of European expansion into the African
continent. Thus also planting the seeds of imperialist ambitions, they traveled the same road as the British abolitionists,
who saw European involvement in Africa as a way of both
making up for the destruction caused by the slave trade and
still enriching Europe.[40] Since the seventeenth century,
officials and traders had at various times, in obscure memoirs
and correspondence, advocated the establishment of a French
imperium in Africa. But it was the abolitionists who made such
a program a truly public affair in France.

A Substitute for the Loss
of Saint-Domingue

By the late eighteenth century, the West Indian colonies
were still deemed important enough for the minister of the
navy to discourage the plantation experiments in Senegal that
had been attempted under the governship of Boufflers. In August 1786 he wrote to the governor that it would be wrong to
set up plantations in Senegal, for if successful they "would be a
damaging competition for our American colonies where the
same products are vigorously grown and which would be deprived of the slaves which would be employed in Senegal."[41]
The uprising of Saint-Domingue in 1791, however, removed

the official reservations about development in Senegal and spurred the search, both official and private, for an alternative to the West Indian colony.

The damage done to the French economy by the loss of the West Indies in the 1790s (Saint-Domingue was in the midst of continuous rebellion, and Martinique was occupied by the British) somehow had to be compensated. It was this very popular theme to which Talleyrand addressed himself in a speech to the National Institute in 1797. France, he declared, should establish "new colonies, whose connection with ourselves may be more natural." Talleyrand foresaw the difficulties of re-establishing slavery and therefore, as did the abolitionists, advised that Europe's need for tropical products could be met by the establishment of plantations "in those very places where the cultivator is born."[42]

Talleyrand supported the establishment of colonies in West Africa and Egypt. The latter was thought to be especially rich, and it had the strategic advantage of being on the trade routes to India and into the center of Africa. Establishing a plantation colony in Egypt to replace Saint-Domingue was advocated not only by Talleyrand but also by many others before and after him.[43] Egypt played a far more important role than West Africa in the attempts to find colonial compensation for the lost Antilles, but once in Egypt the French thought of using it as a base from which to spread their influence to the rest of the continent.[44]

Senegal, the Base for Further Expansion

The interest in the interior helped stress the importance of the Senegambia as a base for expansion of French commercial and political influence to the rest of West Africa. Having established a trading fort at the mouth of the Senegal River in 1659 and believing the river to be the highway to the interior, the French continued to be attracted inland. They knew that the Niger flowed as far inland as Timbuktu. The Arabs believed not only that the Senegal was the Niger but also that it was connected with the Nile.[45] Such beliefs existed also among the French.[46] While the belief that the Nile and the

Niger were the same river was gradually abandoned, most thought the Senegal to be the Niger until the end of the eighteenth century. It was not, of course, that outlandish an idea; the upper reaches of the Senegal are separated from the Niger by only forty miles. And Leo Africanus, in a passage that has always puzzled historians, reported that the Niger, which he had seen in Timbuktu, flowed westward. If that were the case, it made good sense to believe that the Senegal, flowing westward to sea, came from Timbuktu and maybe even beyond.[47] The belief was so deeply rooted that, when the Englishman Mungo Park reported in 1799 that he had seen the Niger and that it flowed eastward, it came as a shock to Frenchmen. Golberry, a former official in Senegal, asked that Park's findings be authenticated, for they undermined French dreams and aspirations.[48] Until Park's exploration, the French were confident that they possessed the only highway into the far interior, and on that basis were tempted to engage in grandiose plans to stretch French influence deep into Africa.

As early as 1716, Brüe had suggested that the French use Galam as a base for further inland penetration. He suggested that an explorer be sent inland to see if the Falémé and the Gambia rivers were connected to the Niger River and to discover the location of Timbuktu. He sent one of his subordinates to explore the gold mines of Bambuk and the route to Timbuktu, whose "wealth . . . is said to be immense. . . ." Brüe's plans were publicized by Father Labat, who also suggested that France extend its trade relations to Timbuktu.[49] It remained an ambition of various officials and, by the end of the eighteenth century, had become an *idée fixe*.

Toward the end of the eighteenth century, either acquaintance with David or, more likely, the works of Labat (who was also a source of David's proposals) influenced officials in Senegal to emphasize the advantages of using Senegal as a means to spread French commerical influence. Governor Boufflers thought the Senegal River could be tied to a trading network that spread all the way to Egypt. He encouraged the plans of one of his subordinates to cross Africa from Senegal to Egypt; the subordinate, disguised as an Arab merchant, would go up the Senegal River all the way to Timbuktu and from there continue his journey eastward as part of a Moorish or Arab caravan.[50] This expedition did not materialize, but it was one of many planned in this period. Under Boufflers, Golberry also had outlined an ambitious program for spreading French influence to the rest of the continent from Senegal. It was felt that the French, in possession of Saint-Louis at the mouth of the Senegal River, had the right to be the first Europeans to explore and acquire the secrets of the inland. Thus Golberry considered Mungo Park's expedition of 1799 a hostile attempt to stake out for England rights that belonged to France. Established in Senegal, the French had the chance to extend their influence to Bambuk and beyond it to Timbuktu and Tocrur. This empire could include the Sahara desert, the area known as Nigritie (the Sudan), and parts of Guinea—in sum, an area occupying one fifth of the entire African continent. And, beyond exercising influence in this area by its penetration inland, France could initiate trade relations to the north with "Morocco, Algiers, Tunis, Tripoli and Cairo, [to the East] with Timbuktu, the land of Hausa, Tocrur, Kaffina, and from there, via Agadès, to Bornu, Senar, and Abyssinia." Golberry suggested that the French recruit young Moors, eight to ten years old, rear them in various trades in Paris, and then, when they were fifteen, send them back to their parents. If the interior could be cultivated to yield cotton, tobacco, indigo, rice, and even coffee, he reasoned, then the Moors, who had been under French influence, could become intermediaries between France and the interior and encourage the growing of these crops.[51]

Senegambia as a Penal Colony

The main reasons for expanding French control over West Africa, especially the Senegambia, were economic and geopolitical. Population problems were rarely mentioned; when they were, it was mostly in regard to finding an outlet for populations no longer wanted by France. Napoleon contemplated evacuating all blacks from the West Indies (since they had been "infected" by the virus of revolution) and sending them to West Africa. Such a possibility was also advocated by a planter who favored restoring slavery in the French colonies.[52]

Senegal was envisioned as an ideal destination for unwanted Frenchmen. Talleyrand suggested that colonization would provide an outlet for Frenchmen overwrought by the Revolution; groups that felt that the Revolution had gone either too far or not far enough would find in colonization a strenuous activity to quench their political passions.[53] Ten years of internal dissension in France, Pelletan argued, could be overcome by giving Frenchmen an outlet in the colonies.[54] Such ideas were by no means original to eighteenth-century thinkers; as early as the seventeenth century, colonies had been seen as a repository for poor people, vagabonds, and criminals—in short, the deviants of society. But both Talleyrand and Pelletan added a new dimension to the argument: not only did colonies provide a convenient place where a nation could rid itself of unwanted elements of society, but also, they asserted, the experience of colonial expansion could overcome domestic dissension and help reunite antagonistic groups and classes within society. They thus anticipated the school of social imperialists that was to develop in the nineteenth century.[55]

Drawing on the example of the English, who in 1788 had established a penal colony in Botany Bay, Australia, the French tried during the Revolution to establish in Africa a colony for political prisoners. On September 17, 1792, the Convention decreed that any cleric denounced by six citizens for *incivisme* ("uncitizenly behavior") would be deported to the coast of Rio d'Oro, an area southwest of Morocco, later to become Spanish Sahara. In December of that year, three ships carrying a total of 550 convicted priests set sail for Rio d'Oro. Unable to complete their journey because of bad weather, the ships returned to port, where the clerics were released.[56] Establishment of a French penal colony in West Africa was thus averted. The plan was revived in 1798 when an official suggested that plantation colonies cultivated by political deportees might be successful in the Upper Senegal.[57] The idea of establishing penal colonies on the West African coast reappeared from time to time, but it was a minor factor in French colonial interests in Africa.

Formal and Informal Empire

It has become common, especially among analysts of British imperialism, to make a distinction between "informal" and "formal" empire. In the eighteenth century, the French themselves debated whether control could better be achieved by indirect French presence through trade or by outright conquest. Both methods were considered, often by the same person, and, rather than forming distinct alternatives, ideas favorable to informal empire and those comprising a more militaristic program often merged in the policies proposed at the time. (It should be noted that "informal empire" is a nineteenth-century British concept; the term is used here in a somewhat anachronous way, but it has its uses as an analytical device.)

Instructing an official commanding the fort at Galam, Brüe wrote that it was necessary to maintain a policy "between firmness and timidity" with the local peoples, and that, when one "is in an area in which one is not the strongest, the attitude of the fox makes more sense than that of the lion."[58] Brüe was a realist who did not want the French to embark on an adventure that had little chance of success. He was not unalterably opposed to conquest; he felt that it just was not timely. Other officials showed far greater willingness to use force. Charpentier did not believe that the gold in the Upper Senegal could be acquired through peaceful means; the local populations were far too intent on keeping their wealth. In Charpentier's opinion, only the use of force could ensure French control over the allegedly rich gold mines. A fort should be built in the region where the mines were located; then, at the least sign of opposition, "we must carry out a horrible carnage . . . destroying them by fire and the sword, it is the only means of taking away their courage and then reducing them to ask for mercy." Charpentier raised the problem of the morality of conquest, only to dismiss it with the remark, "One must not think that this effort will not have its inconveniences, but when one wants to conquer a country, one must ignore many things, which human effort can always restore later."[59]

The plans of the officials in Senegal, especially those of Brüe, were published in 1728 by Father Labat in his *Nouvelle relation de l'Afrique occidentale.* Labat advocated plantation colonies in Senegal. Africans would be unable to develop plantation staples because, he believed, blacks were too lazy to work. He proposed, therefore, that French settlers be sent to Senegal to rent the land from African chiefs and cultivate it. Labat's was a peaceful plan, but he presented it as the first step in a more ambitious program that would culminate in territorial conquest, once the settlers were firmly established: "We will establish ourselves solidly in the country, build cities, and fortresses, which not only will defend us from the insult of the natives, but which will soon reduce them into our tributaries." As for the gold mines of the Upper Senegal, however, Father Labat cautioned against conquest by force: "The law of God forbids us to invade the possessions of others. . . . It is known that for two centuries the Spanish have been unable to wash themselves of the stain of having invaded America."

There were also practical restraints on conquest; the country was too unhealthy to allow a successful military campaign, and the local population had the means to defend itself. Rather, the best means of acquiring the gold was by commercial penetration of the area. Despite his warnings against wars of conquest, Labat, like Charpentier, whom he undoubtedly copied, thought that, once a fort was established in Bondu, the French would be justified in seizing the territory if the fort were attacked.[60] The plan had the moral advantage of providing the excuse for a just, defensive war in subjugating the region.

His initial moral reservations notwithstanding, Labat became an enthusiastic imperialist. Writing in 1730 he proposed that the French conquer the region of Senegal to establish plantation colonies and to seize the gold mines. He favored a system of forts farther south, on the Guinea Coast, to attract the African trade at the expense of other European powers.[61] Whatever the means, the aim was the same, however: to make West Africa dependent upon France. Labat wrote that the French should not teach the Africans how to manufacture the goods sold to them, but should introduce to them as many manufactured products as possible. By making the Africans dependent on these goods, "they will need them so badly that they cannot be without them, and thus will offer . . . all their labor, their trade and their industry." They would be "hooked on French goods in the same manner as Europeans developed a dependency on tobacco."[62]

Informal empire was generally seen as but the prelude to more formal control. Pierre David suggested that the French establish trading posts around the gold mines of the Bambuk that would attract the indigenous peoples. These peoples presumably would take the side of the French, who would then become so powerful that "we shall be able to subjugate the authorities in the country without their being aware." France would "become master of a large country, the closest to Europe and the best known, without spilling blood, without having hunted down any of the natives."[63] Boufflers wanted to establish a plantation colony in Cap Vert by peaceful means, purchasing the cape from the local ruler, the Damel. Pelletan thought that lightly manned forts could easily control an area "two hundred leagues along the coast and three hundred deep," which could then be transformed into a rich plantation colony.[64]

Eager to gain both control over areas reputed to be rich and the support of skeptical officials in Paris, French officials in Senegal implied that certain territorial acquisitions could be made without the expenses of a military expedition. Lamiral argued that the gold of Bambuk could be acquired by trade alone; the inhabitants loved the French and would be glad to have Frenchmen come to the mines and teach them the best means of extracting the gold. He presumed the willingness of the king of Bambuk to negotiate and to give the French the right to the mines if his own sovereignty were respected. Pruneau de Pommegorge, plagiarizing from David, stated that gradual white settlement of the Upper Senegal would make any use of force unnecessary.[65]

Prélong, former director of the Gorée hospital, wrote an essay, which was awarded a prize by the Comité des arts et métiers, to encourage French commercial development. He described the advantages of developing tropical plantations in Senegal, but he adamantly opposed forcible conquest:

Nothing would be more difficult than to seize territory of a certain size in Africa. There would be enough men in this country [Senegal] to chase away the Europeans and to take away their establishments. And second, the climate devours part of our population. And third, the European population would degenerate under the influence of the climate and lose control over the colony.[66]

The moral question also was raised occasionally. Durand, director of the Senegal Company in the 1780s, considered the violent conquest of the gold mines, but a telling combination—morality and French interests—persuaded him to oppose it: "I don't want to give an example of injustice, and the second reason is that our profits would be greater in receiving this gold by exchange than if we had to pay the expenses of mining."[67]

Although few officials condoned the bloody projects suggested in the 1720s, some still advocated the threat of force as the best means of acquiring the fabled gold mines of the Upper Senegal for France. An official in the Ministry of Foreign Affairs suggested the building of forts in the area to house between 700 and 800 Frenchmen and Eurafricans to facilitate the mining operation. It is presumed that he thought the presence of such forts would ensure the cooperation of the local population. Coste d'Arnobat, a military officer and man of letters who had never been to Senegal, echoed in 1789 the militancy of the 1720s. He wrote that it was necessary to send 500 armed men to Bambuk to secure it for France but that war would be unnecessary, for the people of Bambuk were not a fighting people; they were poorly armed and would prefer surrender to battle. Thus the area could be subjugated without shedding any blood.[68] Most French advocates of expansion into West Africa argued that such expansion could be accomplished by peaceful, gradual means. Nevertheless, control was desired, and, in that sense, no matter how peaceful the methods advocated, these proposals were imperialist.

The Civilizing Mission

The spread of French influence, through either trade or conquest, was seen as a French civilizing mission beneficial to

Africa. Many wrote about the benefits for Africa only in terms of trade or other contacts and did not mention outright conquest; their ideas nevertheless merged with the insistence on imperialist aggression. In the seventeenth century, the civilizing mission was viewed mainly as Christianization; in the following century, it was normally viewed as the spread of French secular values, institutions, and material culture.

Conquest for the purpose of converting Africans had been suggested as early as 1402 by Jean de Béthencourt, a Norman who had conquered the Canary Islands. The account of Béthencourt's activities, published in 1630, reported that Béthencourt had intended to use the Canary Islands as a base from which to penetrate the African continent and, "with the help of God, to conquer many peoples and convert them to the Christian faith."[69] Béthencourt wanted to reach the kingdom of Prester John (in Ethiopia), with which Christian Europe wanted to join in the fight against Islam. He shared with his contemporaries the myths of Ethiopian wealth and godliness. The account may not be accurate about Béthencourt's plans, but may rather reflect the missionary zeal prevalent during the Counter-Reformation. This included the desire to bring Africa into the Christian fold. Père Joseph, Richelieu's counselor and the *éminence grise* of the regime, strongly advocated that the French launch a powerful missionary effort that would include Africa.[70]

Secular thinkers also recognized the missionizing duties of France and saw in colonization a way of carrying them out. The theorist Montchrétien declared that conquest would be welcomed by "the many barbarian peoples who stretch out their arms to us, who are ready to subject themselves to us, so that by holy teachings and good examples we can set them on the road to salvation."[71] Such themes were echoed by individual officials, who believed that missionizing by conquest served the political and commercial interests of France.[72] Du Casse suggested that France could gain a near monopoly of the slave trade if it converted the Africans to Catholicism; the converts would hesitate to sell Catholics to non-Catholics, and thus the English, the largest competitors in the slave trade, would be eliminated.[73]

While many philosophes were hostile to organized religion,

they acknowledged Christianity's role in "civilization." Montesquieu wrote that, although Ethiopia's size and harsh climate should have led it to oriental forms of despotism, "the Christian religion has brought to the middle of Africa the mores and laws of Europe." Even Voltaire praised the Jesuits for their activities in the Americas.[74] Thus the spread of Christianity was perceived as part of a larger process of Europeanization, which, from the vantage point of the Enlightenment, was characterized mainly by the adoption of European political and economic institutions, family structures, laws, and material culture.

The civilizing process, it was thought, could be effected by continual contact between Europeans and Africans. Frenchmen could act as tutors, speeding up the evolutionary process, which, it was thought, would bring all societies to the level of Europe. Dralsé de Grandpierre pointed out that the trade between the inhabitants of Whyda and Europeans had affected the former, "considerably civilizing their mores and enlightening their spirit." Labat cited the example of the people of Issiny along the Ivory Coast, who, exposed to European influence, were "quite civilized," while inland another ethnic group, "which sees only Negroes and rarely Whites, are more savage." The European presence on the coast created inevitable transformations in the life of Africans, Labat declared, pointing out that, for instance, chiefs began to build rectangular houses, copying the shapes of the European forts. As for the roofs, Africans "have *not yet* [my italics] thought it appropriate to cover them with shingles," but to Labat it was obvious that this improvement too would occur. The French advance up the Senegal River would change the peoples living on its banks, "awakening them from lethargy and laziness."

The European presence on the coast of Africa, Poivre wrote, explained why agriculture was more successful there than inland; thus, under European influence Africa's agricultural potential would be realized.[75] Pelletan wrote of hardworking peoples on the coast, but believed that, once Africans went inland, they returned "to their indolent life, without concern, and apathetic." Pelletan seems to have been suggesting that only a permanent European presence could change the African's nature. Moreover, the establishment of plantation colonies would give an outlet to labor freed from the scourge of slavery; thus, Africa could be regenerated.[76]

Many philosophes saw European colonial expansion as proof of human progress. Condorcet zealously preached the message. He assumed that the direction of history was toward the increasing perfection of man and the establishment of equality among men and nations. According to Condorcet, all nations would eventually reach the level "achieved by the most enlightened, the freest, the least superstitious, such as the French and the Anglo-Americans"; the distance between that level and the barbarism of Africa would eventually disappear. Condorcet denounced the brutal European conquest of the Americas, Asia, and Africa, but thought that European culture could impose itself in some peaceful manner. He foresaw that, as a result of becoming fully enlightened, Europeans would no longer use their forts as centers for the slave trade, but instead would spread from them "the example of liberty, the enlightenment and reason of Europe." But he did not envision such a program as universally applicable to Africa; he thought that people who were subjected to extreme climates or who were very savage might be intractable to the influence of civilization. Either they would be the last to be civilized, Condorcet thought, or they might even go under. This possibility did not disturb him. It seemed to him a fulfillment of natural law that those who rejected the progress of history—the process by which all peoples were to be civilized—*should* disappear; nothing could come in the way of this law of progress. He foresaw the independence of the Americas and the triumph of the white man on the American continents with the concomitant disappearance of the Indian. He believed that conquest itself could be the means of progress. That was the way Voltaire had viewed the Roman conquest of his ancestors, the Gauls; Julius Caesar and his legions had brought civilization to France.[77]

If military conquest of the rest of the globe was not always praised, the spread of European influence was seen as beneficial to non-Europeans. Dégérando, the founder of the Société des observateurs de l'homme, thought that trade would be

> a means of leading people to civilization . . . witness of our
> riches and at the same time of our superiority, he [the savage]
> will perhaps attach himself to us from gratitude or interest,
> will join in some alliance with us, will call us among his
> people to teach them how to reach our own condition. What
> joy!

Europeans who went overseas would, by their example, bring
enlightenment to the "savages": "perhaps they are laying the
foundations of a new Europe."[78] The civilizing mission was not
merely altruistic; it had commercial advantages too, Golberry
noted: "Savage people are not consumers, but civilized
peoples are becoming increasingly so," and thus the object of
French policy in Africa should be "to create new objects of
exchange, to create new consumers of the products of our
industry."[79]

The overall view of the European impact on Africa was positive, but there were, of course, some dark spots in intercultural contacts, which even enthusiastic imperialists were willing to admit. Labat regarded the poor examples of Europeans
at trading forts as an obstacle to the Christianization of Africa;
drunkenness, he admitted, had been spread by the European
brandy trade.[80] Other regrettable habits, such as stealing, had
also been adopted by Africans as a result of their coming into
contact with Europeans.[81] But individual, episodic results of
intercultural contact did not undermine the basic belief that
contact with Europeans was beneficial to Africa. A greater
threat to that viewpoint came from those eighteenth-century
thinkers who had doubts about the supremacy of Western culture and who waxed enthusiastic about non-Europeans.
Raynal, having generally espoused a Noble Savage ideal of the
black man, saw contact between Europeans and Africans as
having deleterious effects on the latter. In contrast to those
who had argued that the African coast was the most civilized
because it was open to European influences, Raynal argued
that it was the least civilized. Africans in general, he wrote,
were not interested in military conquest or material wealth;
only the peoples on the coast—those exposed to the ideas of
Europe—had degenerated and become warlike and greedy.
Some of these complaints had been made before; what makes
them significant at the time of Raynal's writing is that they had

become part of a more general negative view of Euro-African interaction. Raynal wrote that imposing political and social institutions on Africans would replace a simple, idyllic existence with the tyranny of European conventions. In a rhetorical appeal to the Hottentots, he warned of the advancing white men: "Flee, unfortunate Hottentots, flee! Hide yourselves in the forest. . . . The tiger will eat you perhaps; but he will take only your life. The other will ravage your innocence and your liberty."[82] This passage, actually written by Diderot, foreshadowed the theme Diderot later developed in the *Supplément au voyage de Bougainville,* in which, in even stronger language, he spoke out against European imperialism. In one passage of this work, a wise old man in Tahiti addresses the European explorer:

> This country belongs to you. Why? Because you have set foot on it? If a Tahitian landed one day on your coast and he engraved on one of your rocks or on the bark of a tree "This country belongs to the inhabitants of Tahiti," what would you think?[83]

Rousseau suggested that drastic measures be used to guard blacks against the contamination of European influence: "If I were the chief of one of the peoples of Black Africa, I would set up on the frontier gallows on which I would hang without mercy the first European who dared enter and the first citizen who tried to leave."[84] In their attacks on European expansionism, many writers, however, showed themselves to be ambivalent, as they were about many other subjects involving blacks. The *Ephémérides du citoyen* deplored Euro-African relations as destructive to both parties involved. It pointed out that, by trying to found colonies overseas, Europe had lost population and Africa had been devastated by brandy and gunpowder. On the other hand, the journal did not advocate stopping the process, for, as it noted, Europe needed the raw materials of the non-European world and the latter could not do without European goods.[85] Adamant in his attack on the destructive nature of European contacts with the peoples of the New World, Asia, and Africa, Raynal himself revealed a curious contradiction. He lamented the destruction wrought upon the non-European world, but he also attacked Europe for not spreading enlightenment to the Africans. He was especially severe toward the Portuguese for allegedly perpetuating the ignorance of Africans. While containing long passages deploring expansion and its destructive results in the non-European world, Raynal's work as a whole is a panegyric to European expansion. For Raynal expansion was a sign of Europe's vitality:

> Man carries inside him a natural energy that torments him and that taste, fancy, or weariness turns into the most unusual efforts. Man is curious, he wants to see and to know. The thirst for knowledge is less widespread but more deep than that for gold.[86]

In short, condemning Europe's contact with non-European peoples became a fad, but it was not profound enough to alter basic positions. Coste d'Arnobat seems nearly to have been overcome by melancholy at what European conquest would do to the inhabitants of Africa: "We shall soon have taught you unhappiness, and soon we shall have replaced your touching virtues with all our vices."[87] Still, he advocated the seizure of the Bambuk gold mines by 500 to 600 armed men. Significantly, although he was the most consistent opponent of European expansion, Rousseau, unlike most others who opposed expansion, never called on the French to retreat from their possessions.

The essential imperialist ethos of the era, stimulated by the universal competition for empire in the mid-eighteenth century, unleashed an interest in the colonization of Africa. Officials, abolitionists, and many philosophes were at one in advocating a French advance into West Africa. The ideas developed in this era bore little fruit in the short run, but, after the Revolution and Napoleon, with the establishment of the Restoration, attempts were made to realize what had been merely a dream of empire.

Imperial ambitions cast the African as a passive creature in need of white mastery. His person and his land were to be dominated by the European. The imperial program was yet another manifestation of the tradition of black inequality in French thought.

7

The Nineteenth Century
Confronts Slavery

Slavery, abolished in the French empire in 1794, was reinstated by Napoleon in 1802. For twenty years thereafter, the French government did not completely give up the possibility of reconquering Saint-Domingue, its richest colony, and it retained slavery in the rest of the empire. The problem of slavery had not been resolved with the philosophes and the Revolution; it was only after two more revolutions and the proclamation of the Second Republic in 1848 that slavery was finally abolished. Thus, in the first half of the nineteenth century, the debates on the nature of blacks, to an important degree, still revolved around slavery.

Although slavery inspired both racist literature and the apologia for blacks, the "scientific" literature (discussed in the following chapter) was essentially divorced from the theme of slavery. This had not been true in the United States, where the scientific community was eager to justify slavery.[1] But, in nineteenth-century France, slavery had become such a peripheral institution that it did not affect the work of the scientists. As most of the racist writers were opposed to slavery, it would be wrong to see French racism as an ideology created to justify it. The main racist thinkers found blacks to be inferior, but insisted that, whatever the blacks' failings might be, their enslavement was unjustified. While preaching doctrines of racial inequality, Arthur de Gobineau, for instance, was irritated that his work was used to support proslavery opinion in the United States.[2]

Thus much of the general, speculative literature on Africa and its inhabitants tended to be unaffected by the polemics on slavery that went on in France in the first half of the

181

nineteenth century. The opposite, of course, was not true. Polemicists favoring slavery exploited any negative views of blacks, and their proslavery arguments provided an additional emphasis to the racism developing in the first half of the nineteenth century. To refute the systematic denigration of blacks by proslavery interests, abolitionists attempted to rehabilitate the image of blacks. But the arguments they proffered tended to be inspired less by a conviction of the African's real worth than by the need for a polemical impact to help their own cause. The abolitionist views were contemporaneous with those of the anthropologists and travelers, and were not totally at variance with them. The principles of humanity demanded the abolition of slavery; maintaining human beings in such a condition was a shocking denial of human freedom; slavery degraded not only the slave but also his owner; slavery was an inefficient means of production and a social system that imperiled both French control over the colonies and the lives of white settlers; continued slavery might unleash rebellions as violent as that in Saint-Domingue—such were the arguments for abolition, independent of any assessment of the blacks' worth as human beings.

The Proslavery Image

The abolitionist movement in France, institutionalized in the Société des amis des noirs, dispersed within a few years of the outbreak of the Revolution in 1789. Its membership had consisted largely of nobles or bourgeois with moderate political views, who had to flee France or face persecution at home as the Revolution became more radical. And if that were not enough, their ideas were discredited. Their warnings of slave uprisings, unless slavery were abolished or reformed, were interpreted as calls for the bloody slave revolution that broke out in Saint-Domingue in 1791. Abolitionism, for at least three decades thereafter, ceased to exist in France.

The Saint-Domingue uprising was decisive in strengthening Negrophobia. None of the abolitionists approved of the revolt; some saw it as proof that they had misunderstood the nature of blacks and, consequently, began to reassess them.

Playwright and feminist Marie Gouze, under the pseudonym of Olympe de Gouges, wrote a play in 1786 that, as presented at the Comédie Française in December 1789, proclaimed the nobility of the black race and the barbarity of slavery. But when she published the play in 1792, she provided a preface that essentially negated her earlier stand. Addressing herself to the blacks who had rebelled, she exclaimed, "Men were not born for chains, but you prove that they are necessary."[3] Chateaubriand noted that, after the Saint-Domingue uprising, it was no longer fashionable to talk about the noble black and the indignities he suffered under slavery.[4]

With the re-establishment of slavery in 1802, it again seemed appropriate to cite the condition of blacks as justification for their enslavement. Gouze now presented black enslavement as an enlighted act that saved one's fellow men "from a horrible primitive situation where men not only sold each other but also ate each other." General Baudry Deslozières, a retired officer and planter in the West Indies, wrote a proslavery book dedicated to Empress Josephine in 1802, the year Napoleon tried to reconquer Saint-Dominque. His picture of Africa was one of savage brutality. Embroidering on travelers' accounts of the "customs" in Dahomey, he proclaimed that, when the king died, slaughter took place as

> thousands of slaves [were] strangled on the edge of the grave and the flow of their boiling blood lifts the master's corpse. To shouts of despair this infernal grave is filled with corpses who float in the blood, while the hands of those who in their turn will be strangled cover them with the earth which for a long time will be bloodied by the victims it has swallowed.

Deslozières believed that the custom was common to all of Africa and charged that "these nations have a natural taste for human blood." Hence, he reasoned, the slave trade was a boon, and the slave trader was "the best philosophe since he is the savior of a group of men who would otherwise perish."[5]

In the face of the abolitionist movement in the 1830s and 1840s, proslavery opinion continued to stress the utility of slavery to blacks themselves.[6] The colonial council of

Martinique declared in 1839 that "slavery is a gift of providence to advance religion, a progress for the African race."[7] However, it was not in the interests of the proslavers to imply that the civilizing process had been such a total success that the slaves were ready for emancipation. Therefore, they had to show that, despite contact with European civilization, blacks had not evolved very far. An official in Martinique in 1843 argued that blacks had learned only the vices of European civilization: "Disorder and immorality are the rule." The council of Guadeloupe spoke of the blacks' penchant for promiscuity. It was charged that blacks were so degenerate that they could and should never be freed. The colonial council of Martinique obdurately stated its opposition to "any emancipation at any time whatever," and the Guadeloupe council likewise insisted on "the necessity of indefinitely maintaining the beneficence of slavery."[8]

The Abolitionists and the Slave Trade

The abolitionists were relatively silent during the Empire; few were the men and women who wished to be the object of Napoleonic wrath for agitating on behalf of an issue considered marginal. Anti-Bonapartists of republican and abolitionist convictions were a small group, led by Abbé Grégoire. They spoke out against slavery minimally. Grégoire issued *An Enquiry,* which listed men of achievement who had been black. De Staël, who also was a member of the republican opposition after Napoleon's fall in 1814, penned an introduction to one of Wilberforce's essays on behalf of abolishing the slave trade. She appealed to the sovereigns of Europe meeting to make peace in 1814 for the abolition of the slave trade. The trade carried violence and destruction to Africa; its cessation, De Staël argued, would facilitate the Christianization and civilization of Africa.[9]

The liberal economist Simonde de Sismondi argued against the slave trade on both humanitarian and economic grounds. The end of the slave trade would make it possible for Africans, free from wars, to make rapid progress toward civilization, Sismondi wrote. He denounced the trade as a violation of all the precepts of Christianity and of international law. The eighteenth-century philosophes had drawn up a series of noble traits for the Africans; Sismondi depicted the African way of life, in those areas not scarred by slave raids, as the paragon of the liberal bourgeois state:

> Large commercial and manufacturing cities have been built in the center of the African continent; they are the capitals of powerful kingdoms, where the arts, manufacture and agriculture attest to the progress of the social life, property is assured, civil liberty is guaranteed, justice is administered wisely and the government is respected.

In addition to its inhumanity, slavery was uneconomical, Sismondi wrote. He pointed out that, in order to develop the sugar industry, based on slavery in the Antilles, France would have to invest capital that would otherwise be available for its textile industry; thus it would be involved in an unprofitable rate of exchange.[10]

Opponents of the trade such as De Staël borrowed their arguments from the English abolitionists, and even Sismondi's lacked any real originality. When the French legally abolished the trade, their action was a result of the British example. The British government, under the prodding from its abolitionists in peace negotiations in 1814, demanded that France abolish its participation in the slave trade, as Britain had done in 1807. Not enjoying the benefits of the trade for its own colonies, the British did not wish their rivals across the Channel to revive their economic power in the Caribbean. The British demand was met by stern resistance from the French emissary Caulaincourt, who saw it as an insult to French sovereignty, declaring that such a demand "can never be tolerated by a great people who are not yet in a situation to be insulted with perfect impunity."[11] In 1815 at the Congress of Vienna, however, the French were compelled to accept abolition of the slave trade. The only French possessions that had economies based on slave labor were Martinique, Guadeloupe, and Guiana in the New World and the Ile de Bourbon in the Indian Ocean. None was of crucial importance to the French economy. True, Saint-Domingue, which might yet be recon-

English naval officers informing Africans of the abolition of the slave trade in 1815. Hennin Collection. Photo Bibliothèque nationale, Paris.

quered, represented considerable potential, but it lay beyond France's reach. Since the 1790s, when there had been continuous wars with Britain, the French slave trade had been minimal; thus there were no longer any large interests in France to be damaged by accession to British dictates. In any case, in the face of British control of the seas, the French government was in no position to oppose England. The remaining colonial interests would have to be sacrificed for the more important, continental ones, which required British cooperation.

Louis XVIII's government committed itself to the legal abolition of the slave trade, but it in no way felt a moral obligation to enforce it. French merchants continued the trade, and there seems to have been little public interest in the issue. Between 1814 and 1820, neither of the two legislative chambers received petitions against the slave trade.[12] When the deputy Laisné de Villévêcque raised the issue, the Chamber of Deputies refused to print his speech; the request for its publication was met by an ironic outburst by the deputies: "Yes, by all means let us have a course in African geography."[13] The first law against the slave trade in France was adopted three years after the French government had committed itself to abolition; the law provided very light penalties. As Serge Daget remarks, the fines for trafficking in men were infinitely less severe than those for burning a mill or even for stealing a loaf of bread.[14]

The Restoration, open to the charge of being a regime imposed on France by foreign powers, found in the slave trade issue a convenient means of demonstrating its independence.[15] It looked the other way while slave ships were equipped in French ports and sailed to the West African coast. The abolitionist charges of government complicity in the continuation of the trade have now been substantiated by Daget. Nantes provided the largest proportion of slavers, an average of 43.38 percent of the illegal French trade between 1814 and 1830. In that city slaving was a major industry; 18.52 percent of all ships leaving that port, Daget reveals, were involved in the slave trade. During the whole Restoration period, from 1814 to 1830, he estimates, more of the ships sailing to West Africa were involved in the slave trade than in the legitimate trade.[16]

The French public seemed in no way affected by the accounts of Clarkson and Wilberforce, whose works were translated and circulated in France, on the horrors of the slave trade. The Comte d'Artois, who became Charles X in 1824, declared that he was revolted by accounts of the slave trade, but then quickly added that the main thing "is that they be baptized"—the classic apologia for enslavement.[17] The general French apathy toward the slave trade was so striking that in 1822 the newly founded Société de la morale chrétienne announced a contest in which it offered a prize of 1,000 francs for the best essay explaining why "the abolition of the slave trade enjoys so little popularity" in France.[18]

The apathy toward the issue can be explained by the government's promotion of proslavery writings and its censorship of those opposed to the institution.[19] Moreover, the center of the organized abolitionist movement was gone, undermined by the Saint-Domingue uprising and the demise of the Société des amis des noirs. During the Restoration movements that had in any way been connected with the Revolution were discredited, and the Société was no exception.[20] One of its foremost members survived the vicissitudes of the Revolution, Napoleon, and the Restoration—Abbé Grégoire. But his impact was neutralized by the general suspicion that surrounded him; he was regarded as a turncoat, a churchman accused of having voted for the beheading of Louis XVI and the civil code of the Church (these charges were untrue).[21] Yet the struggle against the slave trade won some respectability when, on March 28, 1822, the Duke de Broglie, in a speech in Parliament, presented himself as a champion of the abolition of the slave trade. He came from an influential, aristocratic family and was a prominent member of the liberal opposition. Much of this opposition was Protestant, drew its ideas from England, and held membership in the Société de la morale chrétienne. Having only 279 members in 1825, the small organization was, however, influential.[22] It counted among its members distinguished men such as François Guizot, Benjamin Constant, and the Duke d'Orléans, the future Louis-Philippe. Like that of its predecessor (the Société des amis des noirs), the importance of the Société de la morale chrétienne was due not to the number of its members, but rather to the influence they exercised.

Another prestigious group throwing its influence against the slave trade was the Académie Française, which in 1823 announced a prize for the best poem decrying the trade. The horrors of the trade and the destruction wrought by slavers on innocent people in a state of nature were stressed in poems and other writings of the era. The poems may have influenced Théodore Géricault in his choice of subjects to paint. Shortly before his death in 1824, he evoked the terrors of the trade in a sketch called "Slave Trade," which showed a black family being separated by slave raiders. Of course, his depiction of blacks in such paintings as "The Raft of the Medusa," "The Boxing Match," "The Black Soldier," "The Black Horseman," and, maybe his finest depiction, "The Negro" was motivated in part by an interest in the special problems of color and shape that Africans posed for the artist. But the very nobility that blacks were given in these paintings was intended equally as a protest against the slave trade, an affirmation of black humanity.[23]

Many liberals who opposed the slave trade came into positions of authority as a result of the Revolution of 1830. They were willing to collaborate actively with the British naval squadrons in repressing the trade. Such policies were due to the commitment of the July Monarchy to abolishing the trade and to its desire to have a visible manifestation of the Anglo-French entente. However, chauvinistic popular opinion insisted that to give the British navy the right to search French ships for slaves was to allow an infringement of French sovereignty. In 1841, when the Guizot government signed an agreement with London renewing and extending previous treaties to combat the slave trade, the agreement was not ratified by the Chamber. Liberals and even abolitionists such as Tocqueville voted against it. Questions of national pride and domestic political advantage were given priority over the human rights of Africans.[24] The failure of abolitionists to support the government seemed to indicate a lack of resolve.

French traders supplied goods that were used by foreign nationals in the slave trade. This practice was well known, and, when it was brought to the attention of Guizot, serving as foreign minister in 1842, he refused to put an end to it. The principles of free trade, he felt, could not be interfered with. When faced with this trade and the practice of selling French ships to Brazilian slavers in African ports, Guizot's liberal abolitionist colleague Victor Destutt de Tracy was to take a similar stance. Serving as minister of the navy in 1849 in the Republic that had abolished slavery, de Tracy declared that "the present sufferings of our maritime commerce impose upon us an absolute reserve on this issue."[25] Economic factors seemed more important than human ones; the priorities of the liberal abolitionists in power were, sadly, not that different from the slaveowning elites of the preceding century.

Liberals continued in their attempts to escape the cost of abolition—the loss of a steady, cheap supply of black labor. With emancipation in 1848 it was correctly anticipated that, since menial labor had for so long been associated with slavery, the new freedmen would only reluctantly continue to cultivate the land, especially in the plantation setting. The need for manpower in the Antilles somehow would have to be met.

A model that came from Senegal and that seemed an appropriate solution was the system of "engagement," begun after 1815 when the slave trade had been abolished. To man its military units and fort-construction work, the government bought slaves from the hinterland, freed them, and contracted them for a fourteen-year period during which the "engagés" were, so to speak, to work off their price. A second group of engagés were slaves freed by French authorities from slave ships; they had to serve seven years.[26] The system had ended in Senegal in 1844, but it was revived for the Antilles and Réunion in 1852. French traders went to West and East Africa, bought slaves, declared them to be free, and shipped them to the Antilles or to Réunion, where they were to work as contract labor for low wages. From 1852 until 1861, between 10,000 and 15,000 Africans were delivered to the Antilles, and 34,700 to Réunion under this system.[27] That this traffic was just another form of the slave trade was obvious to anyone with any discernment,[28] but, characteristically, the voice of French abolitionism was silent on this question. In fact, in 1849 the main organ of the movement, the *Abolitionniste français,* had advocated such a system for Algeria.[29]

The system of transporting African contract labor was ended on the insistence of the British government that the French were continuing—under a new form—the slave trade.[30] Again, not French abolitionism, but British pressure, as it had in 1815, forced the French to abrogate this execrable trade.

These failures to take an outright position of defense of the Africans denotes the absence of a Negrophilism of the intensity that had existed in the eighteenth century. It seems that it was less the plight of the Africans that had motivated the nineteenth-century abolitionist impulse in France than the distaste for an institution so profoundly at variance with the basic principles of liberalism. French abolitionists saw in slavery a basic denial of natural law, a system of constraint that denied the type of human freedom that ought to exist in a rationally ordered society.

The Abolitionists and Slavery:
The Ambiguous Campaign

In the 1820s abolitionist opinion attempted to end the slave trade, which the French government had already ostensibly declared illegal. Some of those advocating an end to the trade also wanted to eradicate slavery, but they kept quiet for fear that their ideas would be rejected as premature. This was the case with the Société de la morale chrétienne, whose founder, La Rochefoucauld-Liancourt, in 1834 explained that the reserve was due "to prudence."[31] This "prudence" not only derived from the fear of being considered out of tune with the times, but also reflected the ambiguities of French abolitionist attitudes toward blacks. The Société de la morale chrétienne spoke of the need to free the black slaves, but insisted that it had to be done "without danger."[32] To precipitate emancipation would endanger the lives of the white planters and lead to a disorganization in the lives of the blacks.

Most writers who favored change wished an amelioration, a humanization of slavery through the abolition of the trade, but they dared not favor outright abolition of slavery. The Enlightenment had been ambiguous in its attitude, attempting rather futilely to reconcile French economic interests with the high ideals it proclaimed. The heirs of this tradition in a way had an easier position. By the nineteenth century Saint-Domingue was lost, and material interests no longer weighed heavily in the balance. Sugar, which had been so important to the colonial economy, was also produced in France from the sugar beet developed by Napoleon; thus France was no longer so dependent on its overseas possession for this valuable commodity.

After Napoleon's fall, beet growing continued. The production of indigenous beet sugar increased dramatically from ten million kilograms in 1830 to nearly thirty million in 1840, and to double that amount in 1847. A law that went into effect in 1847 set equal duties on both sugars in an attempt to favor colonial sugar, but the latter had begun to lose its preeminence.[33] The progress of the beet root was so dramatic in the late 1830s that the caricaturist Honoré Daumier devoted three cartoons to it: one showed "General Beet-root" invading and smashing the forces of "sugarcane"; another showed a healthy beet root attacking a vine, for presumably beet root wine would replace the juice of the grape; in the third cartoon, a black slave in the colonies comfortably reposes on the ground and tells his desperate owner, "Master, I can no longer work your sugar cane; while the French were eating beet sugar I became so fat that I can no longer move."[34] The beet root was seen as a threat to the sugar cane industry, to the wine industry, and to the slave system in the colonies.

The perception of contemporaries was correct in terms of the general thrust of events, but colony-produced sugar on the eve of emancipation still had the bulk of the market. Its share of the market had, however, declined. In the decade 1827–1836, 83 percent of the sugar consumed in France came from the colonies, 2 percent from foreign countries, and 15 percent from the beet roots; in the decade 1837–1846, 63 percent came from the colonies, 1 percent from abroad, and 36 percent from the beet roots.[35]

The interests of the West Indian sugar planters were strongly represented in the port cities and in the government. As had not been the case in the eighteenth century, however, there were strong commercial groups organized in direct opposition to the colonial interests. The beet root growers and the industries depending upon them—there were 400 such factories in the 1830s—especially located in the Département du Nord, carried out a passionate campaign against the colonial interests. In August 1835 the general councils of five départements with commercial interests in the beet root called for the abolition of slavery, arguing that it was inhumane and necessitated the billeting of expensive troops in the Antilles.[36]

The relative decline in the primacy of colonial sugar compared with its position in the eighteenth century and the British example of emancipation in 1833 activated the abolition issue. While the colonial sugar interests were still powerful, Frenchmen could consider abolition without the fear that this measure of humanity would doom France's future as an economic or political force. Yet both the government and the abolitionists were to be most cautious.

One of the earliest and most outstanding spokesmen of French abolitionism was Victor Schoelcher. When he was twenty-five, his father, a porcelain manufacturer, sent him on a sales trip to Mexico, Florida, Louisiana, and Cuba. There he saw plantation slavery and was impressed by the abuses of the system—the mistreatment of slaves and the existence of a racist society. Schoelcher returned to France and wrote an article, "Des noirs," for the *Revue de Paris,* in which he expressed his dismay at the racial nature of slave societies and called for emancipation. But he was very clearly against immediate abolition. Brutalized by enslavement, blacks would be incapable of living in freedom and would be a danger to whites, he wrote; rather, slavery should be abolished gradually; abolition of the slave trade, combined with the high death rate of blacks in slavery, would contribute to an eclipse of the institution; in addition, the young children of slaves should be emancipated immediately and the remaining adults be freed over a gradual period of fifteen to twenty years.[37] Three years later the young Schoelcher became more cautious and proposed abolition over a forty- or sixty-year period; he favored the latter figure.[38] Over a period of time, however, Schoelcher came to realize that the planters' reluctance to educate their slaves was so great that the latter would never be ready for emancipation. Finally, in 1840, Schoelcher advocated immediate freedom, with the proviso that indemnities be provided for the slaveowners.[39]

The liberal poet Alphonse Lamartine showed an even greater reticence toward emancipation. In 1835 he warned that it was necessary to be cautious not only in considering emancipation but even in speaking of it; he seems to have accepted the proslavery argument that the agitation of the Société des amis des noirs had helped lead to the Saint-Domingue uprising. Arguing that the slave should gradually be prepared for freedom, in 1838 he suggested a ten-year transition period.[40]

The development of Alexis de Tocqueville's thought paralleled that of other cautious reformers. His first encounter with slavery was not in the French colonies but in the United States. On a mission to study prison reform, Tocqueville and his friend Gustave de Beaumont traveled in the United States for nine months, beginning in May 1831. They spoke with Americans about the slavery issue and also read American works on it, especially Jefferson's, which had been translated into French. Many Americans echoed Jefferson's thought that slavery was an evil that had to be destroyed but that, when ended, would cause hardships for the blacks and might endanger white society.[41] French observers of American societies may have adopted these attitudes or else have been affected by earlier, French proslavery writings such as those of Malouet, who had declared that freeing slaves would mean the transformation of the colonies into Negro societies. There seemed no way to have a free society in which both races could co-exist. "The more numerous would exclude the weaker group," Malouet had concluded.[42]

Whatever the influence, Beaumont and Tocqueville found confirmation of the blacks' difficulty in adjusting to freedom. Visiting penitentiaries in the United States, they noted the disproportionately large number of freedmen in the prisons. Where there was a large number of freedmen, criminality, they remarked, tended to be unusually high.[43] This observation did not mean that they favored the continuation of slavery, but they stressed that abolition was fraught with the greatest of dangers. They accepted the pessimistic view that blacks and whites could not live freely side by side. Rather, as

Tocqueville wrote in *Democracy in America,* each race struggled for supremacy, and: "wherever the whites have been the most powerful they have maintained the blacks in a subordinate or a servile position; wherever the negroes have been strongest they have destroyed the whites."[44]

From the United States, Beaumont wrote to his sister-in-law that, if the blacks in the United States were freed, "there is good reason to fear that they will avenge themselves with violence for the contempt they have been shown."[45] In his novel *Marie,* published the same year (1835) as *Democracy in America* and intended as its companion piece, Beaumont repeatedly made the same point.[46] It was only in 1839, four years after the publication of *Democracy,* that Tocqueville faced the problem of slavery in the French colonies. With glee the proslavers quoted Tocqueville's predictions of a race war. The author of *Democracy in America* explained that a race war could be avoided after the abolition of slavery if the state intervened.[47]

Other issues faced the emancipationist. The proslavery argument was that colonial wealth, based upon slavery, was crucial to the well-being of France. On this question Tocqueville vacillated. He stated, both in Parliament and in articles in *Le Siècle* in 1843, that the preservation of the colonies was essential to the "strength and greatness of France," but, in a subsequent article, he charged that the colonies' economic value had been exaggerated.[48] Whatever the case, there was another problem of far greater import to this liberal: "If the Negroes have the right to become free it is incontestable that the settlers have the right not to be ruined by the liberty of the Negroes."[49] Tocqueville tried to establish a balance between the principles of human liberty and property rights. In 1839 he came out in favor of immediate emancipation, thus being the first deputy to present such a plan. But he also suggested an indemnity for the slaveowners. His advocacy of emancipation was not free of fears about the outcome:

> France, gentlemen, does not want to destroy slavery only to have the ruined whites leave the soil of the colonies and the blacks fall back into barbarism. She desires not only to give liberty to men who previously were deprived of it but also to constitute civilized, industrious, and peaceful societies.[50]

Tocqueville did not think such goals possible if blacks suddenly were fully emancipated; he therefore suggested an intermediary stage of liberty, which would give slaves some of
the rights of free men as they continued to work on the plantations and then would gradually allow them to gain full rights.
Like European workers, they would be proletarians bereft of
property.[51] The failure of this plan may explain Tocqueville's
willingness to retreat from immediate abolition to gradualism
in 1843, when he supported the government-sponsored plan
of the Duke de Broglie to free the slaves after a ten-year
period, during which they would be prepared for freedom. As
one student of the issue has suggested, Tocqueville, on finding
that immediate freedom of slaves scared the government, may
have decided that gradual emancipation was better than none
at all.[52] It is equally possible, however, to see in Tocqueville's
support of gradualism his continuing fears about emancipation
of blacks. His espousal of immediatism in 1839 had still included many limitations, and his proposal at that time was not
all that different from the Broglie plan of 1843.

That the slaves could be freed without damage to the colonies was finally revealed to Tocqueville by the British example. Following abolition in the British colonies, Tocqueville
wrote in *Le Siècle* in 1843, blacks had not "returned to barbarism"; rather, they had adopted "the mores of the most
civilized people."[53] In 1845, in a speech in the Chamber of
Deputies, Tocqueville proclaimed that British emancipation
had been a total success. Blacks had enthusiastically taken on
the values of the civilized world: there had been a phenomenal
increase in the number of marriages, of schools and churches
built, and of industrial associations formed. Tocqueville noted,
"These million unfortunates who were said to be so close to
brutes . . . have become a million men."[54] The specter of
Saint-Domingue, which had discouraged abolitionism in
France for nearly half a century, vanished before the example
of Britain's emancipation; freedom seemed to be possible.

The British example explains why many French abolitionists
around 1840 embraced immediatism. Tocqueville did so in
1839, and Schoelcher in 1840. No longer fearing the conse-
quences of emancipation, abolitionists could see clearly the

problems inherent in allowing the slaveowners to prepare the slaves for freedom. As one of the immediatists observed in 1846, "The best training for liberty is liberty itself; one cannot prepare for it or be worthy of it in any other way than by exercising it."[55] It was recognized that only by making the decision to emancipate the blacks could France finally be freed of the problem of slavery. Emancipation would cut short the vicious circle created by arguing that blacks were not ready for freedom while allowing slavery to perpetuate the blacks' dependence and their unfitness for freedom. But not all French abolitionists were immediatists, and, even among those who were, immediatism did not necessarily mean a radical reappraisal of the worth of blacks.

The hesitations about emancipation that had plagued abolitionists for so long reflected deep personal doubts about blacks. To show that Africans were not predisposed for slavery, Schoelcher attempted to rehabilitate their image. He sought evidence of the Africans' abilities in the material culture of Africa. He advanced the notion that Volney had already presented, namely, that blacks had founded ancient Egyptian civilization. This achievement proved that Africans were capable of being civilized, of improving themselves, but he noted that it "does not prove, that is clear, that the whole race was civilized." He pointed to African achievements that had been recorded by European travelers: blacks knew how to build two-story houses; they worked hard, weaving cloth, making pottery, brewing beer, tanning skins, dying cloth, using iron; they knew how to read and write. All these accomplishments, however, did not imply equality with Europeans: "That they are as civilized in Africa as in Europe, no one will argue," Schoelcher wrote.[56]

Blacks, Schoelcher wrote, were inferior because of environmental influences. In slavery, he argued, they were stupid because they were enslaved, not because of their race; East Europeans living in serfdom were equally lacking in intellect.[57] He maintained that in Africa the blacks' condition was also due to environment; geographic isolation deprived them of outside influences, and the beneficent climate and fertility of the soil "invite to perpetual rest."[58] Schoelcher thus shared with his contemporaries the belief in African inferiority, but he did not attribute that inferiority to racial differences:

> We do not say that the Negroes are geniuses ... but we say that it is false to make them into idiots, and it signifies a lack of brains to build little physiological theories on whether their [blacks'] facial angles are more or less acute, and thus to deny them nearly all intelligence.[59]

He did not, however, totally deny the claims of the physical anthropologists, and he accepted the notion that blacks had a smaller cranium than whites had. He argued that the difference was not innate, but was caused by a lack of intellectual exercise and by carrying heavy burdens on the head. He wrote that the perfectability of blacks was shown by the physical evolution of the African in the Antilles; the slaves in the West Indies were less prognathic and had "a facial angle more open than among the Africans,"[60] a physical change that also suggested cultural evolution. Schoelcher thus seemed in agreement with the racist notion that the Africans' condition was connected to their physique; a change in physique was necessary before the African could evolve intellectually and morally. Unlike his racist contemporaries, however, he thought—as did thinkers in the eighteenth century—that the African race could change physically, and thus improve, under the influence of environment. As Tocqueville gradually came to favor emancipation, his ideas on the blacks also evolved somewhat. In *Democracy in America,* he wrote that the black's physiognomy "is to our eyes hideous, his understanding weak, his tastes low, and we are almost inclined to look upon him as a being intermediate between man and the brutes."[61] But in an unnoticed footnote, he made clear that the blacks' condition was due to slavery and that their disabilities were due to white prejudice.[62] That slavery was to blame for the blacks' condition was made still clearer by Beaumont, who in *Marie* asked, "How can one compare a race of men brought up in slavery, who transmit through generations a tradition of misery and brutishness, with people who can look back on fifteen centuries of uninterrupted civilization ... ?"[63]

Freed from slavery blacks were capable of improvement, as had been proved to the satisfaction of Tocqueville, who found blacks to have made remarkable advances since being emancipated in the British colonies. He stated that within a short time they had made a greater leap forward "than in any other enlightened nation in the world." Since Africans were thus susceptible to civilization, he condemned the view that they were "a species intermediary between man and monkey."[64] The polemics of antislavery thus made him into an upholder of the black race, but his view of the blacks, apart from the slavery issue, was unclear. When his friend Gobineau sent him a copy of *Inégalité des races humaines,* which proclaimed the inferiority of non-European races, Tocqueville did not refute its ideas; instead he lamented to Gobineau that they could bolster fatalism in Europe thus undermining the possibility for reform, and that in the United States they would be used to justify slavery. Tocqueville's main complaint was not that Gobineau's racial doctrines were wrong, but rather that they were untimely. Beaumont, whose *Marie* was the most important protest novel against racism in his times, was asked why the Société pour l'abolition de l'esclavage did not include Bissette as a member. (Bissette, a man of color, had been unjustly accused of fomenting rebellion in the 1820s and had been ardently defended by the abolitionists.) Independently wealthy and educated, a resident of Paris, and a writer on abolition, Bissette had not been invited to join. Beaumont explained, "Why! He is a colored man!"[65]

The hesitations of the abolitionists were reflected also in the cautious government policy of emancipation. How could blacks be freed without endangering the wealth of the Antilles and the safety of the white planters? The solution that a royal commission produced in 1839 was the indoctrination of the slaves through religious training. Christianity, it was felt, would make the freed slaves less prone to violence and more apt to work. The colonial budget of 1840 provided an additional 200,000 francs to pay for an increase in the colonial clergy. In Martinique the number of priests was increased from fifteen to forty-two, in Guadeloupe from twenty-nine to forty-five, and in Réunion from nineteen to twenty-six.[66]

The gradualist approach was embraced by the government commission on slavery in 1843, which established a ten-year target date for the emancipation of all slaves. According to this plan, all slaves born after 1838 were to be freed immediately, manumission was to be made easier, greater protection was to be extended to slaves, and, by 1853, all those remaining in bondage were to be freed. Concerned lest the planters be deprived of a sufficient labor force by emancipation, the commission recommended that even after being freed the ex-slaves should be bound as wage earners to the service of their former masters for a five-year period.[67] The target date of emancipation was rejected by the government, but otherwise many of the commission's recommendations were set into motion. According to a law of July 1845, slaves could buy their manumission regardless of the wishes of the owner, corporal punishment was limited, slaves were given civil status, and obligatory religious and educational instruction was instituted. The state thus circumscribed the rights of slaveowners, which for so long had been considered sacrosanct. Since 1840 the state had seemed to favor abolition, and in 1845 it set the example by freeing the slaves it owned.[68]

Government policy seems to have been affected little by public feelings, which, once official policy had become clear, also leaned toward emancipation. In 1844 the abolitionist François Isambert presented to the Chamber of Deputies a petition signed by 9,038 laborers in Paris. The language of the petition leads one to suspect that perhaps Isambert worded it himself, for few workers would have had the time to research the slave codes and laws cited in the petition. They may well, however, have been in sympathy with the emotions invoked by the petition, a passage in which declared, "It is in order to follow the grand principle of human fraternity that we come forward to make our voice heard in favor of our unfortunate brothers, the slaves."[69] In 1847 the Chamber received a petition favoring abolition signed by 11,000 people, among them 3 bishops, 19 vicars general, 858 priests, 86 Protestant ministers, 7 members of the Institut de France, 151 elected councillors, and 213 judges and lawyers.[70] Despite such manifestoes, one can say that on the whole the French public was not concerned with the slavery issue. The Société pour l'abolition de l'esclavage founded in 1834 had little impact; as one abolitionist noted in 1844, "until now it has done little, and it seems to accomplish even less as it ages."[71] The abolitionist director of the colonies in the naval ministry concluded in 1848 that French abolitionism had never been affected by the enthusiasm that, for instance, had supported British abolitionism. The press had generally ignored slavery as an issue, and abolitionism had remained the monopoly "of a close-knit circle that was called in derision 'negrophile.'"[72]

In England the fervent evangelicalism of the abolitionist leaders helped shape a popular movement; in France the abolitionist appeal was grounded "in the principles of natural law, in the ideals of reason and the maxims of justice, in the sentiments of humanity and national honor." A French abolitionist argued that these ideas were less potent than the religious appeal of evangelicalism in England for a public acquainted with the Scriptures.[73] Abbé Grégoire, in comparing the two movements, pointed to the continuity of abolitionism in England and the fitful, interrupted character of the movement in France. He seems to have attributed these differences to differences in national character: the English were serious-minded, the French prone to lose interest in even the most important enterprises.[74] The political and social convictions of the two movements have also been compared. In England abolitionists upheld the social order; although the anti-Jacobin sentiment in the 1790s hurt them, they were able to survive as a movement. In France the abolitionists were also wise upholders of the social order; like their English counterparts, they believed in the possibility (and certainly the desirability) of using existing institutions to bring about a gradual improvement in the lot of the slave and, finally, emancipation. But the political climate in France changed far more radically than that in England. True, the Whig abolitionists were out of favor in England in the 1790s, but opposition to them took minor forms, compared with the manner in which the various French regimes, from 1793 to 1830, treated liberals, including those who were members of the abolitionist movements. The different political climates in which the British and the French abolitionists had to function help explain in part the different fates of the two movements.[75]

The very comparison of French abolitionism with the British movement suggests another reason for the French failure: the French movement was seen as but the offshoot of its British counterpart and was regarded with great suspicion. England, it was argued, could perhaps afford to free its slaves; after all, it had other sources of colonial sugar, such as India. Moreover, the British West Indies were seen as already depleted and unable to compete with the French colonies. Thus abolition, the argument ran, would hurt France and give Britain a relative advantage.[76] French abolitionism was tainted by collaboration with "perfidious Albion." The intellectual dependence of French abolitionism on England was historically true; the Société des amis des noirs had been founded to emulate its London counterpart, and the revival of abolitionism in the 1820s was largely due to the influence of Wilberforce and Clarkson. French abolitionism was never able to free itself from its historical origins. The repeated efforts of French abolitionists to claim originality for their cause were attempts to defend themselves against the repeated accusation of being little more than British agents.[77]

The marginality of abolitionism was revealed in its membership. The largest single group represented an equally marginal sector of French society—the Protestant community. The Protestant-dominated Société de la morale chrétienne, launched after Napoleon's fall, combatted the slave trade, but was at first somewhat reluctant to take on slavery; finally, in 1834, it unequivocally did so. At the news of British abolition in 1833, Broglie, Hippolyte, Passy, Odilon Barrot, and Isambert, who were members of both the Chamber of Deputies and the Société, founded the Société pour l'abolition de l'esclavage[78] and, essentially, led the fight against slavery in the Chamber of Deputies. Of course, many non-Protestants also were involved in the abolitionist movement. Considering their small number in France, however, Protestants played a disproportionate role in various humanitarian endeavors.

The Société de la morale chrétienne had several commissions dealing with various social problems; slavery was but one

of them. Although it opposed the most regressive features in
the Restoration, the Société was essentially conservative; it
proclaimed as its goals "To come to the aid of the unfortunate,
to spread in the lower classes of society practical knowledge
that will help them in the conduct of their lives . . . support
the established institutions in the great tasks of suppressing
crime and vice."[79] The Société was interested in implementing
change, but was just as concerned with preserving the established order of society. It announced that, while the lower
classes had improved their lot politically and economically
since the Revolution, they had failed to evolve morally. The
best cure was religion: "Nothing commands the multitude as
much as the knowledge and authority of divine precepts."[80]
The spread of religion, it was reasoned, would keep the masses
under control, but in the meantime reforms would also have to
be introduced; by establishing a rational and humane order,
the authorities would gain and deserve the respect of the
masses.

In their view of the world, members of the Société de la
morale chrétienne tended to be in tune with current economic
developments. They were economic liberals, believing in the
need to allow the free market to regulate itself. They opposed
gambling because it distracted the workers from the necessity
of labor. And that is also why slavery as a means of production
shocked the members of the Société, for it was the opposite of
free labor and free capital—the bases of liberal economics.

Protestants played an important role in the French economy
and were imbued with a strong, Calvinist work ethic. Having
suffered from state persecutions in the past, the Protestants
were especially eager upholders of liberalism, including its
economic program. This is not to deny that they also opposed
slavery because of its inhumanity. Their philanthropy was
genuine enough; the members of the Société de la morale
chrétienne attempted also to improve the lot of the workers in
France. A significant difference, however, suggests itself: in
regard to the evils of slavery, the members advocated not an
improvement in the condition of the slave, but rather the
abolition of the institution that held him in bondage, while,
in regard to the evils of industrial capitalism in Europe,

they suggested not its abolition, but rather a program of amelioration.

Not only economics but also theology explains why Protestants played such an important role in French abolitionism. According to Calvinist doctrine, salvation occurred only by divine grace, and good works were the outward sign of this grace. Protestants had a unique feeling of personal responsibility for their salvation; they especially felt it important not to be complacent in the face of human evil.[81] Such ideas very much paralleled those of British reform movements, and, indeed, the Société de la morale chrétienne had considerable contact with British abolitionist circles. The Société felt that Protestants were especially blessed "by the union of enlightenment with liberty and a return to the pure and fervent zeal of primitive Christianity."[82] The members of the Société were openly sympathetic to the reform-minded evangelicals in England; they shared the same religion. They probably saw the evangelicals as their English equivalents, for, like the Protestants in France, they were in opposition to the majority religion and had fought for the right of individual conscience. The leadership of British evangelical reform groups such as the abolitionists tended to belong to a rather exclusive social milieu, again giving the impression of a common interest. This feeling of kinship with the English explains the willingness of the Société to borrow many ideas from across the Channel. But the Société did not share the same impact. In France antislavery never became a major cause. The weakness of the movement and the ambiguity of its views on freeing the blacks affected the debate on emancipation.

Whereas the July Monarchy had been preparing for eventual emancipation, the Revolution of 1848 brought to power liberals who were sympathetic to immediate abolition. The revolutionary government appointed Schoelcher as undersecretary of colonies; he issued an emancipation proclamation to free the slaves within two months and to give them the rights of French citizens.

*Racial Society in the Nineteenth Century
in the French West Indies*

The status of freedmen was affected by the persistence of slavery in the French West Indies until 1848. The Restoration had been committed to colonial slavery and therefore continued the system of racial discrimination thought to be the necessary underpinning of slavery. The Napoleonic legislation, forbidding blacks to enter France, was kept in force; a ministerial instruction of August 5, 1818, renewed the provision forbidding whites to be accompanied by their black or colored servants to France.[83] In the Antilles efforts at racial separation continued. In 1820 the governor of Martinique, François Donzelot, suggested to Paris a law of seventy-two articles that would verify the title of liberty of persons of color and would make it impossible for them to continue "passing." The law would have thrown back into slavery those families who were unable to prove, for one reason or another, that they had been legally freed; it would have caused such unrest on the island that the Ministry of Marine refused to sanction it.[84]

The white settlers were as adamant as ever in favor of a segregated society: "The whites will never consent to see themselves made the equals of the mulattoes, some . . . of whom have close relatives working in our mills. . . . No matter how little one changes the laws, the colonial system would be undermined. . . ."[85] In Guadeloupe the civil commissioner of Pointe-à-Pitre, the capital, sent troops into a church to ensure that whites and coloreds sat in separate pews. Some of the old laws on racial segregation were not enforced, but many remained, such as those denying freedmen entry into the liberal professions and those promulgating other forms of social and political ostracism. What made the condition of the coloreds more difficult to accept was their comparatively better condition in the independent nation of Haiti, where they ruled themselves, the civil rights acquired by freedmen in the Spanish and British colonies, and the political rights in the latter.[86] In 1823 in Martinique, settlers panicked at rumors of a plot by freed blacks; the purported ringleader of this nonexistent movement, the aforementioned Bissette, was unjustly seized, branded, and sent to the galleys.[87] Eventually the ruling was overturned by a higher court in France, but the incident was a good indication of the continuation of discrimination and hostility against nonwhites in the French colonies. In Guadeloupe the regulation of June 1, 1827, reaffirmed that the punishments for crimes depended upon the race of the criminal.[88] Racial abuses were not limited to the colonies; the metropolitan administration, sympathetic to the planters and their interests, encouraged racial inequality. The governor of Martinique was told in 1824 to maintain the respect of blacks for whites, "for that alone ensures that 80,000 blacks are held in slavery by 10,000 whites." And he was told to ensure that slaves not be dealt with too leniently.[89] The minister of the navy and colonies, the Duke de Clermont-Tonnerre, distrusted the freedmen, seeing them as a source of danger. He opposed granting them political rights, wondered if even generations of freedom would prepare them to enjoy full civil rights, and attempted to confine them to nonurban areas in the slave colonies. The minister did everything possible to allay the fears of the planter class by maintaining the caste system: when his reception of a man of color at a social function caused alarm among the white planters, he assured them that it had happened inadvertently.[90]

With the advent of the July Monarchy, the relationship of race and slavery was perceived in a different light. Minister of the navy and colonies Sebastiani wrote in September 1830 that the best way to preserve slavery was to win the support of free men of color and to make them auxiliaries of white power.[91] The July Monarchy favored a gradual phasing out of slavery and therefore passed legislation to liberalize race relations. In 1848 emancipation legally assured all former slaves and their descendants the full rights of Frenchmen, but considerable time elapsed before blacks in the French Antilles gained a dominant political voice in the selection of deputies. Educational and economic disabilities made the blacks second-class citizens. In Martinique in 1881, Schoelcher discovered that out of 138 government officials, 99 were white, 38 were colored, and ı was black—a policeman.[92] The prejudice of the white settlers continued, and Schoelcher spent much of his later life combatting the racist myths spread by white-controlled newspapers in the Antilles. A generation after slavery had been abolished, slavery and the racial inferiority of blacks were still extolled by certain white groups.[93]

Nineteenth-Century Abolitionism and the Blacks

Schoelcher adamantly insisted on full civic rights for the newly emancipated slaves in the West Indies, but not all abolitionists shared his convictions. Their reluctance to extend full civic rights was due to their ambivalent attitude toward blacks. They thought that blacks should not be slaves, but they were unwilling to admit them to equality. Their attitudes changed little after emancipation. Thus the belief in black inferiority was not just a system of thought upholding the slave system, but rather a far more persistent belief, which was maintained by many abolitionists even after 1848. For instance, Augustin Cochin, a Protestant abolitionist whose history of abolitionism maintained that the success of the movement was the victory of humanity, nevertheless saw Africans in their homeland as a barbarous people bereft of any civilization, as an "inferior race."[94]

The reception of Harriet Beecher Stowe's *Uncle Tom's Cabin* was symptomatic of the prevalence of such attitudes among other abolitionists. The translation triumphed in France. Lucas wrote, "In the first few months of 1853 one had only to advertise a 'black' play to attract a crowd." At the cattle show of Poissy, the winner was a bull named Uncle Tom; among its competitors were Saint-Clair and Shelby.[95] Despite the sentimentalizing, however, the racist opinions of the mid-nineteenth century dominated the same people who wept over Uncle Tom's misfortunes. For instance, in reviewing *Uncle Tom's Cabin,* the literary critic Théophile Gautier declared slavery a means of civilizing the black race, even though he did not wish to justify the institution. Another critic, while agreeing that slavery was an unjust institution, found blacks to be insensitive and incapable of suffering; they were "as stupid as a

LES PHILANTROPES DU JOUR.

Je t'ai déja défendu de m'appeler maître ... apprend que tous les hommes sont frères animal

Honoré Daumier satirizing the abolitionists: "I have forbidden you to call me Master. Know that all men are brothers, animal!" (1844). *Löys Delteil*, Les Peintres graveurs, *23 (Paris, 1926), no. 1303.*

goose."[96] Harriet Beecher Stowe has been taken to task for her "paternalistic" attitude toward blacks and her failure to understand the responsibility of slavery for the degradation of blacks; the "good" blacks were the submissive ones, and blacks not so inclined were depicted negatively.[97] Yet the interesting fact is that the French admirers of Harriet Beecher Stowe felt that she had gone too far in her Negrophilia. Slavery had not caused blacks to become degenerate, declared Alfred Michiels, Stowe's abolitionist translator, but rather it had civilized them. If one were to look at blacks in their natural habitat, in Africa, "far from all European influence," one would discover them to be

> the most stupid, the most perverse, the most bloodthirsty of all human races. It [the black race] is reduced to eternal immobility: no progress, no invention, no desire for knowledge, no pity, no moral sentiment. . . . The black color, the color of darkness, is truly the sign of depravity.[98]

Despite some efforts to rehabilitate the blacks' image, abolitionists as a group were not enthusiastic upholders of racial equality. Their reservations were not due solely to their ambivalence about the institution of slavery; even after abolition in 1848, they continued to share with their contemporaries a generally low opinion of Africans. Honoré Daumier revealed the psychology of many abolitionists when, in a cartoon drawn in 1844, he showed an abolitionist giving a black slave a violent kick in the behind while yelling at him, "I have already forbidden you the right to call me 'master.' . . . Know that all men are brothers, animal!"[99]

8

Scientific Racism

The Continuation of Some Eighteenth-Century Themes

In the first half of the nineteenth century, attitudes toward non-European peoples were influenced by two trends of thought that remained unresolved at the end of the eighteenth century. The first was evolutionist and saw non-European peoples as having differing cultures and civilizations because of environmental factors, but also as being destined to evolve eventually along lines similar to those of Europe. The second was racist and saw the destiny of peoples as shaped by their racial makeup; in this view biology, not environment, was the determinant. By the mid-nineteenth century, the racist view had triumphed. In an era worshipping scientism, the claims racism made of being supported by the findings of science furthered its spread and rooted it firmly in French culture.

The eighteenth-century evolutionary view, which lasted in some cases into the nineteenth century, was a convenient way to account for the humanity of non-Europeans and yet to explain their differences. Africans were viewed as living in an era similar to that of the European Middle Ages. Just as Europe had made progress since then, Africa too would evolve.[1] The analogy made clear that Africans were not doomed to inferiority, but by no means did those who espoused this view see Africans as equal to Europeans, for, occupying a stage of development like that of an earlier Europe, Africans were, in this view, inferior. Grégoire called them barbarians. The history of human progress implied that Europeans had been less perfect in a preceding era; as the important social thinker Henri de Saint-Simon put it, there was a chain of development from "the first men who were necessarily the most ignorant of all until the Europeans of today who, in regard to their civili-

210

zation and scientific knowledge, have infinitely surpassed the peoples who preceded them."[2]

The Africans' failure to develop according to the European pattern was attributed by egalitarians mostly to the forces of environment.[3] But environmentalism asserted that people who lived in different climes—that is, who were subject to different environmental forces—were not the same. The geographers Malte-Brun and Walckenaer suggested that, because Africans lived in a hot climate with fertile soil, they did not have to concern themselves with either planting food or using clothing. The lack of challenge, according to Walckenaer, created a people "forgetful of the past, content with the present and without worries for the future." Malte-Brun was more severe and wrote that the absence of appropriate challenges meant that Africans were not incited to be either industrious or intelligent. The *Magasin pittoresque* announced that the benign climate condemned Africans to "eternal infancy."[4] Whereas, in the seventeenth and eighteenth centuries, it had been common to ascribe the Africans' condition to the severity of their surroundings, in the nineteenth century, nature was viewed as benign. If a society was unregenerative, it was because it had taken advantage of the riches of nature and fallen into sloth. Europe was blessed because it was forced to toil for its subsistence. The work ethic had become so highly valued in the developing industrial society of the nineteenth century that those deprived of the ethic were thought condemned to inferiority. Environmentalists, attributing the Africans' condition not to innate causes but to climate, thus agreed with racists on black inferiority.

Environmentalism itself had taken a new course. In the eighteenth century, people were seen as changing quickly in response to climate; in the nineteenth century, such transformations were seen as slow. Jean-Baptiste Lamarck emphasized environment, which formed and shaped organisms, but proclaimed that characteristics shaped by environment were hereditary and that only over millennia could they be changed. Thus, although the blacks' physique and other attributes deemed inferior to the whites' were attributed to the forces of climate, they now were viewed also as inherited characteristics.[5]

Biological Paradigms and Racism

Toward the end of the eighteenth century, biological racism emerged in a coherent fashion. Although Africans were considered inferior, they were still thought to be capable of evolving physically and, hence, of rising in their social and intellectual accomplishments as well. While never giving up the possibility of physical evolution, nineteenth-century French thinkers strengthened the notion that physical differences were the dominant cause for the different civilizations of the various races, and their view of the future evolution of man was less optimistic than that of the preceding century: the proclaimed inequality of man was to last not for a few generations, as the Enlightenment had thought, but rather for millennia, if not for eternity. In the eighteenth century, the possibility that the evolution of the earth had occurred within the span of 6,000 years or so (an idea derived from the Bible) was still widely accepted. Buffon had posited that the earth might be 50,000 years old, and Voltaire had even suggested that it might date back millions of years, but they had advanced no proof for their claims. By the early nineteenth century, however, the findings of geologists and biologists made it necessary to accept an age for the earth and its creatures beyond what Voltaire had even playfully suggested. The geographer Malte-Brun proclaimed that, if blacks had descended from whites, "it must have taken millions of years to allow the repeated action of the climate to create hereditary black color."[6] One could no longer predict that within a generation or two blacks would turn white and would also change socially and intellectually. Thus, the racism that had emerged in the eighteenth century became in the nineteenth century more deterministic and less flexible; no longer was the physical evolution of blacks seen as a possible solution to their "innate" racial inferiority.

The overriding theme in the eighteenth century was universalism, the brotherhood of man; the nineteenth century was an era of fragmentation. Contemporaries of the revolutionary upheavals saw one civilization collapse and a new order emerge.

It now became common to think of man as having not one civilization but many. The idea of a common human destiny suffered an irreparable blow.[7] The forces of nationalism released by the revolutionary wars stressed the particular at the cost of the universal. So did romanticism. The romantics shunned uniformity and upheld the particular genius and nature of individuals and whole peoples. The romantics believed also that individuals and groups were endowed with innate qualities that determined their destinies. Romanticism thus underscored the movement toward racism in the nineteenth century; it should not, however, be considered its cause. More important was the stress on materialism that had led to biologism in the later part of the Enlightenment.

If eighteenth-century thinkers had seen nature as giving man certain laws by which he should lead his life, nineteenth-century thinkers regarded nature as having a life force of its own. If eighteenth-century thinkers relied on paradigms borrowed from physics, the discipline that made such great headway after Newton, thinkers in the following century looked to biology and borrowed from its lexicon. In trying to understand the differences among human societies, nineteenth-century thinkers employed biology as an explanation. This transformation in thought helped shape the changing anthropology.

Prior to the nineteenth century, a large number of factors were stressed to show the differences between African and European societies. And yet the differences—real or perceived—between the two worlds were not so dramatically distant as they became in the nineteenth century, the climax of Euro-African contact. If, in an earlier period, it had been the Africans' religion, marriage, or social institutions that had shocked Europeans, it was now the Africans' political and material culture. Europe had witnessed a massive political mobilization and a considerable evolution in state structures as a result of the revolutionary wars, as well as an unprecedented growth in the material culture as a result of the industrial revolution. The change in material conditions seemed to create a chasm between Europe and the non-European world. A people's greatness was increasingly measured by its technological achievements, and Europeans began to see material progress as the province of the white race; technological backwardness was identified with other races.

Henri de Saint-Simon wrote that the superiority of a nation was indicated by its military and scientific accomplishments.[8] The lack of such developments in Africa proved African inferiority to Europeans. Africa, wrote the medical doctor Virey, lacked artistic works, organized religion, political systems, and developed languages. Africans had "remained brutish and savage while the other peoples of the earth have more or less embraced the noble career of social perfection." The spread of European power around the globe was a sign of the superiority of the white race: "everywhere it has shown itself to be the most intellectual and industrious." But blacks had "not made known their existence by remarkable works, by superior monuments in the political field, literature, science or industry. . . . it ignores glory." The enslavement of blacks was a sign of their stupidity, for they allowed themselves to "be duped, enchained and sold even by men less strong."[9] Courtet de l'Isle, a reader of Virey and a Saint-Simonian, also asserted that the success of the European slave raiders in Africa was a sign of their "incontestable superiority."

White superiority was so deeply ingrained in the racist thinking of the early nineteenth century that all cultural achievements were credited to whites. Thus, the accomplishments of Chinese and Japanese cultures—state structures and written traditions that Europeans respected because of their outward similarity to European institutions—were attributed to earlier, European influences. The racial explanation for the rise and fall of civilizations did not have to wait for Count Gobineau in the mid-nineteenth century; as early as 1814, Peyroux de la Coudrenière stated that ancient Greece declined because it had become racially impure, mixing its blood with that of blacks.[10]

The increasingly refined means of defining human races that had developed in the eighteenth century led to the notion that races were significant human divisions. Some early classifiers such as Buffon had made clear that the classification of certain groups, races, and subspecies was done for the convenience of the observer and had no intrinsic value, but this was soon forgotten, even by Buffon himself. Instead, it was thought that races were significant biological divisions of humanity and that race, in turn, had profound effects on the social, political, and other collective achievements of the group making up a particular race.

Saint-Simon hoped to find in biology a clue to human variation; science, he was sure, would unlock the mysteries of human societies. And, in the works of contemporary physiologists, Saint-Simon found confirmed the doctrines of racial inequality. Blacks were at different levels of civilization, Saint-Simon stated, because they were biologically inferior to whites. Auguste Comte, the influential founder of positivism and originally a disciple of Saint-Simon, thought that the superiority of European material culture over that of other continents might be due to a difference in the brain structure of whites.[11]

The Ascendance of Race Thinking

In the nineteenth century, race became the main explanation of human variety. The tradition of attributing social differences between the nobility and the third estate to descent from distinctive "racial" groups was already evident in France in the sixteenth century; it continued in the nineteenth century. The Restoration in 1814 and the reassertion of aristocratic privilege brought a revival of racial doctrines as the explanation for domestic history. Historians were particularly drawn to this explanation. François Guizot, looking back at the French Revolution, declared it to have been a struggle between the aristocratic Franks and the commoners, the Gauls, a "war between nations." Augustin Thierry's history of England interpreted all divisions and cleavages among the English people since the Norman conquest as a racial split between Normans and Anglo-Saxons. Ever since its early history, France too had been divided by the conflict between the civilized Gallo-Romans, on the one hand, and the Frankish barbarians on the other. Augustin's brother, Amedée, also wrote of French history as the history of racial strife. Jules Michelet described the French provinces as the creation of different races. The superiority of France over other nations, Michelet argued, was founded upon a unique racial mix of the Celtic and the Roman elements, which made it fit to serve as a model for the world;[12] France's intellectual and political pre-eminence was racially determined. These liberal historians attacked the aristocratic thesis of the civilizing influence of the Germanic invasions, describing the Franks instead as barbaric. And while the argument of the nobles had emphasized purity of blood, the liberals spoke of race mixtures. But even in this attenuated form, some liberals reinforced the belief in race as the determinant of human destiny.

What environment had been in the eighteenth century, race was in the nineteenth—the key to understanding human variety at home and abroad. French middle-class commentators viewed the poor, underprivileged classes in the country and in the cities as forming a different race; the color of their skin, the shape of their skulls, and their innate intellectual capacities were seen as fundamentally different from those of their more fortunate fellow citizens. Biology had condemned the lower classes to their position in society. Lamartine declared, "The more I have traveled, the more convinced I have become that the races are the great secret of history and morals." Hippolyte Taine, in writing his literary studies, resorted to race and physiology as explanations for differences among national literatures and even among the works of individual authors.[13]

In the 1820s and 1830s, the Saint-Simonian Courtet de l'Isle, who, until recently rediscovered by Jean Boissel, had been ignored by intellectual historians, reflected the racial thought of his era in an important way. He declared that "man differs in his faculties and native abilities according to his race . . ." and that the inequality of human groups had an impact on the fate of nations: as their racial stock "improved," so did their power and achievements. (In many of his formulations, Courtet anticipated Gobineau by a generation, and Boissel has suggested that several passages in the works of both men are so closely parallel that one might suspect Gobineau of virtual plagiarism.) Race, as a commentator in the *Revue des deux mondes* pointed out in 1848, had, as never before, become a subject of study and interest to educated men.[14]

The mid-nineteenth century was an age of synthesis: if Karl Marx provided a synthesis in economics, and Darwin one in biology, Arthur de Gobineau, in his *Essai sur l'inégalité des races humaines,* published between 1853 and 1855, conveniently synthesized French thought on race. Gobineau was rarely read in France; the second edition of his book did not appear until 1884. Often depicted as somewhat of a crank at odds with his times, Gobineau nonetheless faithfully reflected the ideas on race of his predecessors and contemporaries. He was an unsuccessful novelist and minor diplomat, an extraordinarily ambitious individual who wanted to set a mark on his age. Politically his family was legitimist, and, seeing all that was pure and worthy as represented by the aristocracy, he identified with the nobility in eclipse, going so far as to add to his name in 1855 the title of count. In his espousal of the legitimist and noble cause, he turned to the racial explanation for the social classes of France, using arguments borrowed from Boulainvilliers—although he strenuously attacked his eighteenth-century predecessor.[15] From having made the claim that nobility had a separate biological lineage apart from the multitude, he developed later in his *Essai* the argument that, because human racial groups were biologically different, they were endowed with different capacities, fated for a different destiny.

As has been pointed out in recent studies, Gobineau's racial thought was largely motivated by a romantic notion about the decadence of civilization.[16] His emphasis on race as a hidden force motivating human history was a romantic revolt against the positivist view of life, which was based on materialism. This latter view was essentially optimistic and saw in the economic progress of Europe a source of confidence; Gobineau's was a pessimistic vision. Unbeknown to the world, he wrote, the real forces in history were not material but racial: "the ethnic question dominates all other problems of history and is the key to it."[17] As races would not be able to remain hermetically sealed from each other, he pointed out, they would mix. In the end, Gobineau gloomily predicted, European civilization, which had been so carefully built, would collapse as a result of racial impurity. Magnifying Gobineau's tragic vision was his belief that race-mixing was necessary for the creation of civilization; the artistic abilities of the blacks were necessary to fertilize the European imagination. But this miscegenation, the very bearer of progress, carried in itself the seeds of destruction. While race-mixing improved the racial stock of the "inferior races" and produced the creativity of the higher ones, it undermined the latter. The higher races "have been lowered, and it is an evil that nothing can compensate, or repair."[18] Thus mankind was doomed; race-mixing would continue and, in the end, the civilizing white race would be so "contaminated" that it would be incapable of sustaining civilization. Although the theme of decadence underpins Gobineau's writings, his *Essai* remains the most comprehensive statement on and the master synthesis of nineteenth-century French racial thought.

That the racism Gobineau expressed was part of the general cultural pattern of nineteenth-century France may be seen in the extent to which views similar to his were expressed in the dictionaries and encyclopedias of the period. Lexicographers, usually cautious in writing their entries, reflect the consensus of their contemporaries. With rare exceptions, French dictionaries throughout the nineteenth century reflected a strong racist bias against the black man.[19]

Science and Race

The developing emphasis on race might be seen in the experience of the Société ethnologique, founded in Paris in 1839 by the Englishman William Frederic Edwards. Edwards served as the first president, the geographer Avézac as vice-president, and the Saint-Simonian Gustave d'Eichtal as secretary. Among the founding members were Courtet de l'Isle, the historian Michelet, the geographers Bertholet and Amedée Jaubert, and the naturalist Isidore Geoffroy Saint-Hilaire. The Société ethnologique's membership was as varied as its purpose was broad—to study "the physical organization, the intellectual and moral character, the languages and historical traditions" of various peoples. In this sense, the Société was very modern in its outlook on the role of ethnology; however, it saw all these aspects as "the principle elements that distinguish human races." The main aim of the Société was to study race and racial variety, and its view that the social organization, language, and history of a people both confirmed and resulted from racial variety was typical of the thought of the period.

The Société ethnologique became deeply involved in the debate on slavery. When slavery was abolished in 1848, the Société—as if it had no more reason for existence—stopped meeting. Failing in France, it had nevertheless stimulated the founding of similar societies in London in 1844 and in New York shortly thereafter.[20] Even before its demise, however, the Société was overshadowed by new trends toward racism that it had contributed to creating. As variations of human culture were increasingly viewed as a function of race, the physical differences of various races received greater attention and were delineated with what was purported to be descriptive accuracy. Yet, while concerned mainly with race, the practitioners of ethnology nonetheless described all aspects of non-European man; ethnology was considered impressionistic and imprecise. The newly emerging discipline of anthropology, however, concerned itself nearly exclusively with "the study of man considered from the point of view of the physical." It was asserted that the physical aspects of humans dictated their behavior. Ever since the end of the eighteenth century, the French word "anthropologie" had signified an emphasis on physiology; the term had been introduced into French in 1788 by Alexandre Chavanne in his book *Anthropologie, ou science de l'homme.* Virey had described an anthropologist as someone who measured the skulls of human races. In France, more than in any other country, anthropology took a definitive turn toward physical anthropology.[21]

In France physiological studies made major strides at the end of the eighteenth century; they far outdistanced comparable work in England. A galaxy of prominent physiologists, from Cabanis in the 1780s to Flourens in the 1840s, inspired great fascination with physiology, which in turn affected the study of anthropology in France. The physiological structures of races were seen as determining their fates. In England the emphasis on the physiological was to come much later, only toward the end of the nineteenth century. The reluctance of British theorists to adopt physical anthropology was due to their background in moral philosophy, whereas the French were strongly grounded in natural philosophy.[22] The strong moral bias in British anthropology derived from antislavery opinion; in France antislavery opinion was less powerful and did not influence the scientific community. Because of their desire to establish a pure science (essentially meaning freedom from religious influences), French scientists had a deep suspicion of any moral constraints on their work. The doctrines of race, they thought, were proven by the methods of "science."

Scientific racism was given an institutional locus with the founding of the Société d'anthropologie de Paris in 1859. Its orientation was shaped by the French tradition of biologism, and by the Société's own origins and membership. It emerged in 1859 as a result of a split in the biological community; its first members were thus biologists. Of the 19 founding members, 16 were physicians. Two years later, when the membership had expanded to 99, 73 were doctors. In the next half-century, there was a gradual reduction in the number of physicians, but in 1909, 51 percent of the 1,102 members were still medical doctors.[23] The presence of so many doctors in the anthropological society reinforced the emphasis on physical anthropology and stifled the possibility of a vigorous ethnological interest that would have emphasized the study of cultures. Biologism, in turn, led to what one critic called "skeletomania," an emphasis on measuring physical features of non-European peoples, with little interest in studying their cultures.[24]

The stress on physical anthropology led to a very serious neglect of ethnography, putting France at a disadvantage in this field, compared with England, Germany, and, especially, the United States. On the eve of the First World War, this gap was noted by one of the earliest French cultural anthropologists, Marcel Mauss, and the historian of French popular culture, A. Van Gennep. They thought that this neglect was due to the lack of government support for ethnographical research and to what they called "the state of mind" of French scientists.[25] Books and articles about non-European peoples were offered by travelers, colonial administrators, and missionaries, but not by the scientific community. Physical anthropology, as a science, had dwarfed and, to all intents and purposes, extinguished ethnographical research.[26] The scientific study of non-European peoples was thus limited to observing the ways in which they physically varied from Europeans. And the French scientific community announced that it was the differences in physique that determined the differences in religion, political systems, and mores.

Physiognomics

The age-old view that the body was the externalization of the soul, an indication of a person's virtues and vices, was strengthened at the end of the eighteenth century. The important advances in anatomical studies showed how various organs of the human body affected each other, and demonstrated the impact of body functions on human behavior. The medical doctor and physiologist Georges Cabanis wrote of the influence of the body on the soul.[27] Since races varied in their physical attributes, it seemed logical that physical differences would lead to intellectual and moral variation too. As Bory de Saint-Vincent put it, the species of men "differed by body structure and their inner structure" and intellectual faculties, which together determined "the degree of moral development that each man may be able to attain."[28] The physical determinants of race included color. The Africans' dark skin continued to intrigue Europeans, who regarded it as a significant sign of the blacks' position in the human family.

The color black continued to have a negative meaning in Western culture. Romanticism, in fact, tended to strengthen the emphasis on the symbolism of the color black. In 1837 the diplomat and historian Frédéric Portal wrote a highly influential book on the symbolism of colors, in which he pointed out the role that black, for instance, played:

> Symbol of evil and falsity, black is not a color, but rather the negation of all nuances and what they represent. Red represents divine love, but black represents infernal love, egotism, hatred and all the passions of degraded man.

... black is [the symbol] of error, of nothingness ... black is the negation of light, it has been attributed to the author of all evil and falsity.

Basing himself on Portal, de Montabert wrote a manual for artists that developed the contrasts between white and black:

White is the symbol of Divinity or God;
Black is the symbol of the evil spirit or the demon.
White is the symbol of light ... ;
Black is the symbol of darkness and darkness expresses all evils.
White is the emblem of harmony;
Black is the emblem of chaos.
White signifies supreme beauty;
Black ugliness.
White signifies perfection;
Black signifies vice.
White is the symbol of innocence;
Black, that of guilt, sin, and moral degradation.
White, a positive color, indicates happiness;
Black, a negative color, indicates misfortune.
The battle between good and evil is symbolically expressed
By the opposition of white and black.

Colors were regarded not as mere symbols, but as the outward manifestation of an object's (or a person's) value. Goethe announced that the superiority of the white race and the inferiority of the black were certainties, for the fact that color "had relation with the differences of character is beyond question."[29] The extent to which the blacks' color was seen as the sign of negative forces may be gauged in the comment by the utopian socialist Charles Fourier, that when blacks would live in harmony, as a result of being "in harmonious rapport with mankind," they would be bleached rather than tanned by the sun. Thus the Africans' blackness indicated some disturbance in the harmony of nature or human relationships. Black civilization was judged to be rising only as blacks changed in physical types and approached that of the whites; it was natural for De Staël, in her play Mirza, to ascribe nobility to her black hero by depriving him of his Negroid features. The same was true of Victor Hugo's Bug Jargal; his nobility was accentuated by his not having a very black and prognathic face. Hugo was an egalitarian who agitated for the emancipation of the slaves and carried on a friendly correspondence with Haitian intellectuals, but he definitely had his aesthetic preferences. In asserting human equality, he wrote to one of his Haitian correspondents that "in front of God, all souls are white."[30] Abbé Grégoire argued in vain against the prejudices of his contemporaries, pointing out that appreciation of color was a relative judgment and that there was no reason to assign an innate inferiority to the color black—in Africa it was the white color that was abhorred. Baron Roger, a friend of Grégoire and former governor of Senegal, shared his outrage at the prejudice against dark-skinned peoples: "Of the thousands of human follies, I have known none more ridiculous, nor more contemptible than that which judges men by the color of their skin." It was, Roger wrote, a "malady of the European spirit." But Roger's fight against white prejudice was futile; his was a minority view. The geographer Jomard, reviewing his friend Roger's novel, concluded that the governor's Negrophilia was "not in accordance [with the view] of most writers."[31]

Despite the long history of French contact with Africa, some Frenchmen, especially the relatively uneducated, suffered a deep cultural shock at suddenly being confronted by black humanity. A member of the teaching order in Senegal, the Frères de Ploermel, wrote to his superior in 1866, "You cannot imagine my surprise when in entering my class for the first time, I saw little children black as bats . . . I could not believe my eyes."[32] Upon landing in Senegal, Julien Viaud, the naval officer who wrote novels under the pen name Pierre Loti, seems also to have been deeply shocked by the black color of the inhabitants; in his novel *Roman d'un spahi,* published in 1881, which deals with Senegal, he mentioned the color black 130 times, revealing the extent to which the Africans' skin color haunted him.[33]

Scientists' attention, however, was directed less at skin color than at the shape of the human face and skull.[34] Theories of physiognomy, which had been so successful in France, focused on the relation of different facial shapes and racial destinies. In nineteenth-century France, the emphasis on head shape was in large part due to the influence of Franz Gall, who has been called by some "the father of phrenology," although he himself never used the term, instead calling his discipline cranioscopy.

Phrenology

Although ideas connected with phrenology had existed ever since the classical age, Franz Josef Gall, a German physician at the turn of the nineteenth century, systemized them. He argued that the main organ of man was the brain and that the back of the head gave a measure of the brain, for "one can recognize different dispositions and inclinations by protuberances or depressions on the head or cranium." In medicine he had an important influence by directing scientific interest to the study of the brain, but in physical anthropology his ideas were taken as confirmation of Lavater's ideas on physiognomy. Gall and his most orthodox disciples battled in vain against having their theories assimilated into theories of physiognomy. For it was not the whole face, Gall insisted, but rather just the brain cage that was an indicator of human accomplishment.[35] Nevertheless, he was readily confused with Lavater and his ideas; significantly, one of his students, who published his lecture notes in 1802, included in the title the expression "physiognomy."[36] The development of the various parts of the brain determined a person's innate abilities, Gall wrote. It so happened that the cranium shaped itself to conform to the brain, and, according to Gall's theory, by feeling the head, one could discover which parts of the brain were the most developed and thus ascertain a person's specific abilities.[37] One part of the brain was the center of love, another of intelligence, third of creativity, and so forth.

Gall's doctrine became popularly known as the study of bumps on people's heads. While Gall focused on individual differences as a function of brain structure, he also speculated on racial differences. And here, curiously, he insisted less on the structures of parts of the brain and spoke more about the sizes of heads and brains; blacks' heads and brains, he asserted, were smaller than those of Europeans. Therefore, he concluded, "generally the Negro is inferior to the European in his intellectual faculties."[38]

Gall was not accepted in French scientific circles (he was to have a dispute with Cuvier, and Napoleon supported the latter), but he was a popular medical practitioner in Paris. He served the Duke Decazes and liberals such as Benjamin Constant, Stendhal, and Saint-Simon.[39] He left a group of devoted disciples; at the time of his death, in 1828, and during the entire July Monarchy, his ideas were especially in vogue. A phrenological society was founded in 1831 to carry forth his ideas.

The pervasiveness in France of phrenological thought was attested by a critic who noted in the early 1840s that the "doctrines of phrenology invade everything." Balzac was influenced by Gall and wrote that Père Goriot's skull contained the bump indicative of a concentration of the attributes of fatherhood. Balzac, like his contemporaries, did not understand the fine distinctions Gall had drawn, and Balzac, too, assimilated him to Lavater and credited Gall with having refined physiognomics. The philosopher and historian Hippolyte Taine also proclaimed a relationship between the shape of a person's skull and his intelligence. Phrenology was employed in politics. When the anarchist thinker Pierre-Joseph Proudhon wanted to dismiss the thought of Fourier, he not only pointed out its weaknesses but also cited his opponent's smaller skull measurements as evidence of an inability to think properly. Fourier's skull, Proudhon sneered, had "dimensions that indicate a mediocre cerebral development."[40]

Gall's ideas were adopted by the Société ethnologique. Edwards, the founder, had announced that the main distinction between the races was "the form of the head and the proportions of the head forms."[41] Head shape not only indicated character, but also formed it. Virey saw in the whole face of both whites and blacks the causes for their attributed differences, as "among us the forehead is pushed forward, the mouth is pulled back as if we were destined to think rather than eat; the Negro has a shortened forehead and a mouth that is pushed forward as if he were made to eat instead of to think." Courtet de l'Isle further observed, "The organs that dominate the head of the Negro are connected with gross instincts, while those that are diminished in size are connected with intellectual powers."[42]

To the professional anthropologists in the 1860s the physique was an external shell indicating internal qualities. At an early meeting of the Société d'anthropologie de Paris, one member declared that "a beautiful race . . . usually has a certain moral superiority." And in the eyes of anthropologists, the European was the norm of beauty, whereas the black was ugly and deformed. Physique, Broca declared, indicated inferiority or superiority: "Prognathism, a more or less black coloring of the skin, wooly hair and intellectual and social inferiority are frequently interconnected. A white skin, straight hair, and non-prognathic face belong ordinarily to the most advanced peoples." Never had a people "with black skin, wooly hair, and prognathic faces been able to lift itself spontaneously to civilization."[43]

It was thought that the further one was removed from the physique of blacks, the closer one was to "genius." Physiognomic theories were so well developed in the Société d'anthropologie that when Broca, the founder, died in 1880, he was depicted in a posthumous portrait as having had a light complexion, blue eyes, and blond hair, even though he had had dark skin, brown eyes, and dark hair.[44]

As early as the eighteenth century, the racial variation in facial shapes was noted, and an attempt had been made to measure these variations. Camper's measurement of facial angles was adopted by a number of naturalists. Virey announced that the white and yellow races had facial angles above eighty-five degrees, whereas the black races had angles between seventy-five and eighty degrees; in fact, he suggested that humanity be divided into two categories: those over eighty-five degrees in facial angle and those below eighty. While he differed slightly from Virey in his measurements, Cuvier concurred that Camper's angles appropriately classified races; he suggested eighty degrees for whites, seventy-five for Mongols, and seventy degrees for blacks. P. P. Broc, a lessknown professor of anatomy, assigned ninety degrees for whites and seventy-five for blacks.[45] The confusion of the naturalists and their disagreement on the measurement for each race gradually discredited the technique. A new measurement was introduced.

André Retzius, a Swede, announced his discovery of essential differences in the skull shape of the various Scandinavian peoples. He presented the very attractive possibilities of expressing statistically, in verifiable measurements, the nature of these differences. The measurements in skull shapes could be expressed, Retzius wrote, as the proportion of the length to the width of the skull. He divided mankind into two categories, the brachycephalic (broadheaded) and the dolichocephalic (longheaded), and proposed that these measurements be combined with Camper's lines for measuring prognathism. Retzius's conclusion was that "since the earliest times the straight facial line has characterized mankind's noblest tribes and those who have been the champions of culture, while prognathism has generally been related to savagery, brutality and paganism."[46] His ideas supported the already existing emphasis on the cranial structure as an indicator and determinant of race and culture.

Retzius's work won wide acceptance in the French scientific community as a result of being championed in the Société d'anthropologie by its president, Broca. He and his disciple Topinard saw, in the ratio of width to length of face, an indicator both of race and of the qualities thought particular to each race; a prognathic head was an indicator of inferiority. By studying human skulls and measuring their prognathism, one could even tell their sex, Topinard stated. Women, who presumably were inferior, were more prognathic than males.

The general size of the head was also an indicator. Isidore Geoffroy Saint-Hilaire found signs of superiority in the developed skull and brain, while developed jaws were a sign of inferiority, of closeness to animality.[47] Intricate displays of the human skull were offered the public. The Museum of Natural History had a skull collection which, one commentator observed, allowed one to "mount or descend the human chain of being." By 1861 the Museum had 1,264 skulls and 117 copies. It was constantly augmenting its collection and, in the short period from 1859 to 1862, added 404 new skulls. In 1877 Broca established a museum of 2,500 skulls.[48]

The skull was thought to tell everything; the Museum of Anthropology in Paris displayed next to each other the plaster

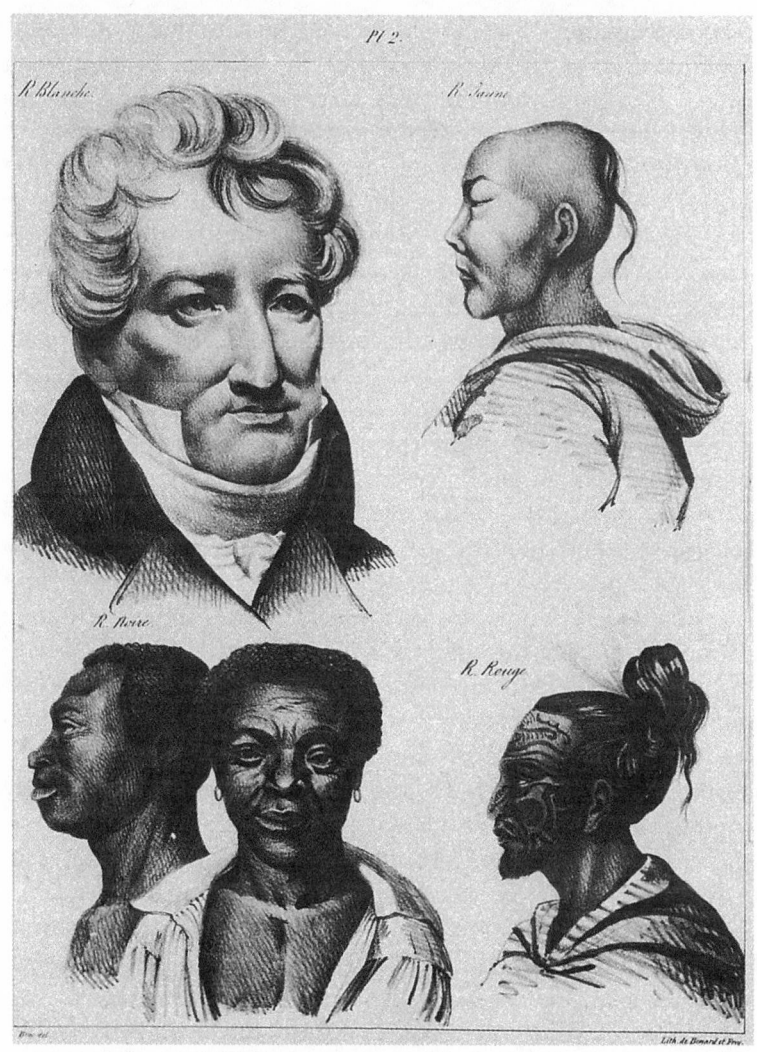

Facial illustration intended to reveal the hierarchy of human
races. *P. P. Broc,* Essai sur les races humaines *(Paris, 1836).*
Photo Bibliothèque nationale, Paris.

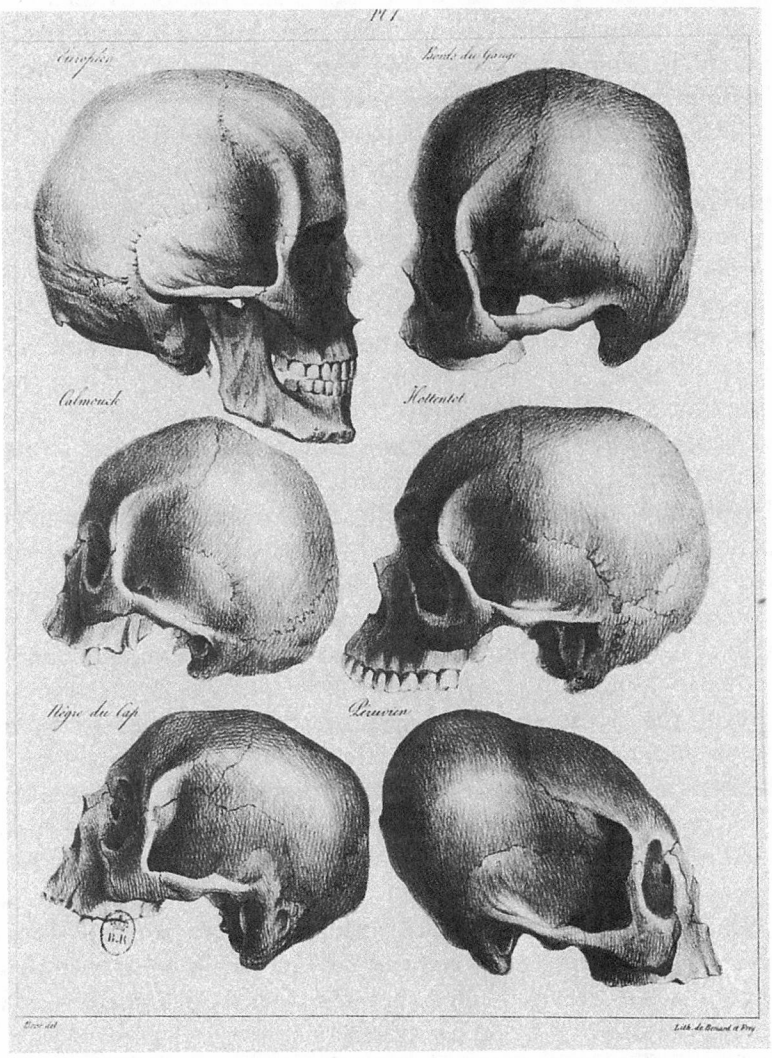

Skull collection intended to reveal the hierarchy of human races. In this scheme the "Peruvian" is considered most distant from the European and closest to the animal.. *P. P. Broc,* Essai sur les races humaines *(Paris, 1836). Photo Bibliothèque nationale, Paris.*

molds of the skull of Sir Walter Scott and that of Lacenaire, a notorious murderer. A view of the two skulls was supposed to be instructive, to explain why one man had turned into a "genius" while the other had become an assassin.[49]

The size of the skull was believed to indicate the size of the brain and, hence, of the intellect. Broca, as a disciple of the phrenologists, measured skulls and proclaimed a 12 percent difference in cranial capacity between the skulls of blacks and of whites, in favor of the latter.[50] Gustave Le Bon, a disciple of Broca and one of the most influential racial sociologists of the late nineteenth century, saw the cranium as an indicator not only of race, but also of sex and even of class. Thus this middle-class, Parisian scientist asserted that his study of skull volumes showed, in descending order, the following strata: first, scientists and men of letters; second, the bourgeois of Paris; third, nobles of old families; fourth, servants; and fifth, peasants.[51] Large skulls indicated a large-sized brain, confirming the law that Le Bon had announced, that "the most voluminous brains belong to the races that are most gifted intellectually and, within each race, to the most intelligent individuals." While the skull was an indicator, the brain was the proof, the irrefutable evidence of the differences between races and individuals. Broca, after dissecting the brain of a black, said he had found it to be darker than those of whites; the German scientist Soemmering had made the same asertion in the late eighteenth century. The implication was (as it had been earlier) that the coloring was an outward sign of black animality and of the essential difference from whites. Moreover, in comparing the weight of a white man's brain with that of a black's, Broca found that the former weighed 1,003 grams, and the latter 925.5 grams.

The differing brain weights of various races showed a hierarchy of abilities and proved, Broca asserted, the superiority of the white race, followed by the Mongol race, and, finally, the race with the smallest brains, the blacks. The Larousse dictionary pointed to brain size as the cause for the lesser intelligence attributed to blacks.[52] More remarkable, perhaps, is that this was the view not only of physiologists and the French anthropologists, but also of those who had had long, practical interaction with Africans. Louis Faidherbe, who

had served in Senegal as governor for nearly a decade, beginning in 1854, and who had had an even longer period of contact with blacks in the West Indies and Africa, noted that Africans were weak-willed and lacking in initiative, "which is why
they can be enslaved. One would never think of enslaving
Arabs, for they would assassinate their masters." The cause for
this lack of will among blacks, Faidherbe wrote, was "the relatively weak volume of their brains."[53]

Physical Anthropology

In the nineteenth-century concern—indeed mania—for
statistics and measurement, physical anthropology triumphed:
measurable physique became the foundation for all the differences perceived between African and European man. Through
statistical methods a search was made for a human norm; deviations from the norm were regarded as signs of inferiority.
The Belgian statistician, Adolphe Quételet, who had a good
following in France, attempted to express in physical measurements the nature of the average man, who, according to
Quételet, was the ultimate in beauty and morality; human perfection would be accomplished when all men approached the
physical dimensions of the "average man."[54] With regard to
race, the white race was established as the norm, deviations
from it were evidence of imperfection. Etienne Serres, professor of anthropology at the Museum of Natural History, wrote
that, in comparison with whites, blacks had unusually short
necks, which made them not only unattractive but also clumsy
and uninventive. Geoffroy Saint-Hilaire and Frédéric Cuvier
found in the skeletons of blacks distinctive marks, which they
claimed separated blacks from whites and showed the animality of blacks; they found blacks' pelvic bones and femur excessively large. Virey, making the same observation, pointed
to pelvic size as the cause for the large sex organs of blacks.[55]
The Dutchman Willem Vrolik developed an index for measuring the pelvic structure, which computed the ratio of the width
to the length of the pelvis; a narrow pelvis was "proof" of
racial superiority.[56] Although the method was not widely
adopted in France, it was referred to from time to time.

A self-avowed follower of Gall pointed to the shape of the

nose as an indicator of human intelligence: "flat, squashed noses announce grave disabilities." Broca agreed with this judgment, but, in tune with the more scientific tendencies of his generation, expressed this aestheticism in measurable terms. He developed a "nose index" that measured the ratio of the width to the length of the nose. A ratio indicating a flat nose was "nearly always the sign of inferiority."[57] No matter that blacks have noses of all shapes; in the nineteenth-century European consciousness, they were perceived to have distinctly flatter noses than whites. Even their noses condemned blacks to inferiority.

The debate over the evolution of races underscored the claim that the white race was the standard by which others should be judged. Thinkers differed as to whether the black or the white race had been created first. Some argued that whites represented the perfected evolution of "lower" races, whereas others, following Buffon, argued that the white race was the original from which others had degenerated.[58] Both views were rooted in one main point: the white race was the norm.

The Victory of Polygenism

The emphasis on biology in the nineteenth century brought to the fore age-old speculations about the causes of racial differentiation. In 1860 the Société d'anthropologie de Paris asked a traveler to West Africa to ascertain whether African children were born black or whether they changed color only gradually, presumably as a result of climatic influences. This question had not been answered even a generation later. In 1882, in a debate reminiscent of those of the seventeenth century, the question was again raised about whether the African child was born black or whether he turned that color as a result of too much sun or of being kept in smokey huts.[59] The method of transmission of physical traits from one generation to the next was not then known. Gregor Mendel published his findings on genetics in 1866, but they were not "discovered" until 1900. As for the cause of the original differences in human races, the solution to that problem is still in dispute.

The origins of race were discussed in terms of whether all

races were descended from one original pair or whether the races really were descended from different species. The monogenist-polygenist debate had been somewhat dampened in the eighteenth century by the Church and by Christian dogma on the unity of mankind. In the nineteenth century, religious constraints were weakened and polygenism made further inroads. It should be noted that, until the mid-nineteenth century, however, the major scientists—Cuvier, Lamarck, and Saint-Hilaire, to mention only the most prominent—were monogenists. The differences in physical features were attributed to environment. Environment was so compelling, argued the monogenists, that races transplanted to different climates changed physical appearance. Thus the anarchist and geographer Elisée Reclus asserted, in a manner that brings to mind Buffon, that the force of the American environment was so strong that in Louisiana both the whites and the blacks he had observed were turning red, becoming like the Indians, the original people of the North American continent. The blacks were less Negroid than in Africa and had gone a quarter way toward the white race as a result of climatic influences. (The whites presumably were "degenerating.")[60]

If the monogenists, explaining physical differences by environmental factors, prevailed early in the nineteenth century, the polygenists began to lay the groundwork for the dominance that they were to win in the second half of the century. Virey, who was publishing when the century began, continued to have an influence through the subsequent editions of his work; he was probably the most-read polygenist. Virey and the naturalist Bory de Saint-Vincent together asserted that, if a naturalist saw insects or four-legged animals as different from one another as were black and white men, he would claim that they belonged to two different species.[61]

By the 1850s polygenism had swept France. The Société d'anthropologie de Paris subscribed to the polygenist dogma, proclaiming it scientifically proven. Quatrefages, a monogenist, stated that the public favored polygenism because it contradicted the Genesis account and therefore appeared to be more scientific. Pierre Larousse, in the first edition of what was to become a very successful encyclopedia, proclaimed the separate speciation of whites and blacks, a view that he noted had the backing of science.[62]

Monogenism was discredited. A. Vernier wrote that monogenism had against it "nearly the whole young school of anthropology, nearly all the doctors, nearly all the classifiers, and entomologists."[63] Whereas in England most men of science were monogenists in the second half of the nineteenth century, in France they were polygenists. To a large degree, this difference seems due to the expressed need among French men of science to turn their backs on the Church and the Church's version of the monogenist origin of the human race. The anthropologist Paul Topinard proclaimed that monogenism was a doctrine embraced by primitive peoples, whereas polygenism was embraced by peoples "with wide horizons."[64]

As Buffon had pointed to the ability of the races to interbreed as evidence of the common membership of all races in a single species, so had other monogenists. But the founder of the Société d'anthropologie, Paul Broca, effectively destroyed that argument in 1859 in a crucial work on hybridity, in which he reminded his readers of something that had been known for at least a century: different species can crossbreed. Thus the donkey and horse, members of different species, could be bred and have offspring. What distinguished interspecies breeding from intraspecies breeding was that the former led to a sterile hybrid. The mule was sterile. But sterility was not necessary to prove hybridization. Wrote Broca, "It is sufficient to prove that certain cross-breeds are inferior to their parent races as regards longevity, vigor, health, and intelligence to render it very probable that the two races are not of the same species."[65]

In regard to the interbreeding of whites and blacks, Broca stated that such mating was usually infertile, but, when it produced offspring, the offspring was stunted both physically and morally, thus proving that the two races were separate species. Broca cited the eighteenth-century English West Indian slaveowner, Edward Long, and the American anthropologist and apologist for slavery, Josiah Clark Nott. The "evidence" for Broca's conviction of the impossibility of a fruitful white and black union was thus somewhat attenuated. He also advanced an earlier idea of Serres that black males had unusually large penises and white females small vaginas and that such conditions would make the mating of black male and white female impossible. Nature had presumably not established corresponding impediments for relations between the white male and black female; such a union was a special form of hybridity that Broca called "unilateral hybridity." The belief of Broca, and of Serres before him, that only the union between a white male and a black female was possible reveals the extent to which they allowed social taboos to influence their anthropology. But the theory of "unilateral hybridity" had to be dropped in the face of the abundant evidence to the contrary.[66]

The theory of the separate speciation of blacks and whites and the hybrid nature of any offspring of the two remained, however. The offspring were seen as sterile hybrids. When statistics were presented to show that in fact they were fertile, the defense was that undoubtedly they belonged to the third or fourth generation. The medical doctor Bérenger-Féraud, who had served in Senegal for many years, lent credence to this theory when he declared that men of color died out when they reached the third or fourth generation.[67]

The definition of races as distinct groups, each with its own innate capacities that could not be changed by environment, seemed confirmed by writers on tropical medicine. The high mortality rate of Europeans in tropical areas indicated to European observers that blacks originating in Africa had a different physical structure that enabled them to bear the tropical environment, whereas whites originating in Europe could not do so. This perceived difference was cited as evidence that each region had its own species of man.[68]

While polygenetic convictions were expressed in specialized works of biology, they were also echoed in popular opinion, as can be seen in the literature of the time in regard to sexual contact between the black and the white races. Novels seemed to assert the impossibility of successful union between the two races. Interracial sex was presented as the violation of the distance between two species; the failure of such unions was proof of the unbridgeable biological gap.[69]

Monogenist-Polygenist Consensus: Black Inferiority

Since whites were upheld as the model, the permanent gap that polygenists had declared existed between what were regarded as two human species seemed to condemn blacks to permanent inferiority. By contrast, however, monogenists were by no means egalitarians; they too stressed the inequality of the races.[70] Armand de Quatrefages, one of the most persistent advocates of monogenism, mounted an attack on polygenism that was to continue throughout his life. He believed that a similar origin of all races did not indicate biological equality; climatic and other environmental factors had shaped the physical characteristics of race and, as a result, had created differences in intellectual and moral faculties. Although all men were members of the same species, Quatrefages emphasized, all races were not equal. The relationship between whites and blacks was similar to that between parent and child.[71]

Saint-Simonians stressed the unity of man, but not the equality. One of the Saint-Simonians most interested in anthropological questions was Eichtal, secretary of the Société ethnologique. In 1839, in a pamphlet that he published with Urbain, a man of color, Eichtal said that the human races had "distinctive characteristics" like those separating the sexes; they formed a couple, in which the white represented the male and the black the female. The Saint-Simonians, for all their interest in science, had a nearly mystical approach to reality, and Eichtal's description of the races certainly was that. In his view Europeans suffered from excessive cerebrality, whereas blacks represented a countervalue, which had its virtues; the simplicity of blacks made them part of "the savage world of Rousseau but without its barbarism." Eichtal, in explaining how blacks were a "female race," revealed, of course, his era's belief in black inferiority and also its attitude toward women:

> Just like the woman, the black is deprived of political and scientific intelligence; he has never created a great state . . . he has never accomplished anything in industrial mechanics. But on the other hand he has great virtues of sentiment. Like women he also likes jewelry, dance and singing.[72]

Those virtues were of limited value to the technocratic Saint-Simonians, who, above all, saw human perfection mirrored in the splendid material achievements of nineteenth-century Europe.

The racism of the monogenists can be seen in their solution to alleged African inferiority. Their proposal was to change the black race by infusing into it "white blood." Eichtal declared that the black race could overcome its barbarism only if it were "married" to the white race. But he seems to have seen this union only as a means of improving the black race, not of ensuring its equality with whites; inequality was destined to be a permanent human condition: "there will always be superior and inferior races." Humans, so the argument went, would never be able to overcome their dependence upon their biological structures, which were different for every race. Gobineau declared that man could change his level of civilization only by changing race.[73]

Race and Culture

Physical inferiority, according to racist doctrine, was accompanied by cultural inferiority. Courtet de l'Isle wrote that "the more beautiful a race is, the more its civilization is advanced; the uglier it is, the more imperfect its civilization."[74] The model for beauty was Apollo; that for ugliness was resemblance to the brute. Gobineau proclaimed the white race as the model for all humanity, the model by which the aesthetic qualities of all races were to be measured. Outer physical beauty was thought to express internal capacities that were as different as physical types.

History proved, Gobineau asserted, that all civilizations were created by whites; none could ever develop without the help of the white race. He maintained that whites had migrated to Egypt and had helped build its civilization; the center of human history had always been in the areas inhabited by whites; they had developed civilization, and only their spread to the corners of the globe expanded civilization. He flatly declared, "History develops only as a result of contact with the white race."[75]

Any proof of African accomplishment could always be dismissed, as it was by Courtet: accomplished Africans were not "real Africans," for they were, he stated, not totally Negroid. Thus Courtet willingly accepted that indeed the Mandingoes, Ashantis, Fulani, and others had achieved a number of impressive feats, but these peoples, he insisted, were mixed with European stock. In other words, Africans could accomplish impressive feats only when they had been racially "uplifted" by the infusion of "European blood."[76] Such an "infusion" was assumed for blacks with relatively light skin or aquiline noses, and therefore they were more highly regarded than other Africans. This differentiation was especially true in the case of the Fulani, who enjoyed a good French "press." Because of the Fulani's light skin, the explorers Caillié and Raffenel thought them superior to other Africans. When an explorer found a people of whom he was fond, he would ascribe to them Caucasian features that they might not necessarily possess. Hecquard, traveling in the Senegambia, met a king and found him to be congenial: "he has European features. His face exudes goodness, he is said to be generous."

The extent to which Caucasian facial features were considered an indication of internal qualities may be seen in a report written in the Ministry of the Navy and Colonies. Basing his account on the travel notes of an adventurer sent to Dahomey, a ministry clerk wrote that King Ghezo was "very light-skinned." The clerk's superior crossed out those words and wrote instead that the king was "a very intelligent black."[77]

Africans as Animals or Children

The inferiority of blacks was emphasized by claiming their affinity to the animal world or comparing them with European children. Thinkers in the eighteenth century, when establishing a chain of being, had placed the black man close to the animal, but the chain as perceived then was evolutionary and allowed for ascension. By the nineteenth century, it was believed that, if there were a chain of being, it was stationary and condemned people to remain fixed in the hierarchy. Bory de Saint-Vincent divided man into fifteen races, according to hair color; the lowest three races were African (Ethiopian, number thirteen; Kaffir, number fourteen; Hottentot, number fifteen). Then began the animals, the most evolved of which were thought to be the orangutans.

In the chain of being, Virey asserted, a greater distance lay between blacks and Newton, Montesquieu, and Buffon than "between monkeys and these stupid peoples."[78] The old idea that placed blacks close to apes was reinforced by the great Cuvier's dissection of a South African woman, known as the Hottentot Venus. As a result of his reports, she became famous in French naturalist circles and dominated much of the French scientific thought about blacks. Her life had been tragic. An Englishman had brought her from South Africa to Europe to show her off in public and then had handed her over to an animal show in Paris. After eighteen months in Paris, she died of tuberculosis. Her ordeal was not over; she was taken to Cuvier's laboratory and dissected. Her reproductive organs were prepared in alcohol and given to the Academy of Sciences, and Cuvier carefully studied her face. When she was alive, her movements had appeared to Cuvier to be "brusque and capricious like those of a monkey." Her lips were pouted forward, supposedly like those of an orangutan. Of the dead woman, Cuvier wrote, "I have never seen a human head more resembling a monkey's than hers."[79]

The physical characteristics of the Hottentot are to an outside observer unique. He is short, has small hands and feet, and is of yellowish hue. The female has elongated vaginal lips and fat-padded buttocks, steatopygia. By the time Cuvier was describing the Hottentot Venus, the Hottentot population had been considerably reduced and formed a very small proportion of the African population. But Cuvier and his readers saw her as possessing characteristics typical of the black populations of Africa in general.

The parallel that Cuvier drew between the Hottentot woman and animals struck a familiar note. Virey and Bory de Saint-Vincent proclaimed an affinity between a black's prognathism and an animal's snout. Serres, in his lectures at the Museum of Natural History, spoke of a black's face as resembling that of a monkey, because of the black's flat nose and

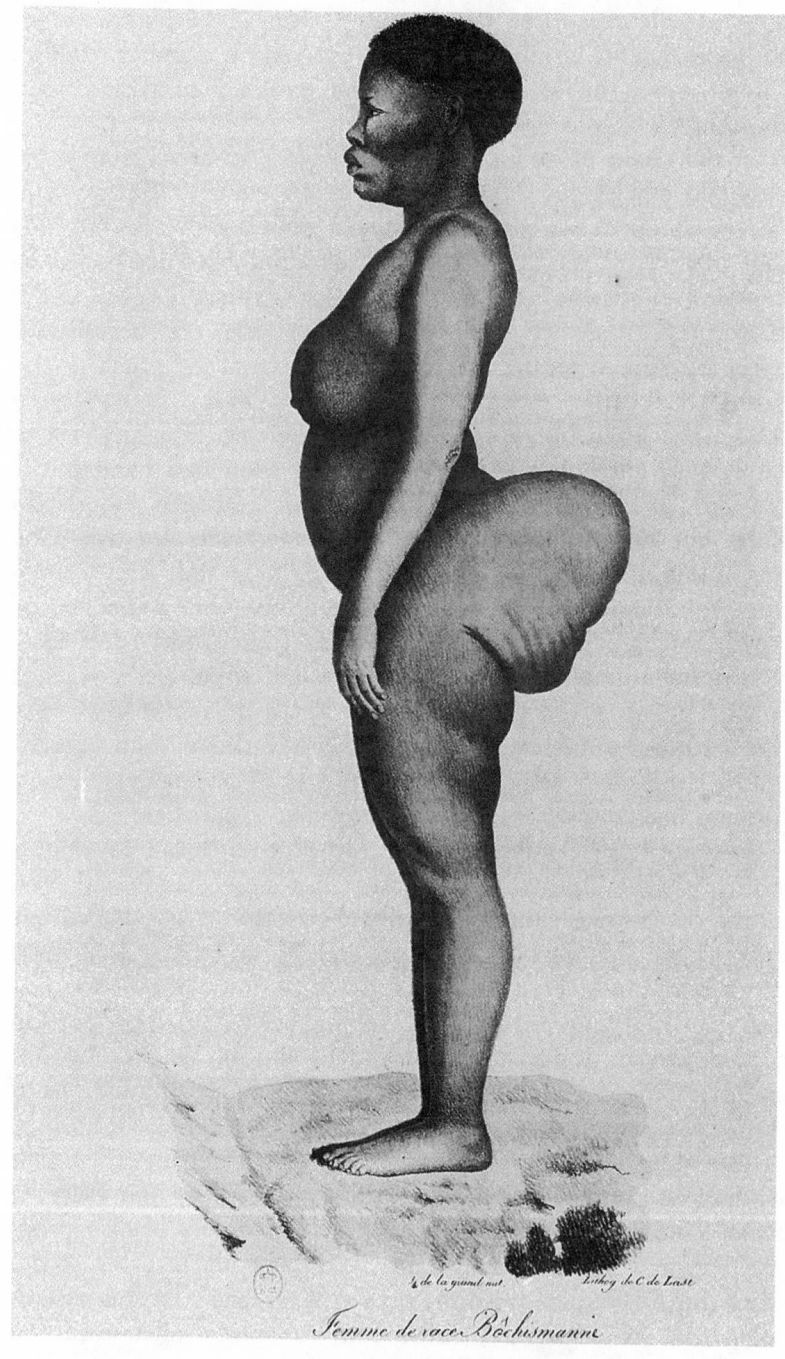

Georges Cuvier's Hottentot Venus. *Geoffroy Saint-Hilaire and Frédéric Cuvier*, Histoire naturelle des mammifères avec des figures originales, colorées, dessinées d'après des animaux vivans *(Paris, 1824). Photo Bibliothèque nationale, Paris.*

prognathism. Looking at blacks, Serres said, "one notices that sad calm without intelligence that some monkeys have." Gobineau also maintained that blacks had simian features.[80] Broca found that Africans had longer arms than Europeans— they do—and saw this as evidence of black animality; he prefaced his work with a quotation from the Englishman Charles White, who had believed that, in possessing long arms, the black was a link between the monkey and the European. Perhaps not entirely convinced, Broca nonetheless announced to the Paris anthropological society the finding of others, that the penises of black men had cartilage structures like those of monkeys and that black women did not have hymens at the entrance of the vagina.[81] According to Bérenger-Féraud, chief medical officer of Senegal, the angle formed by the pelvic bones and the backbones of Wolof women was such that it looked more natural for them to be walking on all fours than to walk upright as bipeds. He further asserted that the big toes of Africans were large and capable of independent movement—far more so than those of Caucasians.[82]

The blacks' behavior, it was believed, confirmed animality. Their speech reminded Serres and others of animals; of the Hottentots, the group considered the lowest of the black race, it was frequently said that they could not speak, but rather could only articulate some guttural sounds. Malte-Brun characterized African languages in general as consisting of "barely articulated yells, many strange sounds, roars, whistling sounds imitated from the animals."[83] Louis Figuier found that blacks were endowed with thick skins and insensitive nervous systems, making them impervious to pain. And what was most similar to the animal, Figuier declared, was the blacks' smell: "These emanations are as hard to endure as those which some animals exhale."[84] Blacks, by their perceived nearness to animality, were also, it was thought, endowed with an excess of sensuality. Gobineau wrote that blacks were voracious eaters: "All foods are good, nothing repulses [them]. What [they] want is to eat, eat with excess, fury." A black person was regarded as the victim of violent passions and desires that he or she could not control, being merely a "human machine."[85]

The supposed animality of blacks also, however, gave them

certain qualities. Virey and Serres maintained that blacks were endowed with a better sense of smell than were whites. Gobineau developed a whole philosophy of history around the passionate, spontaneous character of blacks: their passions were not totally a sign of degeneracy, for they had their role in the development of humanity; for all their inability to develop an independent civilization, blacks had brought an important contribution to humanity—art; the passion and animality of blacks, which made them inept, simultaneously led to the creation of great works of art and literature, when crossed with the cerebrality of whites.[86]

It was the belief in the blacks' closeness to the animal that made it possible for Europeans to put credence in accounts about the Niam-niams, a Central African people who, it was commonly believed, had tails; Niam-niams were alleged to own one piece of furniture, a small bench with a hole in it for the tail. The halls of the Société de géographie de Paris, of the Académie des sciences, and of the Société orientale resounded with the echo of the Niam-niam controversy. In 1854 the adventurer Du Couret, who later was exposed as a fraud, provided an illustration of a Niam-niam with his tail. The apparent basis for the belief in the Niam-niam tail is that the Niam-niams wore tail-like ornaments made out of leather, but that fact was not revealed until 1860 in the *Tour du monde*.[87]

The affinity between blacks and apes was thought to be so close that some writers asserted that the two could interbreed. An Englishman at the beginning of the nineteenth century spread the rumor that several members of the Institut de France had requested an explorer in Africa to "make the experiment of a connection between a male orangutan and an African woman."[88] It should be noted that there is no corroborative evidence to give substance to the rumor; nevertheless, that it was aired at all is revealing. Cuvier's and later Geoffroy Saint-Hilaire's clarification of the definitions and relationships of species prevented continued scientific speculation about the possibility of sexual interaction between blacks and apes, but the idea continued to have a long life in popular literature.

Some anthropologists who were disciples of Buffon were

very uncomfortable with the notion of establishing a link between humans, including Africans, and animals. Instead of proclaiming variance from the white norm as proof of an affinity with animals, they equated the adult black with the white child. Quatrefages said that Africans had a cephalic index equal to that of a Parisian child. Once Africans arrived at a cerebral stage akin to that of a European child, they seemed incapable of further evolution. An African was like a "big child."[89]

The idea of black animality was reflected in the popular literature. Balzac, who frequently resorted to biological analogies, found parallels in the animal kingdom for the society and characters he described. He depicted one character as dumb as a "pasture animal, the savages of America, or some native of the Cape of Good Hope." Blacks in fiction were presented as just above the ape or as variant types of one. The hero of a children's book, published in 1837, told of his shocked reaction at seeing Africans: "they seemed hideous, I would have thought of them as monkeys of the worst species if their bodies, which had no clothing, had not had a human form."[90]

This view was not foreign even to the humanitarians in France. Thus the abolitionist translator of *Uncle Tom's Cabin* depicted, in one of his own works, Africans less sensitive than animals and "certainly more stupid." His hero examined simultaneously the physique of an African king and that of a monkey and concluded that "they both had a short forehead, a flat nose, eyes closely together . . . were it not for differences in skin and the dignity that the prince had acquired as a result of being used to command, the monarch and the animal would have been exactly alike."[91]

Jules Verne, in a telling dialogue in *Five Weeks in a Balloon* (which, published in 1863, established the author's fame), revealed his belief in the close physical resemblance between blacks and monkeys:

> "There was an attack!" said Joe. "We began to think that you were besieged by the natives."
> "They were only apes, fortunately," replied the doctor.

"At a distance the difference is not striking, my dear Samuel."

"Not even when you are close," said Joe.[92]

Verne elaborated on the same theme in *The Mysterious Island,* which tells of the capture of an orangutan that is made the helpmate of the black servant, Neb. As presented in the novel, Neb and the animal are very close to each other; Neb is simple-minded enough and the monkey intelligent enough so that there could be a link in the chain of being. The animal, Verne wrote, "belonged to the family of anthropoid apes, of which the facial angle is not much inferior to that of the Australians and the Hottentots."[93]

The racial views of the physical anthropologists, who saw the physical appearance of the black as bestial and thus proof of a lowly position in the chain of being, were developed furthest by Pierre Loti in his well-known, dream-like, exotic novel, *Roman d'un spahi,* published in 1881. According to Roland Lebel, Loti's novels crystallized French thought on exoticism and, according to Fanoudh-Siefer, they specifically defined French thought on Africa.[94] *Roman d'un spahi* is the story of a French soldier, Jean, billeted for service in Senegal, who falls under what is described as the sensuous spell of a young Wolof girl, Fatou-Gaye. One of the main themes of this popular novel is that blacks are unnatural, animalistic, and akin to apes in both their physical appearance and their behavior. *Roman d'un spahi* had a widespread influence, going through eight editions in the first seven years; subsequently, in less than a century, it has been printed in 150 editions. Read by young and old, it was popular enough to be made into a musical that was presented at the Opéra Comique in 1897. The French literary establishment bestowed on Loti the highest honor available when in 1891 he was elected to the Académie Française. The award was all the more striking in light of the fact that Loti's competitor for the coveted seat was Emile Zola.

The view of blacks as childlike also was echoed in the fiction of the time. Blacks were depicted as loyal servants, desiring nothing but to serve their white masters. Jules Verne's Neb is the loyal servant; thinking that his master is lost, he falls into deep grief and "was like the dog that will not leave the place where his master is buried"; upon finding his master, Neb is filled with joy and "danced like a Negro." The Sambo image was present also in the works of the popular children's novelist, Comtesse de Ségur, who wrote of the loyal servant Rome, who when happy, "in the accustomed manner of Negroes, jumped, somersaulted, and let out discordant yells." Maupassant depicted a black named Tombouctou, a soldier in the French army during the Franco-Prussian War, as a large, smiling child. Whenever this child of nature became hungry, he ate a Prussian.[95]

Sexuality

Africans in the French view were oversexed beings, constantly prey to their lusts. The passions of blacks were believed to be due to large sex organs; the black man was said to have a larger penis and the black woman a larger vagina than whites.[96] Although literate nineteenth-century Europeans were rather reticent about their own sexuality, they eagerly projected their sexual fantasies onto Africans. Blacks, Europeans believed, were wont to indulge in sexual orgies and lusted after whites. In the many travel accounts that described black women as avid for intercourse with white men,[97] one can detect the fantasies of celibate white Frenchmen in Africa.

Sexual contact between black men and white women was rejected as a violation of the natural order of things. One may suspect that the objection to interracial sex of that kind was due to essentially primitive reactions to all intergroup relationships. In patriarchal societies group A will object to one of its women having intercourse with a male from group B, because she would then be lost to the group, integrated into her male partner's reference group. By contrast, if a male from group A has contact with a woman from group B, she then becomes part of the community of group A. If group B is considered inferior to group A, the differences between the two groups is more acute, and it is even more important to group A that one of its females does not have contact with a male from group B. If the members of the group allowed that, it would signify their powerlessness to protect one of their women from the contamination that comes from contact with men deemed inferior. Governor Faidherbe, an enlightened man and, for his time a rather liberal-minded official, could not imagine that Shakespeare's Othello was black; he conceded only that at most Othello was a Moor:

> For if you put in his place a Negro with curly hair, he becomes nothing but a monster with depraved tastes. . . . One can only be shocked at the idea of a young aristocratic Venetian woman enamored of a man whom in our country the girls would look upon with fright.[98]

Nearly all novels that contained black characters included a discussion of interracial sex. The blacks' presumed excessive sexuality was usually expressed in an attack on innocent white womanhood. The good black was the one who had the chance to have sexual contact with a white woman but who resisted. In Hugo's play *Bug Jargal,* the hero's nobility of character is shown partly by his refusal to express openly his love for a young white woman. The depiction of such self-abnegation was rare, however, as most blacks were believed unable to control themselves in their desire to rape white women.[99]

Curiously enough, works that protested against racism contained some of the same ingredients of black madness, black violence against white womanhood, and, finally, the death of the black man brazen enough to violate what was seen almost as nature's law, namely, the separation of the races. Anicet-Bourgeois and Dumanoir's *Le Docteur noir,* a play first produced at the Porte Saint-Martin theatre in 1846, inveighs against race prejudice. In every sort of way, the doctor of the title, Fabien, is superior to the white males around him, but, being kind and gentle, he is understood to be a unique black man. Although speaking generally against racial discrimination, the play contains some of the racist elements of other works: Fabien's love for the white girl is presented as a form of madness; he kidnaps her and threatens to kill her before he wins her avowal of her secret love for him. As is not the case in most other works of the period, however, this play shows the two married; and yet they do not live together, for Fabien perishes while saving his wife in an accident.

Two novels—Alexandre Dumas' *Georges* (1848) and Anatole France's *Le Chat maigre* (1879)—present miscegenation, not as an abomination against nature, but rather as no different from any other relationship between the sexes. (However, that the principal male in each novel is a mulatto may reveal an underlying notion of closer biological and social affinity between whites and nonwhites of light color. Dumas himself was a man of color. France was very deeply and genuinely an egalitarian; his characters are only very incidentally colored, and color is not an issue in the novel.) In these two novels normal love relationships develop between members of the two races and lead to happy marriages. In all other novels that were published during the same era and that depict similar situations and sexual contact, however, the black, once having dared to touch a white woman, dies violently: in Balzac's *The Negro* he commits suicide; in Balzac's *Le Vicaire des Ardennes* and in Anicet-Bourgeois and Dumanoir's *Le Docteur noir* he is shot; in *Le Mulâtre* (1824), attributed also to Balzac, he is brought down by a posse; in Cashin's *Amour et liberté* (1847) and in Thouret's *Toussaint, le mulâtre* he is killed by fire.

Most novels of the period that deal with interracial sex depict a black man and a white woman. The reverse was rarely a subject of interest (although it was closer to social reality), but two novels of the early nineteenth century depict the relationships of white males and nonwhite females. Rather than presenting the relationships as violations of the laws of nature, Mme Duras' *Ourika* (1824) and Gustave de Beaumont's *Marie, or Slavery in the United States* (1835),[100] are romantic tales of the impossible love between white and black in a racist society. *Ourika* is the sentimental account of a black girl in Paris who falls in love with her mistress's grandson; knowing the prejudice against her race, she does not reveal her secret love and dies of a broken heart. This novel, twice reprinted in 1824 and adapted as a play, was at least twice translated into Spanish. The novel by Beaumont, the famed travel companion of Alexis de Tocqueville during his voyage to the United States, depicts the horrors of racism in the United States. The

hero, Ludovic, a Frenchman, falls in love with Marie, a beautiful girl reputed to have some "black" blood in her veins.
Hunted by violent mobs, the young couple flees into the
wilderness, where Marie dies from exhaustion—a victim of
American racism. *Ourika* and *Marie* are protest novels
affirming the need for racial equality, but they represented a
minority view in a predominantly racist age.

Darwinism and Racism

The introduction of Darwinist thought reinforced the doctrines of racial inequality, but by no means created them. They
had existed in France for centuries, at least. In fact, there was a
strong resistance to Darwin in France. *The Origin of Species*
never had the impact on French thought that it had, for instance, on the English-speaking world.

The French never quite understood in what way Darwin differed from their own Lamarck and even, for that matter, from
Buffon, who had already admitted the possibility of the evolution of species. A certain amount of national pride lay behind
the French insistence that Lamarck had already said what was
significant about evolution; the French tended to see Darwin
as but a disciple of the great French scientist. Darwin's monogenist stand on species made him unpopular with the Société
d'anthropologie, most of whose members were polygenist.
The few monogenists distrusted Darwin, for they believed
in the immutability of species, whereas the Englishman, of
course, denied it.[101]

There were, of course, a few convinced Darwinists in
France, who professed to base their belief in the doctrines of
racial inequality on a reading of the English scientist. Mme
Clémence Royer, who introduced Darwin to France when she
translated the third edition of *The Origin of Species* in 1862,
asserted that his theories proved the falseness of the doctrines
of racial equality. "Nothing is more self-evident than the inequalities of the various human races," she wrote, proclaiming
that there was a law in nature that ordained the supplantation
of inferior races by stronger ones and that races were well-
defined entities whose destinies could be deflected only by

race-mixing, which, however, posed a danger to the superior races who would lose their dominance if they married inferior ones.[102]

Some Frenchmen who read Darwin saw in his writings specific evidence of a forthcoming struggle for existence among the races. In 1864, two years after the Royer translation appeared, Georges Pouchet cited Darwin's ideas as evidence that Africans were doomed eventually to disappear in favor of the stronger, European race. The young journalist Georges Clemenceau was well acquainted with the scientific writings of the Anglo-Saxon world (he had spent the second half of the 1860s in the United States), and, although he did not cite Darwin, he appears to have been influenced by Darwin. Clemenceau wrote, "In this ruthless struggle for existence carried on by human society, those who are weaker physically, intellectually, or morally must in the end yield to the stronger. The law is hard but there is no use in rebelling." He was unsure whether blacks would be able to survive in the struggle with whites and wrote that "time alone can show of what the black race is capable." Clemenceau was less categorical than Pouchet in condemning blacks to oblivion, but he nevertheless was convinced that forces such as those he had described were in operation.[103]

Other Frenchmen held similar ideas without any apparent connection with Darwinian thought. The Saint-Simonian journalist and proponent of imperialism Jules Duval wrote, "It is a fatal law that the inferior races will disappear in the face of the superior ones; the former gradually disappear from the surface of the earth. . . . they silently are extinguished without violence, victims of destiny." The novelist Jacolliot cited Broca as an authority on black inferiority, but, in developing a doctrine of a competitive struggle among races, he did not mention Darwin. Jacolliot proclaimed that the black race was in the throes of extinction; incapable of further development and unable to adapt, it was dying out and leaving the globe to "the white race, that is, the race with straight hair and of an Indo-European type."[104] Such ideas seemed naturally to develop from the doctrines of racial inequality, and Darwinism was not essential to their formulation.

Europeans in Africa

There were two challenges to scientific racism. The first, which was the more effective, came from within the scientific community. The proliferation of measurements revealed the contradictions in the claims that had been made, the unreliability of many of the measurements, and the arbitrariness with which the significance of the measurements had been endowed. By the 1880s racist anthropology had been undermined and was slowly giving way to different interpretations for the variety of humankind. The second challenge, which was less effective but which carried perhaps the greater potential to discredit scientific racism, was the experience of Frenchmen in Africa proper. Rarely, however, was the travel literature of the period consulted. The emphasis on physical anthropology, of course, seemed to make such excursions unnecessary. In the confines of a Parisian laboratory, the various organs of the African could be more exactly measured. These measures were considered the most important sources of information, for biology, it was thought, was the determinant of all human behavior.

French travel accounts could have been of use to those who wanted to learn about Africa. Many were generally sympathetic accounts of African life and mores. In an account published in 1814, R. G. Villeneuve, the former aide of Boufflers, gave a positive and detailed description of rites during marriage, death, and birth and of agricultural methods, handicrafts, and amusements. The account showed that the people of the Senegambia were able to build bridges. In his description of nearly all states in the Senegambia as feudal political systems, Villeneuve pointed out that other writers on Africa were thus wrong in characterizing those African governments as the "most revolting despotism." This part of Africa, he wrote, had a political order that showed that, in some ways, it was "already civilized."[105] Traveling through the Senegambia in the early 1820s, Mollien repeated many of the remarks about the virtues of Africans that had been made earlier. Mollien wrote that Africans were stalwart and capable of enduring the hardships of life, yet they were sensitive and showed "extreme emotion for the loss of their parents." The Wolofs were kind to their slaves, he pointed out, and the Fulani were hospitable and generous.[106]

No matter how sympathetic, however, direct observers applied European measures to African societies and found them wanting. Villeneuve wrote of the royal court in Cayor:

> Does one want to have a just idea of a royal court in Africa that some travelers have described in such a pompous manner? Here it is: The palace is a collection of thirty or forty huts surrounded by dead thorn bushes. . . . [Inside] A Negro smoking his pipe clothed in four yards of cotton cloth . . . there is the sovereign; princes begging for rum, powder, and tobacco, slaves half-naked, that is the court and the valets.

For Villeneuve, a large distance from European norms opened the society he observed to ridicule: its similarities to European societies lent it respectability. Mollien, whose political sympathies were with ultraroyalist Restoration France, explained why the Fulani of Bondu were a people gentler than those of Futa Toro: the former lived under a monarchy, the latter under a republic.[107] Thus was European wisdom confirmed in Africa.

Exploratory trips, such as those of Mollien and later of René Caillié, were intended to reach geographic goals. Mollien's destination was the sources of the Gambia, Senegal, and Niger rivers; Caillié's was Timbuktu. Until the goal was reached, every village, every people, was an obstacle in the way, not groups of people worthy of study. Still, Mollien and Caillié were amazingly patient and persevering.

The problems of early-nineteenth-century exploration can be seen in the accounts of Mollien and others. Mollien's ability to observe the cultures and institutions of Senegambia was limited by the short duration of his stay in various villages and by the problems of being a white man in areas that rarely, if ever, had seen Europeans. On arrival in a village, he would frequently be surrounded by crowds eager to touch him, to see if his color were real, to feel the shape of his nose, to examine the cut of his clothes.[108] Sometimes the crowds would mob him (in one town he estimated the crowd at

1,200), and he has left a graphic account of how the children often beset him:

> Some took off my shoes, and almost flayed my feet by putting them on and pulling them off again; others tried on my hat and were making merry in this covering, some unbuttoned my clothes, and but for three aged duennas, I suppose I might have been stripped stark naked.[109]

Sick with malaria, delirious with fever, lying in a hut with the rain leaking in, Mollien wrote his will one evening, in the belief that the night would be his last. The villagers agreed with his assessment of his condition; the children came, threw stones at him, and pillaged all his provisions. Raffenel, a more hostile observer who traveled in Senegal two decades later, was nearly crushed to death by a curious crowd. Later, in the Upper Senegal, he was held virtual prisoner for three months and, during the rainy season, had to share a leaking hut with various domestic animals.[110] Mollien recovered, and Raffenel was saved from the crowd and eventually released in the Khasso, but such ordeals were not ideal settings in which to observe the customs and traditions of other peoples.

What made Mollien and Caillié remarkable as travelers was that they did not ascribe their difficulties to African perfidy, but rather attempted to understand African behavior toward them in terms of an African rationale. The people of Bambuk were distrustful in particular circumstances, wrote Mollien: "continued invasions have rendered them so suspicious that they seldom permit strangers to enter their rich country, especially Europeans with whose cupidity they are well acquainted."[111]

All travelers were by no means so understanding; many were affected by the difficulties they encountered. Despite long, previous experience in West Africa, Anne Raffenel, once he set out on his journeys, found himself easily discouraged and irritated.[112] Feeling isolated in the midst of a culture he did not understand, he concluded that the peoples surrounding him were savages, and he judged blacks as credulous and dominated by fear and superstition.[113] Still, Raffenel's account included evidence of the genius of the people he was visiting:

the king of Bondu was a consummate diplomat, who also knew how to construct elaborate fortresses and who encouraged the fine arts; the peoples of Kaarta had a militia of four armies commanded by superior officers, and there was an organized administration. All these institutions won Raffenel's praise, but they did not change his overall image of the African; the virtues noted were considered exceptions to the rule. Thus the organization of the armies appeared to him "truly remarkable in a country so little civilized."[114] Having a preconceived notion of African savagery, Raffenel was unwilling to change his initial opinion of Africans.

The formative years of the early explorers occurred at a time when France was an agrarian society in which rural values still dominated. By the mid-nineteenth century, France had become industrialized and urbanized. The explorers were time-conscious, impatient with hindrances in Africa. Eugène Mage, sent on an official mission to Ségu in 1863, revealed an obsession with time in his scrupulous record of it: "two o'clock," "twenty minutes past four," "quarter to seven," "five minutes past nine." The traveler Paul Soleillet, moving through the Sudan a decade later, also noted the time with nearly the precision of a railroad timetable—"ten to three," "twenty past three"—and then recorded the exact interval between various observations—"ten minutes later," "five minutes later." The reader of the account is relieved when Soleillet's watch finally broke down, but Soleillet heroically continued his attempt to give the exact time by looking at the sun.[115]

Despite his apparent compulsiveness, Soleillet revealed an essentially sympathetic attitude toward Africans. After describing the African tradition of carrying amulets, he noted that it was no different from the custom practiced by French Catholics. After telling of how an African woman had come running toward his horse to get it to urinate on her to ward off rheumatism, he admonished, "We should not laugh at such a belief; in all of France, in all of Europe, thousands of people in groups often travel long distances to accomplish acts that are as unclean and far more dangerous." Africans, he wrote, were in no way inferior to Europeans; they only lacked proper education. They were, he advised, capable of all the progress that the white man had accomplished; significantly he noted also that progress would be possible only through the tutelage of Europeans. By not believing Africans capable of evolution by themselves, Soleillet reflected the racial doctrines of his era.[116]

Soleillet's generally positive attitude was exceptional, however, compared with the grotesque racism of other French travelers, who in no way conceded the humanity of the peoples with whom they came into contact. Shocked by the differences in the civilization and material culture of the Africans, they reverted to the abstractions of the racists at home. Victor Largeau, explorer of the Sahara, could not hide his sense of disgust at seeing blacks. He described a black child as "a kind of little monster, all naked, having a head that had nothing human about it." Charles Hertz, who had been sent to the Gold Coast, resorted to comparisons with the animal world in describing individual Africans; one of them was a "horrible darkie" who put "his paw on his heart while smiling at me in the manner of a cannibal," and a chief laughed "with this Negro laugh, which reveals the teeth of a crocodile."[117]

Europeans who remained for protracted periods in Africa shed the abstract nature of racist thought. These missionaries, merchants, and administrators knew the Africans far more intimately and realistically; to them the Africans' humanity was obvious. They were in Africa because they essentially intended to transform the African; that is, to make him into a Christian, to make him into a consumer of European goods, to make him into a French subject. Their very presence in Africa affirmed the notion that the Africans could be transformed; to them the Africans were not immutable and unchangeable, as the racists at home had declared. Of course Europeans in Africa were not free of hostility. At times they were impatient with the slow progress of their work in Africa and blamed the Africans for their failures; they were sick and tired and often ill tempered. Hostilities were triggered also by political friction. In the 1850s and 1860s, during the war with the Tukolor empire of El Haj Umar, the French in Senegal were hostile toward the interior Sudan. The official explorer Mage thought the Upper

Senegal rich and wanted it annexed to France. As did many travelers before him, he blamed the lack of development of the region on the shortcomings of the local inhabitants:

> The hand of man has not known how to extract anything from this world of wealth; the natives have not even known how to make anything to dress themselves. Their women go naked, their most advanced art being their miserable hovels, their clumsy tools. . . .

Another advocate of expansionism, the surgeon Bérenger-Féraud, saw the Africans as victims of "a thousand little tyrants" who spread terror and mayhem. Only a French advance, presumably, could save the Africans. Colonel Gallieni, on his mission to the Tukolor empire, had to cross the regions inhabited by the Bambara, who attacked and robbed him of most of his baggage. Meeting such hostility, Gallieni could speak of the Bambara only as "these highway robbers," "these stupid people," "these barbarians."[118]

Missionaries often found it hard to accommodate themselves to African institutions and mores, which they viewed as antithetical to Christianity. The missionizing effort was a very frustrating one, for little continuous work could be done in the disease-ridden environment. Of the seventy-four missionaries sent to the Senegambia between 1844 and 1854 by the Congrégation du Saint-Esprit and of the Saint-Coeur de Marie, twenty died and nineteen more had to be repatriated within a short time of their arrival. Between 1859 and 1875, thirty-two missionaries in Dahomey and Sierra Leone died. Nowhere else on earth, noted Father Desribes, was missionary work so difficult.[119]

Few Africans flocked to hear the missionaries, and efforts to educate the young also often were in vain. In 1854 in Gabon, six priests taught six to eight boys, and seven nuns taught fifteen to twenty girls.[120] Despite lengthy missionary work in some areas, notably Senegal, few were converted. Having an exaggerated sense of the size of the populations with which they were dealing, the missionaries must have felt that the number of their converts was truly insignificant. (In a general report on Catholic missions in 1869, it was estimated that the situation in West Africa was as shown in Table 2.) Some missionaries revived seventeenth-century notions of Africa as devil-infested or as subject to divine curse to explain the Africans' resistance to conversion.[121]

Table 2

Missionary Estimates of Population and Converts in Africa, 1869

Areas	Mission	Number of Missionaries	Population	Converts
The Two Guineas	Congrégation du Saint-Esprit and Saint-Coeur de Marie	8	30 million	1105
Sierra Leone	Congrégation du Saint-Esprit	3	Unknown	280
Dahomey	Société des missions africaines de Lyon	14	Unknown	Unknown
Senegambia	Congrégation du Saint-Esprit and Saint-Coeur de Marie	9	20 million	5000

Statistiques: Tableau générale des missions catholiques en 1869 (Lyons, 1869), pp. 22–24.

The failure of Christianity to have an impact on Africa was especially irritating in view of the spectacular success of Islam. By proselytization and jihad, Islam spread throughout West Africa in the nineteenth century. The advance of Islam lent a sense of urgency to the Christian missions' task. In 1881 Father Lavigerie declared that, in the preceding hundred years, fifty million people had converted to Islam: "Now the tribes conquered by the Crescent are lost for centuries to come." The lowly condition of the African was in part due to Islam, Lavigerie announced: "The Moslem creed is the masterpiece of Satan, for whilst satisfying to a certain extent the religious needs of the human heart, . . . it legitimizes the baser cravings of our lower nature."[122]

The hostility to Islam may have stemmed partly from anti-Islamic traditions in Christianity, which had begun with the Crusades and which were revived by contemporary military confrontations with Islam. From 1830 on, the French clashed with the Islamic populations of Algeria. In Senegal in the 1850s, the competition for the Senegambia with the Tukolor empire again brought the French into conflict with an Islamic group. Officials in Senegal also were at times affected by the struggle. Although Faidherbe had called for a "crusade against cruel and intolerant fanaticism" of Islamic forces, he was an exception among those who supported anti-Islamic policy. Rather than oppose Islam, he tried to use it as a means of spreading French influence; during his governorship he attempted to underwrite and modernize the Koranic schools in Senegal. Within the African context, Faidherbe viewed Islam as a progressive force, far preferable to animism. Bouët-Willaumez, one of Faidherbe's predecessors, had written that the Koran had introduced a "half civilization certainly superior to the barbarism and absurdities of fetishism."[123] In general Islam was seen as inherently more civilized than animism because its religious tradition appeared more systematic: it was based on a written text, and its origin was linked to Judaism and Christianity; its literacy allowed for record-keeping and commerce with distant areas. Its tendency to encourage the formation of relatively large states also impressed Europeans as evidence of civilization. The political authorities thus saw the potential value of Islam, but the missionaries, of course, were adamant in their opposition.

Dahomey

The varying attitudes of Frenchmen who had visited Africa came into sharp focus in their accounts of Dahomey. Here was represented everything that Europeans had explicitly or subconsciously stated about blacks for several centuries. Here savagery, bestiality, cannibalism, irreligion, and a political mixture of unbridled despotism and anarchy were documented by credible witnesses such as missionaries and other visitors to the court of Dahomey. Europeans were present at the "customs," the traditional yearly feasts at which human sacrifices were made; under King Ghezo (1818–1858) and King Glélé (1858–1889), the festivals attained a complexity and display unequaled in earlier times.[124] The "grand custom" of 1860, which several Europeans attended and described, seems to have been particularly bloody. It is possible that the Dahomean ruler, sensing the oncoming European onslaught on the continent, wanted to discourage any attacks against his kingdom by deliberately fostering an image of unparalleled savagery and ferociousness.[125] If that was his aim, he succeeded.

To the missionaries human sacrifice symbolized the extent to which the devil reigned over Africa; to secular observers it was a reminder of what the lack of civilization and the unchecked reign of savagery could lead man to. The missionaries found that the practice of human sacrifice in Dahomey underscored the importance of their work in West Africa and could be used to attract financial aid to their efforts. In an appeal for funds from the faithful for missionary work, the Bishop of Autun spoke of Dahomey as a place where "murderous Satan rules through human hecatombs."[126]

Travelers played on the public curiosity for tales of violence and savagery. The illustrations accompanying their accounts attempted to capture in great detail the horror of the "customs." This pictorial sensationalism had become such a tradition that in 1863, when naval surgeon Dr. Répin published his account of a visit to Dahomey made seven years earlier, the text was illustrated by a picture of bloody, human decapitations, even though the only religious sacrifice made during his visit was the killing of a hyena.[127] The king of Dahomey, noted the authoritative *Le Temps,* had become notorious for "his unheard of cruelty and the numerous human sacrifices." Vivien de Saint-Martin, secretary of the Société de géographie de Paris, charged that such sacrifices "measured not by hundreds but thousands."[128]

Although the prosaic truth about the human sacrifices should have been sufficient, they were rather imaginatively embellished. In what should have been an objective study, Louis Figuier wrote of the Dahomeans, "To kill and slay is to them a pleasure. . . . the post of executioner is sought for by the richest and most powerful in the land as affording the opportunity for the most coveted enjoyments."[129] Children's novels also included descriptions of the "customs." Armand Dubarry described them as the result of the inhabitants' having

Sacrifices humains au Dahomey. — Dessin de Foulquier, d'après un croquis de MM. Répin et Boulanger.

Although he personally did not witness any atrocities, the author included in his travel account this illustration of the Dahomey "customs." *Dr. Répin, "Voyage au Dahomey," Tour du monde 7 (1863); 101. Photo Bibliothèque nationale, Paris.*

a "bloodlust" and being deprived of civilization: "Man is worth nothing more than the animals when civilization has not shaped him." In his novel Jacolliot reflected the general notion that the "customs" were a daily, rather than yearly, phenomenon.[130]

Only a small number of Frenchmen actually traveled to Dahomey, and the French stake in that area was minimal, but the accounts' impact on the image of Africans in general was significant; few Frenchmen noted geographic or ethnic distinctions among Africans. In their blackness and their lack of European traditions and institutions, all Africans appeared the same to Europeans. Vivien de Saint-Martin wrote that, as with the civilized nations that differed only by a nuance of civilization, the blacks differed only by a nuance of barbarism. And Rabaud, president of the Marseilles geographical society, declared that blacks "have conserved from region to region great traits of resemblance in physique, customs and languages from one extremity of Africa to another."[131] The most horrible stories of one people thus could be believed of all Africans. The stories of human sacrifice of one group somehow confirmed the general view of Africans as brutal and bestial.[132]

Racism and Imperialism

The racist themes developed in the second half of the nineteenth century have been viewed as a backdrop to imperialism. Yet many believers in black inferiority were opponents of expansion overseas. Gobineau warned against imperialism when he charged that the fall of both the Greek and the Roman civilizations occurred when they conquered Asia Minor and became racially "contaminated" by those whom he saw as inferior people. In the Société d'anthropologie, Périer argued that the inferiority of blacks justified not oppression but rather goodwill by those who considered themselves to be civilized. Pellarin, attributing the destruction overseas to the spread of European power, called for restraint "in the zeal which makes us concern ourselves with distant peoples with the goal of religious propaganda and social interference." Broca attacked slavery, but he as well could have been speaking of other forms of control when he inveighed against the "subordination of one race to another." And Figuier wrote, "The Negro race possesses less intelligence . . . but this fact affords no justification for the hateful persecutions to which these unfortunate people have been the victims in every age."

Outside the Société d'anthropologie were a number of people who upheld the doctrines of the racial inferiority of blacks, but who still opposed imperialism. Clemenceau, when he became a deputy, denounced colonial expeditions as a betrayal of the rights of man.[133] (Once in government, however, he favored overseas conquest.) The novelist Pierre Loti, adamantly opposed to empire, saw the Africans as bereft of both ability and a worthy homeland; he depicted Africa as a barren desert where European military expeditions were sent without purpose or meaning. Some men concerned with Africa were, of course, imperialists, among them, Caillié, Raffenel, Verne, Mage, and Bérenger-Féraud, who saw European conquest as necessary and the logical result of racial differences. Thus until the 1880s, when empire building started in earnest, the racists were divided on whether Africans should be conquered. Racism, therefore, cannot be seen as a rationalization of the growing imperialist ambitions of European states. Rather, racist thought often reflected "pure scientific" observation. That is what made it so pernicious. Racist doctrine found support in the convictions of disinterested men presenting the findings of their research.

Conclusion

Frenchmen who had actually met Africans and lived among them did not resort to the extreme racist abstractions so common among the anthropologists of the mid-nineteenth century. Outright racism derived from the belief in the primacy of biological determinants of human variation. The French experience reveals the limited applicability of the sociological model that suggests that racism is the rationalization for conflict between competing human groups.[134] If the sociological model were true, one could expect that the Frenchmen who had actually experienced the traumas of culture contact would have been more racist than the theorists in France. The opposite was true.

The development of scientific racism in the late eighteenth century, which became fully accepted by the mid-nineteenth century, does not necessarily reflect a radical departure in attitude toward blacks. Racism should be interpreted as a natural result of the rise of the biological sciences, which desired to explain everything in terms of biology, to explain differences between humans in terms of race. In the twentieth century, we are more accustomed to view religion in a latitudinarian manner and to think of political and economic institutions as unstable, changing variables; therefore, criticisms of Africans in religious, political, or material terms do not seem so serious and hostile as those couched in the language of biology. But it is perfectly possible to assume that the fully developed racism of the nineteenth century, rather than expressing a radical departure in attitude, reflected the new predominance of biological theory. The hostility toward blacks, which had already existed in the seventeenth century, was now expressed in language borrowed from biology.[135]

9

The Lure of Empire

The nineteenth century was an era of dramatic expansion. The revolutionary and Napoleonic wars had given Frenchmen the exhilarating experience of seeing their national power extended throughout the European continent. Although the defeat of Napoleon put an end to that particular hegemony, political expansion still exercised the French imagination, especially among military officers wanting to avenge the trauma of Trafalgar and Waterloo. Whereas such action was now precluded in Europe, it was presumably possible overseas and would compensate for military defeat. Having brought the principles of liberty and equality to the rest of Europe during the revolutionary wars, France believed that it could affect the non-European world in the same manner, that it could become a beacon for human progress, hastening the day when all mankind would be united at the highest level of human culture. With the dramatic growth of industry and world trade, and the revolution in communications manifest in the steamship, the railroad, and the telegraph, Europeans generally were in an expansionist mood.

In France several groups helped to concentrate public attention on Africa. They intensified their efforts by focusing on specific regions. French officials and traders on the coast of Africa developed plans for inland expansion that merged with the more general imperialist ethos developed by geographers, abolitionists, the political left, missionaries, and writers of fiction. The action and thought of all these groups helped create the ideology to justify the piecemeal, haphazard expansion that actually occurred.

Geographers

The geographers were natural advocates of expansion. Occupationally concerned with overseas activities, they not only encouraged exploration, but also developed a well-articulated program of colonization. Even before the end of the Napoleonic wars, the influential geographer Malte-Brun, editor of the *Précis de la géographie universelle* and of the journal *Nouvelles annales des voyages,* called for the establishment of European colonies along every major African river. He was on the lookout for useful sites on which to establish plantation colonies, suggesting Senegal and Cyrenaica as possibilities. Later he cast his eyes toward the Western Sudan, advocating its conquest by an armed French expedition; as for the coast of Africa, he suggested colonies in Dahomey and the Ivory Coast.[1] Malte-Brun spelled out the rationale for conquest: France had the obligation to spread civilization and Christianity. And there were also advantages to the colonizing power; colonies would provide an outlet for excess population, a market for European goods, and an escape valve for "a monarchy . . . peopled by an ambitious and turbulent race."[2]

Ideas such as Malte-Brun's were given the prestige of institutional backing after the founding of the Société de géographie de Paris in 1822. From the time it organized, it was an active force in favor of French expansion overseas. Its members helped popularize imperialist ideas and at the same time worked for their realization by advising the government on expeditions. As they declared in their founding program, the members of the geographical society were convinced that "the perfection of geographic sciences is intimately tied to the advancement of the other sciences, the progress of civilization, the destruction of all hatred and all national rivalries and the betterment of the human species."[3]

European civilization would thus be "bringing to the whole universe the law of God and humanity."[4] Such action was not disinterested; the spread of European influence would draw the non-European world into the white man's orbit and ensure its dependency. Edmé Jomard, the distinguished geographer, famous for his scientific accomplishments while accompanying Napoleon on the Egyptian expedition, declared, "We want . . . Africa with the rest of the world to pay its tribute to our industry, to send to our cities overfilled with men its treasures, products, precious metals. . . . Africa must in its turn fall to modern civilization."[5] In an 1856 article in the *Revue des deux mondes*, Alfred Jacobs wrote that geographical explorations were motivated by a desire for "the conquest . . . of souls living under the darkness of the greatest barbarism; it is the desire to open for commerce and industry new roads, it is also the hope to have a whole race of men participate some day . . . in this social amelioration and intellectual development meant by civilization."[6]

Europeans conceived of civilization as a stage of development in which trade was carried on extensively. In Europe life had become gentler since the Renaissance, as a result of the increase in commerce. Trade had become possible as a result of increased production and, by allowing for new divisions of labor, had helped the growth of the European economy.[7] It was possible to think that, if exploration promoted "civilization," it would also bring about an increase in trade, which in turn would further advance "civilization." At times this interest in spreading trade and civilization may have been altruistic, but it was also motivated by economic interests. Baron Las Cases, president of the Société de géographie, called for French penetration into central Africa in order to spread French values there, "values that are the forerunners of our material products." France would thus be assured of "new outlets for our industry."[8] These notions suggested the establishment of economic, but not necessarily political, predominance. Occasionally, however, the Société de géographie articulated the need for overseas territorial conquest; the editor of its bulletin declared in 1859:

> We forget too often that no matter how rich a country may be, its own territory is never sufficient for its activities; its population would not be able to grow, its influence to maintain itself if it did not constantly expand its relations and extend its enterprise.[9]

The interest in geography spread in the 1870s; membership in the Paris organization grew from 600 in 1871 to 1,352 by 1875 and to 2,000 by 1881. Outside the capital eleven societies were founded in the provinces, as well as two in Algeria.[10] As in the 1820s, geographers in the 1870s played an important role in advising the government and in expounding imperialism.[11] Admiral La Roncière, president of the Société de géographie de Paris, served on one of the important sub-commissions of the trans-Sahara railroad commission that advised the government about building the railroad and insisted on the railroad's role in ensuring control of the Sudan. The close connection between the Société de géographie and the government seemed natural; in 1878 at least a quarter of the members were government officials.[12] Every Friday at the Petite Vache restaurant, Maunoir, secretary general of the Société, informally presided over social gatherings attended by both geographers and explorers, and here, in the 1870s and 1880s, the two groups shared ideas and affected each other's thinking about France's role overseas.[13]

In 1876 an offshoot of the Société de géographie de Paris organized under the name of the Société de géographie commerciale. It was even more imperialist than the parent organization, upholding a program of "militant geography."[14] Less interested in the scientific aspects of geography, it was devoted exclusively to exploring those areas that were of commercial benefit to France and that could be colonized.[15] It did not, however, disagree in any way with the parent organization, whose president, La Roncière, declared, "Providence has dictated that we know the world and conquer it. This supreme commandment is one of the imperious duties inscribed on our intelligence and on our activity."[16]

The Slavery Debate and Colonialism

In the first years after the turn of the nineteenth century, the notion of the utility of colonies was upheld by slave interests eager to see France regain Saint-Domingue.[17] Although the defeat of Leclerc's expedition had sealed the French fate in Saint-Domingue, the French did not give up the idea of regaining the former colony, either by force or by more peaceable means.[18] By 1815 the defeat of France in Europe made it unlikely that France would engage in a military venture against Haiti, which had bested even Napoleon. The other French possessions in the Caribbean continued to be important to France, and the debate over whether slavery ought to be preserved in them led to the proslavery forces' continued stress on the advantages of colonies to the national interest.[19]

The abolitionists also believed in empire. Continuing the themes developed in the eighteenth century, they pushed for colonies in Africa for two reasons: first, to find a substitute for the slave plantation colonies of the Antilles and, second—more pronounced after emancipation in 1848—to extirpate slavery and the slave trade from African soil. As was the case with their eighteenth-century predecessors, the abolitionists in the nineteenth century wished to show that slavery not only contradicted the laws of humanity, but also went against French self-interest. Instead of transporting blacks as slaves to the New World to grow tropical staple goods, the French could cultivate such goods in Africa by using free black labor. In Africa, the abolitionists argued, the plantations would flourish even better than in the Caribbean. The blacks would retain their freedom and France would make a profit.

The possibility of establishing colonies based on free black labor was an old concept that was given an added boost by the British founding of Sierra Leone. In France this experiment was thought successful, its failure largely unknown.[20] Whereas Sierra Leone had been the model of colonization at the end of the eighteenth and the beginning of the nineteenth centuries, Liberia came to occupy that position in the 1820s. The Liberians were seen as a virtuous and hardworking people, thus demonstrating that blacks could be producers without having to be enslaved. The founding of colonies similar to Liberia, it was thought, would further the interests of French trade and ensure the spread of Christianity to the African continent as a whole.[21] Tocqueville, among others, found that transporting free blacks from the United States was an inadequate solution to the potential race problems of America, but that it probably secured the introduction "of the arts and sciences of the Whites" into Africa.[22]

Schoelcher suggested that the blacks seized off the African

coast by French antislavery patrols be declared free and be
settled on the African coast in colonies such as Liberia and
Sierra Leone. The French government at times considered
setting up such colonies.[23] The colonization movement was
given added impetus by the founding in 1841 of the Institut
de l'Afrique, patterned after the African Institute in London.
The Institut's goals were to work for the cessation of the slave
trade and of slavery itself, to promote European commerce
with Africa, and to encourage Europeans to settle on the West
African coast, "on this soil rich in all the products of nature."
By spreading Christianity and civilization in Africa, Frenchmen
would win the populations over to France and "so to speak
make Frenchmen out of them."[24]

Such ideas influenced Admiral Edmond Bouët-Willaumez to
found Libreville in 1849. Slaves recaptured from the illegal
slave ships were freed by Bouet-Willaumez's antislavery patrols and were brought to settle in the town named after
Freetown, its namesake in Sierra Leone. Like Freetown, it was
to be an asylum for freed slaves, to be the means, Bouët-
Willaumez declared, "to spread as much as possible Christian
and French ideas on the shores of Gabon." And also like Sierra
Leone, the settlement was initially a failure, falling prey to internal dissension. A few of the liberated Africans, however,
stayed behind, becoming the nucleus of a growing settlement
that by 1865 had 1,800 inhabitants, of whom 100 were
Europeans.[25]

The possibility of using former slaves to advance French interests in Africa was a panacea embraced by Frenchmen of all
walks of life. Father Boilat suggested that black West Indians
be brought to Senegal, where, since they were already Catholic and knew French, they could serve as an example to Africans and help speed their conversion and civilization. In 1850,
two years after the abolition of slavery, the trader V. Verneuil,
in a petition to Louis Napoleon, declared that 30,000 blacks in
the French West Indies wished "to return to their fatherland,
Senegal"; if they were settled there, they would "civilize and
convert to Christianity their compatriots."[26]

Most hopes of using former slaves as intermediaries for
spreading French culture and influence, however, centered on

the purchase and freeing of indigenous African slaves. Missionaries were especially enamored with this solution. Finding little success in their work, they hit upon the idea of buying slaves, especially children, converting and educating them, and then using them as the intermediaries through which to spread their missionary work. Father Bessieux suggested doing so in Dahomey.[27] In the 1870s a special missionary foundation was established to purchase slaves, free them, and then try to convert them.[28] Begun in North Africa, such ventures spread to East Africa, notably Zanzibar. The founder of the White Fathers order, Father Lavigerie, sponsored a program of purchasing young slaves to be converted to Christianity, trained in medicine, and sent out to preach "faith and civilization." These plans, while well-intentioned, did not take into account the extent to which purchasing slaves—even in order to free them—encouraged the internal slave trade. The French were shocked when the British consul in Zanzibar charged them with encouraging the trade.[29]

That such programs of emancipation could never have a great effect on indigenous slavery was apparent. It was thought that African slavery could best be rooted out by transforming African society *in toto*. The opponents of the Atlantic slave trade argued that, if Europe established plantation colonies based on free labor, then slaves would no longer be needed for plantations in the Antilles. The same argument was presented as the remedy for indigenous slavery. Adopting ideas similar to those expounded by T. F. Buxton in *The African Slave Trade and Its Remedy*, French abolitionists pointed to the advance of French commerce as an alternative to the slave trade and a cure for indigenous slavery in Africa.[30] Most of the opponents of indigenous slavery thought it would disappear gradually as European ideas and institutions penetrated Africa. Some had a more radical program, however. Raffenel, shocked by the African slavery he had observed in the Upper Senegal, called for European intervention to eradicate it. He was somewhat unclear on the form such intervention should take, but his writings give the impression that he had in mind political conquest. The abolitionist Alfred Michiels called for an all-out war against Africans engaged in the slave trade: "all these monsters should be destroyed like the wolves in England." The explorer Mage, having observed slavery in the Sudan, felt that conquest of the area was the only way to eradicate the long, cruel slave caravans.[31]

The Political Left

Optimism about the advantages to Africa of the European advance into the continent came from a general faith in the possibility of human progress, especially among those on the political left. They saw Europe as having been transformed by the spread of the philosophes' ideas and by the industrial revolution. They pointed to Europe as the beacon to the rest of the world. The political left foresaw a time when the world would be one, tied together by modern means of communication and by shared values. The utopian socialists in particular held on to that vision and played a significant role in exploration. To prepare for the active interaction of the peoples of the world, they publicized the idea of a canal through the Suez isthmus; they studied the wealth of the countries along the route to India and explored Upper Egypt, Ethiopia, the East African coast, and Arabia. One of the Saint-Simonians, Prax, was the first Frenchman to penetrate to Mecca.

The socialists enthusiastically supported the conquest of Algeria in the 1830s, seeing the possibilities of establishing model socialist societies and of expanding into the rest of Africa. In 1831 Philippe Buchez, a Saint-Simonian who later became a "Christian socialist," welcomed the conquest that had just taken place in Algeria, because it would allow France to dominate the Mediterranean; the new holding could serve as a base for "direct communications with the interior of Africa."[32] Enfantin, Saint-Simon's official successor, desired to see the day when "four Europeans leaving from Cairo, Algiers, Senegal, and the Cape of Good Hope can meet in Timbuktu." He hoped that, once France was well established in Algeria, it could build railroads southward and expand its influence to the Niger Valley and Timbuktu.[33]

The utopian Charles Fourier, in a proposal to the Société de géographie de Paris, asserted that, if the model communes he

was suggesting for Europe, the *phalanstères,* were established
in Africa, they would civilize the population, thus allowing
explorers to go inland unhindered. As social organizations the
phalanstères would encourage production and ensure France a
tripling of its wealth within a year. In his theoretical writings,
he speculated on the possibility of settling four million Frenchmen in Africa, to be aided by blacks who would work in
their own *phalanstères.* [34] The disciples of Fourier followed
their master's ideas; a Fourierist paper announced that "the
motto for a nation situated like France . . . must be: colonize
everywhere and always." In 1848 Fourierists in Algeria, cele-
brating the new Republic, declared, "The colonization of Africa
is, we are profoundly convinced, the providential destiny of
France in the nineteenth century."

Other forms of socialism also favored a program of expansionism. Louis Blanc upheld a Jacobin ideal of empire: wherever France conquered, human progress was ensured. In 1839
he wrote that France had not passed anywhere "without leaving behind the signs of its spirituality." France was motivated
by an urge to expand, to project itself onto the rest of the
globe. According to Proudhon, Europe's predestined role was
teaching the non-European peoples the need for work; with
regard to the Africans, whom he accused of being adverse to
labor, he announced, "it is our right to compel them to do
so."[35]

All these socialist schemes were part of the conviction that
France had a special mission in the globe; as one Saint-
Simonian, Guillain, put it, the mission chosen for his countrymen was "the civilization of territories as yet in the grip of
savagery and barbarism."[36] Saint-Simonians would later play an
important role in trying to expand French influence overseas.
Prominent among them was de Lesseps, who, in building the
Suez Canal, thought of his efforts not only as a technical feat
but also as the opening of an era in which European influence—especially that of France—would radiate throughout
the world. He called for the partition of Africa among the
European powers.[37]

Saint-Simonian concerns became the main themes of publicists who wrote specifically on colonial questions. In 1864

Jules Duval, a Saint-Simonian and, at other times, a Fourierist journalist, proclaimed a colonial program for France. He deplored the fact that France's role overseas was inferior to that of other powers, notably England, and he suggested that France could recapture its position as a great world power by conquest overseas. Duval pointed out that an empire would provide trade opportunities, but his main emphasis was on national glory: "There is honor in participating in the exploration and exploitation of the globe, which is the supreme mission of humanity on earth."[38]

While many others echoed Duval's message, the work of one publicist in particular serves as an example of the kinds of colonial themes that were fostered. Paul Leroy-Beaulieu, an economist with Saint-Simonian connections (he was the son-in-law of the Saint-Simonian Michel Chevalier), declared in his comparative study, *De la colonisation,* that "the future of France is in great part in Africa."[39] Essentially, his message was that expansion was necessary for economic and political reasons; providing France with an outlet for manufactured goods, it would help stimulate population growth. While much of Africa might not be climatically suited for emigration, nevertheless, even French acquisition of Africa would stimulate population growth by providing greater opportunities for French commerce. Joined to this economic appeal was a strong nationalist motive. Only by acquiring parts of Africa, he declared, could France "maintain its grandeur."[40] If France failed to colonize, "What will be our importance? What weight shall we hold in this world?" Leroy-Beaulieu, seemingly affected by social Darwinist notions, predicted that, if France did not expand as other nations—here he pointed to the spectacular growth of continental powers such as the United States and the Russian empire and the overseas expansion of Britain— then France was doomed. He wrote, "What holds for individuals, hold for nations . . . it is necessary to ascend ceaselessly if one does not want to descend on the social ladder."[41] Owing many of his thoughts to the expansionist ideology of the Saint-Simonians, Leroy-Beaulieu was also very much a political liberal.

In fact, nineteenth-century liberalism as a whole was sympathetic to an overseas mission. Originally, however, French liberals hesitated on the issue of expansion. Many adopted the critical attitude of their British counterparts toward the mercantilist empire.[42] The economist Jean-Baptiste Say had done so, but in 1826, in the fifth edition of his *Traité,* he abruptly and significantly reversed his previous position, stating that one day Europeans would set up colonies in the heart of Africa, cultivate tropical staples at modest prices, and civilize the continent.[43]

The conquest of Algeria in 1830 troubled many liberals, but, in the end, the desire to preserve and advance French power and prestige led to the decision of the special parliamentary commission established to investigate the Algerian question to retain the colony. Tocqueville, who was a member of that commission, wrote to an American friend that American expansion westward was a good example for France to follow in Africa.[44] Schoelcher scolded Europeans for not founding large and important colonies in Africa; if that were done, he maintained, the continent could be quickly civilized. A generation later, when France was considering penetrating inland from Senegal, Schoelcher welcomed France's opportunity to gain a market of "200 million consumers" and to play a role "in this magnificent movement of civilization that will be an added glory for the nineteenth century." And when the military conquest began, he described colonization as the advance of civilization into Africa, a form of reparation for the evils of the slave trade.[45] The poet Alfred de Vigny spoke of the Europeans' duty to civilize "savage races" and to make sure that the whole globe was inhabited only by civilized men.[46]

Other liberal writers also saw such a responsibility thrust upon Europeans, especially upon Frenchmen. In 1849 Victor Hugo's newspaper, *L'Evénement,* urged the conquest of Madagascar, so that from that island and Algeria, which France already possessed, there could be a two-pronged assault on the African continent. Regardless of the savagery of this conquest, it would benefit the Africans:

> France is composing a magnificent poem that has as its title: the colonization of Africa. . . . She resorts to war . . . only to

the extent that is necessary for civilization. What reassures her is that she knows that she bears in her hand light and liberty; she knows that, for a savage people, to be occupied by France is to begin to be free, for a city of barbarians, to be burned by France is to begin to be enlightened. That she should wage war, invade territories, bombard fortifications, this is not important if she silences her guns with books.

Hugo, like all those on the left, was deeply affected by Jacobin nationalism, and saw in the spread of French power the work of providence. When military actions began, he served as honorary president of a projected Compagnie coloniale française, which was designed to exploit the wealth of the new empire and to carry overseas "the renown of France and its generous ideals."[47] In the 1830s Lamartine, impatient with the conservatism of Louis-Philippe's foreign policy, urged that the powers of Europe gather in congress and divide Asia and Africa among them:

Let Europe colonize Asia and Africa; let it expand on these wild shores the excess of its activity with its noble passions and its progressive civilization and religion; let it expand in these wild regions . . . and you, gentlemen, place yourselves at the head of this holy crusade of mankind.[48]

These attitudes were widespread. In 1859 the liberal journal Le Siècle declared that "everywhere France has set her foot, she has made herself loved," and it called for France to unleash in Africa "this great crusade of reason and liberty."[49] Two decades later Léon Gambetta's official publication, the République française, consistently advocated overseas expansion to every corner of the earth, proclaiming the desirability of a new empire "to replace the one which the Monarch lost in India and America a century ago."[50]

The Republic, founded after the defeat of France in the Franco-Prussian War of 1870, was an ardent proponent of imperialism, but the defeat itself had not suddenly caused French imperial ambitions. True, the defeat was sometimes singled out as a humiliation that needed to be compensated for overseas. In an editorial published almost exactly a year after the outbreak of what had been a disastrous war for France, a writer for *Le Temps* announced that, "cruelly dwarfed in Europe, we must look for compensation elsewhere." Having also in mind the recent experiences of the Commune uprising, the author hoped that an overseas empire would provide an outlet for the poor and would help France to avoid future "social explosions."[51] In their attempts to expand French influence overseas, numerous explorers and military officers cited the defeat of 1870 as a motive for their actions.[52] Their strong nationalist feelings, however, were no different from earlier motives for imperialism,[53] which had also been strongly influenced by the desire to see France uphold its rank as a great power. The only difference was that until 1870 colonial expansion had been seen as a way to preserve great power status vis-à-vis England. After 1870 Germany also entered the picture.[54]

The Missionary Impulse

Missionary sentiments and activities also led to an emphasis on expansion overseas. During the Restoration piety and formal religion, regarded as a way to combat revolutionary ideas inside France, played an important part in society. This stress on religion led to a renewed interest in missionary activities, one of the most important of which was the founding in Lyons in 1822 of the Société de la propagation de la foi, an organization of clergy and laymen. The Société raised money for Catholic missions around the world; its journal, which chronicled its activities, came out in editions of 100,000, a very high figure for the time.[55] Supporters of missionary activity received copies of the *Annales de la propagation de la foi*, which gave its readers a vivid sense of participation in a great adventure overseas. As the Bishop of Carcassonne wrote, "Edifying and curious accounts will give you from time to time information on the progress of the faith in barbarous and savage countries . . . you will applaud the triumph of these laborers of the Gospel."[56] There was also an element of competition: the faithful were asked to contribute more than the Protestants and more than neighboring dioceses.[57]

The missionary zeal in France was well developed. It is es-

timated that between 1820 and 1914 five or six hundred
pastoral letters on the missions were issued by French bishops.
Frenchmen in large numbers went overseas to serve as missionaries; in 1900 over two thirds of all Catholic missionaries
were French.[58]

Missionizing was presented as glorifying France: "France . . .
has been chosen by God." France, a cleric declared, had declined in power and prestige as a result of revolution and irreligion, but missionary activity would re-establish its glory.[59]
Father Lavigerie, who established the White Fathers in
Algeria, proclaimed in his first pastoral letter of 1867 that "in
His providence God has chosen France to make of Algeria the
cradle of a great and Christian nation, a nation like unto herself, her sister, and her child, happy to walk by her side in the
paths of honor and justice." He envisioned spreading Christianity from Algeria to the rest of Africa. The entire continent,
declared Father Desribes, a missionary in Dahomey, had been
reserved by providence for France to evangelize.[60]

Most missionaries, especially those in the first half of the
nineteenth century, were not advocating French conquest of
Africa, but their own ambitions added to the expansionist tone
of the era. In the early years of missionary activity, however,
some French missionaries were remarkably wary of becoming
the instruments of French power or even of European civilization. They shunned such a role for fear that it would interfere
with their religious success. Father Libermann, founder of the
Saint-Coeur de Marie, an order of missionaries to the black
peoples of the world, instructed his staff: "Do not judge according to what you have seen in Europe; lay aside the mores
and spirit of Europe; become Negroes with the Negroes." And
one of Libermann's missionaries, Father Truffet, made clear
that his activity in West Africa was in no way intended to
spread European influence there: "We are not going to Africa
in order to establish Italy, France or any other European country there; but to spread the Holy Catholic Church, free of
nationality or any other human system."[61] Truffet shunned
European culture because he wanted to overcome the Africans' suspicion that priests were just the spearhead of French
expansionism. And there was a second reason for missionaries

to fear the spread of the European culture: having imposed on the Africans its worst elements, that culture had been destructive of African life:

> All they have received from Europeans is the love of money, and the knowledge of how to use guns and tobacco. Add to that the abuse of brandy ... and you will know what the Europeans have done for the civilization of this country.[62]

Despite these strictures against European civilization and the attempt by some missionaries to be "Negroes, with the Negroes," the Christianizing effort was generally seen as part of the spread of European culture, which in turn was regarded as beneficial to Christianity. Even Father Libermann, who had enjoined against identifying Christianity wholly with Western culture, stated that the missionary effort was an attempt not only to spread religion

> but also to initiate peoples to our European civilization. Faith, Christian morality, education, knowledge about agriculture and mechanical arts will mutually aid each other ... and will finally lead the black populations to benefit from Christianity, the mores and the civilization of the peoples of Europe.[63]

Some missionaries hoped that, by attracting Africans to plantation colonies in Senegal, they could isolate Africans from native religious influences, teach them European methods of production, "civilize" them, and, presumably, make them more receptive to Christianity.[64] The introduction of Western social organization was thought useful to the Christianizing effort.

Although sometimes ambivalent, the missionaries' generally positive attitude toward Western culture led them to believe that certain values could best be spread through the expansion of European political power. At times, Libermann was even willing to see his missionaries cooperate with and help to further the interests of the French authorities overseas. While he warned his missionaries against taking any action that might give Africans the impression that the priests were "political agents of the French government," he also advocated close collaboration with French administrators, as long as it was not "opposite to the interests of God and your conscience."[65]

Missionaries were willing to collaborate with the colonial authorities because they saw French imperialism as helping the evangelization of the world.[66] On the local level, of course, there often were disputes between missionaries and officials who disagreed on policies and were entangled in personality conflicts. A notable example was the perennial dispute between Father Bessieux and the authorities of the fort in Gabon.[67] For all these local difficulties, however, churchmen as a group looked to France to help them spread the gospel. The willingness of Napoleon III to espouse the cause of missionaries overseas and to come to their rescue with military help (as in Cochin-China in 1858) showed how empire and religion could cooperate. Bishop Dupanloup in 1860 described the developing European imperialism as "a partition of the universe among the sons of Christ." Overseas conquests followed "the designs of Providence."[68]

In order to strengthen the prestige of his missionaries in Dahomey, Father Planque, the superior of the Missions africaines, which after the middle of the nineteenth century was responsible for missionary work south of the Gambia, called for French naval demonstrations.[69] And in Dahomey, Father Borghero attributed the failure of the missionary to the "diabolic powers of the fetishist chiefs" and the physical weakness and lethargy of the Africans. It was his view that only strong European tutelage could change those conditions, and that Christianity in Africa would be successful if it were spread by conquest, as had been the case in the Americas and in Europe itself.[70] Later Father Laffitte wrote that in 1862 he had hoped that France would take over Porto Novo: "With France there, I thought Christianity would implant itself strongly in the country and, with Christianity, civilization."[71]

In the 1860s French conquests in Senegal, Indochina, and Mexico were welcomed by churchmen in France; one announced that the sword of France was "carrying out the work of God."[72] The close relationship between church and state overseas did not cease with the collapse of the Second Empire and the founding of the Third Republic. In the 1870s the regime was not particularly anticlerical; when it became so in the 1880s, Catholics nevertheless continued to support the efforts of the Republic overseas, seeing the conquests as leading to the spread of the faith.[73]

French Protestant missions also emphasized the need for the expansion of European values and civilization. The Société des missions évangéliques supported explorations in Africa as preparatory to its conversion. The Protestant ambition for the conquest of Africa was total: "The day is not far . . . when the missionaries from the South in the Cape of Good Hope, from the West on the coast of Guinea, from the North in the Barbary states, and from the East in Abyssinia will join in the center of these unknown regions."[74] The Protestants, exactly like the Catholics in stressing the need to spread their message to the four corners of the earth, helped to fuel the expansionist ethos of the times.

Fiction

Expansionist themes appeared in the fiction of the era. One can discount a novel by Baron Roger, *Kélédor* (1828), for, after all, the author was the governor of Senegal and had written the book to propagandize his plantation schemes there. But novels by authors with no colonial connections show that expansionist ideas were common enough to be taken up by writers of fiction. The desirability of French influence in Africa was a prominent theme in the novel by de Préo, *Les Youlofi* (1842), which tells of a soldier and a priest who make friends with the Wolofs in Senegal and build them a church and a bath house with mineral water. The bathing place, they hope, will attract people from surrounding regions, "who will return home with the most happy and favorable disposition toward Christianity and Civilization."[75] The two heroes reform the government and set up a music school; the Africans live in eternal bliss, and the French make decisive inroads into the continent.

A dissent from the imperialist attitude came, surprisingly enough, from a writer of children's books, Léon Guérin, who, in *Le tour du monde* (1851), reminded his young readers that "it

is not always . . . civilization that Europeans bring to distant
countries. To Africa it is rum; to China opium." But this minor
instance of disagreement should not obscure the overriding
consensus with which novels portrayed the benefits that Africa
gained from the meeting of the two cultures. "If agriculture
and industry developed in Guinea," wrote A. E. de Saintes in
another children's book, *Voyages du petit André en Afrique*
(1852), "this country would be one of the most flourishing in
the world."[76]

Fictional accounts assumed that with hard work whites overseas could transform savage nature and create a facsimile of
the distant, beloved homeland, for Africa was destined to be
exploited and settled by whites. This idea was presented with
strong conviction in the works of Jules Verne, whose fiction
paralleled the program of the Société de géographie, of which
Verne was a member. In *Five Weeks in a Balloon,* Dr. Ferguson,
flying over the Sudan, speculated:

> The people of the future ages may come here when the coun-
> tries of Europe can no longer support their inhabitants. . . .
> Africa will offer to new generations the accumulated treasure
> of centuries . . . the climate . . . will yield to the purifying
> influence of distribution of crops and drainage . . . this dis-
> trict over which we are passing, more fertile, richer, more
> quickly productive than the others, will become some great
> kingdom.[77]

Verne saw no moral dilemma in colonization. Louis Jacolliot,
however, in his rather tedious travel novel, *Voyage au pays
mystérieux,* at least raised the moral question, but then he
quickly disposed of it by invoking natural law:

> Every nation has the absolute right to extend its influence as
> far as possible to bring progress to the savage peoples . . . in
> the face of these immense lands that are not being exploited
> by their inhabitants; nations have the natural right that allows
> the acquisition of the land to every new arrival. . . . A people
> then has the right to extend itself outside, to open new
> routes for the days when the home will be too small.[78]

If conquest was perceived as a benefit to French trade and a
potential outlet for surplus French population, it was viewed

also as an added strength in France's continental rivalry with Germany. In Armand Dubarry's children's book, *Voyage au Dahomey* (1879), the hero goes to Dahomey intending to make a fortune, put his wealth at the disposal of the Republic, and thus enable France to buy enough cannons to carry out a *revanche* against Germany and win back Alsace-Lorraine.[79]

The valiant white men who in nineteenth-century novels conquered land, sea, and sky by heroic action and discipline of mind were the fictional models of the explorers and officers whom the Third Republic sent forth into the Sudanic and equatorial belts of Africa. When the colonial officer Hubert Lyautey spoke of a large and ambitious project in Indochina, a high official exclaimed, "But that is pure Jules Verne," whereupon Lyautey retorted, "Good Lord, yes sir, of course, it is Jules Verne. For twenty years the people who march forward have been doing nothing else but Jules Verne."[80]

Territorial Expansion

While imperialist ideas were prevalent among many groups in France, they were not necessarily the opinion of the majority of the French public. Colonies, even in the heyday of imperial expansion in the 1880s and 1890s, did not receive popular acclaim.[81] Rather, throughout the century an intellectual climate had developed among the generally well-educated segments of French society; it was from their midst that the policy makers and the apologists of imperialism came. The imperial ambitions expressed in the years 1800–1880 focused on three specific regions in Africa: the Senegambia, Western Sudan, and the west coast of Africa south from Senegal to Gabon.[82]

After the middle of the nineteenth century, the French became particularly active, sending expeditions inland and down the coast in the hope of spreading commercial and political influence. The French acquired some territory in the years 1840–1880, but it is especially after the latter date that they seized significant parts of real estate. The late-nineteenth-century change in attitude and course of action was in response to a perceived change in British policy; to prevent areas from falling under British control, the French launched a conquest of their own.

The French acquisition of territory in Africa occurred piecemeal and was influenced by both local considerations and perceived French interests. It would be a mistake to see this expansion as the fruit of an overall imperialist strategy that had captivated either the French public or the government. Throughout the nineteenth century, imperialist thought had developed among well-informed, specialized groups such as the missionaries and the abolitionists and had been intensified by the agitation by traders and administrators for inland expansion from the modest coastal positions that the French already occupied. These groups helped form a body of thought that could be used to rationalize the imperialist activities of the 1880s and gave the various overseas activities a coherence that they otherwise would not have had. Though developed in a fragmentary manner and presented by individuals and specific interest groups, the expansionist ideas enunciated prior to 1880 had already created an imperial consciousness in France. It could be called on to justify the "scramble" once it was launched.

Plans for imperial control and finally conquest itself continued to present Africans as passive, as the objects of French activity, thus reinforcing the existing images of blacks. White domination was thus still regarded as a natural result of the perceived inequality between Europeans and Africans.

Afterword

Imperialism and the Black Image

In the late nineteenth century, explorers, administrators, and soldiers in Africa retained many of the views that had become customary among Europeans confronting people whose appearance and customs seemed so different from their own. Their observations lacked originality; they reiterated centuries-old complaints about African laziness, lasciviousness, godlessness, and savagery.[1] It is possible that, under the impact of imperialism, these stereotypes were increasingly emphasized to justify conquest. Jean Bayol, governor of newly conquered Dahomey, emphasized the savagery and barbarism of that kingdom in order to show that "France, by putting an end to such atrocities, will have carried out a humanitarian mission." In the 1890s, while the conquest was underway, the French popular press reproduced illustrations of Dahomean human sacrifice that had been circulated a generation earlier.[2] Such images served to justify imperialism by underscoring the age-old view of Africans as savage, inferior peoples. Commandant Edmond Ferry declared that France's continued presence in West Africa was necessary, for "if tomorrow we were to disappear from this part of Africa, he [the black man] would slide back into barbarism where his demi-savage instincts lead him."[3] Imperialism did not cause any reassessment of blacks, but rather helped to preserve the negative images that had existed since the earliest stages of Franco-African contact.

In some cases, however, imperial control provided the opportunity for long-term contacts between the French and Africans, which led to sympathetic assessments of blacks and their societies.[4] Some colonial administrators developed a close sympathy for African societies and in their writings dissented from the prevailing image of blacks. The best known was Maurice Delafosse, who in several works showed the capacity of Africans to erect complex states, economies, and systems of philosophy, religions, and aesthetics. He fought against ethnocentric judgments of Africa, although his eagerness to show African accomplishments in statecraft and philosophy still reveals a certain ethnocentrism.[5] Missionaries, so apt to be disturbed by non-Christians, in some cases even showed sympathetic insights into animism. In 1927 Father Aupiais wrote that, although Europeans had been blinded by their prejudices toward Africans, the latter in fact had a code of morality, basic wisdom, respect for each other, and love of the divine.[6]

Delafosse and Aupiais were, however, in the minority and their views did not make any significant impact on the general public or, in fact, on most of the writings about Africa. School textbooks in the 1920s and 1930s, by emphasizing the civilizing mission of French imperial rule in Africa, reinforced the notions of black barbarism and savagery.[7] Colonial novels in the interwar years were particularly powerful in conveying an image of African savagery and bestiality; their accusations of black cannibalism were even stronger than those made prior to the colonial era. Films about Africa represented whites heroically; African societies were merely the backdrops providing the French an opportunity to show love of adventure and resoluteness.[8] Anthropological thought had abandoned racism, but French popular opinion during the first three quarters of the twentieth century not only placed Africans low on the evolutionary scale of humanity, but also often embraced the racist view that, condemned by their biology to an inferior existence, blacks were suited only to serve whites and to live dependent on them.

Blacks in France

In their personal relations with black Africans, French individuals, of course, often departed from the negative stereotypes; if they held ideas about black inferiority, these did not prevent them from being friendly to Africans. The combat of black troops on France's behalf in World War I opened an era of good feeling toward blacks. Prime Minister Clemenceau was deeply moved to see the black troops after a battle and is supposed to have said, "There is not a 'Boche,' not a doctor of the University of Berlin or Munich, who in beauty and grandeur is equal to any Senegalese."[9] Lucie Cousturier published a novel, *Les Inconnus chez moi* (1920), which dealt with the brave sacrifices of the black troops, the so-called *tirailleurs Sénégalais* (they did not all come from Senegal); *Force Bonté* (1926), the autobiography of one of the *tirailleurs,* Bakari Diallo, was a minor literary success.

Among intellectuals and artists, Africa had already gained a certain renown before and in the years following World War I. Seeing the culture of the West as decadent, many intellectuals looked elsewhere for inspiration. They admired African art, for instance, for its simplicity and spontaneity of expression. The works of Matisse, Vlaminck, Derain, and Picasso were all influenced by African forms. In 1917 the art critic and poet Guillaume Apollinaire, together with Paul Guillaume, published *Le premier album de sculptures nègres;* in 1930 the prestigious *Cahiers d'art* dedicated an issue to African art.[10] Jazz became popular and black musicians and entertainers such as Josephine Baker conquered the hearts of Parisians.

Black intellectuals issued manifestoes on the meaning of blackness; in the cafés of Paris, Aimé Césaire and Léopold Sédar Senghor formulated their doctrines of négritude. Many American blacks felt comfortable in Paris, finding it free of the racial discrimination then so pervasive in the United States. Richard Wright declared, "There is more freedom in one square block of Paris than in all of the United States."[11]

The apparently easy social mixing of whites and blacks in Paris gave the impression of an egalitarian society free of racism. The French had proclaimed doctrines of equality since the Revolution and sincerely believed that they had been true to them. Seeing the acceptance of blacks in Paris in the 1920s and 1930s, foreigners concurred with the French view that there was no color prejudice in France. Yet egalitarianism had not been followed in either the Antilles or after the mid-nineteenth century in Africa, and Frenchmen, like other Europeans, had for centuries maintained a negative image of blacks.

How can one explain the apparent contradiction between the legacy of antiblack thought and the apparent openness toward blacks in the French capital in the interwar years? The answer seems to lie in the lack of a necessary correlation between intellectual convictions and actual social relations. In the abstract the French might well have thought that blacks were inferior, but in actual contacts they could treat Africans with affection and esteem.

It must be remembered that until the 1960s blacks composed a very small minority in France. Many came from the educated elites of Africa, with refined culture and taste. They were often young students or artists who were assimilated with relative ease into the cosmopolitan and nonconformist circles of the Left Bank. They were a guest group, not in competition with the French for scarce goods. They were exotic additions to the French scene. After spending a few years in Paris, they left. The French could relate to them as temporary residents, without considering whether they could or wanted to live with them permanently.

Traditional views of black inferiority continued, despite the contribution of African colonies to the war effort and the liberation of France during World War II, or the colonies' subsequent achievement of independence. Moreover, existing negative stereotypes were exacerbated by the large immigration of blacks into France after World War II, especially in the 1960s. In the 1970s, 200,000 blacks, of whom roughly half came from the French Antilles and the other half from the independent African states, resided in France. Most of them, because of low salaries, difficulties in finding adequate housing, and the need to send home a large proportion of their earned income, lived in crowded slum conditions. The majority were single males. Their life-style in France created a great gap between them and the white host population. In addition, of course, were the barriers of language and culture, for, despite decades of colonial rule, little effort was made to spread French education in Africa. The blacks' occupation of the lowest and most menial jobs in the French economy created a certain contempt for them.

Many of the problems of African migrants were shared by

migrants from other parts of the world who came to work in France. The black migrants from the Antilles, however, should not have suffered most of these problems: they knew French and French culture, they were French citizens, and their life-style was not significantly at variance from that of their white compatriots. To the extent that they suffered ostracism, they were victims not of xenophobia but of racism, for race seemed to be the only characteristic that distinguished them from countless other Frenchmen.

The persistence of the negative image and the confrontation with a large, apparently permanent black population sharpened racial feelings in France and revealed antiblack prejudice. Projections of an increase in the black population—some commentators have predicted that by 1985 there will be one million blacks in France—have raised tensions.[12] A public-opinion poll of 1962 showed that one out of five Frenchmen felt that there were too many blacks in France; a poll of 1967 revealed that 52 percent of Parisians had antiblack feelings.[13] At least half of those interviewed in an in-depth survey conducted for the Ministry of Cooperation (in charge of foreign aid to former African colonies) believed in the superiority of whites over blacks, and a fifth of the total sample thought that this superiority was racial or in some other way innate. The survey revealed also that

> the great majority of those interviewed have aggressive feelings toward blacks and the countries of black Africa. These take the form of repulsion or desire for domination or superiority. They are extremely widespread since we have hardly found more than one interviewee out of ten who did not show such a reaction.

The image of Africans after some three centuries of contact has not improved significantly. One woman seemed to summarize the deep prejudices accumulated in French culture over the centuries; she told the interviewer that an African

> evokes something dark which repels me. . . . He is too primitive to be attractive . . . scenes of cannibalism . . . I think all of this comes from childhood education. . . . What

repels me especially is the physical appearance of these
people; I have a horror of darkness, of their color of skin and
flattened nose . . . a black man makes me frightened, it is
physical.[14]

Such feelings seem to have multiplied with the increased
number of blacks in France; they are no longer viewed as interesting and exotic, but rather as a threat. The American
journalist Roi Ottley apparently sensed the thin veneer of
French acceptance when he wrote that blacks were accepted
mainly for their exotic appearance.[15] But as the black population has increased, blacks have met with open discrimination
and expressions of collective hostility.[16] A black American
visiting Paris in the 1960s described racism in France as "but
an attenuated form of what I have known in the USA."[17]

The increased hostility against blacks is not exclusively the
result of the long intellectual tradition of antiblack feeling, but
also the response to the perceived threat of a growing new
population. That intellectual legacies are not the sole determinants of group interaction may be seen in the French response
to the North African migrant workers whom they call "Arabs."
Compared to blacks, Arabs historically enjoyed a far better
reputation in French thought (except, of course, among the
settlers in Algeria). In their political and religious institutions,
they seemed closer to the European mode and could be appreciated in those terms. Nor were the differences in outward
appearance so acute. Yet, despite the higher position Arabs
have historically occupied in French thought, the popular response to them since World War II has been far more hostile
than to black Africans. To some degree this hostility may result from feelings engendered by the Algerian war, but mainly
it is due to the North Africans' longer presence and greater
numbers in France. In 1950, 200,000 Algerians lived in
France; by the 1970s over 800,000 did so.

North Africans, by religion, language, and slightly darker
skin color, stood apart from the French. The French had a
mixture of fear and contempt toward them that was even
greater than that toward blacks. In 1966 a poll of representative French individuals revealed that 18 percent thought there

were too many blacks in France and that 62 percent thought there were too many North Africans.[18] A poll of Parisians showed 65 percent "having a racist attitude toward Arabs"; 26 percent would be "very discontent" if their daughters were to marry black men; 38 percent would be if they married Arabs.[19] In southern France, where a large proportion of both the North African population and the former white settlers in Algeria have settled, hostility toward North Africans has been particularly acute. In a series of terrorist incidents against North Africans in the autumn of 1973, several were murdered; the authorities showed themselves to be remarkably lax in attempting to discover the killers.[20] Although blacks suffered from discrimination, they did not meet hostility on this scale. As the greater intensity of hatred toward the North Africans was due to their presence in larger numbers in France, the hostility against blacks was not due solely to the legacy of centuries of contempt, but also to current social tensions between groups—on the one hand, a white native group; on the other, an easily identifiable migrant group of blacks.

The role of earlier ideas was mainly that they were available to rationalize the frictions that had developed. The traditional prejudices against blacks now have had an opportunity to play an active role in the modern interaction of whites and blacks. But even with no history of negative feelings, human groups can quickly develop xenophobia when they are brought into contact with an alien people whom they perceive as a threat. Moreover, an alien group of only minimal size can be the target of considerable prejudice, as is the Jewish population in Eastern Europe, which, during World War II, was almost wiped out. Yet, with hardly any Jews left in Eastern Europe, anti-Semitism, the result of a centuries-old heritage of prejudice deeply implanted in East European culture, is still rife.[21]

There seems to be considerable variation in the patterns of prejudice. It is possible for prejudice to have deep cultural roots or to emerge suddenly in the face of what are perceived as threatening foreign elements in the society. Or it may develop as a mixture of both elements, as has been the case in the current attitude toward blacks in France.

Until very recently, the French vociferously denied that

they were racists. That some of the main racist thinkers of the nineteenth century were Frenchmen and that the Jews were persecuted under Vichy have been proclaimed accidental phenomena in no way connected to the legacy of French culture. However, the considerable hostility that since the 1960s the French have shown to the migrant workers has been recognized as a form of racism. In a series that was widely commented upon, journalist Jean Lacouture published articles entitled "Les français sont-ils racistes?"—a question that he answered in the affirmative.[22]

Sociologists and other commentators have labeled French hostility toward migrant workers as racism. In many cases, such use of the term has produced semantic nonsense. One might ask, how can the French be "racist" toward the Portuguese or the Spanish, who belong to the same race as the French? The only racially different immigrant group in France is the black one, yet it seems that other groups are nonetheless also viewed as different races. The desire to lump Algerians and Portuguese into a race other than that of the French shows the persistence of racial thinking. The transformation of Algerians and Portuguese into another race seems to demonstrate and prove their inferiority to the general public.

The efforts of intellectuals and public authorities to combat the growing hostility toward migrant workers have met with varying success. Intellectuals write books and publish manifestoes that, as one worker writing in *L'Esprit* wryly noted, have had little effect on the French worker living in daily contact and sometimes conflict with his foreign neighbors.[23]

For thirteen years the French parliament had under consideration a bill to outlaw discrimination in housing and hiring on the basis of race or religion, and, almost yearly since 1959, it was defeated. The opposition to the bill was based on the argument that its passage would be a shameful admission of something that officially did not exist in France—racism. The lack of such legislation was in fact cited by the French representative to the United Nations Security Council as a source of pride:

There are few traditions that are so much a part of the history of my country as the concept of equality between the

races. . . . Every place where French laws and mores are the
rule, there is no racial discrimination. It has not even been
forbidden because it is not necessary to do so.[24]

A bill outlawing racial discrimination finally passed in 1972.
It is now widely recognized that the French are capable of racism. The suggested remedy has been unusual, however; it is
generally thought that reducing black migration into France
will be the best cure for further manifestations of racism.[25] By
agreement with African countries, the French government has
limited the immigration of blacks but has increased the
number of Portuguese and Spanish workers allowed entry.
The liberal journal *L'Express* greeted this policy as "maybe a
good preventive of racism," but added that it was "an abandonment of the national tradition of hospitality without discrimination."[26] Ironically, the best remedy for discrimination
has been a further extension of it.

A Retrospective

Racial attitudes are often deeply rooted in a culture, the result of all the feelings experienced and expressed over centuries. As one looks back at the history of French-black relations through the ages, one is struck by the hardy life that the
belief in black inferiority has enjoyed. The belief was shaped
and reinforced during the centuries of the white-black encounter and took forms very similar to those of other Western cultures. French reactions were in no way unique; they were part
of and contributed to the general Western reaction to blacks.
Europeans held common values and were struck by the same
aspects in African society, and drew similar conclusions from
them. Especially in the early years, the limited literature on
Africans was translated and shared by the literary public in
several European countries. Portuguese, Dutch, and English
travelers' accounts were translated into French, and these nations, in turn, showed an awareness of the contributions made
by the French. The French establishment of a slave society in
the Caribbean presented problems that all European slaveowning societies were to experience. Wishing to justify slavery and
observing the degraded condition of the black slaves, Frenchmen posited the idea of the blacks' inferiority. For purposes

of social control over the growing slave and free-colored populations, the French, like other Europeans, established a racial
society based on the claims of white supremacy. And, as did
other European states, France developed a program of overseas conquest. Their ambitions, when aimed at Africa, portrayed the continent and its inhabitants as objects of European
desires and denied them an independent and sovereign existence. In the nineteenth century, European scientists rather uncritically adopted racism (for reasons peculiar to the concerns
of French science, racism seems to have had an even more
profound impact in France than elsewhere), and many Frenchmen shared their view.

French opinion about blacks was often fragmented. Some
saw the Africans' variance in physique and mores from the
European norms as evidence of a separate creation and a different ultimate destiny. Others saw these differences as
superficial, ephemeral variations; they stressed the common
humanity and the equality of all. Some saw the Africans as
destined for slavery, while others found slavery a revolting institution, a criminal assault on the rights of man. Nor did all
Frenchmen agree on empire; some thought Africa should be
conquered and put under white rule, while others saw the
European advance into Africa as a calamity. Despite such fundamental cleavages in French opinion, there was a consensus
on the essential inferiority of blacks.

The criteria by which blacks were averred to be inferior
shifted throughout the centuries, reflecting changing values in
France. In the sixteenth and seventeenth centuries, Africans
struck the French as infidels, sinners, and miscreants. The
philosophes were horrified by what they perceived as a lack of
civilization and refinement among Africans. In the nineteenth
century, the inferiority ascribed to Africans was viewed as the
result of biological makeup. Racism was not a constant in
French reactions to the African, but prejudice was. Racism was
but a variant of the essential traditional French consensus on
black inferiority. Over the years the French developed a belief
system that, in the face of what is seen as an influx of a large
foreign population, has recently expressed itself openly.

On the whole, the increasing awareness of French attitudes

toward blacks in the 1970s is a healthy development. This new consciousness might include an examination of the role that blacks have historically played in French thought. To overcome one's legacy, no matter how somber, one has to know it. And one should face that legacy with the hope that comes from knowing that the past does not condemn the future.

NOTES

Preface

1. Henri Blet, *France d'outre-mer: L'oeuvre coloniale de la troisième république*, 3 (Paris, 1950), p. 284.
2. *La Conférence africaine française, Brazzaville (30 janvier 1944–8 février 1944)* (Algiers, 1944), p. 65; q. in Wilmot Alfred Fraser, "Lettre de Paris," *L'Express* (January 23, 1964).
3. Martine Astier Loutfi, *Littérature et colonialisme: L'expansion coloniale vue dans la littérature romanesque française, 1871–1914* (Paris, 1971); Ada Martinkus Zemp, *Le Blanc et le noir: Essai d'une description de la vision du Noir par le Blanc dans la littérature française de l'entre deux guerres* (Paris, 1975).
4. William Howard Schneider, "The Image of West Africa in Popular French Culture, 1870–1900" (Ph.D. diss., University of Pennsylvania, 1976). I wish to thank Dr. Schneider for his kindness in lending me a copy of this valuable study.

1. The Impulse to Inequality

1. Frank M. Snowden, *Blacks in Antiquity* (Cambridge, Mass., 1969); a slight corrective is Jehan Desanges, "L'Afrique noire et le monde méditerranéen dans l'Antiquité (Ethiopiens et Gréco-Romains)," *Revue française d'histoire d'outre-mer* (henceforth *RFHOM*) 62 (1975):391–414.
2. Herodotus, *History*, Bk IV, chs. 171–94, trans. J. Enoch Powell, 1 (Oxford, 1949), pp. 341–48.
3. Pliny, *The Natural History*, Bk V, ch. 8, ed. and trans. John Bostock and H. T. Riley, 1 (London, 1893), pp. 405–06.
4. Caius Julius Solinus, *The Excellent and Pleasant Worke*, trans. Arthur Golding (London, 1587), ch. 42.
5. Robert Lucas, "Medieval French Translations of the Latin Classics to 1500," *Speculum* 45 (1970):226.
6. J. K. Wright, *Geographical Lore* (New York, 1925), reprint ed. (New York, 1965), pp. 41, 55.
7. M. Benabou, "Monstres et hybrides chez Lucrèce et Pline l'Ancien," in *Hommes et bêtes: Entretiens sur le racisme*, ed. Léon Poliakov (Paris, 1975), p. 146.

8. Rabelais, *Pantagruel,* in *Oeuvres complètes* (henceforth *OC*), 3 (Paris, 1873), p. 19.

9. Bernard Lewis, *Race and Color in Islam* (New York, 1970), pp. 25–29. There has, however, always been in Islamic thought a strong universalism; a convenient summary of this aspect is S. D. Goitien, "The Concept of Mankind in Islam," in *History and the Idea of Mankind,* ed. W. Warren Wager (Albuquerque, 1971), pp. 72–91.

10. Tenth-century writer Mutahar Ibn Tahir al Maqdisi, q. in Lewis, p. 35.

11. Leo Africanus, *Description de l'Afrique,* ed. and trans. A. Epaulard, 1 (Paris, 1956), p. 65; these themes are also found in ibid., 2, pp. 461–62, 482.

12. Jean Bodin, *Method for the Easy Comprehension of History,* trans. Beatrice Reynolds (New York, 1945), pp. 54, 377.

13. G. R. Crone, "Notes on the Texts," in *The Voyages of Cadamosto,* ed. G. R. Crone (London, 1937) (Hakluyt Society, 2d ser., no. 80), p. xliii.

14. Roger Mercier, *L'Afrique noire dans la littérature française: Les premières images (XVIIe–XVIIIe siècles)* (Dakar, 1962), pp. 11–13.

15. *The Voyages of Cadamosto,* p. 54.

16. Ibid., pp. 62–63.

17. For the debate on the claims for French contacts with West Africa in the fourteenth century, see Charles de la Roncière, *La découverte de l'Afrique au moyen âge,* 2 (Cairo, 1925), pp. 10–17; Raymond Mauny, "Les prétendus navigations dieppoises à la côte occidentale d'Afrique au XIVe siècle," *Bulletin de l'Institut français d'Afrique noire* (henceforth *BIFAN*) 12 (1950): 122–34; Théodore Monod, "Un vieux problème: les navigations dieppoises sur la côte occidentale d'Afrique au XIVe siècle," *BIFAN* 25 (July-October 1963):427–34. A modification of this view is found in Léonard Sainville (who argues that some contact did begin in the fourteenth century, but who would hold that it was sporadic and unimportant), *Histoire du Sénégal depuis l'arrivée des Européens jusqu'à 1850* (Saint-Louis, Senegal, 1972), pp. 5–11.

18. J. A. Rogers, *Sex and Race: Negro-Caucasian Mixing in All Ages and All Lands,* 1 (New York, 1940), p. 230.

19. *Histoire chronologique des parlements de Languedoc écrite par moi, Guillaume Badin,* q. in La Roncière, *La découverte de l'Afrique,* 3, pp. 9–10.

20. Ibid., 3, p. 5.

21. Rogers, 1, p. 230.

22. Shelby T. McCloy, *The Negro in France* (Lexington, Ky., 1961), p. 12.

23. Q. in Jules Mathorez, *Les étrangers en France sous l'Ancien Régime,* 1 (Paris, 1919), p. 388.

24. Geoffroy Atkinson, *Les nouveaux horizons de la Renaissance française* (Paris, 1935), p. 136.

25. Alphonse de Saintonge, *Cosmographie* (Paris, 1544), ed. Georges Musset (Paris, 1904), p. 342.

26. André Thévet, *Cosmographie universelle* (Paris, 1575), p. 52.

27. Vincent Le Blanc, *Les Voyages fameux de . . . ,* 2 (Paris, 1649), p. 2.

28. Atkinson, pp. 10–11.

29. Léon Deschamps, *Histoire de la question coloniale en France* (Paris, 1891), p. 196.

30. Jean Meyer, *Les Européens et les autres de Cortès à Washington* (Paris, 1975), p. 6.

31. Roger Mercier, "Les débuts de l'exotisme africain en France," *Revue de littérature comparée* 36 (1962):192, 194.

32. Guy Turbet-Delof, *L'Afrique barbaresque dans la littérature française aux XVIe et XVIIe siècles* (Paris, 1973).

33. Albert Chinard, *L'Amérique et le rêve exotique dans la littérature française au XVIIe et XVIIIe siècles* (Paris, 1913), p. 139.

34. W. G. L. Randles, *L'image du sudest africain dans la littérature européene au XVIe siècle* (Lisbon, 1959), p. 153.

35. Maurice Besson, *L'influence coloniale sur le décor de la vie française du moyen âge à nos jours* (Paris, 1944), p. 12.

36. Chinard, p. 20; Cornelius J. Jaenen, *Friend and Foe* (New York, 1976), pp. 22–23.

37. Pierre J. Simon, "Portraits coloniaux des vietnamiens (1858–1914)," in *L'idée de race dans la pensée politique française contemporaine*, ed. Pierre Guiral and Emile Temime (Paris, 1977), p. 222. [François Bernier], "Nouvelle division de la terre, par les différentes espèces, ou races d'hommes qui l'habitent, envoyée par un fameux voyageur à Monsieur XXX à peu près en ces termes," *Journal des savans* (1684):133–40.

38. Thévet, *Cosmographie,* p. 77.

39. Jean Barassin, *Naissance d'une chrétienté: Bourbon des origines jusqu'en 1714* (Paris, 1954), p. 7.

40. P. F. X. de Charlevoix, *History and General Description of New France,* trans. John G. Shae, 1 (New York, 1866), p. 126.

41. R. P. Boussingault, *Le nouveau théâtre du monde ou abrégé des états et empires de l'Univers, Afrique,* 4 (Paris, 1681), p. 121; Father Margat, "Explication physique de la noirceur des nègres," in *Mémoires pour l'histoire des sciences et des beaux arts* (Trévoux) (June 1738), p. 35.

42. *Moeurs des sauvages amériquains* (Paris, 1724), q. in Edward D. Seeber, *Antislavery Opinion in France during the Second Half of the Eighteenth Century* (Baltimore, 1937), p. 48.

43. Jean-Baptiste Dutertre, *Histoire générale des antilles,* 2 (Paris, 1667), p. 508; C. de Rochefort (*Histoire naturelle et morale des îles antilles de l'Amérique* [Rotterdam, 1658], p. 321) blamed the midwife. Carminella Biondi (*Mon frère tu es mon esclave: Teorie Schiaviste e dibattiti antropologico-razziali nel Settecento francese* [Pisa, 1973], p. 149, fn. 47) has suggested that the real author of Rochefort's work was either Dutertre or the governor of Saint-Christophe, de Poincy.

44. Louis Moreau de Chambonneau, "Traité de l'origine des nègres du Sénégal, coste d'Afrique, de leur pays, religion, coutumes et moeurs," in "Notes et documents: Deux textes sur le Sénégal (1673–1677)," ed. Carson I. Ritchie, *BIFAN* 30 (1968):321; Godefroy Loyer, "Relation du voyage du royaume d'Issigny, côte d'or, pais de Guinée en Afrique" (Paris, 1714), in

L'établissement d'Issiny, 1687–1702, ed. Paul Roussier (Paris, 1935), p. 177; Villault de Bellefond, *Relation des costes d'Afrique appellées Guinée* (Paris, 1669), p. 235; Jean-Baptiste Labat, *Voyage du Chevalier Des Marchais,* 1 (Paris, 1730), pp. 63, 317; Claude Jannequin, *Voyage de Lybie au royaume de Senéga* (Paris, 1643), q. in G. G. Beslier, *Le Sénégal* (Paris, 1935), p. 63.

45. Léon-François Hoffmann, *Le nègre romantique* (Paris, 1973), p. 47.

46. Jean-Baptiste Labat, *Nouvelle relation de l'Afrique occidentale,* 2 (Paris, 1728), p. 255.

47. Winthrop D. Jordan, *White Over Black: American Attitudes Toward the Negro, 1550–1812* (Baltimore, 1969), pp. 17–20.

48. Chambonneau, p. 309.

49. Léon Poliakov, *The Aryan Myth: A History of Racist and Nationalist Ideas in Europe,* trans. Edmund Howard (London, 1974), pp. 7–8.

50. The problem of slavery and the image of the black is dealt with in chapter 2.

51. "Dissertation sur l'origine des nègres et des américains," Ms., Bibliothèque nationale, Paris (henceforth BN), Nouvelles acquisitions françaises (henceforth NAF), 1041, folio 75; *Mémoires* (Trévoux) (November 1733), pp. 1927–77.

52. Labat, *Nouvelle relation,* 2, pp. 256–62.

53. *Académie royale des sciences* (1702):30–32.

54. M. N., *Voyages aux côtes de Guinée et en Amérique* (Paris, 1719), p. 149.

55. A convenient summary and translation of some of these texts appears in James S. Slotkin, ed., *Readings in Early Anthropology* (New York, 1965), pp. 5–43.

56. Q. in "Remarques du père Tournemine, jésuite, sur le mémoire touchant l'origine des nègres et des américains, inséré dans ce journal le mois de Novembre 1733," in *Mémoires* (Trévoux) (June 1734), p. 627; the mystical origin of La Peyrère's thought is revealed in Poliakov, *The Aryan Myth,* pp. 132–33.

57. [Bernier], pp. 133–40, translation available in Slotkin, p. 95, and in M. L. Dufrenoy, "A Precursor of Modern Anthropology: François Bernier (1620–1680)," *Isis* 41 (March 1950):27–29.

58. Simon Tyssot de Patot, *Voyages et aventures de Jacques Massé* (Paris, 1710), pp. 32–33, translation available in Slotkin, pp. 191–92.

59. "Voyages de Jean Ovington à Surate et en d'autres lieues de l'Asie et de l'Afrique, Paris 1725," *Journal des savans* (1725):499.

60. Kenneth J. Gergen, "The Significance of Skin Color in Human Relations," in *Color and Race,* ed. John Hope Franklin (Boston, 1968), p. 121.

61. Jean Filliosat, "Classement des couleurs et des lumières en Sanskrit," in *Problèmes de Couleur,* ed. Ignace Meyerson (Paris, 1957), p. 304.

62. Louis Gernet, "Dénomination et perception des couleurs chez les Grecs," in ibid., pp. 315, 323.

63. J. André, "Sources et vocabulaire des couleurs en Latin," in ibid., p. 329; Snowden, p. 179. Not all cultures have perceived the color black negatively; thus ancient China in its paintings saw it as an essential part of cosmic

harmony; Jacques Gernet, "Expression de la couleur en Chinois," in Meyerson, ed., pp. 296–97. Cultures not speaking Indo-European languages have also seen black negatively; P. Metais, "Vocabulaire et symbolisme des couleurs en Nouvelle Calédonie," in ibid., pp. 354–55; Hiroshi Wagatsuma, "The Social Perception of Skin Color in Japan," in Franklin, ed., pp. 129–65.

64. G. R. Dunstan and R. F. Hobson, "A Note on an Early Ingredient of Racial Prejudice in Western Europe," *Race* 6 (April 1965):335.

65. Roger Bastide, "Color, Racism, and Christianity," in Franklin, ed., pp. 38–39.

66. *La Chanson de Roland*, ed. Giulio Bertoni (Flòrence, 1935), st. 143, p. 218.

67. Pierre Corneille, *Medée*, in *Oeuvres de P. Corneille*, ed. Charles Marty Laveaux, 2 (Paris, 1862), p. 360; Racine, *Britannicus*, in *Oeuvres de J. Racine*, ed. Paul Mesnard, 2, 2d ed. (Paris, 1886), p. 339; *Phèdre*, in ibid., 3 (Paris, 1885), p. 373. Molière, *Tartuffe*, in *Oeuvres complètes de Molière*, ed. Charles Lorandre, 2 (Paris, n.d.), p. 415; *L'Ecole des femmes*, in ibid., 1, p. 468.

68. Ignacy Sachs, "L'Image du noir dans l'art européen," *Annales, économies, civilisations, sociétés* 24 (July-August 1969):886, fn. 2. It also became part of French folklore; Max Milner, *Le diable dans la littérature française de Cazotte à Baudelaire, 1772–1861*, 1 (Paris, 1960), p. 74. For the continuity of this tradition in contemporary French folklore, see Claude Seignolle, *Le diable dans la tradition populaire* (Paris, 1959), pp. 17–18, 24, 40.

69. Louis Du May, *Le prudent voyageur*, 1 (Geneva, 1681), p. 19.

70. Labat, *Nouvelle relation*, 3, p. 170.

71. E. T. Hamy, "Les Cent quarante nègres de M. d'Avaux à Munster (1644)," *Bulletins et mémoires de la société d'anthropologie de Paris*, 5th ser., 7 (1906):271–75.

72. Jules La Mesnardière, *La Poétique* (Paris, 1639), p. 125, q. in Marcel Paquot, *Les étrangers dans les divertissements de la cour de Beaujoyeulx à Molière (1581–1673)* (Brussels, 1932), p. 195.

73. Thévet, *Cosmographie*, p. 66. For similar opinions, see *Journal du corsaire Jean Doublet de Honfleur*, ed. Charles Bréard (Paris, 1883), p. 257, and Labat, *Voyage du Chevalier*, 1, p. 65.

74. Sieur Froger, *Relation d'un voyage fait en 1695, 1696 et 1697 aux côtes d'Afrique* (Paris, 1699), p. 18; Pierre François Xavier Charlevoix, *Histoire de l'île espagnole ou Saint-Domingue*, 2 (Paris, 1731), p. 501.

75. Alexis de Saint-Lo, *Relation du voyage au cap vert* (Paris, 1637), p. 183.

76. "Relation inédite d'un voyage en Guinée adressé en 1634 à Peiresc par le P. Colombin de Nantes," ed. P. Ubald d'Alençon, *Revue de Bretagne* (1906), p. 10; Labat, *Voyage du Chevalier*, 1, p. 341; M. N., pp. 62–63.

77. Saint-Lo, p. 2.

78. Pierre Martino, *L'orient dans la littérature française au XVIIe et XVIIIe siècles* (Paris, 1906), pp. 105–30.

79. Loyer, pp. 173, 175.

80. Dralsé de Grandpierre, *Relation de divers voyages faits dans l'Afrique, dans l'Amérique, et aux Indes occidentales* (Paris, 1718), p. 134.

81. Paul Masson, "Un double énigme: André Brüe," *Revue de l'histoire coloniale française* (henceforth *RHCF*) 20 (January-February 1932):9–34; Mercier, p. 55.

82. Abdoulaye Ly, "Conséquences des cas Labat et Loyer," *BIFAN* 15 (1953):751–66.

83. Mercier, p. 57.

84. Some of the earliest efforts, failed attempts by both Spain and France, are described in Henri Labouret and Paul Rivet, *Le Royaume d'Arda et son évangélisation au XVIIᵉ siècle, Travaux et mémoires de l'Institut d'ethnologie*, 7 (Paris, 1929), pp. 16–30.

85. Labat, *Nouveau voyage aux îles de l'Amérique*, 4 (Paris, 1743), p. 435.

86. Labat, *Voyage du Chevalier*, 1, p. 66; ibid., 2, p. 87.

87. Ibid., 1, pp. 68–69.

88. Labat, *Nouveau voyage aux îles*, 4, p. 436; Charlevoix, *Histoire de l'île espagnole*, 2, p. 502; Villault de Bellefond, p. 11.

89. Labat, *Nouveau voyage aux îles*, 4, p. 422. Missionaries in their correspondence also alluded to it; *Règlement de discipline pour les nègres adressé aux curés dans les isles françaises de l'amérique*, q. in Gabriel Debien, *Les esclaves aux antilles françaises* (Basse Terre, Guadeloupe, 1974), p. 252, fn. 3.

90. André Thévet, *Les singularitez de la France antarctique* (Paris, 1558), ed. Paul Gaffarel (Paris, 1878), p. 77.

91. Bodin, pp. 112–13.

92. *La Méthode de l'histoire*, ed. and trans. P. Mesnard (Paris, 1941), p. 88, q. in Hoffmann, p. 17. This passage is rendered slightly differently in the English translation of the Latin text: "Because self-control was difficult . . . they gave themselves over to horrible excesses. Promiscuous coition of men and animals took place wherefore the regions of Africa produce for us so many monsters"; Bodin, p. 105.

93. Thévet, *Les singularitez*, p. 80.

94. Froger, p. 15.

95. Loyer, pp. 143–44. The same ideas appear in M. N., pp. 79–80. François de Paris, "Voyage à la Coste d'Affrique dite de Guinée et aux Isles de l'Amérique fait en années 1682 et 1683," Ms., ed. Guy Thilmans, "La Relation de François de Paris (1682–1683)," *BIFAN* 38 (1976):41.

96. A. Pherotée de la Croix, *Relation universelle de l'Afrique ancienne*, 2 (Lyons, 1688), p. 350; Labat, *Voyage du Chevalier*, 2, p. 46.

97. La Croix, 2, p. 532; ibid., pp. 368–69.

98. Labat, *Voyage du Chevalier*, 1, p. 67.

99. Idem, *Nouveau voyage aux îles*, 4, p. 434.

100. R. P. Perbal, *Le missionnaire français et le nationalisme* (Paris, 1939), pp. 18–19.

101. Du Casse, "Mémoire ou relation du Sr Du Casse sur son voyage de Guynée avec la Tempeste en 1687 et 1688," in Roussier, ed., pp. 26–27.

102. Labat, *Nouveau voyage aux îles*, 4, p. 443.

103. Bruce L. Mouser, "Landlords-Strangers: A Process of Accommoda-

tion and Assimilation," *International Journal of African Historical Studies* 8 (1975):425–40.

104. Du Casse, p. 38.

105. Lemaire, *Les voyages de Sieur Lemaire aux îles Canaries, Cap Vert, Sénégal, et Gambie* (Paris, 1695), pp. 125, 126; "Relation du voyage fait sur les costes d'Afrique aux mois de novembre et décembre de l'année 1670," in *Receuil de divers voyages* (Paris, 1670), p. 4; Du Casse, pp. 26–27; Labat, *Voyage du Chevalier*, 2, pp. 5–6; ibid., 1, p. 327. François de Paris, p. 12.

106. Ibid., p. 17; Dralsé de Grandpierre, p. 166.

107. A. G. Hopkins, *An Economic History of West Africa* (London, 1973), pp. 17–20.

108. Chambonneau, p. 320.

109. M. N., p. 361; La Croix, 2, p. 410.

110. Froger, p. 15; M. N., pp. 36, 78; Loyer, pp. 142–51, 193, 197; D'Estrées, "Mémoire, tant sur l'arrivée des vaisseaux du royaume au cap vert . . . ," in C. Thilmans and N. I. de Moroes, "Passage à la petite côte du vice—Amiral d'Estrées (1670)," *BIFAN* 39 (1977):60; *Receuil de divers voyages faits en Afrique et en Amérique, qui n'ont point esté encore publiez* (Paris, 1674), pp. 3–7.

111. Labat, *Nouvelle relation*, 2, p. 303.

112. The best discussion of money and measures in precolonial Africa is in Philip D. Curtin, *Economic Change in Precolonial Africa: Senegambia in the Era of the Slave Trade* (Madison, Wisc., 1975), ch. 6.

113. Lemaire, p. 126; Charlevoix, *Histoire de l'île espagnole*, 2, p. 499; Labat, *Voyage du Chevalier*, 2, pp. 201–02.

114. Chambonneau, p. 337.

115. La Croix, 2, p. 368.

116. Walter Rodney, *A History of the Upper Guinea Coast, 1545–1800* (Oxford, 1970).

117. Loyer, pp. 134–35, 168; François de Paris, p. 24.

118. Claude Meillassoux, ed., *L'Esclavage en Afrique précoloniale* (Paris, 1975).

119. Lemaire, p. 82; François de Paris, p. 25.

120. See chapter 2.

121. For instance, M. N., pp. 74, 97, which several times refers to Africans as "ces animaux."

122. There is some dispute about the extent to which it continued to be triangular, but general indications are that, rather than decline, it grew; Dieudonné Rinchon, *Pierre-Ignace-Liéven Van Alstein, capitaine négrier* (Dakar, 1964), p. 367; Hopkins, pp. 98–99.

123. On these attitudes, see chapter 2.

124. The affirmation "During the sixteenth century black Africa becomes a reservoir of slaves for the European nations and the era of contempt for the black race starts" contains a lot of truth, but is overschematic as an explanation; Michèle Duchet, "Esclavage et préjugé de couleur," in *Racisme et société*, ed. Patrice Comarmond and Claude Duchet (Paris, 1969), p. 121.

125. "Relation inédite . . . ," p. 9; La Croix, 2, p. 350; Le Blanc, 2, p. 7.

126. Labat, *Nouvelle relation*, 4, p. 87; idem, *Nouveau voyage aux îles*, 4, pp. 189, 424–25; idem, *Voyage du Chevalier*, 2, pp. 125, 129; also Charlevoix, *Histoire de l'île espagnole*, 2, p. 498. For a discussion of the ethnic repartition of slaves in the French West Indies, see Debien, *Les esclaves*, pp. 39–68; idem, "Les Colons des antilles et leur main d'oeuvre à la fin du XVIIIᵉ siècle," *Annales historiques de la révolution française* 27 (1955):263.

127. La Croix, 2, p. 350.

128. Kenneth E. Boulding, *The Image* (Ann Arbor, 1956).

129. M. N., p. 32.

130. Leo Africanus, 1, p. 63; Thévet, *Cosmographie*, p. 77; Lemaire, p. 127; La Croix, 2, p. 532; Labat, *Nouveau voyage aux îles*, 4, p. 457.

131. Labat, *Voyage du Chevalier*, 1, p. 319; ibid., p. 125.

132. Ibid., 2, p. 158.

133. Loyer, p. 111.

134. J. Mendez-Castro and R. Mauny, "Godefroy Loyer (1714), plagiare de le Maire (1695)," *Notes africaines*, no. 55 (July 1955):88–90; Ly. The recent publication of the Chambonneau manuscript reveals the extent to which it was the source for plagiarization by Father Gaby in his *Relation de la nigritie* (Paris, 1689); Charles Becker, "A propos d'un plagiare, le père Gaby," *Notes africaines*, no. 133 (January 1972):17–21. G. Thilmans and N. I. Moroes, "Villault de Bellefond sur la côte occidentale d'Afrique: Les deux premières campagnes de l'Europe (1666–1671)," *BIFAN* 38 (1976): 261.

135. Ly.

136. This new emphasis is treated in François de Dainville, *La Géographie des humanistes* (Paris, 1940; reprinted Geneva, 1969), pp. 209–55.

137. Nicholas Sanson, *L'Afrique et plusieurs cartes nouvelles et exactes et en divers traictés de géographie et d'histoire* (Paris, 1666), n.p.

138. Randles.

139. Some of these arguments have been borrowed from the provocative Michel Foucault, *Madness and Civilization* (New York, 1965).

140. Poliakov, *The Aryan Myth*, pp. 148–54. This theme is more fully examined in idem, ed. It is also suggested in an essay that deserves a larger audience; Hayden White, "The Forms of Wildness: Archeology of an Idea," in *The Wild Man Within*, ed. Edward Dudley and Maximilian E. Novak (Pittsburgh, 1972), pp. 3–38.

2. The Establishment of Slave Societies

1. The phrase, also appearing as the title of this section, is borrowed from Winthrop D. Jordan, *White Over Black: American Attitudes Toward the Negro, 1550–1812* (Baltimore, 1969), ch. 2.

2. For the Antilles, typical was Jean-Baptiste Dutertre, *Histoire générale des antilles*, 2 (Paris, 1667), p. 357; Cornelius J. Jaenen, *Friend and Foe* (New York, 1976), ch. 1.

3. Jacques Bouton, *Relation de l'établissement des françois depuis l'an 1635 en*

l'isle de la Martinique, l'une des Antilles de l'Amérique (Paris, 1640), pp. 115–16; Marcel Trudel, *L'esclavage au Canada français* (Montreal, 1960), p. 46.

4. Lucien Peytraud, *L'esclavage aux antilles françaises* (Paris, 1897), pp. 27–30.

5. Gabriel Debien, *Les engagés pour les Antilles, 1632–1715* (Paris, 1951), p. 215.

6. Ibid., pp. 45, 206.

7. Q. in Charles de la Roncière, *Nègres et négriers* (Paris, 1933), p. 19.

8. Louis-Philippe May, "Le plus ancien voyage aux Antilles françaises," *La Géographie* 18 (July-August 1932):16.

9. Q. in Debien, *Les engagés, pp.* 206–07; Dutertre (2, p. 477) had made a similar comment.

10. Debien, ibid., p. 257.

11. Ibid., p. 254.

12. Ibid., p. 251.

13. Bouton, p. 99.

14. C. de Rochefort, *Histoire naturelle et morale des îles antilles de l'Amérique* (Rotterdam, 1658), p. 323; Blénac to the Minister of the Marine, November 19, 1681, Ms., BN, NAF, 9328, and q. in Debien, *Les engagés,* p. 215.

15. Debien, ibid., p. 253. The early development of Barbados is described in Richard S. Dunn, *Sugar and Slaves: The Rise of the Planter Class in the English West Indies, 1624–1713* (Chapel Hill, 1972), ch. 2.

16. Peytraud, p. 23.

17. Q. in La Roncière, *Nègres et négriers,* p. 19.

18. Philip D. Curtin, *The Atlantic Slave Trade: A Census* (Madison, Wisc., 1969), p. 75.

19. David Brion Davis writes about slavery and race prejudice in the New World as follows: "Although the questions are of compelling importance, we cannot begin to determine whether slavery was a source of racial prejudice or prejudice a source of slavery . . ."; "The Comparative Approach to American History: Slavery," in *The Comparative Approach to American History,* ed. C. Vann Woodward (New York, 1968), pp. 121–33, reprinted in *Slavery in the New World: A Reader in Comparative History* ed. Laura Foner and Eugene D. Genovese (Englewood Cliffs, N. J., 1969), p. 65.

20. M. I. Finley, "The Idea of Slavery: Critique of David Brion Davis' *The Problem of Slavery in Western Culture*," *New York Review of Books* 2 (1967), reprinted in Foner and Genovese, eds., p. 261.

21. Jordan, ch. 2.

22. David Brion Davis, *The Problem of Slavery in Western Culture* (Ithaca, N. Y., 1966), chs. 2–3.

23. Bouton, p. 103.

24. These instructions date from 1705 and 1721; Mme Marchand-Thébault, "L'esclavage en Guyane française sous l'ancien régime," *RFHOM* 47 (1960):10–11.

25. The earliest experiments had been attempted with slave labor in Madeira, Canary Islands, and in the Cape Verde Islands. But the real model

for the Americas was Sao Thomé, an island in the Bight of Biafra; Marian Malowist, "Les débuts du système de plantations dans la période des grandes découvertes," *Africana Bulletin* (1969):9–30.

26. Stewart L. Mims, *Colbert's West India Policy* (New Haven, 1912), p. 17.

27. Léonard Sainville (*Historie du Sénégal depuis l'arrivée des Européens jusqu'à 1850* [Saint-Louis, Senegal, 1972], p. 32) states that this situation persisted until 1664, but in fact it continued throughout the century; Curtin, *The Atlantic Slave Trade*, p. 121.

28. De Gallitzer, "Motifs et moyens de traiter beaucoup de nègres," n.d., Ms., BN, NAF, 21393, folio 59; although it is not dated, it seems reasonable to assume that it was written somewhere between 1660 and 1680.

29. This measure was written into the charter of the Compagnie de Saint-Christophe in 1635; C. W. Cole, *Colbert and a Century of French Mercantilism*, 1 (New York, 1939), pp. 187–88. The measure was by no means necessarily followed, for in fact both a Protestant and a Jewish community prospered in the French Antilles.

30. Davis, *The Problem of Slavery*, p. 100; Noel Deerr, *The History of Sugar*, 2 (London, 1950), p. 292.

31. Bouton, p. 102. Similar ideas can be found in Dutertre, 2, p. 501; Pierre Pelleprat, *Relations des missions des pères de la Compagnie de Jésus* (1655), q. in Antonine Gisler, *L'esclavage aux Antilles françaises (XVIIᵉ–XVIIIᵉ siècles): Contribution au problème de l'esclavage* (Fribourg, 1965), p. 153, fn.; Jacques Savary, *Le parfait négociant*, 7th ed. (Paris, 1713), p. 540.

32. Paul W. Bamford, *Fighting Ships and Prisons* (Minneapolis, 1973), p. 139.

33. Ibid., pp. 140–52.

34. Trudel, pp. 101–02.

35. Bamford, pp. 164–65.

36. Ibid., pp. 152–54, 167–72.

37. Germain Fromageau, *Le dictionnaire de cas de conscience*, 1 (Paris, 1733), p. 1444.

38. Jean-Baptiste Labat, *Nouveau voyage aux îles de l'Amérique*, 4 (Paris, 1743), p. 436.

39. Jacques-Bénigne Bossuet, *Cinquième avertissement aux Protestants sur les lettres de M. Jurieu*, q. in Gisler, p. 12, fn. 2.

40. Shelby T. McCloy, *The Negro in France* (Lexington, Ky., 1961), p. 12.

41. Peytraud, pp. 374–75.

42. Q. in Alfred Rosset, *Les premiers colons de l'île Bourbon* (Paris, 1967), pp. 17–18.

43. Adolphe Cabon, *Histoire d'Haïti*, 1 (Port au Prince, 1930), pp. 40–43, 54–59.

44. De Cussy, "Mémoire pour Mgr le Ministre, Seignelay, October 18, 1685," Ms., BN, NAF, 7485.

45. Q. in Pierre de Vaissière, *Saint-Domingue: La Société, 1629–1789* (Paris, 1909), p. 16.

46. Peytraud, pp. 14–15, 294.

47. Léon Vignols, "L'institution des engagés," *Revue d'histoire économique et sociale* 14 (1928):33.

48. Deerr, 2, p. 318; Debien, *Les esclaves*, p. 394; Gwendolyn M. Hall, *Social Control in Slave Plantation Societies: A Comparison of Saint-Domingue and Cuba* (Baltimore, 1971), p. 62.

49. Hall, p. 62.

50. Dutertre, 2, p. 477.

51. Debien, *Les engagés*, p. 257.

52. Rennard, "Arrivée des femmes aux Antilles," *RHCF* 23 (1935): 135–48.

53. Q. in Pierre de Vaissière, "Origines de la colonisation à Saint-Domingue," *Revue des questions historiques*, no. 79 (January-April 1906):517, fn. 5.

54. Q. in May, p. 16.

55. Vaissière, "Origines de la colonisation," p. 518.

56. Q. in Jean Barassin, *Naissance d'une chrétienté: Bourbon des origines jusqu'en 1714* (Paris, 1954), p. 105.

57. Ibid., p. 107.

58. Peytraud, p. 208.

59. Q. in Lothrop Stoddard, *The French Revolution in San Domingo* (New York, 1914), pp. 41–42; Peytraud, p. 205.

60. Labat, *Nouveau voyage aux îles*, 2, p. 190.

61. Article 6, reprinted in Jean-Baptiste Labat, *Voyage du Chevalier Des Marchais*, 4 (Paris, 1730), pp. 179–80.

62. Dutertre, 2, p. 513.

63. Q. in Stoddard, p. 41.

64. Hall, p. 141.

65. Jacques Ghestin, "L'action des parlements contre les 'mésalliances' au XVIIᵉ et XVIIIᵉ siècles," *Revue historique de droit français et étranger* 24 (1956):74–110, 196–224.

66. That it really did so is often averred; Hall, p. 139.

67. Peytraud, pp. 165–66.

68. Ibid., p. 163.

69. For instance, Hall, pp. 114–19.

70. That was done in the American colonies, too, although practices varied from colony to colony, and, in real desperation during the American Revolution, both the colonists and the British resorted to arming slaves; Jordan, pp. 125–26, 411–12.

71. Marvin Harris, *Patterns of Race in the Americas* (New York, 1964); Carl N. Degler, *Neither Black Nor White* (New York, 1971).

72. Peytraud, p. 369.

73. Article 29, reprinted in Labat, *Voyage du Chevalier*, 4, pp. 189–96.

74. A. Lebeau, *De la condition des gens de couleur libres sous l'ancien régime* (Paris, 1903), p. 78.

75. Léo Elisabeth, "The French Antilles," in *Neither Slave Nor Free: The*

Freedmen of African Descent in the Slave Societies of the New World, ed. David
W. Cohen and Jack P. Greene (Baltimore, 1972), pp. 153–54.

76. Q. in ibid., p. 140. While citing this ordinance, Elisabeth sees this
evolution as coming later, after the mid-eighteenth century (ibid., pp.
134–35).

77. Peytraud, p. 407; Elisabeth, pp. 137–42; Gabriel Debien, "Les affran-
chissements aux Antilles françaises aux XVIIᵉ et XVIIIᵉ siècles," *Annuario de
Estudios Americanos* 23 (1958):1180.

78. Suggestive are the proportions of people of color Gabriel Debien (*Les
esclaves aux antilles françaises, XVIIᵉ–XVIIIᵉ siècles* [Basse Terre,
Guadeloupe, 1974], pp. 65, 67) finds as slaves in the later part of the
eighteenth century: for the northern part of Saint-Domingue, examination of
some plantation lists revealed 4.8 percent as colored; a more extensive
number of plantation lists from the 1790s showed 2.8 percent of the slaves
as colored. Writing about the entire era of slavery in the French West Indies,
Debien speaks of the difficulty of knowing the exact racial composition of
freedmen, but concludes, "It is certain that the number of free blacks was
infinitely less than that of mulattoes"; ibid., p. 380.

79. My calculations are based on Cohen and Greene, eds., Table A 5, p.
337.

80. Deerr, 2, pp. 424–25. Comparing the yields given by writers of various nationalities, Ward Barrett has noted that the French were the most
demanding; "Caribbean Sugar Production Standards in the Seventeenth and
Eighteenth Centuries," in *Merchants and Scholars,* ed. John Parker (Minneapolis, 1965), pp. 147–70.

81. Debien, *Les esclaves,* p. 121.

82. Peytraud, p. 307.

83. S. Linstant, *Essai sur les moyens d'extirper les préjugés des blancs contre la
couleur des Africains et des sang-mêlés* (Paris, 1841), p. 28.

84. Dutertre, 2, p. 497.

85. Labat, *Nouveau voyage aux îles,* 6, p. 199.

86. Robin Winks, *The Blacks in Canada: A History* (New Haven, 1971),
pp. 11–13.

87. Trudel, p. 94.

88. It is hard to estimate what the proportion of slaves to free population
was at any given time because of the lack of a proper census. Trudel (p. 97)
presents as maybe indicative the first census of 1784, which showed the slave
population of 304 to constitute .3 percent of the total population.

89. Labat, *Nouveau voyage aux îles,* 6, p. 199.

90. Ibid., 1, pp. 65–66.

91. Dutertre, 2, p. 493.

92. Ibid., pp. 497–98.

93. The theme of slave deviancy as a means of survival is stressed in Jean
Fouchard, *Les marrons de la liberté* (Paris, 1972), pp. 253–55.

94. Bouton, p. 100; *Les desseins de son éminence le cardinal de Richelieu pour
l'Amérique, ce qui s'est passé de plus remarquable dépuis l'établissement des colonies*
(Rouen, 1658), p. 68, q. in Debien, *Les esclaves,* p. 254; Dutertre, 2, p. 500.

3. The Philosophes and Africa

1. The dialectical situation inherent in the Enlightenment view of non-Europeans was well put by René Pomeau, who remarked that "the Enlightenment allows the coexistence of myths and a critic that destroys these myths"; in regard to China, for instance, he wrote, "The Chinese myth was developed at the same time as Sinology developed as a science"; "Voyage et lumières dans la littérature française du XVIIIe siècle," *Studies on Voltaire and the Eighteenth Century*, 57 (1967):1287.

2. Claude Lévi-Strauss, *A World on the Wane*, trans. John Russell (New York, 1961), pp. 308–10, one of many translations of *Tristes Tropiques* (Paris, 1955).

3. Voltaire, "Eléments de la philosophie de Newton," *OC*, Moland ed. (Paris, 1879), 22, p. 420. "Voyage," *Encyclopédie* (Paris, 1751–1765), 17, p. 477; Jean-Jacques Rousseau, "Discours sur l'origine et les fondements de l'inégalité," *OC*, ed. V. D. Musset-Pathay (Paris, 1823), 1, pp. 342–43.

4. Edmé Jomard, "Note sur une société de géographie projetée à Paris en 1785," *Bulletin de la société de géographie* (henceforth *BSG*), 2d ser., 1 (1834):409.

5. Joseph Marie Dégérando, *The Observation of Savage Peoples*, trans. F. C. T. Moore (Berkeley and Los Angeles, 1969), pp. 67–70.

6. J. A. Perreau, *Considérations physiques et morales sur la nature de l'homme et ses facultés*, 2 (Paris, 1802) pp. 186–87, 212.

7. Gaston Martin, *Nantes au XVIIIe siècle: L'ère des négriers (1714–1774)* (Paris, 1931), p. 43; Philip D. Curtin, *The Atlantic Slave Trade: A Census* (Madison, Wisc., 1969), p. 283; Dieudonné Rinchon, *Le Trafic négrier, d'après les livres de commerce du capitaine gantois Pierre-Ignace-Liéven van Alstein*, 1 (Paris, 1938), pp. 248–302.

8. Pruneau de Pommegorge, *Description de la nigritie* (Amsterdam, 1789), p. 150.

9. Abbé A. F. Prévost, *Histoire générale des voyages*, 3 (Paris, 1746), p. 139.

10. Louis Desgraves, *Catalogue de la bibliothèque de Montesquieu* (Paris, 1954), pp. 185–88, 195.

11. Pierre Martino, *L'orient dans la littérature française au XVIIe et XVIIIe siècles* (Paris, 1906), p. 184, fn. 1; Michèle Duchet, *Anthropologie et histoire au siècle des lumières* (Paris, 1971), pp. 68–69; there was of course some information on Africa in the nineteen travel collections that he owned.

12. *Histoire de Louis Anniaba, roi d'Essenie en Afrique sur la côte de Guineé*, 1 (Paris, 1740), pp. 9, 45.

13. Marie Gouze, *L'Esclavage des noirs, ou l'heureux naufrage* (Paris, 1792), p. 32; the play was written in 1786 and first produced at the Comédie Française in December 1789. Mirza was also the name of Anne-Louis Germaine de Staël-Holstein's heroine; "Mirza, lettres d'un voyageur," *OC*, 1 (Paris, 1861; reprinted Geneva, 1967), pp. 72–78.

14. Roger Mercier, "Les débuts de l'exotisme africain en France," *Revue de littérature comparée* 36 (1962):193–94.

15. Robert Mandrou, *De la culture populaire au XVIIe et XVIIIe siècles: La Bibliothèque de Troyes* (Paris, 1964), p. 66.

16. Henri Roddier, *L'Abbé Prévost* (Paris, 1955), pp. 44–45.

17. Duchet, *Anthropologie*, pp. 81–95.

18. Michèle Duchet, "L'Histoire des voyages: Originalité et influence," *L'Abbé Prévost: Actes du colloque d'Aix-en-Provence* (Aix-en-Provence, 1965), pp. 147–54; G. Pire, "Jean-Jacques Rousseau et les relations des voyages," *Revue d'histoire littéraire de la France* 56 (July-September 1956):355–78; Roddier, p. 180.

19. Prévost, 3, pp. 236, 595.

20. Daniel Mornet, "Les Enseignements des bibliothèques privées (1750–1780)," *Revue d'histoire littéraire de la France* 17 (1910):460.

21. Georges-Louis Leclerc, Comte de Buffon, *Natural History*, 4, trans. Barr (London, 1811), pp. 284–85, 291.

22. Charles de Secondat, Baron de Montesquieu, *De l'esprit des lois, OC,* 2 (Paris, 1951), p. 602; Voltaire, *Essai sur les moeurs, OC,* 12, p. 357; Voltaire to J. J. Paulet, April 23, 1768, *Voltaire's Correspondence,* 69, ed. Theodore Bestermann (Geneva, 1961), no. 14025; René Hubert, *Les Sciences Sociales dans l'Encyclopédie* (Lille, 1923), p. 86; Jaucourt, "Sénégal," *Encyclopédie,* 15, p. 13; "Afrique," *Encyclopédie,* Supplement, 1 (Amsterdam, 1780), p. 194 (this supplement was a clever attempt to trade on the popularity of the *Encyclopédie,* but except for sharing two collaborators, d'Alembert and Marmontel, it had little in common with its predecessors); Antonelli Gerbi, *The Dispute of the New World,* trans. Jeremy Moyle (Pittsburgh, 1973), p. 99, fn. 76.

23. Abbé Proyart, *Histoire de Loango, Kakongo et autres royaumes* (Paris, 1776), pp. 1–3, 57, 64–65, 71–72, 83–88, 358.

24. Abbé Demanet, *Nouvelle histoire de l'Afrique française,* 2 (Paris, 1767), p. 4.

25. Sylvain Meinrad Xavier de Golberry, *Fragmens d'un voyage en Afrique, fait pendant les années 1786, 1787, dans les contrées occidentales de ce continent,* 2 (Paris, 1802), pp. 359–60. Dominique Harcourt Lamiral, *L'Affrique et le peuple afriquain* (Paris, 1789), pp. 49, 57, 192.

26. See chapter 4.

27. Pire, pp. 355–78.

28. Michel Adanson, *A Voyage to Senegal, the Isle of Gorée and the River Gambia,* trans. from the 1756 French edition (London, 1759), p. 54.

29. Golberry, 2, pp. 355–56, 395, 504–05, 373; ibid., 1, pp. 41–42; Mercier, "Les débuts de l'exotisme africain en France," p. 209.

30. Jean-Baptiste Léonard Durand, *Voyage au Sénégal* (Paris, 1802), illustration 27; Grasset Saint-Sauveur, *Encyclopédie des Voyages,* 4 (Paris, 1796).

31. Pétion de Villeneuve, "Discours sur la traite des noirs" (April 1790), reprinted in *La Révolution française et l'abolition de l'esclavage* (henceforth *RFAE*), 8 (Paris, 1968), pp. 10–11.

32. Hennin Papers, Ms. 1266, folio 253, Bibliothèque de l'Institut. I am grateful to my colleague Michael Berkvam for showing me this letter, which is part of the Hennin papers he is currently editing.

33. Paul-Henri Holbach, "Serpent fétiche," *Encyclopédie,* 15, p. 108; Denis Diderot, "Hottentot," *Encyclopédie,* 7, pp. 320–21; "Nègres—caractère des nègres en général," *Encyclopédie,* 11, p. 82.

34. Guillaume Thomas Raynal, *Histoire philosophique et politique des établissements et du commerce des européens dans les deux Indes,* 1 (Geneva, 1780), pp. 392–93; Abbé Grégoire, *An Enquiry concerning the Intellectual and Moral Faculties, and Literature of Negroes . . . ,* trans. D. B. Warden (Brooklyn, 1810), p. 125; Adanson, p. 43.

35. Mercier, "Les débuts de l'exotisme africain en France," p. 205.

36. Michèle Duchet, "Voltaire et les sauvages," *Europe* 38 (May-June 1959):88–96.

37. For the Enlightenment commitment to civilization, see N. Golubtsova, "Le Problème de la culture dans quelques oeuvres de la philosophie des lumières au XVIIIᵉ siècle," *Journal of World History* 11 (1969):657–74; Abbé Genty, *L'Influence de la découverte de l'Amérique sur le bonheur du genre humain* (Paris, 1787), p. 12; C. F. Volney, *La loi naturelle ou catéchisme du citoyen français* (Paris, 1793), p. 27.

38. Claude Adrien Helvétius, *De l'homme, de ses facultés intellectuelles et de son éducation* (London, 1773), p. 457.

39. Roger Mercier, "La Théorie des climats, des 'Réflexions critiques' à *l'Esprit des lois,*" *Revue d'histoire littéraire de la France* 53 (January-March 1953):17–37.

40. Roger Mercier, *La Réhabilitation de la nature humaine,* 1700–1750 (Villemonble, 1960), p. 161.

41. Charles de Secondat, Baron de Montesquieu, *The Persian Letters,* ed. and trans. J. Robert Loy (Cleveland, 1961), p. 236; Raynal, 1, pp. 121–22.

42. Montesquieu, *De l'esprit,* 2, p. 562.

43. Helvétius, p. 457.

44. "Afrique," *Encyclopédie,* Supplement, 1, p. 194.

45. Ibid.; Grégoire, p. 249.

46. Buffon, 4, pp. 291–92.

47. Arthur O. Lovejoy and George Boas, eds., *A Documentary History of Primitivism and Related Ideas* (Baltimore, 1935).

48. Q. in François de Dainville, *La Géographie des humanistes* (Paris, 1940; reprinted Geneva, 1969), p. 307.

49. Lecture by Jacques Roger, Indiana University, Bloomington, November 10, 1971.

50. Charles De Brosses, *Du culte des dieux fétiches* (Paris, 1760), pp. 192–94 (the copy at Northwestern University Library was owned by the nineteenth-century anthropologist Abel Hovelacque); Proyart, pp. 184–87.

51. Q. in Jean Etienne Martin-Allanic, *Bougainville navigateur et les découvertes de son temps* (Paris, 1964), p. 652.

52. De Brosses, p. 206; Pierre Poivre, *Voyages d'un philosophe* (Paris, 1769), p. 9; Médéric Louis Elie Moreau de Saint-Méry, *Danse* (Philadelphia, 1796), p. 9; Lamiral, *L'Affrique,* p. 197.

53. Paul-Henri Thiry Holbach, *Essai sur les préjugés* (Paris, 1770), p. 273.

54. Villeneuve, pp. 9–10; Marie-Jean de Condorcet, *Esquisse d'un tableau historique des progrès de l'esprit humain* (Paris, 1795), p. 328.

55. *Pour et contre* 12 (1737):316–17; Prévost, 4, pp. 324–25, 350–51; ibid., 9, p. 16; Buffon, 4, pp. 306, 319, 345–46.

56. Louis Daubenton, *Encyclopédie méthodique*, 1 (Paris, 1782), p. xxxiii; C. F. Volney, *Travels Through Syria and Egypt*, 1, trans. from the French (London, 1787), p. 80.

57. Abbé Joseph Delaporte, *Voyageur français*, 13 (Paris, 1772), p. 449.

58. P. M. J. à Saint-Domingue, "Explication physiognomique de la noirceur des nègres," *Mémoires pour l'histoire et des sciences et des beaux arts* (Trévoux) (June 1738), pp. 1180–82; Buffon, 4, p. 304; ibid., 9, pp. 315–16.

59. Cornelius de Pauw, *Recherches sur les américains*, 2 (Paris, 1774), p. 56, and ibid., 1, p. 52, q. in Michèle Duchet, "Esclavage et préjugé de couleur," in *Racisme et société*, ed. Patrice Comarmond and Claude Duchet (Paris, 1969), p. 123. The most extensive treatment of de Pauw's thoughts on blacks is contained in Carminella Biondi, *Mon frère tu es mon esclave: Teorie Schiaviste e dibattiti antropologico-razziali nel Settecento francese* (Pisa, 1973), pp. 230–35.

60. Pierre Barrère, *Dissertation sur la cause physique de la couleur des nègres* (Paris, 1741), p. 4; Claude-Nicolas Le Cat, *Traité de la couleur de la peau humaine en général* (Amsterdam, 1765), pp. 128, 173–75. An attempt at rescuing Le Cat from his well-deserved obscurity is G. S. Rousseau, "Le Cat and the Physiology of the Negroes," *Racism in the Eighteenth Century, Studies in Eighteenth-Century Culture*, 3 (Cleveland, 1973), pp. 369–86.

61. Pierre de Maupertuis, *Venus physique* (1745), *OC*, 2 (Lyons, 1756), pp. 106–10, 128–30. The existence of albinism among Africans had exercised the European imagination; Winthrop D. Jordan, *White Over Black: American Attitudes Toward the Negro, 1550–1812* (Baltimore, 1969), pp. 249–52; Biondi, pp. 218–37. Albinism in Africa as proof of the original color of man was also advanced by the missionary Demanet (2, pp. 217, 294).

62. "Nègre," *Encyclopédie*, 11, p. 77.

63. "Humaine espèce," *Encyclopédie*, 8, pp. 347–48.

64. "Nez," *Encyclopédie*, 11, p. 127.

65. Buffon, 4, p. 317; Emile Guyénot, *Les Sciences de la vie au XVIIᵉ et XVIIIᵉ siècles*, 2d ed. (Paris, 1957), pp. 365–66.

66. "Nègre," *Encyclopédie*, 11, pp. 76–77; Maupertuis, *OC*, 2, new ed. (Lyons, 1768), pp. 106–07.

67. Voltaire, *Essai sur les moeurs*, *OC*, 11 (Paris, 1878), pp. 5–6; ibid., 12, pp. 357, 380–81; idem, "Homme," *Dictionnaire philosophique*, *OC*, 19 (1879), p. 377; idem, *Singularité de la nature*, *OC*, 27 (1879), p. 184.

68. On the problem of species, see John C. Greene, "Some Early Speculators on the Origin of Human Races," *American Anthropologist* 56 (February, 1954):31–41. The lack of a clear delineation among the species may be seen in an experiment that Réaumur conducted when he attempted to cross a rabbit with a chicken, or in the suggestion later in the century by a scientist of even greater reputation for his research in anatomy, Bonnet, who suggested the possibility of crossing plants with animals; L. Poliakov, "Le

fantasme des hybrides et la hiérarchie des races," in *Hommes et bêtes: Entretiens sur le racisme*, ed. Léon Poliakov (Paris, 1975), pp. 168–70.

69. Voltaire, "Homme," pp. 357, 377, 380–82.

70. Yves Benot, "Diderot, Pechmenja, Raynal et l'anti-colonialisme," *Europe* 41 (1962):140.

71. S. J. Ducoeurjoly, *Manuel des habitants de Saint-Domingue*, 1 (Paris, 1802), p. 17; Baudry Deslozières, *Les égarements du négrophilisme* (Paris, 1802), p. 65. In my opinion Urs Bitterli (*Die Entdeckung des Schwarzen Afrikaners* [Zurich, 1970], p. 110) is wrong to insist on the interconnection of proslavery thought and polygenism. In America, too, there was no necessary connection between polygenism and slavery; John C. Greene, "The American Debate on the Negro's Place in Nature, 1780–1815," *Journal of the History of Ideas* 15 (June 1954):384–96; rather, it seemed to depend on attitudes toward the Scriptures.

72. Peyroux de la Coudrenière, "Observations sur la couleur des nègres," *Journal de Monsieur* (January 1780):190.

73. Arthur O. Lovejoy, *The Great Chain of Being: A Study of the History of an Idea* (Cambridge, Mass., 1936; reprinted New York, 1960).

74. Carl Linné, *Systema naturae per regna tria naturae*, 1 (Stockholm, 1758; reprinted London, 1956), pp. 24–25.

75. Lovejoy, p. 235; Rousseau, 1, pp. 337–41.

76. J. B. Robinet, *Considérations philosophiques de la gradation naturelle des formes de l'être* (Paris, 1768), p. 168. Robinet's contribution to chain-of-being thought is examined in Lovejoy, pp. 269–83.

77. Rousselot de Surgy, *Mélanges intéressants et curieux* (Paris, 1763–1765), 10, p. 161, q. in Duchet, "Esclavage et préjugé," p. 122.

78. Demanet, 2, p. 125; Lamiral, *L'Affrique*, p. 183.

79. Voltaire, *Lettres d'Annabed*, *OC*, 21, p. 462; idem, "Traité de métaphysique," *OC*, 22, p. 192.

80. Q. in Paul Topinard, *Eléments d'anthropologie générale* (Paris, 1885), p. 43.

81. Gabriel Mailhol, *Le Philosophe nègre* (London, 1764), p. 50; A. Pherotée de la Croix, *Relation universelle de l'Afrique ancienne*, 2 (Lyons, 1688), p. 519; Voltaire, *Essai sur les moeurs*, p. 7; Lamiral, *L'Affrique*, p. 46.

82. F. Tinland, "L'homme sauvage vu par l'homme des lumières," in Poliakov, ed., pp. 183–99.

83. Elizabeth C. Evans, "Galen the Physician as Physiognomist," *American Philological Association, Tracts and Proceedings* 76 (1945): 294–96. I wish to thank Professor Glanville Downey for bringing this article to my attention.

84. G. Lanteri-Laura, *Histoire de la phrénologie* (Paris, 1970), p. 21. Transferring these attitudes to pharmacology, Porta believed that plants shaped like human organs could cure the organs they resembled; thus liver-shaped leaves would cure liver disease; Guyénot, pp. 14–15.

85. Q. in E. T. Hamy, "Recherches sur les origines de l'enseignement de l'anatomie humaine et de l'anthropologie au Jardin des plantes," *Nouvelles archives du Muséum*, 3d ser., 7 (1905):9.

86. *Essai sur la physionomie destiné à faire connaître l'homme et le faire aimer,*

4 vols. (The Hague, 1781–1803): *L'Art de connaître les hommes par la physionomie* (1806; new eds. 1806–1809, 1807–1810, 1820); *Règles physiognomiques ou observations sur quelques traits caractéristiques* (1838); *Nouveau manuel de physiognomie et de phrénologie* (1838; new ed. 1845); *Des signes physiognomiques* (1801).

87. Jordan, pp. 27–28; Léon-François Hoffmann, *Nègre romantique* (Paris, 1973), pp. 61–62, 109.

88. James Walwin, *Black and White: The Negro and English Society, 1555–1945* (London, 1973), p. 71.

89. "Nègre," *Encyclopédie*, 11, p. 76; Maupertuis, 2, p. 98; Daubenton, 1, p. xxxi.

90. Bougainville q. in Duchet, "Esclavage et préjugé," p. 122, and in Martin-Allanic, p. 749; François Levaillant, *Voyage dans l'intérieur, de l'Afrique, par le cap de Bonne espérance dans les années 1780, 1781, 1782, 1783, 1784, et 1785*, 2 (Paris, 1791) p. 98. Though protesting against physiognomics, Levaillant still held on to many of its presuppositions, thus tending to see the less Negroid peoples he met as nobler; ibid., pp. 1, 103.

91. Peter Mark, *Africans in European Eyes: The Portrayal of Africans in Fourteenth- and Fifteenth-Century Europe, Foreign and Comparative Studies, Eastern Africa*, 16 (Syracuse, N. Y., 1974); Hamy, p. 11.

92. "Relation du voyage fait sur les costes d'Afrique," in *Receuil de divers voyages* (Paris, 1674), p. 16.

93. Saint Lambert q. in Hoffmann, p. 86; de Staël-Holstein, p. 73.

94. Golberry, pp. 101–10; ibid., 2, p. 132; Durand, 1, pp. 368–69.

95. Linné, 1, p. 22; de Pauw q. in Duchet, "Esclavage et préjugé," p. 123.

96. D. J. Cunningham, "Anthropology in the Eighteenth Century," *Journal of the Royal Anthropological Institute* 38 (1908):20, 26.

97. A. C. Haddon, *History of Anthropology*, 2d ed. (London, 1934), pp. 16, 31; Philip D. Curtin, *The Image of Africa: British Ideas and Action, 1780–1850* (Madison, Wisc., 1964), p. 40.

98. Georges Cuvier, *Tableau élémentaire de l'histoire naturelle des animaux* (Paris, 1798), p. 71; Cuvier q. in George W. Stocking, "French Anthropology in 1800," *Isis* 55 (August 1964):146; Cuvier q. in M. Bouteiller, "La Société des observateurs de l'homme," *Bulletin et mémoires de la Société d'anthropologie de Paris*, 10th ser., 7 (1956):454. Similar ideas were expressed by the founder of the Society for Observers of Man, Louis Jauffret, q. in Georges Hervé, "Le Premier programme de l'anthropologie," *Revue scientifique* 30 (October 23, 1909):523.

99. J. J. Virey, *Histoire naturelle du genre humain*, 2 (Paris, 1801), pp. 132, 147, 428.

100. Pierre L. Van den Berghe, *Race and Racism: A Comparative Perspective* (New York, 1967), p. 11.

101. The most thorough study of the development of the racial idea among the French nobility is André Duvevyer, "Le Sang épuré: La naissance du sentiment et de l'idée de race dans la noblesse française (1560–1720)," 3 vols., Ms., mimeo., Brussels, n.d. (1970), copy Ms. in BN. Still an excellent

survey, but emphasizing less the early period is Jacques Barzun, *The French Race* (New York, 1932).

102. Barzun, pp. 114, 139–140, 201; Duvevyer, 2, pp. 282–95.
103. Lenard R. Berlanstein, *The Barristers of Toulouse in the Eighteenth Century (1740–1793)* (Baltimore, 1975), p. 120.
104. Barzun, p. 248.
105. Virey, *Histoire naturelle*, 1, pp. 167–68; ibid., 2, pp. 131–34; ibid., pp. 293–94.
106. Hervé, p. 525.

4. Three Patterns of Interaction: West Indies, France, Senegal

1. Among others who support this view is Gwendolyn M. Hall, *Social Control in Slave Plantation Societies: A Comparison of Saint-Domingue and Cuba* (Baltimore, 1971), pp. 139–46; Laura Foner, "The Free People of Color in Louisiana and Saint-Domingue," *Journal of Social History* 3 (1970):406–30.
2. Gabriel Debien, *Les esclaves aux antilles françaises, XVIIe-XVIIIe siècles* (Basse Terre, Guadeloupe, 1974), p. 374.
3. On these statistics, see chapter 2.
4. Jean Fouchard, *Les marrons de la liberté* (Paris, 1972), p. 347.
5. Adolphe Cabon, *Histoire d'Haïti*, 1 (Port au Prince, 1930), p. 145.
6. A comparative study similar to that of H. Hoetink ("Diferencias en Relaciones Raciales entre Curazao y Surinam," *Revista de Ciencias Sociales* 5 [December 1961]:499–514, trans. in *Slavery in the New World: A Reader in Comparative History,* ed. Laura Foner and Eugene D. Genovese [Englewood Cliffs, N. J., 1969], pp. 178–88) would be very appropriate for the French Caribbean.
7. Y. Debbash, "Le Crime d'empoisonnement aux îles pendant la période esclavagiste," *RFHOM* (1963):138–44. Hall (pp. 68–74) feels that poisoning was a means of black resistance and thus suggests that the white fears were grounded in some reality. Debien (*Les esclaves,* pp. 399–403) is more cautious, ascribing the poisoning neither to white hysteria nor to black machinations.
8. Q. in Lucien Peytraud, *L'esclavage aux antilles françaises* (Paris, 1897), pp. 193–94; Gaston Martin, *Histoire de l'esclavage dans les colonies françaises* (Paris, 1948), p. 122.
9. Peytraud, p. 428; S. Linstant, *Essai sur les moyens d'extirper les préjugés des blancs contre la couleur des Africains et des sang-mêlés* (Paris, 1841), p. 38; Antonine Gisler, *L'esclavage aux Antilles françaises (XVIIe–XVIIIe siècles): Contribution au problème de l'esclavage* (Fribourg, 1965), p. 93; Léo Elisabeth, "The French Antilles," in *Neither Slave Nor Free: The Freedmen of African Descent in the Slave Societies of the New World,* ed. David W. Cohen and Jack P. Greene (Baltimore, 1972), p. 162.
10. M. J. Morénas, *Précis historique de la traite* (Paris, 1828), p. 233;

Linstant, p. 40; Decree of February 9, 1779, A. Lebeau, *De la condition des gens de couleur libres sous l'ancien régime* (Paris, 1903), pp. 80–81.

11. Peytraud, p. 422.

12. Ibid., p. 423; Martin, p. 115; Lothrop Stoddard, *The French Revolution in San Domingo* (New York, 1914), p. 43.

13. E. Hayot, "Les Gens de couleur libres du Fort Royal, 1679–1823," *RFHOM* 56 (1969):126–28.

14. Hall, p. 79; Michel René-Hilliard d'Auberteuil, *Considérations sur l'état présent de la colonie française de Saint-Domingue: Ouvrage politique et législatif*, 2 (Paris, 1782), p. 73.

15. Hilliard, 2, p. 94.

16. June 29, 1734, q. in Elisabeth, p. 139.

17. Michèle Duchet, "Esclavage et humanisme en 1787: Réflexions sur les moyens de rendre meilleur l'état des nègres ou des affranchis de nos colonies," *Annales historiques de la révolution française* 37 (1965):350–51.

18. Foner (pp. 428–29) seems to subscribe to such an interpretation.

19. Instruction of 1766, q. in Cabon, 2, p. 306. Such a policy was again advocated in 1778, in the same words; Martin, p. 153.

20. Peytraud, p. 424; Gisler, pp. 99–100; Hall, p. 136.

21. Frank Tannenbaum, *Slave and Citizen* (New York, 1946). This influential work has had a large following among others; Herbert S. Klein, "Anglicanism, Catholicism, and the Negro Slave," *Comparative Studies in Society and History* 8 (April 1966):295–307.

22. Stanley Elkins, *Slavery: A Problem in American Institutional and Intellectual Life* (Chicago, 1959).

23. Marvin Harris, *Patterns of Race in the Americas* (New York, 1964); Carl N. Degler, *Neither Black Nor White* (New York, 1971).

24. Gilberto Freyre, *The Masters and the Slaves: A Study in the Development of Brazilian Civilization,* trans. Samuel Putnam, revised, 2d ed. (New York, 1966); A. J. R. Russell-Wood, "Iberian Expansion and the Issue of Black Slavery: Changing Portuguese Attitudes, 1440–1770," *American Historical Review* 83 (February 1978):38–42.

25. H. Hoetink, *The Two Variants in Caribbean Race Relations: A Contribution to the Sociology of Segmented Societies* (London, 1967). As this interpretation is also open to criticism, Stanley W. Mintz ("Groups, Group Boundaries and the Perception of 'Race,'" *Comparative Studies in Society and History* 13 [1971]:437–50) has argued that the differences between the treatment of slaves to be found in Spanish-controlled Cuba and that in Puerto Rico show that the cultural attitude of the colonizing country was less important than the material conditions; in Cuba sugar was king, but Puerto Rico was a far less important plantation society.

26. Peytraud, pp. 380–81.

27. André Corvisier, "Les Soldats noirs du maréchal de Saxe: Le problème des antillais et africains sous les armes en France au XVIIIe siècle," *RFHOM* 55 (1968):372.

28. Ibid., pp. 367–413.

29. Police officials, on the basis of a census of 1777–78, estimated that there were 5000 blacks and people of color in the kingdom. Shelby T. McCloy (*The Negro in France* [Lexington, Ky., 1961], p. 5) thinks this figure too high and suggests a figure of 1000.

30. Ernest Nys, "L'Esclavage noir devant les jurisconsultes et les cours de justice," *Revue de droit et de législation comparée*, 1st ser., 22 (1896):146.

31. Elisabeth, p. 138.

32. Peytraud, p. 388.

33. Ibid., p. 390; Lebeau, pp. 75–76.

34. Maurice Besson, "La police des noirs sous Louis XVI en France," *RHCF* 16 (July-August 1928):433–46; McCloy, pp. 47–49.

35. This figure is high and unreliable, but it represented the estimate of contemporaries and therefore had some influence on shaping possible reactions to blacks; James Walwin, *Black and White: The Negro and English Society, 1555–1945* (London, 1973), pp. 46–47.

36. Philip D. Curtin, *The Image of Africa: British Ideas and Action, 1780–1850* (Madison, Wisc., 1964), pp. 98–99; Walwin, pp. 144–58.

37. Q. in Dr. Lemaire, "Dunkerque et la traite des noirs au XVIIIᵉ siècle," *Union faulconnier, société historique et archéologique de Dunkerque et de la Flandre maritime* 31 (1934):106.

38. Pierre Victor Malouet, *Mémoire sur l'esclavage des nègres* (Neufchatel, 1788), p. 4. Similar arguments appear in César de l'Escale de Vérone, *Observations sur les hommes de couleur des colonies* (Paris, 1790), cited in Léon Poliakov, *The Aryan Myth: A History of Racist and Nationalist Ideas in Europe,* trans. Edmund Howard (London, 1974), p. 360; Dominique Harcourt Lamiral, *L'Affrique et le peuple afriquain* (Paris, 1789), pp. 211–12; Jean-Baptiste Léonard Durand, *Voyage au Sénégal,* 1 (Paris, 1802), p. 166.

39. Léon-François Hoffmann, *Le nègre romantique* (Paris, 1973), p. 107.

40. G. Debien, *Les colons de Saint-Domingue et la Révolution: Essai sur le club Massiac* (Paris, 1953), p. 107.

41. P. Caron, *Paris sous la Terreur,* 3 (Paris, 1943), pp. 315–23, 332–33.

42. "Mémoire en faveur des gens de couleur ou sang-mêlés de Saint-Domingue, et des autres îles françaises de l'Amérique" (Paris, 1789), reprinted in *RFAE,* 1.

43. For the legislative struggle, see J. Saintoyant, *La Colonisation française pendant la Révolution, 1789–1799,* 1 (Paris, 1930), pp. 115–29; Mitchell B. Garrett, *The French Colonial Question, 1789–1791* (Ann Arbor, 1916), p. 105; Thomas O. Ott, *The Haitian Revolution, 1789–1804* (Knoxville, Tenn., 1973), pp. 28–42. A short, concise summary is presented in David B. Davis, *The Problem of Slavery in the Age of Revolution, 1770–1823* (henceforth *The Problem of Slavery* 2) (Ithaca, N. Y., 1975), pp. 137–48.

44. Saintoyant, 1, pp. 127–28.

45. Q. in Stoddard, p. 126.

46. A recent study in English that brings new details to the story is Ott, chs. 1–4.

47. G. Debien, "Les colons des Antilles et leur main-d'oeuvre à la fin du

XVIIIᵉ siècle," *Annales historiques de la révolution française* 28 (1955): 276–77; address, November 28, 1789, q. in Saintoyant, 1, p. 109.

48. Michel Leiris, *Contacts de civilisations en Martinique et en Guadeloupe* (Paris, 1955), pp. 117–92.

49. Garrett, pp. 127–33; Saintoyant, 2, pp. 53–74, 133; Ott, ch. 4.

50. 16 Pluviose, II (debate of February 4, 1794), *Archives parlementaires,* 1st ser., 84 (1962):284.

51. Marcel Garaud, *La Révolution et l'égalité civile* (Paris, 1953), p. 35.

52. Pluviose, II (February 5, 1794), *Moniteur universel* (1794):388.

53. Antoine C. Thibadeau, *Mémoires sur le Consulat, 1799 à 1804, par un ancien conseiller d'état* (Paris, 1827), p. 120, q. in Ott, p. 144.

54. Peytraud, p. 399.

55. Victor Schoelcher, *Des Colonies françaises* (Paris, 1842), p. 211.

56. Comte de Montholon, "Réflexions de Napoléon sur la politique coloniale," *Revue libérale,* no. 11 (1955):98.

57. Baudry Deslozières, *Les égarements du négrophilisme* (Paris, 1802), pp. 29, 156–57.

58. Peytraud, p. 398.

59. Paul Frédéric Grunebaum-Ballin, *Henri Grégoire, l'ami des hommes* (Paris, 1948), p. 153.

60. André-Charles de Lajaille, *Voyage au Sénégal pendant les années 1784 et 1785 d'après les mémoires de Lajaille avec des notes sur la situation de l'Afrique jusqu' à l'an X,* ed. P. Labarthe (Paris, 1802), p. 177.

61. Q. in Paul Marty, "Tentatives de Christianisation," *Etudes sénégalaises* (Paris, n.d.), p. 224.

62. Sylvain Meinrad Xavier de Golberry, *Fragmens d'un voyage en Afrique, fait pendant les années 1786, 1787, dans les contrées occidentales de ce continent,* 1 (Paris, 1802), pp. 154–55; George E. Brooks, Jr., "The Signares of Saint-Louis and Gorée: Women Entrepreneurs in Eighteenth-Century Senegal," in *Women in Africa: Studies in Social and Economic Change,* ed. Nancy J. Hafkin and Edna G. Bays (Stanford, Calif., 1976), p. 33.

63. Q. in Marty, p. 230.

64. Minister to Governor Schmalz, Christian Schefer, *Instructions générales données de 1763 à 1870 aux gouverneurs et ordonnateurs des établissements français en Afrique occidentale,* 1 (Paris, 1927).

65. Denise Bouche, *L'enseignement dans les territoires français de l'Afrique occidentale de 1817 à 1920,* 1 (Lille, 1975), pp. 82, 114–15.

66. H. Oludare Idowu, "Assimilation in 19th-Century Senegal," *CEA* 9 (1969):194–218; Saliou M'Baye, "La représentation du Sénégal au parlement français sous la seconde république (1848–1851), *BIFAN* 38 (1976): 517–51.

67. For the development of the office of mayor, François Zucarelli, "Les maires de Saint-Louis et Gorée de 1816 à 1872," *BIFAN* 35 (1973):551–73.

68. Lamiral, *L'Affrique,* p. 43.

69. John D. Hargreaves, "Assimilation in Eighteenth-Century Senegal," *Journal of African History* 6 (1965):177–84; idem, *West Africa: The Former French States* (Englewood Cliffs, N. J., 1967), pp. 62–72; Bouche, 1, p. 83.

70. Lamiral, *L'Affrique*, pp. 1–3, 37–40, q. in *France and West Africa*, ed. John D. Hargreaves (London, 1969), p. 84. The editions of Lamiral available to me have similar sentiments, but not exactly as quoted in Hargreaves.

71. J. Monteilhet, "Au Seuil d'un empire colonial," *Bulletin du comité d'études historiques et scientifiques de l'Afrique occidentale française* (henceforth *BCEHSAOF*) 1 (1918):148.

72. Q. in Léonce Jore, *Les établissements français sur la côte occidentale d'Afrique de 1758 à 1809* (Paris, 1964), p. 423.

73. P. Alquier, "Saint-Louis du Sénégal pendant la révolution et l'empire (1789–1809)," *BCEHSAOF* 5 (1922):309–10.

74. Abbé Boilat, *Esquisses sénégalaises* (Paris, 1853), pp. 7–8.

75. Ibid., pp. 236–37, and q. in Bouche, 1, p. 186.

76. Q. in M'Baye, "La représentation," p. 534.

77. André Delcourt, *La France et les établissements français au Sénégal entre 1712 et 1763* (Dakar, 1952), p. 123.

78. Boilat, p. 226.

79. Brooks, "The *Signares*," in Hafkin and Bays, eds., 19–44; idem, "Artists' Depictions of Senegalese Signares: Insights Concerning French Racist Attitudes in the Nineteenth Century," paper delivered at the Fourth Berkshire Conference on the History of Women, August 24, 1978; Marie-Hélène Knight-Baylac, "La Vie à Gorée de 1677 à 1789," *RFHOM* 57 (1970): 401–03. Further details of signare wealth are provided in idem, "Gorée au XVIIIᵉ siècle: L'appropriation du sol," *RFHOM* 64 (1977):33–54.

80. Françoise Deroure, "La vie quotidienne à Saint-Louis, par ses archives (1779–1801)," *BIFAN* 26 (1964):409; Knight-Baylac, "La vie à Gorée," p. 414.

81. Knight-Baylac, "La Vie à Gorée," pp. 402–03; idem, "Gorée au XVIIIᵉ siècle," pp. 44–46.

82. De Lajaille, p. 177; Durand, 2, p. 26; Saugnier, *Relations de plusieurs voyages à la côte d'Afrique à Maroc, au Sénégal, à Gorée, à Galam . . .* (Paris, 1791), p. 178.

83. Pruneau de Pommegorge, *Description de la nigritie* (Amsterdam, 1789), pp. 2–3.

84. Jore, pp. 216–17, fn. 2.

85. Ibid., p. 211; Alquier, p. 318.

86. Durand, 2, pp. 34–36; Jore, pp. 295–96.

87. Michel Adanson, *A Voyage to Senegal, the Isle of Gorée and the River Gambia*, trans. from the 1756 ed. (London, 1759), p. 50.

88. Louis Lamiral, "Mémoire pour servir à celui qui a été présenté au ministère de la marine pour des établissements aux côtes occidentales d'Afrique," n.d. (1780s), T 1393, Archives nationales (henceforth AN).

5. The Issue of Slavery

1. David Brion Davis, *The Problem of Slavery in Western Culture* (Ithaca, N. Y., 1966), p. 108.

2. Guy Turbet-Delof, *L'Afrique barbaresque dans la littérature française au XVIe et XVIIe siècles* (Paris, 1973), pp. 131–32, 235–38; idem, *La presse périodique française et l'Afrique barbaresque au XVIIe siècle (1611–1715)* (Paris, 1973), p. 73; idem, "L'antiesclavagisme bordelais en 1571," *Revue historique de Bordeaux et du département de la Gironde* 24 (1975):75–78.

3. Richelet, *Dictionnaires français,* eds. of 1719, 1728, and 1732, q. in Simone Delesalle and Lucette Valensi, "Le Mot 'Nègre' dans les dictionnaires français de l'ancien régime: Histoire et léxicographie," *Langue française* 15 (September 1972):86; idem, "Nègre/Negro: Recherches dans les dictionnaires français et anglais au XVIIe siècle," in *L'idée de race dans la pensée politique française contemporaine,* ed. Pierre Guiral and Emile Temime (Paris, 1977), p. 158–62.

4. *Dictionnaire des arts et sciences,* eds. of 1776, 1798, 1811, 1814, 1825, q. in Delesalle and Valensi, "Nègre/Negro," p. 87; "Nègre," *Dictionnaire de l'Académie française* (Paris, 1789), p. 171, and ibid., 5th ed. (Paris, 1813), p. 156.

5. Serge Daget, in a word-content analysis of 143 texts between 1770 and 1845 examining the varying uses of the terms *esclaves, nègres,* and *noirs,* shows that the term *noirs* was introduced by the abolitionists and that its rise in usage roughly coincided with the rise of abolitionist sentiment, but that the other terms also persisted; "Les mots esclave, nègre, noir, et les jugements de valeur sur la traite négrière dans la littérature abolitionniste française de 1770 à 1845," *RFHOM* 60 (1973):511–48.

6. Poivre and Mirabeau q. in Michèle Duchet, *Anthropologie et histoire au siècle des lumières* (Paris, 1971), pp. 149–50; Marmontel, *Les Incas, ou la destruction de Pérou* (Lyons, 1810, [1st éd. 1777]) 1, p. 144, q. in Carminella Biondi, *Mon frère tu es mon esclave: Teorie Schiaviste e dibattiti antropologico-razziali nel Settecento francese* (Pisa, 1973), p. 44.

7. Charles de Secondat, Baron de Montesquieu, *De l'esprit des lois, OC,* 1 (Paris, 1951), p. 494; Voltaire, "Esclaves," *Dictionnaire philosophique, OC,* 30 (Paris, 1880), p. 446. On Quakers, see Voltaire's letter to René François Doigny du Ponceau, October 12, 1775, *Voltaire's Correspondence,* 42, ed. Theodore Bestermann (Geneva, 1964), no. 18580; "Esclavage," *Encyclopédie* (Paris, 1751–1765), 5, pp. 934–39; "Humaine espèce," *Encyclopédie,* 8, p. 347; "Traite des nègres," *Encyclopédie,* 16, pp. 532–33, written by the chevalier de Jaucourt, who was indirectly influenced by Montesquieu, having read similar passages in the work of an English disciple of Montesquieu, George Wallace (see David Brion Davis, "New Sidelights on Early Antislavery Radicalism," *William and Mary Quarterly,* 3d ser., 28 [October 1971]: 588–89).

8. Montesquieu, *De l'esprit, OC,* 1, p. 496; Davis, *The Problem of Slavery,* p. 403. The contradiction of Montesquieu's thought on slavery was due to the tension between his sense of pity for the individual and his conviction that natural law dictated the utility of slavery in certain regions, and in fact was probably not that destructive of the individual, argues Jean-Pierre Despin, "Montesquieu était-il esclavagiste?" *Pensée,* no. 193 (June 1977):102–12.

9. Voltaire, *Essai sur les moeurs, OC*, 12, pp. 380–81; idem, "Esclaves," *Dictionnaire philosophique, OC*, 30, p. 446. Michèle Duchet ("Voltaire et les sauvages," *Europe* 38 [May-June 1959]:95–96) rather vehemently argues that Voltaire opposed serfdom because it no longer served the interest of the bourgeoisie, which found this form of labor outmoded, but that as a spokesman for the business classes Voltaire favored slavery, which played an essential role in the accumulation of wealth.

10. Davis, *The Problem of Slavery*, pp. 416–17.

11. "Nègres considérés comme esclaves dans les colonies de l'Amérique," *Encyclopédie*, 11, p. 80. See also the matter-of-fact descriptive account of how to make slaves work in a sugar mill in "Sucrerie," *Encyclopédie*, 15, pp. 618–19. Jean-Jacques Rousseau, "*Du Contrat social*," *OC*, ed. V. D. Musset-Pathay (Paris, 1823), 5, p. 158; Abbé Grégoire, *An Enquiry concerning the Intellectual and Moral Faculties, and Literature of Negroes. . .* , trans. D. B. Warden (Brooklyn, 1810), p. 152. This tension of thought is explored in the recent article by Daniel Whitman, "Slavery and the Rights of Frenchmen: Views of Montesquieu, Rousseau and Raynal," *French Colonial Studies* 1 (Spring 1977):17–33; interesting, but not proved to my satisfaction, is Whitman's thesis that the debate on slavery was a veiled discussion of the French political system and that the ambiguity was due to the bourgeois ambivalence toward full equality at home.

12. The fusion of the Enlightenment and the "Establishment" after the mid-eighteenth century is described in Robert Darnton, "The High Enlightenment and the Low Life of Literature in Prerevolutionary France," *Past and Present*, no. 51 (May 1971):81–115.

13. Geneviève Charpentier, *Les Relations économiques entre Bordeaux et les antilles au XVIIIe siècle* (Bordeaux, 1937); François Georges Pariset, ed., *Bordeaux au XVIIIe siècle*, 5 (Bordeaux, 1969), p. 224. On its role in Nantes, see Jean Meyer, *L'Armement Nantais dans la deuxième moitié du XVIIIe siècle* (Paris, 1969); Pierre H. Boulle, "Slave Trade, Commercial Organization, and Industrial Growth in Eighteenth-Century Nantes," *RFHOM* 59 (1972): 70–112; idem, "Marchandises de traite et développement industriel dans la France et l'Angleterre du XVIIIe siècle," *RFHOM* 62 (1975):309–30; Thomas M. Doerflinger, "The Antilles Trade of the Old Regime: A Statistical Overview," *Journal of Interdisciplinary History* 6 (Winter 1976):397–415.

14. Louis-Philippe May, "La France, puissance des Antilles," *Revue d'histoire économique et sociale* 18 (1930):451–81.

15. Pariset, 5, pp. 231–33.

16. Duchet, *Anthropologie*, pp. 151–60.

17. Jean Hurault, "Histoire des noirs refugiés Boni de la Guyane française," *RFHOM* 47 (1960):76–77; Mme Marchand-Thébault, "L'esclavage en Guyane française sous l'ancien régime," *RFHOM* 47 (1960):67.

18. For Diderot as bourgeois, see Jacques Prost, *Diderot et l'Encyclopédie* (Paris, 1962), ch. 3 and *passim*.

19. Edward D. Seeber, *Antislavery Opinion in France during the Second Half of the Eighteenth Century* (Baltimore, 1937), p. 66; Jacques Donvez, *De*

Quoi vivait Voltaire? (Paris, 1949); Léon Kozminski, *Voltaire financier* (Paris, 1929).

20. Fernand Caussy, "Les Manuscrits de Voltaire, à Saint Petersbourg," *Correspondence* (March 25, 1914), pp. 1129–56.

21. Duchet, *Anthropologie*, pp. 129–30.

22. Hans Wolpe, *Raynal et sa machine de guerre: L'histoire des deux Indes et ses perfectionnements* (Stanford, Calif., 1957).

23. Ibid., p. 158.

24. Guillaume Thomas Raynal, *Histoire philosophique et politique des établissements et du commerce des européens dans les deux Indes,* 10 (Geneva, 1780), p. 297, q. in Davis, *The Problem of Slavery,* p. 16.

25. Raynal, ibid., 6 (Paris, 1821), p. 109 ff., q. in Charles Minguet, "L'Esclavage et les problèmes de l'indépendance dans les Antilles (1810–1820)," *Mélanges à la Mémoire de Jean Sarrailh,* 2 (Paris, 1966), pp. 184–85. One of the rare scholars to have noticed the lack of a specifically anti-French-colonial posture is Thomas Cassilly, "The Anticolonial Tradition in France: The Eighteenth Century to the Fifth Republic" (Ph. D. diss., Columbia University, 1975).

26. Raynal, ibid., pp. 157–58.

27. Jacques Henri Bernardin de Saint-Pierre, *Voyage à l'Ile de France, OC,* 1 (Paris, 1818), pp. 152–63; Karl Noël, "L'Esclavage à L'Île de France pendant l'occupation française (1715–1810)" (thèse de doctorat de l'université de Paris, 1953), pp. 198–99; Anna Cooper, *L'Attitude de la France à l'égard de l'esclavage pendant la révolution* (Paris, 1925), pp. 16–17.

28. Raynal, 6, p. 221. On Diderot's collaboration with Raynal, see Michèle Duchet, "'Le Supplément au Voyage de Bougainville'" et la collaboration de Diderot à l'Histoire des deux Indes," *Cahiers de l'Association internationale des études françaises,* no. 13 (1961), pp. 173–87; Yves Benot, "Diderot, Pechmeja, Raynal et l'anticolonialisme," *Europe* 41 (January-February 1963):137–53; idem, *Diderot* (Paris, 1970).

29. "Règlements de la Société des amis des noirs, 1789," *RFAE,* 6, n.p.

30. C. Perroud, "La Société française des amis des noirs," *Révolution française* 69 (1916):122–47.

31. Daniel P. Resnick, "The Société des amis des noirs and the Abolition of Slavery," *French Historical Studies* 7 (1972):558–69.

32. The connection of evangelicalism and abolitionism in Britain is shown in Roger Anstey, *The Atlantic Slave Trade and British Abolitionism, 1760–1810* (Atlantic Highlands, N. J., 1975), chs. 7–9; Gaston Martin, *Histoire de l'esclavage dans les colonies françaises* (Paris, 1948), p. 171.

33. J. Meyer, "Le Commerce négrier nantais (1774–1792)," *Annales, économies, sociétés, civilisations* 15 (January-February 1960):120–29; J. Everaert, "Les Fluctuations du trafic négrier nantais (1763–1792)," *Cahiers de Tunisie* 11 (1963):37–62.

34. Philip D. Curtin, *The Atlantic Slave Trade: A Census* (Madison, Wisc., 1969), Table 60, p. 200. A 9.3-percent higher range is suggested by Roger Anstey, "The Volume of the North American Slave-Carrying Trade from Africa, 1761–1810," *RFHOM* 62 (1975): 47.

35. J. Vidalenc, "La Traite des nègres en France au début de la Révolution

(1789–1793)," *Annales historiques de la révolution française* 29 (1957):56–69. The opposite is argued by Léon Vignols, who claimed that the enormous increase of the slave trade was proof of the success of abolitionist ideas; he argued that the spread of abolitionist ideas unsettled European governments and made them believe that slavery, or at least the slave trade, would end imminently; to ensure a good supply of labor prior to this expected calamity, the planters and the public authorities radically increased the importation of slaves; "Etudes négrières de 1774 à 1928: Pourquoi la date de 1774?" *Revue d'histoire économique et sociale* 16 (1928):8.

36. Roger Mercier, *L'Afrique noire dans la littérature française: Les premières images (XVIIe-XVIIIe siècles)* (Dakar, 1962), pp. 121–71; Léon Deschamps, *Histoire de la question coloniale en France* (Paris, 1891), p. 329.

37. Beatrice F. Hyslop, *French Nationalism in 1789 according to the General Cahiers* (New York, 1934), p. 142.

38. Q. in ibid.

39. Cahier, Etats généraux, Senéchaussé de Mont-de-Marsan, *Archives parlementaires,* 1st ser., 4 (1868):36.

40. Cahiers de doléance, 3d Estate, Amiens Bailliage, *Archives parlementaires,* 1st ser., 1 (1879):754.

41. R. Simonin, "Le Problème noir au XVIIIe siècle vu par des paysans comtois," *Nouvelle revue franco-comtoise* 7, no. 25 (1962):9–13.

42. See chapter 4 for strategic considerations of emancipation. "La liberté des nègres," in *Histoire de France par les chansons,* 4, ed. Pierre Barbier and France Vernillat (Paris, 1957), pp. 154–57. I wish to thank my colleague Michel Berkvam for bringing it to my attention.

43. *Dictionnaire universel français et latin* (1705), q. in Delesalle and Valensi, "Le Mot 'nègre,'" p. 86.

44. Charles de Secondat, Baron de Montesquieu, *The Persian Letters,* ed. and trans. J. Robert Loy (Cleveland, 1961), letter 118.

45. *Dictionnaire de Trévoux,* eds. of 1728, 1732, 1740, q. in Delesalle and Valensi, "Le Mot 'nègre,'" p. 94; idem, "Nègre/Negro," pp. 162–63.

46. Delesalle and Valensi, "Le Mot 'nègre,'" p. 89.

47. Grasset Saint-Sauveur, "Sénégal," *Encyclopédie des voyages,* 4 (Paris, 1796), pp. 2, 15.

48. Jean-Gabriel Pelletan, *Mémoire sur la colonie française du Sénégal, avec quelques considérations historiques et politiques sur la traite des nègres,* ed. Marc-Françoise Guillois (Paris, 1801), p. 56; "Mémoire sur les nègres pour servir de matériaux au cahiers des colonies," F7. 4344, AN; Dominique Harcourt Lamiral, *L'Affrique et le peuple afriquain* (Paris, 1789), pp. 158–59, 167, 180, 204, 209.

49. Montesquieu, *De l'esprit des lois, OC,* 1, p. 490; "Esclavage," *Encyclopédie* 5, pp. 934–39; Abbé Roubaud, *Histoire générale de l'Asie, de l'Afrique, et de l'Amérique,* 10 (Paris, 1771), p. 41.

50. Jacques Doumet, "Mémoire historique sur les différentes parties de l'Afrique dépendant de l'île de Gorée depuis la rivière du Sénégal . . . 1769," in "Mémoire inédit de Doumet (1769)," ed. C. Becker and V. Martin, *BIFAN* 36 (January 1974):34.

51. Bellon de Saint-Quentin, *Dissertation sur la traite et le commerce des*

nègres (Paris, 1764), p. 20, q. in Michèle Duchet, "Esclavage et préjugé de couleur," in *Racisme et société*, ed. Patrice Comarmond and Claude Duchet (Paris, 1969), p. 122.

52. Pierre Victor Malouet, "Mémoire présenté au ministère" (1775), cited in Deschamps, p. 328; Malouet, "Du traitement et de l'emploi des nègres aux colonies" (1776), q. in Lucien Peytraud, *L'esclavage aux antilles françaises* (Paris, 1897), p. 238; Pierre Victor Malouet, *Mémoire sur l'esclavage des nègres* (Neufchatel, 1788), p. 22; M de C., *Mémoire sur l'esclavage et sur la traite des nègres* (London, 1798), p. 9.

53. Moreau de Saint-Méry, *Considérations présentées aux vrais amis du repos et du bonheur de la France* (Paris, 1791), pp. 50–54.

54. Dubuc de Marentille, *De l'esclavage des nègres dans les colonies de l'Amérique* (Point-à-Pitre, Guadeloupe, 1790), pp. 4–6, q. in Pierre de Vaissière, *Saint-Domingue: La Société, 1629–1789* (Paris, 1909), pp. 154–55, fn. 2.

55. "Mémoire sur l'esclavage des nègres par MDLDMFY" (Paris, 1790), p. 36, q. in Vaissière, p. 206.

56. Doumet, p. 44.

57. Voltaire to Charles De Brosses, January 2, 1760, *Voltaire's Correspondence*, 41 (Geneva, 1958), no. 7956; Curtin, *The Atlantic Slave Trade*, pp. 265–66.

58. Voltaire to *Gazette de l'Europe* (October 1764), *Voltaire's Correspondence*, 56 (Geneva, 1960), no. 11306.

59. Pruneau de Pommegorge, *Description de la nigritie* (Amsterdam, 1789), pp. 207–08, 213, 262–63.

60. Raynal, 6, pp. 175–76. The double of that was suggested by Brissot de Warville, "Discours sur la traite des noirs" (April 1790), *RFAE*, 8, p. 8.

61. Benjamin-Sigismond Frossard, *La cause des esclaves nègres et des habitants de la Guinée*, 1 (Lyon, 1789), p. 26; idem, "Observations sur l'abolition de la traite des nègres présentées à la Convention nationale" (1793), *RFAE*, 8, p. 20; Abbé Sibire, *L'aristocratie négrière, ou réflexions philosophiques et historiques sur l'esclavage et l'affranchissement des noirs, dediées à l'Assemblée nationale* (1789), *RFAE*, 2, p. 4.

62. Sibire, p. 52. A biographical sketch of Sibire appears in Jean Vinot-Préfontaine," *Revue des études historiques* (April-June 1932):127–64.

63. Frossard, *La cause des esclaves*, 1, p. 121.

64. "Adresse aux amis de l'humanité par la Société des amis des noirs sur le plan de ses travaux" (1790), *RFAE*, 8, p. 2.

65. Raynal, 6, p. 207; Larivallière, *Les Africains, ou le triomphe de l'humanité, comédie en un acte et en prose* (Paris, 1795), *RFAE*, 5.

66. Lecointe-Marsillac, *Le More Lack, ou essai sur les moyens les plus doux et les plus équitables d'abolir la traite et l'esclavage des nègres d'Afrique, en conservant aux colonies tous les avantages d'une population agricole* (Paris, 1780), pp. 26–27, 132; Pétion de Villeneuve, "Discours sur la traite des noirs" (April 1790), *RFAE*, 8, p. 9.

67. Lecointe-Marsillac, p. 132; J. P. Brissot de Warville, "Mémoire sur les

noirs de l'Amérique septentrionale, lu à l'assemblée de la Société des amis des noirs, le 9 février 1789" (Paris, 1789), *RFAE,* 7; Grégoire, *An Enquiry.*

68. Raynal, 6, p. 207; Sibire, p. 102.

69. Duchet, *Anthropologie,* pp. 154, 170–71.

70. Raynal, 6, pp. 216–17; Wolpe, pp. 155–56.

71. Wolpe, p. 157.

72. Sibire, p. 104; "L'esclavage des nègres aboli, ou moyens d'améliorer leur sort" (Paris, 1789), *RFAE,* 1.

73. Lecointe-Marsillac, p. 223; Anthony Benézet, *Some Historical Account of Guinea* (London, 1788), pp. 116–17; J.-B. Sanchamau, *Ecole des peuples et des rois, ou essai philosophique sur la liberté, le pouvoir arbitraire et les noirs* (Paris, 1790), p. 68, fn.; "Adresse aux amis de l'humanité par la Société des amis des noirs sur le plan de ses travaux" (1790), *RFAE,* 8, p. 2; E. Clavière, "Adresse de la Société des amis des noirs à l'Assemblée nationale," *RFAE,* 9, p. 108, and *Le Patriote français* (July 28, 1789), q. in Mitchell B. Garrett, *The French Colonial Question, 1789–1791* (Ann Arbor, 1916), p. 6, fn.

74. "Réflexions sur l'esclavage des nègres par M. Schwartz" (pseud. of Condorcet) (Paris, 1788), *RFAE,* 6, pp. 29–31, 44.

75. M. L'abbé Grégoire, "Lettre aux philanthropes" (Paris, October 1790), *RFAE,* 4, p. 3; Grégoire q. in Ruth F. Necheles, *The Abbé Grégoire, 1787–1831* (Westport, Conn., 1971), p. 81.

76. Danton speech, February 4, 1794, *Archives parlementaires,* 1st ser., 84 (Paris, 1962):284.

77. Grégoire, *Memoirs,* q. in A. Brette "Les Gens de couleur libres et leurs députés en 1789," *Révolution française* 29 (1895):392.

78. G. T. Raynal, *Essai sur l'administration de Saint-Domingue* (Paris, 1785), p. ix, q. in Seeber, p. 23, fn. 42.

6. The Rise of Imperialism

1. Robert Mandrou, *Introduction à la France moderne (1500–1640): Essai de psychologie historique* (Paris, 1961), p. 65; Marc Lescarbot, *Histoire de la nouvelle France* (Paris, 1609), pp. 143–45; Jean Bodin, *Method for the Easy Comprehension of History,* trans. Beatrice Reynolds (New York, 1945), pp. 359–62. De la Morandière entitled his book *Police sur les mendiants, les vagabonds, les joueurs de profession, les intrigants, les filles prostituées, les domestiques hors de maison depuis longtemps et les gens sans aveu;* on this work see Alfred Sauvy, "Some Lesser Known French Demographers of the Eighteenth Century: De la Morandière, de Caveirac, Cerfvol, and Pinto," *Population Studies* 5 (July 1951):8–9.

2. D'Argenson cited by Joseph J. Spengler, *French Predecessors of Malthus: A Study in Eighteenth-Century Wage and Population Theory* (Durham, N. C., 1942), p. 74.

3. Jean Meyer, *Les Européens et les autres de Cortès à Washington* (Paris, 1975), p. 137.

4. Antoine de Montchrétien, *Traicté de l'oeconomie politique* (Paris, 1615), q. in Charles W. Cole, *Colbert and a Century of French Mercantilism,* 1 (New York, 1939), p. 98.

5. Charles de Secondat, Baron de Montesquieu, *The Persian Letters,* ed. and trans. J. Robert Loy (Cleveland, 1961), p. 219; *Ephémérides* 2 (1765–1766):34–35, 63–64; ibid., 8 (1771):105–06.

6. Spengler, p. 290.

7. "Commerce," *Encyclopédie,* 3 (Paris, 1753), p. 691.

8. G. Hubrecht, "Les Colonies et Bordeaux au XVIIIᵉ siècle," *Annales de la faculté de droit de l'université de Bordeaux* 2 (1934):41.

9. Paul Roussier, ed., *L'établissement d'Issiny, 1687–1702* (Paris, 1935), pp. xii–xiii.

10. Damon, "Relation du voyage de Guynée fait en 1698 par le chevalier Damon," in ibid., p. 78.

11. Louis Moreau de Chambonneau, "Traité de l'origine des nègres du Sénégal, coste d'Afrique de leur pays, religion, coutumes et moeurs," in "Notes et documents: Deux textes sur le Sénégal (1673–1677)," ed. Carson I. Ritchie, *BIFAN* 30 (1968):337.

12. Savary, *Le parfait négociant,* 7th ed. (Paris, 1713), p. 541; Godefroy Loyer, "Relation du voyage du royaume d'Issigny, côte d'or, pais de Guinée en Afrique" (Paris, 1714), in *L'établissement d'Issiny, 1687–1702,* ed. Paul Roussier (Paris, 1935), p. 145; Jean-Baptiste Labat, *Voyage du Chevalier Des Marchais,* 1 (Paris, 1730), pp. 315–16.

13. A. Pherotée de la Croix, *Relation universelle de l'Afrique ancienne,* 2 (Lyons, 1688), p. 428.

14. Damon, p. 78.

15. Du Casse, "Mémoire ou relation du Sr Du Casse sur son voyage de Guinée avec la Tempeste en 1687 et 1688," in Roussier, ed., pp. 39–42; Labat, *Voyage du Chevalier,* 1, pp. 260–62.

16. Henri Froidevaux, "La Découverte de la chute de Félou (1687)," *Bulletin de géographie historique et descriptive,* no. 2 (1898):12–13, 19.

17. André Delcourt, *La France et les établissements français au Sénégal entre 1712 et 1763* (Dakar, 1952), p. 108.

18. M. N., *Voyages aux côtes de Guinée et Amérique* (Paris, 1791), pp. 39–40, 136–37.

19. Simone Berbain, *Etudes sur la traite des noirs au Golfe de Guinée: Le Comptoir français de Juda au XVIIIᵉ siècle* (Paris, 1942), p. 67.

20. J. Machat, *Documents sur les établissements français de l'Afrique occidentale au XVIIIᵉ siècle* (Paris, 1906), p. 90.

21. Du Casse, p. 38.

22. Philip D. Curtin, "The Lure of Bambuk Gold," *Journal of African History* 14 (1973):623–31; idem, *Economic Change in Precolonial Africa: Senegambia in the Era of the Slave Trade* (Madison, Wisc., 1975), pp. 198–206; Michel Perron, "Un Eldorado africain: Le Bambuk," *Bulletin de l'agence générale des colonies* 19 (1926):192–206.

23. Memoir of October 8, 1734, Machat, p. 46.

24. Pierre David, *Journal d'un voiage fait en Bambouc en 1744*, ed. André Delcourt (Paris, 1974).

25. Pierre David, "Estimation du produit des mines, 1780," Mémoires et documents, Afrique, XI, Archives du Ministère des Affaires étrangères (henceforth AMAE). Calculation on gold is based on declaration by Daru in 1810 that 986,643,000 livres were coined from gold between 1726 and 1806; Meyer, p. 265.

26. Lafeuillade d'Aubuisson, "Mémoire sur le Sénégal, Galam et Bambouc" (1780?), Mémoires et Documents, Afrique, XI, AMAE.

27. "Mémoire du Roi pour servir d'instructions au Sr Chevalier de Boufflers, novembre 1785," 13G 22, Archives nationales, Sénégal (henceforth ANS).

28. Anonymous Memorandum, 1778, Machat, pp. 117, 127; Pierre David, "Moyen à employer par le ministère pour assurer à la France tous les avantages qu'elle doit tirer d'un établissement sur les mines de Bambouk," August 14, 1778, AMAE; idem, "Mémoire," September 1, 1780, AMAE.

29. The British seemed to have shared that assessment, for it was reported that "the British government actually toyed with the idea of trading Canada back to the French . . . in exchange for Guadeloupe"; *Gentleman's Magazine* (October 1764), q. in Edward Scobie, *Black Britannia: A History of Blacks in Britain* (Chicago, 1972), p. 15.

30. "Mémoire sur la concession du Sénégal," Ms., NAF, 22085, folio 410, BN; Delcourt, pp. 81–83; Léonce Jore, *Les établissements français sur la côte occidentale d'Afrique de 1758 à 1809* (Paris, 1964), pp. 350–51.

31. Delcourt, pp. 81–82. Philip D. Curtin (*The Atlantic Slave Trade: A Census* [Madison, Wisc., 1969], Table 49, p. 170), estimates that the Windward Coast provided in the 1750s 38.9 percent of all French slave imports, whereas Senegambia by then was reduced to 8.7 percent of the French trade. Idem, *Economic Change*, p. 112.

32. Paul M. Bondois, "Un Essai de culture exotique sous l'ancien régime: La peste du riz de Thiers (1741)," *Revue d'histoire économique et sociale* 16 (1928):586–655. The military aspects of the Guiana experiment are stressed in John R. Singh, "French Foreign Policy, 1763–1779: With Special Reference to the Caribbean" (Ph.D. diss., 1972); E. Daubigny, *Choiseul et la France d'outre-mer après le traité de Paris* (Paris, 1892); Gustave Reynaud, *Hygiène des établissements coloniaux* (Paris, 1903), p. 4; Jean Chaïa, "Echec d'une tentative de colonisation de la Guyane au XVIIIᵉ siècle (étude médicale de l'expédition de Kourou, 1763–1764)," *Biologie médicale* 47 (April 1958):i–lxxxii; Francisco Guerra, "The Influence of Disease on Race, Logistics and Colonization in the Antilles," *Journal of Tropical Medicine and Hygiene* (February 1966):30–34.

33. Abbé Roubaud, *Histoire générale de l'Asie, de l'Afrique, et de l'Amérique*, 12 (Paris, 1771), pp. 202–16.

34. Edward D. Seeber, *Antislavery Opinion in France during the Second Half of the Eighteenth Century* (Baltimore, 1937), p. 115.

35. *Ephémérides du citoyen* 7 (1771):243–44; Guillaume Thomas Raynal,

Histoire philosophique et politique des établissements et du commerce des européens dans les deux Indes, 6 (Geneva, 1780), p. 215.

36. "Discours sur la nécessité d'établir à Paris une société pour concourir avec celle de Londres," *RFAE,* 6, pp. 18–19.

37. Abbé Sibire, *L'aristocratie négrière, ou réflexions philosophiques et historiques sur l'esclavage et l'affranchissement des noirs, dediées à l'Assemblée nationale* (1789), *RFAE,* 2, p. 117; Benjamin-Sigismond Frossard, *La cause des esclaves nègres et des habitants de la Guinée,* 1 (Lyon, 1789), p. 190; ibid., 2, pp. 372–78. Frossard mentioned Sierra Leone as a model in "Observations sur l'abolition de la traite," *RFAE,* 8, pp. 21–22.

38. Marie Jean de Condorcet, *Esquisses d'un tableau historique des progrès de l'esprit humain* (Paris, 1795), pp. 333–35.

39. Ruth F. Necheles, *The Abbé Grégoire, 1787–1831* (Westport, Conn., 1971), pp. 159–63.

40. Ralph A. Austen and Woodruff D. Smith, "Images of Africa and British Slave and Trade Abolition: The Transition to an Imperialist Ideology, 1787–1807," *African Historical Studies* 2 (1969):79.

41. Jore, p. 351.

42. Charles Talleyrand, *Memoir concerning the Commercial Relations of the United States with England to which is added An Essay upon the Advantages to Be Derived from New Colonies in the Existing Circumstances* (Boston, 1809), pp. 15–22.

43. Carl Ludwig Lokke, *France and the Colonial Question* (New York, 1934), p. 95; idem, "The Agricultural Mission to Egypt," *Agricultural History* 10 (1936):111–17. Not as compensation for the Antilles, but to make up for any advantages that other European powers might win from the collapse of the Ottoman empire, the French planned to take Egypt; François Charles-Roux, *Le projet français de conquête de l'Egypte sous le règne de Louis XVI, Mémoires de l'Institut de l'Egypte,* 14 (Cairo, 1929).

44. Lokke, *France and the Colonial Question,* pp. 212–14; F. Charles-Roux, *Bonaparte: Governor of Egypt* (New York, 1937), pp. 115–16; Jean-Gabriel Pelletan, *Mémoire sur la colonie française du Sénégal, avec quelques considérations historiques et politiques sur la traite des nègres,* ed. Marc-Françoise Guillois (Paris, 1801), p. xiv; Emmanuel Las Cases, *Memorial de Saint-Hélène,* 1 (Paris, 1968), pp. 625–26; Jore, p. 305; Pelletan, p. iv; Pierre F. Page, *Traité d'économie politique et de commerce des colonies,* 1 (Paris, 1801–1802), pp. 271–72.

45. C. K. Meek, "The Niger and the Classics," *Journal of African History* 1 (1960):15.

46. Roland Fréjus, *The Relation of a Voyage Made into Mauritania in Africk by the Sieur Roland Fréjus* (London, 1671), p. 18; Pruneau, p. 80.

47. Jean-Baptiste Labat, *Nouvelle relation de l'Afrique occidentale,* 2 (Paris, 1728), pp. 125–26; "Niger," *Encyclopédie,* 11, p. 140; P. Cultru, ed., *Premier voyage du Sieur La Courbe fait à la coste d'Afrique en 1685* (Paris, 1913), p. 16; D'Anville's map, "Carte de la Barbarie et Nigritie, 1738," is reproduced in Youssouf Kamal, ed., *Monumenta cartographica Africae es Aegypti,* 5, pt. 2

(Cairo, 1951):1590; Guillaume de l'Isle papers, Ms. 2304, Institut de France; Jerome Lalande, *Mémoires sur l'intérieur de l'Afrique* (Paris, 1791), p. 13.

48. Sylvain Meinrad Xavier de Golberry, *Fragmens d'un voyage en Afrique, fait pendant les années 1786, 1787, dans les contrées occidentales de ce continent*, 1 (Paris, 1802), p. 26.

49. Delcourt, pp. 170–75; Labat, *Nouvelle relation de l'Afrique*, 3, pp. 267–68.

50. R. G. Villeneuve, *L'Afrique ou histoire, moeurs, usages et coutumes des africains*, 1 (Paris, 1814), pp. 144–47.

51. Golberry, 1, pp. 2–6, 25, 54–55; ibid., 2, pp. 333–34, 503.

52. *Bulletin de la Société de géographie de l'Est* (1883); Baudry Deslozières, *Les égarements du négrophilisme* (Paris, 1802), pp. 138–39.

53. Talleyrand, pp. 16–17.

54. Pelletan, p. xvi.

55. Bernard Semmel, *Imperialism and Social Reform: English Social-Imperial Thought, 1895–1914* (Cambridge, Mass., 1960).

56. Jore, pp. 40–41. Whereas West Africa was abandoned as a possible penal colony for political prisoners, Guiana was used for that purpose by the Directorate, which in April 1795 condemned 4 Robespierrists, 16 members of the former Conseil des anciens, and 193 ex-deputies to that colony, where they nearly all succumbed to disease; M. Bresson, *Le Domaine colonial français*, 1 (Paris, 1929), pp. 115–17.

57. Cultru, ed., p. 295.

58. André Brüe, "Instructions pour M. Jean-Baptiste Collé, commandant et directeur particulier du Galam, décembre 9, 1716," Ms., NAF, 9341, folio 41, BN.

59. Sr. Charpentier, "Mémoire au Sénégal, 1725," Ms., NAF, 9339, folio 163, BN.

60. Labat, *Nouvelle relation de l'Afrique*, 3, pp. 202–05, 336; ibid., 4, pp. 59–61.

61. Idem, *Voyage du Chevalier*, 1, pp. 127, 260–61.

62. Idem, *Nouvelle relation de l'Afrique*, 3, pp. 267–68.

63. David, *Mémoire*.

64. Pelletan, pp. vii-xii.

65. Dominique Harcourt Lamiral, *L'Affrique et le peuple affriquain* (Paris, 1789), pp. 324–25; Pruneau, pp. 93–94. Pruneau took this passage verbatim from David, *Mémoire*.

66. Prélong, "Mémoire sur les îles de Gorée et du Sénégal," *Annales de Chimie* 18 (September 1793): 290.

67. Jean-Baptiste Léonard Durand, *Voyage au Sénégal* (Paris, 1802), p. 366.

68. Lafeuillade d'Aubuisson; Coste d'Arnobat, *Voyage au pays de Bambouc, suivi d'observations intéressantes sur les costes indiennes, sur la Hollande, et sur l'Angleterre* (Paris, 1789,) pp. 52–53. Coste seems to have made his own the account by Boucard, a company official serving in 1730–31 in the Upper Senegal close to the gold mines; André Delcourt, "Appendix, III," in

Delcourt, ed., p. 247; the discovery of this authorship belongs to Philip Curtin, who edited Claude Boucard, "Relation de Bambouc (1729)," *BIFAN* 36 (1974):246–75. Though not identifying the author, R. Pageard ("Un mystérieux voyage au pays de Bambouc, 1789," *Notes africaines,* no. 89 [January 1961]:23–27) had earlier denied Coste's authorship of this section.

69. Jean de Béthencourt, *Histoire de la première découverte et conqueste des canaries,* 1 (Paris, 1630), p. 107; this account was written by two monks, Pierre Bontier and Jean Le Verrier.

70. G. Vaumas, *L'éveil missionnaire de la France au XVIIe siècle* (Paris, 1939), p. 106.

71. Montchrétien q. in Cole, 1, p. 98.

72. *Relation du voyage du sieur Montauban capitaine des filibustiers en Guinée en l'année 1695* (Amsterdam, 1698), p. 363; Dralsé de Grandpierre, *Relation de divers voyages faits dans l'Afrique, dans l'Amérique, et aux Indes occidentales* (Paris, 1718), p. 134; Villault de Bellefond, *Relations des costes d'Afrique appellées Guinée* (Paris, 1669), p. 11.

73. Du Casse, pp. 44–45.

74. Charles de Secondat, Baron de Montesquieu, *De l'esprit des lois, OC,* 2 (Paris, 1951), p. 717; Michèle Duchet, *Anthropologie et histoire au siècle des lumières* (Paris, 1971), pp. 210–11.

75. Dralsé de Grandpierre, p. 165; this view is already evident in Thomas Corneille, "Nègres," *Dictionnaire universel géographique et historique,* q. in Simone Delesalle and Lucette Valensi, "Nègre/Negro: Recherches dans les dictionnaires français et anglais du XVIIe siècle," in *L'idée de race dans la pensée politique française contemporaine,* ed. Pierre Guiral and Emile Temime (Paris, 1977), p. 159; Labat, *Voyage du Chevalier,* 1, pp. 224, 331; idem, *Nouvelle relation de l'Afrique,* 2, p. 155; Pierre Poivre, *Voyages d'un philosophe* (Paris, 1769), pp. 9–11. Similar ideas are expressed in a memorandum by Governor Eyriès in 1783; Léon Pierre Raybaud, "L'administration du Sénégal de 1781 à 1784 (l'affaire Dumontet)," *Annales africaines* (1968):150.

76. Pelletan, pp. 67–71.

77. Condorcet, pp. 328–36; Voltaire, *Essai sur les moeurs, OC,* 11 (Paris, 1879), pp. 158–59.

78. Joseph Marie Dégérando, *The Observation of Savage Peoples,* trans. F. C. T. Moore (Berkeley and Los Angeles, 1969), pp. 97, 102.

79. Golberry, 2, p. 335.

80. Labat, *Voyage du Chevalier,* 1, p. 68.

81. Paul Erdmann Isert, *Voyages en Guinée et dans les îles caraïbes en Amérique* (Paris, 1793), p. 200.

82. Raynal, 6, pp. 86, 94; ibid., 10, p. 341; ibid., 1, p. 339.

83. Denis Diderot, *Supplément au voyage de Bougainville,* in *Chefs-d'oeuvre de Diderot,* ed. Louis Asseline and André Ufivre, 2 (Paris, n.d.), p. 128.

84. Jean-Jacques Rousseau, "Dernière Réponse à M. Bordes," *OC,* 1 (Paris, 1823), p. 152.

85. *Ephémérides du citoyen* 1 (1765–1766):120–21.

86. Raynal, 1, p. 52; ibid., 3, pp. 144–45.

87. Coste, pp. 35–36, 62. The expansionist program is only implicit in Boucard's account, in which he pointed out the military weakness of the states in the Bambuk; Coste saw the weakness as an invitation to conquest.

7. The Nineteenth Century Confronts Slavery

1. George M. Fredrickson, *The Black Image in the White Mind: The Debate on Afro-American Character and Destiny, 1817–1914* (New York, 1971), pp. 71–96.

2. J. J. Virey, *Histoire naturelle du genre humain*, 2 (Paris, 1801), pp. 65–66; Bory de Saint-Vincent, "L'Homme," *Dictionnaire* 8, p. 318; Auguste Comte, *Cours de philosophie positive*, 3d ed., 5 (Paris, 1869; 1st ed. between 1830 and 1842), p. 135; Armand de Quatrefages, "La Floride," *Revue de deux mondes* (henceforth *RDM*), n.s., 1 (1843):760; Eichtal, "Types de races humaines," *BSG*, 4th ser., 9 (January-February 1855):64; Peyroux de la Coudrenière, *Mémoire sur les sept espèces d'hommes* (Paris, 1814), pp. 17, 48; Gobineau letter to Prokesh-Osten, June 20, 1856, q. in Jean Boissel, ed., *Gobineau polémiste* (Paris, 1967), p. 32.

3. Marie Gouze, *L'Esclavage des noirs, ou l'heureux naufrage* (Paris, 1792), p. 4.

4. *De la nécessité d'adapter l'esclavage en France* (Paris, 1797), pp. 11–13; René Périn, *L'Incendie du cap, ou le règne de Toussaint L'Ouverture* (Paris, 1802), pp. 52–53, 59; René Chateaubriand, *Génie du Christianisme, OC,* 6, p. 185. The reflection of this Negrophobia in the fiction of the era is examined in Léon-François Hoffmann, *Le nègre romantique* (Paris, 1973), pp. 116–30.

5. Gouze, p. 7; Baudry Deslozières, *Les égarements du négrophilisme* (Paris, 1802), pp. 18, 21–22. Similar ideas are expressed in S. J. Ducoeurjoly, *Manuel des habitants de Saint-Domingue*, 1 (Paris, 1802), pp. 21–22; J. Abeille, *Essai sur nos colonies et sur le rétablissement de Saint-Domingue* (Paris, 1805), pp. 24–25; *Journal de l'empire* (May 20, 1812); "De l'utilité des colonies par Mazières, colon" (Paris, 1814), q. in Etienne Servais, *Les sources de 'Bug Jargal'* (Brussels, 1923), p. 64.

6. Félix Patron, *Des noirs, de leur situation dans les colonies françaises: L'esclavage n'est-il pas un bienfait pour eux et un fardeau pour leurs maîtres?"* (Paris, 1831).

7. Q. in Antonine Gisler, *L'esclavage aux Antilles françaises (XVIIe-XVIIIe siècles): Contribution au problème de l'esclavage* (Fribourg, 1965), p. 68, fn. 4.

8. Q. in ibid., pp. 68, 130; Ministère de la marine et des colonies, *Commission pour l'examen des questions relatives à l'esclavage et à la constitution politique des colonies* (Paris, 1843), pp. 2–3.

9. Germaine de Staël, "Préface pour la traduction d'un ouvrage de M. Wilberforce sur la traite des nègres," *OC,* 17 (Paris, 1820), pp. 369–75; idem, "Appel aux Souverains réunis à Paris pour en obtenir l'abolition de la traite des nègres (1814)," ibid., pp. 376–82.

10. J. J. L. Simonde de Sismondi, *De l'intérêt de la France à l'égard de la traite des nègres* (Geneva, 1814), pp. 7, 20–24, 27–28, 32.

11. On domestic British pressure for international abolition, see Seymour Drescher, *Econocide: British Slavery in the Era of Abolition* (Pittsburgh, 1977), pp. 148–61. Martha Putney, "The Slave Trade in French Diplomacy from 1814 to 1815," *Journal of Negro History* 60 (July 1975):411.

12. Melvin Dow Kennedy, "The Suppression of the African Slave Trade to the French Colonies and Its Aftermath, 1814–1848" (Ph.D. diss., University of Chicago, 1947), p. 10.

13. Q. in Serge Daget, "La France et l'abolition de la traite des noirs de 1814 à 1831" (thesis, University of Paris, 1969), p. 173.

14. Ibid., p. 106; idem, "L'Abolition de la traite des noirs en France de 1814 à 1831," *Cahiers d'études africaines* (henceforth *CEA*) 11 (1971):28–29.

15. Idem, "L'Abolition de la traite," p. 57.

16. Ibid., p. 53; idem, "Long cours et négriers nantais du trafic illégal (1814–1833)," *RFHOM* 17 (1975):111; idem, "An Exceptional Document: Legitimate Trade of the Ship 'Africain' on the West Coast of Africa in 1823," *Journal of African Studies* 2 (Summer 1975):177.

17. Yvan Debbash, "Poésie et traite: L'opinion français sur le commerce négrier au début du XIXᵉ siècle," *RFHOM* 48 (1961):318, 320–21.

18. "Programme d'un prix de mille francs," *Journal de la Société de la morale chrétienne* (henceforth *JSMC*) 2 (1822):352.

19. Jean Vidalenc, "La Traite négrière en France sous la Restauration, 1814–1830," *Actes du 91ᵉ congrès national des sociétés savantes, Rennes 1966, section d'histoire contemporaine* (Paris, 1969), pp. 220–21; Minister of the Marine to Prefect, November 5, 1821, Généralités, FOM, 53/472, ANSOM; Moreau du Jonnès, "Recherches sur la prospérité des colonies françaises" (1823), Ms., FOM, 296/1972, ANSOM; Debbash, p. 324, fn. 1.

20. Serge Daget ("Esclave, nègre et noir," p. 530) found only one article produced during the Restoration, in which a French abolitionist traced his movement back to the Société des amis des noirs.

21. Ruth F. Necheles, *The Abbé Grégoire, 1787–1831* (Westport, Conn., 1971), pp. 195–97.

22. Debbash, pp. 326–32.

23. Ibid., p. 343. The first prize was won by A. B. Bignan, *L'abolition de la traite des noirs* (Paris, 1823). Sophie Doin, *La Famille noire ou la traite et l'esclavage* (Paris, 1825), pp. 9, 70; Klaus Berger, *Géricault et son oeuvre*, trans. Maurice Beerblock (Paris, 1952), p. 27.

24. A good study of this topic, but in my opinion too sympathetic to the opponents of the treaty, is Lawrence C. Jennings, "France, Great Britain, and the Repression of the Slave Trade, 1841–1845," *French Historical Studies* 10 (Spring 1977):101–25. On Tocqueville's nationalist priorities in foreign policy, see Seymour Drescher, *Tocqueville and England* (Cambridge, Mass., 1964), pp. 152–69.

25. Lawrence C. Jennings, "French Policy toward Trading with African and Brazilian Slave Merchants, 1840–1853," *Journal of African History* 17 (1976):518–19, 525.

26. François Zucarelli, "Le Régime des engagés à temps au Sénégal (1817–1848)," *CEA,* 2 (1962):420–30.

27. Philip D. Curtin, *The Atlantic Slave Trade: A Census* (Madison, Wisc., 1969), p. 82; Dorvault, "Régime de la main-d'oeuvre," in *Les Colonies françaises,* ed. Imbart de la Tour et al. (Paris, 1900), p. 131.

28. It was obvious to Victor Régis, the Marseilles trader, for instance; Séance, November 4, 1853. Délibérations de la Chambre de commerce de Marseille, L, 176. (Later, however, Régis became a transporter of the engagés; Minister to Governor of Guadeloupe, September 30, 1858, Senegal, XIV, 24, ANSOM). The Minister of the Marine also recognized the extent to which the engagés system might be confused with the slave trade; Minister to Governor of Senegal, November 30, 1854, 1 B64, ANS.

29. Review by Dutrone of Jacob Oxeda, "Projet de colonisation au moyen des ouvriers noirs applicables à l'Algérie et aux colonies, Algiers, 1847," *Abolitionniste français* 6 (1849):143–45.

30. Charles J. Balesi, "A 19th-Century Anglo-French Dispute: The Issue of African Free Laborers," in *Proceedings of the Second Annual Meeting of the French Colonial Historical Society,* ed. Alf Andrew Heggoy and David Gardinier (Athens, Ga., 1977), pp. 75–86.

31. La Rochefoucauld-Liancourt, "Rapport fait à la société française pour l'abolition de l'esclavage," *JSMC,* 2d ser., 6 (July 1834):301.

32. "Comité pour l'abolition de la traite des noirs," *JSMC* 2 (1823):46.

33. Augustin Cochin, *The Results of Emancipation,* trans. Mary L. Booth, 2d ed. (Boston, 1863), p. 177; Noel Deerr, *The History of Sugar,* 2 (London, 1950), pp. 479–80.

34. Löys Delteil, *Les peintres graveurs,* 22 (Paris, 1926), nos. 749, 750, 748.

35. Cochin, pp. 186–87.

36. Kennedy, pp. 224–28. Commercial interests in France such as beet growers' associations also mounted a campaign against slavery in pamphlets denouncing the "un-French" nature of slavery, suggesting that the planters in the Antilles did not have the right of economic protection as long as they owned slaves; "Observations sur la question des sucres présentées aux chambres des pairs et des députés par les agriculteurs-fabricants de sucre des arrondissements de Valenciennes et d'Avesnes" (Valenciennes, 1849), pp. 14, 62.

37. Victor Schoelcher, "Des Noirs," *Revue de Paris* 20 (1830):82.

38. Idem, *De l'esclavage des noirs et de la législation coloniale* (Paris, 1833) p. 84.

39. Idem, *Abolition de l'esclavage: Examen critique du préjugé contre la couleur des Africains et des sang-mêlés* (Paris, 1840), p. 156.

40. Speech, April 22, 1835, and February 15, 1838, reprinted in *La France parlementaire,* ed. Louis Ulbach, 1 (Paris, 1864), p. 147, and in ibid., 2, pp. 35–41. In 1842 he was still cautious; Speech at banquet, March 10, 1842, ibid., 2, p. 172.

41. The influence of American thought on Tocqueville is shown in Benedict Gaston Songy, "Alexis de Tocqueville and Slavery: Judgments and Predictions" (Ph.D. diss., St. Louis University, 1969).

42. Pierre Victor Malouet, *Mémoire sur l'esclavage des nègres* (Neufchatel, 1788), p. 43.

43. Alexis de Tocqueville and Gustave de Beaumont, *On the Penitentiary System in the United States and its Application in France,* trans. Francis Lieber (Carbondale, Ill., 1964), pp. 93, 210.

44. Alexis de Tocqueville, *Democracy in America,* trans. Henry Reeve, 1 (New York, 1899), p. 383. Similar ideas are expressed in ibid., pp. 399, 403.

45. Letter of October 26, 1831, q. in Songy, p. 18.

46. Gustave de Beaumont, *Marie, or Slavery in the United States,* trans. Barbara Chapman (Stanford, Calif., 1958), pp. 60, 172, 216.

47. Mary Lawlor, *Alexis de Tocqueville in the Chamber of Deputies: His Views on Foreign and Colonial Policy* (Washington, D. C., 1959), p. 174; Alexis de Tocqueville, "Intervention dans la discussion de la loi sur le régime des esclaves dans les colonies," *OC,* 3 (Paris, 1962), p. 114.

48. Lawlor, pp. 114–15. Similar ideas are expressed in Tocqueville, "Rapport fait au nom de la commission chargée d'examiner la proposition de M. de Tracy relative aux esclaves des colonies," *OC,* 3, pp. 85–86.

49. Tocqueville, "De l'émancipation des esclaves," *OC,* 3, p. 105.

50. Idem, "Rapport," p. 57. Such an indemnity was already suggested by Beaumont, p. 207.

51. Tocqueville, "Rapport," p. 73; Seymour Drescher, *Dilemmas of Democracy: Tocqueville and Modernization* (Pittsburgh, 1968), pp. 187–88.

52. Songy, p. 217. This point of view is furthest developed by Sally Gershman, who sees Tocqueville as fully committed to abolitionism, his departures from that position but a tactic to convince his opponents; "Alexis de Tocqueville and Slavery," *French Historical Studies* 9 (Spring 1976):467–83. The conservative nature of Tocqueville's attitude toward abolition is best described in Drescher, *Dilemmas of Democracy,* pp. 151–95.

53. Lawlor, p. 120.

54. Tocqueville, "Intervention," *OC,* 3, p. 122.

55. G. de Félice, *Emancipation immédiate et complète des esclaves: Appel aux abolitionnistes* (Paris, 1846), p. 35.

56. Schoelcher, *Abolition de l'esclavage,* pp. 24, 38, 42, 71–72.

57. Ibid., pp. 21–22.

58. Ibid., p. 76.

59. Ibid., p. 72; idem, *Des Colonies françaises* (Paris, 1842), pp. 139–46.

60. Ibid., pp. 146–47.

61. Tocqueville, *Democracy in America,* 1, p. 382. A study of Tocqueville's attitude toward blacks is Richard W. Resh, "Alexis de Tocqueville and the Negro," *Journal of Negro History* (October 1963):251–59; it tends, however, to view Tocqueville outside the context of his writings.

62. Tocqueville, ibid., p. 415, fn. 31.

63. Beaumont, p. 59.

64. Tocqueville, "Intervention," pp. 122–23.

65. *Correspondance d'Alexis de Tocqueville et A. de Gobineau, OC,* ed. J. P. Mayer, 3d ed., 9 (Paris, 1959), pp. 276–77; Beaumont q. in Drescher, *Dilemmas of Democracy,* p. 163.

66. J. Rennard, "1848–1948, Centenaire de la liberté," *RHCF* 35 (1948):44–45.

67. Ministère de la marine et des colonies, *Commission pour l'examen des questions relatives à l'esclavage et la constitution politique des colonies* (Paris, 1843), pp. 48, 361.

68. Gaston Martin, *Histoire de l'esclavage dans les colonies françaises* (Paris, 1948), pp. 281–90.

69. "Pétitions des ouvriers de Paris en faveur de l'abolition de l'esclavage," *Abolitionniste français* 1 (1844):121–25.

70. Martin, p. 50.

71. Félice, p. 50.

72. Henri Galos, "Les Colonies et l'émancipation depuis la révolution de février," *RDM* 23 (September 1848):742.

73. Félice, p. 58.

74. Abbé Grégoire, "Observations préliminaires," Preface of Thomas Clarkson, *Histoire du commerce homicide appelé traite des noirs ou cri des africains* (Paris, 1822), p. 7.

75. In comparing the two movements, David Brion Davis (*The Problem of Slavery in the Age of the Revolution, 1770–1823* [henceforth *The Problem of Slavery* 2] [Ithaca, N. Y., 1975], p. 346) suggests that the success of the British and the failure of the French abolitionism in the 1780s was due to the conservatism of the British and the egalitarianism of the French movement, but I see the political environment in which both movements had to function as more important in explaining their varying impacts and fail to see the radicalism of either the Société des amis des noirs or its successors.

76. Thomas-Marie-Adolphe Jollivet, *De la Philanthropie anglaise* (Paris, 1842), pp. 6–8.

77. "L'Emancipation des noirs est-elle une idée anglaise?" *Abolitionniste français* 1 (1844):105–09; Victor Schoelcher, *Polémique coloniale* 1 (Paris, 1882), p. 227.

78. "Nouvelles de l'abolition de l'esclavage," *JSMC*, 2nd ser., 6 (July 1834):111–15.

79. Victor Broglie, "Discours d'ouverture," séance April 25, 1825, *JSMC* (1825):3.

80. "Rapport de M. Périer," *JSMC* 4 (1825):26–27.

81. These arguments are based on the valuable insights into British abolitionism of Davis, *The Problem of Slavery* 2, pp. 46–47, 358–61.

82. "Comité pour l'abolition de la traite des noirs," *JSMC* 2 (1823):46.

83. Ministerial instruction, August 5, 1818, Senegal, IX, I, ANSOM.

84. Léonard Sainville, "La Condition des noirs à Haïti et dans les Antilles françaises de 1800 à 1850" (Dr. d'état, University of Paris, 1970), p. 1198.

85. "Adresse des colons au Général Donzelot, présentée le 22 décembre 1823," q. in M. J. Morénas, *Précis historique de la traite* (Paris, 1828), p. 289.

86. Sainville, "La Condition des noirs," pp. 1186–88.

87. Melvin D. Kennedy, "The Bissette Affair and the French Colonial Question," *Journal of Negro History* 45 (January 1960):1–10.

88. Sainville, "La Condition des noirs," p. 1202.

89. Christian Schefer, *La France moderne et le problème colonial* (Paris, 1907), pp. 294–98.

90. Ibid., pp. 299–300.

91. Letter of September 14, 1830, q. in Sainville, "La Condition des noirs," p. 1205.

92. Schoelcher papers, Ms. 22134, NAF, folio 96, BN.

93. *La Défense,* February 28, 1882, q. in Victor Schoelcher, *L'Immigration aux colonies* (Paris, 1883), p. 14.

94. Cochin, pp. 14–15.

95. E. Lucas, *La littérature antiesclavagiste au dix-neuvième siècle: Etude sur Madame Beecher Stowe et son influence en France* (Paris, 1930), pp. 155–56.

96. Ibid., pp. 142, 150.

97. John O. Killens, "The Myth of the 'Black Psyche,'" *New York Times Magazine* (June 7, 1964), reprinted in *Negro Protest Thought in the Twentieth Century,* ed. France L. Broderick and August Meier (Indianapolis, 1965), p. 349.

98. Alfred Michiels, *Le capitaine Firmin, ou la vie des nègres en Afrique* (Paris, 1853), pp. 8–12.

99. Delteil, 23, no. 1303.

8. Scientific Racism

1. René Chateaubriand, *OC,* 6 (Paris, 1827), p. 27; Baron Jacques Roger, *Kélédor, histoire africaine* (Paris, 1828), p. xiii (the copy of the novel in the possession of the BN had been presented by Roger to Grégoire); idem, *Fables sénégalaises recueillies de l'Ouolof* (Paris, 1828), p. 114; Abbé Grégoire, *An Enquiry concerning the Intellectual and Moral Faculties, and Literature of Negroes . . . ,* trans. D. B. Warden (Brooklyn, 1810), p. 134; Roger, *Kélédor,* p. x; Pierre Blanchard, *Récréations utiles, ou récits d'un voyageur offrant des détails instructifs et curieux sur l'Afrique* (Paris, 1856), p. 29; Anne Raffenel. *Nouveau voyage au pays des nègres* (Paris, 1856), 1, p. 83; ibid., 2, p. 235.

2. Henri de Saint-Simon, "Mémoire sur la science de l'homme," *OC,* 5 (Paris, 1966), pp. 115–16.

3. Pacho, "Essai sur la civilisation de l'intérieur de l'Afrique," *Nouvelles annales des voyages,* 2d ser., 5 (1827):189–93.

4. Charles A. Walckenaer, *Recherches géographiques sur l'intérieur de l'Afrique septentrionale* (Paris, 1821), p. 182; Conrad Malte-Brun, *Précis de la géographie universelle, ou description de toutes les parties du monde,* 4 (Paris, 1813), p. 436; "De l'homme considéré à l'état de nature," *Magasin pittoresque* 22 (1854):392.

5. Jean-Baptiste P. A. Lamarck, *Philosophie Zoologique,* 2 vols. (Paris, 1809; reprinted New York, 1960). A convenient introduction are his unpublished lectures in Max Vachon, Georges Rousseau, and Yves Laissus, eds., *Inédits de Lamarck* (Paris, 1972).

6. Malte-Brun, *Précis de la géographie universelle,* 2, pp. 545–48.

7. Lucien Febvre, "Civilisation, le mot et l'idée," in *Civilisation, le mot et l'idée*, ed. Lucien Febvre (Paris, 1930), pp. 24–25.

8. Saint-Simon, "Mémoire," *OC*, 5, p. 56.

9. J. J. Virey, *Histoire naturelle du genre humain*, 1 (Paris, 1801), pp. 434–35; ibid., 2, pp. 52–57, 170; idem, "Des Causes physiologiques," *Bulletin de l'académie royale de médecine* 6 (1841):11.

10. Victor Courtet de l'Isle, *La Science politique fondée sur la science de l'homme, ou étude des races humaines* (Paris, 1838), p. 208; Peyroux de la Coudrenière, *Mémoire sur les sept espèces d'hommes* (Paris, 1814), pp. 45–46.

11. Saint-Simon, "Introduction aux travaux scientifiques du dix-neuvième siècle, II," *OC*, 6, p. 129; Auguste Comte, *Cours de philosophie positive*, 3d ed., 4 (Paris, 1869; 1st ed. between 1830 and 1842), pp. 276–77; ibid., 5, p. 20.

12. François Guizot, *Du Gouvernement de la France depuis la Restauration et du ministère actuel*, 2d ed. (Paris, 1820), pp. 1–2, cited by Léon Poliakov, *The Aryan Myth: A History of Racist and Nationalist Ideas in Europe*, trans. Edmund Howard (London, 1974), p. 31; G. P. Gooch, *History and Historians*, new ed. (Boston, 1959), pp. 163–66; Jules Michelet, *The People*, trans. John P. McKay (Urbana, Ill., 1973), pp. 151, 193.

13. Louis Chevalier, *Laboring Classes and Dangerous Classes in Paris During the First Half of the Nineteenth Century*, trans. Frank Jellinek (New York, 1973), pp. 409–17; Eugen Weber, *Peasants into Frenchmen: The Modernization of Rural France, 1870–1914* (Stanford, Calif., 1976), pp. 3–7; Lamartine q. in Poliakov, *The Aryan Myth*, p. 230; François Léger, "L'idée de race chez Taine," in *L'idée de race dans la pensée politique française contemporaine*, ed. Pierre Guiral and Emile Temime (Paris, 1977), pp. 89–99.

14. Jean Boissel, *Victor Courtet (1813–1867): Premier théoricien de la hiérarchie des races* (Paris, 1972); Courtet, pp. ix, 361; Alphonse Esquieros, "Des études contemporaines sur l'histoire des races," *RDM*, n.s., 21 (March 1848):982–83.

15. Michael D. Biddiss, *Father of Racist Ideology: The Social and Political Thought of Count Gobineau* (New York, 1970), pp. 105–06, 245.

16. Janine Buenzod, *La Formation de la pensée de Gobineau et l'Essai sur l'inégalité des races humaines* (Paris, 1967); Biddiss; Jean Boissel, "Introduction," in *Gobineau polémiste*, ed. Jean Boissel (Paris, 1967); Colette Guillaumin, "Aspects latents du racisme chez Gobineau," *Cahiers internationaux de sociologie* 42 (January–June 1967):145–58.

17. Arthur de Gobineau, *Essai sur l'inégalité des races humaines*, repr. of 1854 ed., 1 (Paris, 1967), p. 29.

18. Ibid., pp. 208, 317–20.

19. Paule Brasseur, "Le mot 'nègre' dans les dictionnaires encyclopédiques français du XIXᵉ siècle," *Cultures et développement* 8 (1976):579–94.

20. *Mémoires de la Société ethnologique* 1 (1841):iii–xiv; H. V. Vallois, "La Société d'anthropologie de Paris, 1859–1959," *BSAP*, 11th ser., 1 (July–September 1960):295–96; Paul Topinard, *Eléments d'anthropologie générale* (Paris, 1885), p. 147.

21. Vivien, "Recherches sur l'histoire de l'anthropologie"; *Mémoires de la Société ethnologique* 2:46; Paul Topinard, "Un Mot sur l'histoire de l'anthropologie en 1788," *Revue d'anthropologie* (March 15, 1888):197–201; Virey, 1, p. 416; Donald Bender, "The Development of French Anthropology," *Journal of the History of the Behavioral Sciences* 1 (April 1965):139–51. A much less satisfactory summary is Nicole Bernageau, "L'Anthropologie physique en France au XIXᵉ siècle" (thesis, Ecole pratique des hautes études).

22. Philip D. Curtin, *The Image of Africa: British Ideas and Action, 1780–1850* (Madison, Wisc., 1964), p. 387.

23. M. L. Manouvrier, "La Société d'anthropologie de Paris depuis sa fondation," *BSAP*, 6th ser., 1 (July 8, 1909):321–23.

24. Clémence Royer, "Du caractère spéciale des études ethnographiques et des études anthropologiques," *Congrès international des sciences ethnographiques: Comptes rendus* (Paris, 1881), p. 438.

25. Marcel Mauss, "L'Ethnographie en France et à l'étranger," *Revue de Paris* (October 1, 1913):537–60 and ibid. (October 15, 1913):815–37; A. Van Gennep, "Un ethnographe oublié du XVIIIᵉ siècle: J. N. Demenunier," *Revue des idées* (1910):18–28.

26. Bender; Bernageau.

27. P. J. G. Cabanis, *Rapports du physique et du moral*, 2 vols. (Paris, 1802).

28. Bory de Saint-Vincent, *L'Homme*, 1 (Paris, 1827), p. 72. Bory used the term *species* rather than *race* because he was a polygenist.

29. Frédéric Portal, *Des Couleurs symboliques dans l'antiquité, le moyen age, et les temps modernes* (1837), new ed. (Paris, 1957), pp. 21, 103; De Montabert, "Du caractère symbolique des principales couleurs employées dans les peintures chrétiennes: Question empruntée au savant ouvrage de M. Frédéric Portal, et simplifiée et disposée à l'usage des artistes," *Mémoires de la société d'agriculture, science, arts et belles lettres du département de l'Aube* 17 (1838):19; J. W. Goethe, *Theory of Colours*, trans. Charles Lock Eastlake (London, 1840), p. 265.

30. Fourier q. in Nicholas V. Riasanovsky, *The Teaching of Charles Fourier* (Berkeley and Los Angeles, 1969), p. 235, fn. 33; Victor Hugo, *Bug Jargal*, *OC*, 1 (Paris, 1910), p. 398; Hugo q. in Dantès Bellegarde, "Lamartine et Victor Hugo, amis d'Haïti," *Conjonction*, no. 45:5–13.

31. Abbé Grégoire, *De la littérature des nègres* (Paris, 1808), p. 28. Grégoire devoted a whole pamphlet to combat the prejudice in favor of white skin; "De la noblesse de la peau" (Paris, 1826). Roger, *Fables sénégalaises*, notes, 193; "Kélédor, histoire africaine, receuillie et publiée par M. le baron Roger," *Revue encyclopédique* 37 (March 1828):675.

32. Q. in Bouche, *L'enseignement dans les territoires français de l'Afrique occidentale de 1817 à 1920*, 1 (Lille, 1975), p. 127.

33. Léon Fanoudh-Siefer, *Le mythe du nègre et de l'Afrique noire dans la littérature française* (Paris, 1968), p. 79.

34. T. K. Penniman, *A Hundred Years of Anthropology*, 2d ed. (London, 1952), p. 55.

35. Q. in G. Lanteri-Laura, *Histoire de la phrénologie* (Paris, 1970), p. 84; F. J. Gall, *Anatomie et physiologie du système nerveux*, 1 (Paris, 1818), p. iv.

36. *Darstellung der neueren, auf Untersuchungen des Berrichtungen des Gehirns gegrundeten Theorie des Physiognomik des Herrn Dr. Gall in Wien* (Weimar, 1802).

37. F. J. Gall and Johann Caspar Spurzheim, *Anatomie et physiologie du système nerveux en général*, 2 (Paris, 1810 ed.) p. 355; ibid., 3 (1818 ed.), pp. 15, 71.

38. Ibid. (1818), 4, p. 283.

39. Erwin A. Ackerknecht and Henry Vallois, *Franz J. Gall, Inventor of Phrenology, and His Collection*, trans. Claire St. Leon (Madison, Wisc., 1956), p. 10.

40. P. Flourens, *Examen de la phrénologie* (Paris, 1845), p. 9; Donald L. King, *L'Influence des sciences physiologiques sur la littérature française de 1670 à 1870* (Paris, 1929), p. 113; Hippolyte Taine, *Vie et correspondance*, 1 (Paris, 1904), p. 330, cited in Léger, p. 92; P.-J. Proudhon, *De la Création de l'ordre dans l'humanité, ou principes d'organisation politique* (Paris, 1843), p. 435.

41. William Edwards, *Des caractères physiologiques des races humaines considérés dans leurs rapports avec l'histoire: Lettre à M. Amedée Thierry* (Paris, 1839), p. 45.

42. Virey, 2, p. 41; Courtet, p. xii.

43. Jean-André-Napoléon Périer, "Sur les croisements ethniques," *BSAP* 1 (1860):196; Paul Broca, "Anthropologie," *Dictionnaire encyclopédique des sciences*, 5 (Paris, 1866), reprinted in *Mémoires d'anthropologie*, 1 (Paris, 1871), pp. 8, 33.

44. L. Manouvrier, "L'indice céphalique et la pseudosociologie," *Revue mensuelle de l'école d'anthropologie de Paris* 9 (1899):289.

45. Virey, 1, p. 438; Georges Cuvier, *Leçons d'anatomie comparée*, 2 (Paris, 1805), p. 6; P. P. Broc, *Essai sur les races humaines* (Paris, 1836), p. 71.

46. André Retzius, *Om formen af nordboernes cranier* (Stockholm, 1843); A. Retzius, *Om formen af huvudets benstomme hos olika folkslage* (Christiana, Norway, 1847), p. 21 (the copy of this book in the BN has in it a dedication to Gustave d'Eichtal, secretary of the ethnological society).

47. Paul Topinard, *L'anthropologie* (Paris, 1876), pp. 541–42; idem, "Du prognathisme alvealo sous nasal," *BSAP* (January 2, 1873):28–29; Isidore Geoffroy Saint-Hilaire, "Sur la classification anthropologique et particulièrement sur les types principaux du genre humain," *Mémoires de la Société d'anthropologie de Paris* 1 (1860–1863):133.

48. "Cabinet anthropologique du Muséum d'histoire naturelle," *Nouvelles annales de voyages* 140 (1853):358–60; Paul Topinard, *La Société, l'école, le laboratoire, et le musée Broca* (Paris, 1890), p. 8.

49. H. Didon, "L'homme et la bête," *Revue de France* 31 (September 15, 1878):230.

50. Paul Broca, "Etudes sur le cerveau d'un nègre," *BSAP* 1 (1860): 53–55; idem, "Sur le volume et la forme du cerveau suivant les individus et suivant les races," *BSAP* 2 (1861):185.

51. Gustave Le Bon, "Recherches anatomiques et mathématiques sur les

lois des variations," *Revue d'anthropologie*, 2d ser., 2 (1879):103–04; idem, "Recherches expérimentales sur les variations de volume du cerveau et de crâne," *BSAP* (July 18, 1878):310–15.

52. Idem, "Etudes sur le cerveau d'un nègre," *BSAP* 1 (1860):53–55; idem, "Sur le volume et la forme," 139–207; Armand de Quatrefages, *The Human Species*, 6th ed. (London, 1903; first appeared in French 1880), p. 401; Pierre Larousse, "Nègre," *Grand dictionnaire universel* (Paris, 1866), p. 903.

53. Louis Faidherbe, *Essai sur la langue poul* (Paris, 1875), p. 14.

54. Adolphe Quételet, *Sur l'homme*, 2 (Paris, 1835), pp. 274, 326–27. On Quételet there are a couple of older studies; Frank H. Hankins, *Adolphe Quételet as Statistician, Studies in History, Economics, and Public Law*, 31, no. 4 (New York, 1908), and Joseph Lottin, *Quételet statisticien et sociologue* (Paris, 1912).

55. Serres q. in Alphonse Esquieros, "Du mouvement des races humaines: Cours de M. Serres," *RDM*, n.s., 10 (April–June 1845):163; Geoffroy Saint-Hilaire and Frédéric Cuvier, *Histoire naturelle des mammifères avec des figures originales, colorées, dessinées d'après des animaux vivans* (Paris, 1824), p. 6; Virey, 2 (1824), p. 162.

56. R. Verneau, *Le bassin dans les sexes et dans les races* (Paris, 1875); Paul Topinard, "Le bassin chez l'homme et les animaux," *BSAP*, 2d ser., 10 (October 21, 1875):504–08. Though maintaining that there was no such clear difference between black and white, E. Verrier did see it between the more developed peoples (including Europeans and Africans such as Wolofs) and the less developed peoples such as the Bushmen of South Africa and the Kanakas; "Nouvelle classification du bassin suivant les races au point de vue de l'obstétrique: Conséquences qui en découlent," *BSAP*, 3d ser., 10 (May 1, 1884):317–24.

57. Dr. Jean-Baptiste Bourdon, *Physiognomonie et phrénologie* (Paris, 1842), p. 236; Paul Broca, "Recherches sur l'indice nasale," *Revue d'anthropologie* 1 (1872):1–4.

58. Among those believing that the black race was the original one from which others evolved are Reiset, comments in Gustave d'Eichtal, "Quels sont les caractères distinctifs de la race noire et blanche et les conditions d'association de ces deux races," *Bulletin de la Société ethnologique de Paris* (1847):86; Serres, q. in Esquieros, p. 16. Serres, however, was not consistent, for in 1855 he described the black race as a "degradation of other races"; Dr. Deramond, "Cours d'anthropologie de M. Serres," (extract of *Presse littéraire*, 1855), p. 5. In the opposite camp can be cited Isidore Geoffroy Saint-Hilaire, lecture at Sorbonne, April 1851, Ms. 2297, MHN; Dr. B. A. Morel, *Traité des dégénérescences de l'espèce humaine*, 1 (Paris, 1857), pp. 428–48; L. F. Maury, *La Terre et l'homme* (Paris, 1857), pp. 410–11.

59. Geoffroy Saint-Hilaire, de Castelnau, Broca, "Instructions pour le Sénégal," *BSAP* 1 (1860):131; G. Delaunay, "De la méthode en anthropologie," *BSAP*, 3d ser., 2 (January 19, 1882):55–66.

60. Elisée Reclus, "Le Mississipi: Etudes et souvenirs," *RDM*, 2d ser., 5 (August 1, 1859):624.

61. Virey, 1 (1824), p. 429; Bory de Saint-Vincent, 1, p. 74.

62. Armand de Quatrefages, *Rapport sur les progrès de l'anthropologie* (Paris, 1867), pp. 98–99; idem, "Discussion sur l'action des milieux," *BSAP,* 1st ser., 4 (April 16, 1863):243–44; Larousse, p. 903. Larousse does not seem to have appreciated the full scope of polygenist thought, for he also stated (p. 904) that whites and blacks could sexually mate, "a striking sign of our common nature."

63. A. Vernier, "Causerie scientifique: L'espèce humaine," *Temps* (March 22, 1877).

64. Paul Topinard, "Histoire de l'anthropologie de 1830 à 1839," *Revue internationale des sciences* (1878).

65. Paul Broca, *On the Phenomena of Hybridity in the Genus Homo* (London, 1864), pp. 27–28; idem, "Documents rélatifs au croisement des races très différentes," *BSAP* 1 (May 1860):255–68.

66. Broca, *On Hybridity,* pp. 28, 32–37. Simonot revealed the absurdity of this doctrine, but subscribed to the notion that people of color were an inferior breed destined to disappear; "Les métis aux colonies," *BSAP,* 6 (March 2, 1865):116.

67. Eugène Dally, "Recherches sur les mariages consanguins et sur les races pures," *BSAP,* 4 (November 5, 1863):550; Simonot, pp. 113–17; L. J. B. Bérenger-Féraud, *Peuplades de la Sénégambie* (Paris, 1879), pp. 394–97. A similar thought appears in idem, "Note sur la fécondité des mulâtres au Sénégal," *Revue d'anthropologie,* 2d ser., 2 (1879):580–88. Confirmation seemed also to come from the naval officer Vallon, "Séance," *BSG,* 5th ser., 7 (1864):371.

68. Jean-Christian Boudin, "Sur le non-cosmopolitanisme des races humaines," *BSAP,* 1 (1860):167–78; idem, "Du non-cosmopolitanisme des races humaines," *Mémoires de la Société d'anthropologie de Paris,* 1 (1860–1863), p. 122; idem, "Des races humaines considérées au point de vue de l'acclimatement et de la mortalité dans les divers climats," *Journal de la société de statistique de Paris* 2 (1860):4–5; L. J. B. Bérenger-Féraud, *Traité clinique des maladies des Européens au Sénégal,* 2 (Paris, 1875), pp. 325–31.

69. Léon-François Hoffmann, *Le nègre romantique* (Paris, 1973), pp. 136–40, 229–51; William B. Cohen, "Literature and Race: Nineteenth-Century French Fiction, Blacks and Africa, 1800–1880," *Race and Class* 16 (October 1974):181–205.

70. Herbert H. Odom, "Generalizations on Race in Nineteenth-Century Physical Anthropology, *Isis* 58 (Spring 1967):5–18; John S. Haller, "The Species Problem: Nineteenth-Century Concepts of Inferiority in the Origin of Man Controversy," *American Anthropology* 72 (December 1970): 1319–29.

71. Quatrefages, *Rapport,* pp. 153, 380; idem, "Histoire naturelle de l'homme," *RDM,* 2d ser., 8 (March 1, 1857):160; idem, "La Floride," *RDM,* n.s., 1 (1843):757–59.

72. Gustave d'Eichtal and Ismail Urbain, *Lettres sur la race noire et la race blanche* (Paris, 1839), pp. 15–16, 22. The Saint-Simonians posited eventual sexual equality when the "supreme father" and the "supreme mother" ruled

the world, but in the meantime they practiced male supremacy; Dominique Deanti, "Misère de la femme dans la famille saint-simonienne," *Le Monde* (April 16, 1976). On the mysticism of Eichtal, see Barrie M. Ratcliffe, "Saint-Simonism and Messianism: The Case of Gustave d'Eichtal," *French Historical Studies* 9 (Spring 1976):484–85.

73. Eichtal and Urbain, pp. 47–48; Eichtal, "Quels sont les caractères," p. 69; Quatrefages, "Histoire naturelle," p. 163; idem, *Rapport*, pp. 482, 492–93; idem, *The Human Species*, pp. 449–50; Quatrefages comment in Broca, "Sur le volume et la forme du cerveau suivant les individus et suivant les races," *BSAP* (1861):207; Gobineau, pp. 60–62.

74. Courtet de l'Isle, *Tableau ethnographique du genre humain* (Paris, 1849), p. 2; idem, comment in *Bulletin de la Société ethnologique de Paris* (1847):184.

75. Gobineau, pp. 124, 159, 162, 446–47.

76. Eichtal and Urbain, pp. 36–37; Courtet, *Tableau ethnographique*, p. 14. Although he was sympathetic to blacks, Omalius d'Halloy expressed similar views; *Des races humaines, ou éléments d'ethnographie* (Paris, 1845), pp. 19, 171–72, 178. Henri Hollard, *L'Homme et les races humaines* (Paris, 1855), pp. 167–68, 181, 250; Dominique Godron, *De l'espèce et des races dans les êtres organisés*, 2 (Paris, 1853), pp. 217, 229–30; Maury, pp. 353–55; Vivien de Saint-Martin, "Revue géographique," *Tour du monde* (1866):419.

77. René Caillié, *Journal d'un voyage à Tembouctou et à Jenné dans l'Afrique centrale*, 2 (Paris, 1830; reprinted in Anthropos edition, 1965), p. 326; Anne Raffenel, *Voyage dans l'Afrique occidentale exécuté en 1843 et 1844* (Paris, 1846), p. 138; Hecquard, "Voyages notes," p. 54, NAF, Ms. 11347, BN, p. 54; "Voyage au Dahomey de M. Christophe Colomb" (1850?), Missions, I, ANSOM.

78. Bory de Saint-Vincent, 1, p. 83; ibid., 2, pp. 123–24; Virey, 1, pp. 413–15, 428.

79. G. Cuvier, "Extraits d'observations faites sur le cadavre d'une femme connue à Paris et à Londres sous le nom de Vénus Hottentote," *Mémoires du Muséum d'histoire naturelle* 3 (1817):259–74.

80. Bory de Saint-Vincent, "Sur l'anthropologie de l'Afrique française," *Académie des sciences* (June 30, 1845):14; Virey, 1 (1824), p. 409; Etienne Serres, "Observations sur la race nègre," Ms. 165, MHN; Gobineau, p. 124.

81. Charles White, *An Account of the Regular Gradations in Man* (London, 1799); Paul Broca, "Sur les proportions rélatifs du bras, de l'avant bras et de la clavicule chez les nègres et les Européens," *BSAP*, 3 (April 3, 1862): 162–72; idem, "Polygénisme et transformisme," *BSAP*, 2d ser., 4 (June 30, 1869):443.

82. L. J. B. Bérenger-Féraud, *Peuplades*, pp. 2–4.

83. Serres, q. in Esquieros, pp. 164–65; Malte-Brun, *Précis de la géographie universelle*, 4, p. 435.

84. Louis Figuier, *Races of Man* (New York, 1872), p. 506.

85. Gobineau, pp. 205–06.

86. Virey, 2, p. 41; Flourens, Duperrey, and Serres, "Rapport sur les

races nègres de l'Afrique orientale au sud de l'équateur, *Compte rendu des séances de l'Académie des sciences* 30 (1850):688; Gobineau, pp. 208, 317–20.

87. F. de Castelnau, *Renseignements sur l'Afrique centrale sur une nation d'hommes à queue qui s'y trouveraient d'après le rapport des nègres du Soudan, esclaves à Bahia* (Paris, 1851), p. 6; idem, "Sur les Niam-niams ou hommes à queue," *BSG*, 4th ser., 2 (1851):25–27; Séance, 20 August, *Académie des sciences, Compte rendus*, 29 (1849):207–14; *Revue de l'orient* (1848):427; Louis Du Couret, *Voyages au pays des Niam-Niams ou hommes à queue* (Paris, 1854); *Tour du monde* (1860).

88. Henry Redhead Yorke, *Letters from France in 1802*, 2 (London, 1804), pp. 210–11.

89. Quatrefages, *Human Species*, p. 376; Pruner-Bey, "Mémoire sur les nègres," *Mémoires de la Société d'anthropologie de Paris*, 1 (1860–1863), p. 334; Ernest Renan, *L'Avenir de la science*, OC, 3, pp. 859–60; Bérenger-Féraud, *Peuplades*, p. 416; Figuier, p. 508.

90. Honoré de Balzac, *Comédie humaine*, 7 (Paris, 1956), p. 776; C. H. de Mirval, *Le Robinson des sables du desert, ou un voyage d'un jeune naufragé sur les côtes et dans l'intérieur de l'Afrique* (Paris, 1837), p. 101.

91. Alfred Michiels, *Le capitaine Firmin, ou la vie des nègres en Afrique* (Paris, 1853), pp. 88, 91, 107, 113–14, 201, 205, 207, 238, 249, 271, 282.

92. Jules Verne, *Five Weeks in a Balloon, Works*, trans. Charles F. Horne, 1 (New York, 1911), p. 242.

93. Verne, *The Mysterious Island, Works*, 6, p. 116.

94. Roland Lebel, *Histoire de la littérature coloniale en France* (Paris, 1931), p. 69; Fanoudh-Siefer, pp. 12–13.

95. Verne, *Mysterious Island, Works*, 6, p. 81; Comtesse de Ségur, *Après la pluie, le beau temps* (Paris, 1871), p. 111; Guy de Maupassant, "Tombouctou," *Contes du jour et de la nuit*, OC (Paris, 1909), pp. 221–33 (first appeared in *Le Gaulois*, August 2, 1883).

96. J. B. Henry Savigny and Alexandre Corréard, *Narrative of a Voyage to Senegal in 1816* (London, 1968), p. 21; Dr. J. P. F. Thévénot, *Traité des maladies des europèens dans les pays chauds et spécialement au Sénégal* (Paris, 1841), p. 122; Bory de Saint-Vincent, *L'Homme*, 2, p. 31; Virey, 2 (1824), pp. 46, 128, 162; Broc, p. 72.

97. Bory de Saint-Vincent, *L'Homme*, 2, pp. 42–43.

98. General Louis Faidherbe, "Les Berbères et les arabes," *BSG*, 4th ser., 7 (1854):91–92.

99. Cohen ("Literature and Race," pp. 192–98) covers this in some detail.

100. Trans. Barbara Chapman (Stanford, Calif., 1958).

101. Yvette Conry, *L'Introduction du darwinisme en France au XIXᵉ siècle* (Paris, 1974), pp. 37, 84–85. A contemporary complaint is Dally, "Discussion sur le transformisme," *BSAP* (March 17, 1870):149–57. In English two studies have delineated the failure of Darwinism in France; Linda Loeb Clark, "Social Darwinism and French Intellectuals, 1860–1915" (Ph.D. diss., University of North Carolina, 1968), and Robert Ernest Stebbins, "French Reactions to Darwinism, 1859–1882" (Ph.D. diss., University of Minnesota,

1965). Idem, "France," in *The Comparative Reception of Darwinism*, ed. Thomas F. Glick (Austin, Texas, 1974), pp. 117–63.

102. Clémence Royer, "Préface," in Charles Darwin, *De l'origine des espèces* (Paris, 1862), pp. lx-lxi.

103. Georges Pouchet, *The Plurality of the Human Race*, trans. J. C. Beavan, 2d ed. (London, 1864), p. 102; Georges Clemenceau, *American Reconstruction, 1865–1870*, ed. Fernand Baldensperger, trans. Margaret MacVeagh (New York, 1928), pp. 298–99.

104. Jules Duval, *Les colonies et la politique coloniale de la France* (Paris, 1864), p. 449; Louis Jacolliot, *Voyages aux rives du Niger* (Paris, 1879), pp. 137–39.

105. R. G. Villeneuve, *L'Afrique, ou histoire, moeurs, usages et coutumes des africains*, 4 (Paris, 1814), pp. 12–16, 168–69, 188–89.

106. G. Mollien, *Travels in Africa to the Sources of the Senegal and Gambia in 1818*, trans. from the French (London, 1820), pp. 22, 35.

107. Villeneuve, 3, pp. 111–12; Mollien, p. 78.

108. Mollien, pp. 16, 25, 32, 47, 95.

109. Ibid., pp. 16, 53.

110. Ibid., pp. 101–03; Raffenel, *Nouveau voyage*, 1, pp. 225, 333.

111. Mollien, p. 80.

112. Raffenel to L. Vélis, Kogué, May 3, 1847, copy in Senegal, III, 7, ANSOM; idem, *Voyage dans L'Afrique occidentale*, pp. 303–04.

113. Idem, *Voyage*, pp. 159, 180; idem, *Nouveau voyage*, 1, pp. 136, 209, 393.

114. Idem, *Voyage*, pp. 123–25, 144–47, 300–01.

115. E. Mage, *Relation du voyage d'exploration de MM. Mage et Quintin au Soudan occidental de 1863 à 1866* (Paris, 1867), pp. 125–26, 329; Paul Soleillet, *Voyage à Ségou, 1878–1879*, ed. G. Gravier (Paris, 1887), pp. 134–35, 307, 310.

116. Soleillet, *Voyage*, pp. 29, 308; Soleillet letter, Segu-Sikoro, October 19, 1878, *Exploration* 7 (1879):647–50.

117. Victor Largeau, "Exploration française du Sahara," *Exploration* 4 (1877):32; Charles Hertz, "Une excursion à la côte de Guinée," *Exploration* 5 (1878):392–98, 492–96.

118. Mage, p. 30; Bérenger-Féraud, *Peuplades*, pp. 402–03; Gallieni to Governor, Nango, July 3, 1880, no 4, pp. 10, 14, 15; Gallieni to Governor, no. 5, p. 29, 1G50, ANS.

119. "Vicariat apostolique de la Sénégambie," *Annales de la propagation de la foi* (henceforth *APF*) 48 (1876):124; Father Bouche, *Sept ans en Afrique occidentale* (Paris, 1885), p. 209; Desribes, *L'évangile au Dahomé et à la côte des esclaves* (Clermont-Ferrand, 1877), pp. 169–70, 489.

120. Elikia N. M'Bokolo, "La France et les français en Afrique équatoriale, le comptoir de Gabon, 1839–1874" (thesis, Ecole des hautes études en sciences sociales, 1974), p. 230.

121. Libermann, Paris, May 8, 1851, *Lettres spirituelles du R. P. Libermann* (Paris, 1945), pp. 647–48; Borghero to Planque, September 30, 1861, *APF*, 34 (1862):217; Bessieux to Libermann, *APF*, 19 (1847):104; Abbé

Borghero, Whydah, December 3, 1863, *APF*, 36 pt. 1 (1864):420; Félicité Robert de Lamennais, *Essai sur l'indifférence*, *OC*, 3 (Paris, 1836), p. 80, q. in Pierre Charles, S.J., "Les Noirs: Fils de Cham le maudit," *Nouvelle revue théologique* 55 (1928):735–36; Letter from Bouche, Porto Novo, November 1, 1867, *Annales de L'Institut d'Afrique* (May-June 1868); Laffitte, pp. 42, 106; Desribes, pp. 18, 29, 40, 119, 486; Lavigerie q. in François Renault, *Lavigerie, l'esclavage africain, et l'Europe, 1868–1892*, 1 (Paris, 1971), p. 168.

122. Q. in Richard F. Clark, *Cardinal Lavigerie and the African Slave Trade* (London, 1889), p. 155.

123. Raffenel, *Nouveau voyage*, 2, pp. 246–48; Louis Faidherbe, "Récit de la bataille d'Isly," *BSG*, 4th ser., 7 (1854):278; Dénise Bouche, "L'école française et les Musulmans au Sénégal de 1850 à 1920," *RFHOM* 61 (1974): 218–25; Louis Faidherbe, "MM. Mage et Quintin dans l'intérieur de l'Afrique," *Annales des voyages* 4 (1866):14; Mage, pp. 300, 456, 486–87; Gallieni to Governor, Saint-Louis, November 17, 1879, p. 29, Senegal III, 10 bis, ANSOM; Gallieni to Governor, Nango, October 14, 1880, no. 14, 1G50, ANS; E. Bouët-Willaumez, *Commerce et traite des noirs aux côtes occidentales d'Afrique* (Paris, 1848), p. 77.

124. Cathérine Coquery-Vidrovitch, "La Fête des coutumes au Dahomey," *Annales, économies, sociétés, civilisations* 19 (1964):698–716.

125. Suggested by John D. Hargreaves, *Prelude to the Partition of West Africa* (London, 1963). p. 17.

126. Mgr. Perraud, in letter to the faithful, *APF* 50 (1878):147.

127. Dr. Répin, "Voyage au Dahomey," *Tour du Monde* 7 (1863):65–112. This illustration was copied from an account by the Englishman Forbes in 1850.

128. L. Legault, "Chronique et faits divers," *Temps* (September 25, 1863); Vivien de Saint-Martin, "Variétés: Quelques publications récentes sur le haut Nil et l'Afrique occidentale," *Temps* (October 14, 1861).

129. Figuier, p. 510.

130. Armand Dubarry, *Voyage au Dahomey* (Paris, 1879), pp. 63, 89; Louis Jacolliot, *Voyage au pays mystérieux* (Paris, 1880), p. 20.

131. Vivien de Saint-Martin; Rabaud, "Population de l'Afrique," *Bulletin de la Société de géographie de Marseille*, reprinted in *Exploration* 8 (1879):591.

132. Mainly stressing the later period, Véronique Champion-Vincent also presents some valuable material on Dahomey for the period covered here; "L'image du Dahomey dans la presse française (1890–1895): Les sacrifices humains," *CEA* 7 (1967):27–58.

133. Gobineau letter to Tocqueville, January 15, 1856; Jean-André-Napoléon Périer, "Réprise de la discussion," *BSAP* 1 (1860):428–29; Pellarin, "Ce qu'il faut entendre par le mot civilisation," *BSAP* (July 18, 1867):456; Broca, *Phenomena of Hybridity*, p. 70; Figuier, p. 516; Clemenceau speech, *Chambre des députés, débats, Journal officiel, République française* (July 19, 1882), p. 1326.

134. This is conveniently summarized, but not unconditionally supported, by John Rex, "The Concept of Race in Sociological Theory," in *Race and Racialism*, ed. Sami Zubaida (New York, 1970), pp. 35–55.

135. This line of reasoning, suggested by ibid., p. 50, is more fully developed by Gavin Langmuir, "Prolegomena to the Study of Prejudice against Jews," a study kindly lent me prior to its publication.

9. The Lure of Empire

1. Conrad Malte-Brun, *Précis de la géographie universelle, ou description de toutes les parties du monde*, 4 (Paris, 1813), p. 440; idem, "Perspective coloniale du Sénégal," *Annales des voyages* 24 (1814):98–104, 339–41; idem, "Idées sur les colonies en général et particulièrement sur celles qui conviennent à la France," *Nouvelles annales des voyages* 16 (1822):350–55; idem, "Coup d'oeil sur la description géographique," *Nouvelles annales des voyages* 1 (1819):42–47; idem, "Variétés" (Review of Mollien's *Voyages*), *Journal des débats* (February 18, 1820):4.

2. Idem, "Coup d'oeil," p. 8; idem, "Idées sur les colonies," p. 346.

3. *BSG* 1 (1822):2.

4. Villemain, "Discours," *BSG*, 2d ser., 16 (1841); Amédée Jaubert, "Discours d'ouverture," *BSG*, 2d ser., 4 (1837):250; Berthelot, "Rapport sur les travaux de la société de géographie de Paris, *BSG*, 2d ser., 20 (1843):334; Mackau, "Discours," *BSG*, 3d ser., 3 (1845):275.

5. *BSG* 2 (1824):240.

6. Alfred Jacobs, "Les voyages d'exploration en Afrique," *RDM*, 2d ser., 5 (October 15, 1856):908.

7. For this development see Immanuel Wallerstein, *The Modern World System: Capitalist Agriculture and the Origins of the European World Economy in the Sixteenth Century*, 1 (New York, 1974).

8. Baron Las Cases, "Discours d'ouverture," *BSG*, 2d ser., 15 (1841):215.

9. L. F. Alfred Maury, "Rapport sur les travaux de la société de géographie et sur les progès des sciences géographiques pendant l'année 1858," *BSG*, 4th ser., 17 (1859):81.

10. "La Société de géographie, 1821–1921," *BSG* 26 (July-August 1921): 137–287.

11. Donald V. McKay, "Colonialism in the French Geographical Movement, 1871–1881," *Geographical Review* 33 (1943):214–32.

12. Of 1700 members in 1878, 160 belonged to the army, 139 to the navy, 105 to the diplomatic corps; membership in other government services was not given, but may have swelled the ranks of the civil servants to constitute between a third and a half of the total membership of the geographical society; James Jackson, "Statistique des membres de la société de géographie de Paris," *BSG*, 6th ser., 18 (1879):187–93.

13. Henri Malo, *A l'Enseigne de La Petite Vache: Souvenirs, gestes et figures d'explorateurs* (Paris, 1945), pp. 30–34. For instance, Brazza, Ballay, Mizon, and Crampel were frequent visitors (ibid., pp. 46, 62).

14. A phrase used in its publication, *Exploration* 5 (1878):366.

15. *Exploration* 1 (December 1876–February 1877):1–7.

16. Q. in Agnes Murphy, *The Ideology of French Imperialism, 1871–1881* (Washington, D. C., 1948), p. 25.

17. "Mémoire sur la seconde des questions proposées le Ier Frimaire, an X, par M. le Ministre de l'intérieur," Mémoires et lettres de Chambre de Commerce de Bordeaux, 1802–1839, pp. 4–6, Archives, Chamber of Commerce, Bordeaux; Alexis Albert, *Des véritables causes qui ont amené la ruine de la colonie de Saint-Domingue* (Paris, 1814), p. 3.

18. In 1814 alone several dozen essays were published on the colony; they are conveniently listed by Gabriel Debien, "Les Projets d'un ancien planteur cotonnier de Saint-Domingue (1814)," *RHC* 41 (1954):83. In 1814 the Chamber of Commerce of Le Havre suggested a military expedition, as cited by the Marseilles Chamber of Commerce, séance, August 9, 1814, Délibérations de la Chambre de commerce de Marseille, IX, 52, Archives, Marseilles Chamber of Commerce. In 1804 the Paris Chamber of Commerce, which represented far fewer colonial interests, suggested the renunciation of force; Chambre de commerce de Paris to General Humbert, March 17, 1804, Etat de correspondance, I, 73, Archives, Chamber of Commerce, Paris.

19. Séance, April 10, 1838, Délibérations de la Chambre de commerce de Marseille, XXXIV, 379, Archives Chamber of Commerce, Marseilles; Petit de Baroncourt, "Première lettre à M. le duc de Broglie et sur la ruine de notre marine et de nos colonies par suite de l'émancipation des noirs" (Paris, 1843), p. 6.

20. "Quelques détails sur l'état actuel de la colonie de Sierra Leone," *Annales des voyages* 10 (1810):328–39; Charles Coquerel, "Sur la Sociabilité de la race noire," *JSMC* 5 (1825):363.

21. "Notice sur la colonie américaine de Libéria et sur la côte d'Afrique," *BSG* 12 (1829):35; Edmé Jomard, *"Kélédor, ou histoire africaine,* recueillie et publiée par M. le baron Roger," *Revue encyclopédique* 37 (March 1828): 676; G. de Félice, "Notice sur la colonie de Libéria fondée par la société américaine de colonisation sur les côtes occidentales de l'Afrique," *Revue encyclopédique* 50 (May 1831):241–66; "De l'établissement des colonies," *JSMC*, 2d ser., 3 (1833):340–43. On the impact of Liberia, there is a fine analysis by Jean-Claude Nardin, "Le Libéria et l'opinion française (1821–1847)," *CEA* 5 (1965):96–143.

22. Alexis de Tocqueville, *Democracy in America,* trans. Henry Reeve (New York, 1899), i, p. 403.

23. Victor Schoelcher, *Esclavage des noirs* (Paris, 1833), p. 87; Minister to Governor of Senegal, July 6, 1833, 1B20, ANS.

24. *Annales de l'Institut d'Afrique* 1 (January 1841):1. Similar ideas are expressed in *Annales de l'Institut d'Afrique* 2 (July 1842):49–51; "Note sur la civilisation de l'Afrique," *Annales de l'Institut d'Afrique* 10 (July-August 1850):49–52.

25. Elikia N. M'Bokolo, "La France et les français en Afrique équatoriale: Le comptoir de Gabon, 1839–1874" (thesis, Ecole des hautes études en sciences sociales, 1974), pp. 218–19, 221, 254.

26. Abbé P. D. Boilat, *Esquisses sénégalaises* (Paris, 1853), pp. 474–75; V. Verneuil to President of Republic, April 25, 1850, Missions, I, ANSOM, published as idem, "Mémoire explicatif et statuts d'une société ayant pour but de christianiser et de faire produire l'Afrique centrale" (Paris, 1850), pp. 5–6, 11–20.

27. Anne Raffenel, *Voyage dans l'Afrique occidentale exécuté en 1843 et 1844* (Paris, 1846), p. 359; Bessieux to Libermann, Gabon, October 15, 1845, APF 19 (1847):110–11.

28. Emile Leguay, *Notice sur l'oeuvre de rachat des esclaves* (Paris, 1847); *Notice sur la vie de la jeune soeur négresse Bakita Macca décédée au monastère de la visitation de Montélimar (Drôme)* (Riom, 1879); Mgr. Gaume, *Suéma ou la petite esclave africaine enterrée vivante* (Paris, 1870).

29. François Renault, *Lavigerie, l'esclavage africain, et l'Europe, 1868–1892,* 1 (Paris, 1971), pp. 140–41, 157, 206.

30. Paul Merruau, "Le Dahomey et le roi Guezo," *RDM*, n.s., 12 (October-December 1851):1041; statement by deputy Bourner, December 30, 1850, Commission des comptoirs, Senegal, XIII, 3a, ANSOM; Minister to Penaud, commandant des stations des côtes occidentales d'Afrique, May 23, 1850, Senegal, XIII, 2 ANSOM.

31. Anne Raffenel, "Esclavage chez les africains de la Haute Sénégambie," *Annales de l'Institut d'Afrique* 7 (July-August 1847):55–56; Alfred Michiels, *Le capitaine Firmin, ou la vie des nègres en Afrique* (Paris, 1853), p. 81; Eugène Mage, speech, August 26, 1867, *Special Report of the Antislavery Conference held in Paris on the Twenty-Sixth and Twenty-Seventh August, 1867* (London, n.d.), pp. 17–19.

32. *Journal des sciences et morales politiques* (December 31, 1831), q. in Thomas A. Cassilly, "The Anticolonial Tradition in France: The Eighteenth Century to the Fifth Republic" (Ph.D. diss., Columbia University, 1972), p. 312.

33. Ibid., pp. 300, 302.

34. Fourier to Count Amédée de Pastoret, Paris, February 6, 1823, and Fourier to Marquis de Laplace, Paris, February 6, 1823, Archives of the Société de géographie (henceforth ASG), 6; Marcel Emérit, "L'Idée de colonisation dans les socialismes français," *L'Age nouveau,* no. 24 (1948):104.

35. Q. in Cassilly, pp. 318–21; A. Loubère, "Les idées de Louis Blanc sur le nationalisme, le colonialisme et la guerre," *Revue d'histoire moderne et contemporaine* 5 (1957):50–52; Proudhon q. in Cassilly, pp. 334–35.

36. Charles Guillain, *Documents sur l'histoire, la géographie et le commerce de l'Afrique orientale,* 1 (Paris, 1856), pp. xxv, xxix, q. in Marcel Emerit, "Les Explorations Saint-Simoniens en Afrique orientale et sur la route des Indes," *Revue africaine* 87 (1943):115. In a recent article the general contribution of Saint-Simonianism to imperialism was traced by Marcel Emerit, "Diplomates et explorateurs Saint-simoniens," *Revue d'histoire moderne et contemporaine* 22 (July-September 1975): 397–415.

37. De Lesseps, cited in Henry Bionne, "La civilisation en Afrique," *Exploration* 7 (1879):225.

38. Jules Duval, *Les colonies et la politique coloniale de la France* (Paris, 1864), pp. 23, 445.

39. Paul Leroy-Beaulieu, *De la colonisation chez les peuples modernes* (Paris, 1874), p. 356; the same phrase appears in his journal, *Economiste* (August 15, 1874), q. in Dan Warshaw, "Paul Leroy-Beaulieu, Bourgeois Ideologist: A Study of the Social, Intellectual and Economic Sources of Late Nineteenth Century Imperialism" (Ph.D. diss., University of Rochester, 1966), p. 139.

40. *Journal des débats* (November 5, 1872; June 5, 1873), q. in Murphy, pp. 140, 143.

41. *Journal des débats* (November 17, 1875; January 26, 1879), q. in Murphy, pp. 149, 154.

42. René Valet, *L'Afrique du nord devant le parlement au XIXe siècle* (Algiers, 1924), pp. 101–02.

43. Jean-Baptiste Say, *Traité*, 5th ed., 2 (Paris, 1826), pp. 192–93, q. in Cassilly, p. 296.

44. Valet, pp. 88–99; Tocqueville, in letter to Lieber, q. in Benedict Gaston Songy, "Alexis de Tocqueville and Slavery: Judgments and Predictions" (Ph.D. diss., St. Louis University, 1969), p. 144.

45. Victor Schoelcher comment appears in *Bulletin de la Société ethnologique de Paris* (1847):163–64. Earlier, Schoelcher had thought colonization could be done by peaceful means; *Abolition de l'esclavage: Examen critique du préjugé contre la couleur des Africains et des sang-mêlés* (Paris, 1840), p. 76. Schoelcher speech in Senate, April 1, 1879, reprinted in *Polémique coloniale, 1871–1881*, 1 (Paris, 1882), p. 28; *Les Colonies* (January 3, 1883), reprinted in *Polémique coloniale*, 2 (Paris, 1886), p. 119.

46. R. A. Lochore, *History of the Idea of Civilization in France (1830–1870)* (Bonn, 1935), pp. 53–54.

47. *Evénement* (March 16, 1849), q. in Cassilly, p. 465. Equally aggressive was his speech in front of a group of Parisian businessmen in 1879, q. in Sanford Elwitt, *The Making of the Third Republic, Class and Politics in France, 1868–1884* (Baton Rouge, 1975), p. 275. "Compagnie coloniale de l'Afrique française–Statuts provisoires, Paris, 1882–Président d'honneur, Victor Hugo," ASG, Carton II, 37.

48. Lamartine speech of 1839, q. in Cassilly, p. 446.

49. *Le Siècle* (September 12, 1859), q. in Cassilly, p. 514.

50. *République française* (February 26, 1881). For the general position of the *République française*, see William B. Cohen, "Gambettists and Colonial Expansion before 1881: The *République française*," *French Colonial Studies* 1 (Spring 1977):54–64.

51. *Le Temps* (July 3, 1871).

52. For example, Paul Soleillet, *L'avenir de la France en Afrique* (Paris, 1876), p. iv.

53. Studying colonial ideas in the late 1860s, André Masson concluded that indeed 1870 did not constitute a particular break in French imperialist thought; "L'Opinion française et les problèmes coloniaux à la fin du second Empire," *RFHOM* 49 (1962):366–437.

54. H. Brunschwig, *L'avènement de l'Afrique noire* (Paris, 1963), pp. 54–58; Henri Brunschwig, "Anglophobia and French African Policy," in *France and Britain in Africa,* ed. Prosser Gifford and W. R. Louis (New Haven, 1971), pp. 3–29.

55. L. Jardin, "Les Archives de la propagation de la foi de Paris et de Lyon," *Bulletin des séances, Académie royale des sciences d'outre-mer* (Brussels) (1969):240.

56. *APF* 9 (1836):430.

57. *APF* 11 (1838):365; *APF* 31 (1859):264; *APF* 23 (1851):20–21.

58. André Rétif, "Les évêques français et les missions," *Etudes,* no. 295 (1957):362–65; M. H. Vicaire, "Un grand débat: Le catholicisme français au XIXe siècle," *Annales, économies, sociétés, et civilisations,* n.s., 4 (July-September 1949):317.

59. *APF* 8 (1835):435–36.

60. Q. in Richard F. Clarke, *Cardinal Lavigerie and the African Slave Trade* (London, 1889), p. 33; Father Desribes *L'évangile au Dahomey et à la côte des esclaves* (Clermont-Ferrand, 1877), p. 18.

61. Letters of November 19, 1847, and March 28, 1847, q. in Paule Brasseur, "A la recherche d'un absolu missionnaire: Mgr. Truffet, vicaire apostolique des Deux Guinées (1812–1847)," *CEA* 15:263–64, fn. 22.

62. Truffet letter, July 7, 1847, q. in Brasseur, p. 271. A similar report on Gabon is Father Bessieux, June 29, 1845, *APF* 19 (1847):105; on Senegambia, Father Kobès, "Mission de la Guinée," *Annales d'Afrique* 14 (November-December, 1854):82.

63. Letter of Libermann to l'Institut d'Afrique, *Annales de l'Institut d'Afrique* 6 (October 1846):76–77.

64. Arlabosse, "Observations et projet de civilisation pour le Sénégal," Saint-Louis, July 28, 1846, Senegal XIII, 17 ANSOM. Arlabosse was given 9000 francs for his scheme, but died before he could try it out; Georges Hardy, *La mise en valeur du Sénégal* (Paris, 1921), p. 287. "Missions d'Afrique confiées à la congrégation du Saint-Esprit et de l'immaculé coeur de Marie," *APF* 36 (1864):110; "Vicariat apostolique de la Sénégambie," *APF* 38 (1866):33.

65. Georges Goyau, *La France missionnaire,* 2 (Paris, 1948), pp. 214–15.

66. Abbé Pierre Paul Castelli, *De l'esclave en général et de l'émancipation des noirs* (Paris, 1844), p. 3.

67. Hubert Deschamps, "Quinze ans de Gabon: Les débuts de l'établissement français, 1839–1853," *RFHOM* (1963):318; (1965):102–04. A fine study treating the general relationship of the missionaries and the colonial administration is Paule Brasseur, "Missions catholiques et administration française sur la côte d'Afrique de 1815 à 1870," *RFHOM* 62 (1975):415–46; I think, however, the article unduly minimizes the extent to which the missionaries were interested in the spread of French power.

68. Pastoral letter of Mgr. Dupanloup, Bishop of Orléans, *APF* 32 (1860):64–65.

69. A. Planque to Minister of Marine, July 13, 1862, October 28, 1862, Afrique, IV, 9d, ANSOM.

70. Borghero to Planque, December 3, 1863, *APF* 36, pt. 2 (1865): 104–06.

71. Abbé J. Laffitte, *Pays des nègres* (Paris, 1876), p. 103.

72. *APF* 38 (1866):238.

73. Charles A. Perkins, "French Catholic Opinion and Imperial Expansion, 1880–1886" (Ph.D. diss., Harvard University, 1964).

74. "Voyage des découvertes dans l'intérieur de l'Afrique," *Journal des missions évangeliques* 7 (1832):256; "Décision du comité relatif au départ de trois frères pour le sud de l'Afrique," *Journal des missions évangeliques* 7 (1832):162–63; "Afrique occidentale," *Journal des missions évangeliques* 16 (1841):256.

75. De Préo, *Les Youlofi: Histoire d'un prêtre et d'un militaire français* (Lille, 1842), p. 228.

76. Léon Guérin, *Le Tour du monde ou les mille et une merveilles des voyages: Voyages des deux enfants avec leur père sur les côtes occidentales et orientales de l'Afrique* (Paris, 1851), p. 60; A. E. de Saintes, *Voyages du petit André en Afrique* (Paris, 1852), p. 84.

77. Jules Verne, *Five Weeks in a Balloon, Works,* trans. Charles F. Horne, 1 (New York, 1911), pp. 255–56.

78. Louis Jacolliot, *Voyage au pays mystérieux* (Paris, 1880), pp. 118–21.

79. Armand Dubarry, *Voyage au Dahomey* (Paris, 1879).

80. Hubert Lyautey, *Lettres du Tonkin et Madagascar,* 1 (Paris, 1920), p. 224, q. in Martine Astier Loutfi, *Littérature et colonialisme: L'expansion coloniale vue dans la littérature romanesque française, 1871–1914* (Paris, 1971), p. 53.

81. The continued weakness of the proimperial groups even after the scramble for empire was begun is shown in C. M. Andrews and A. S. Kanya-Forstner, "The French Colonial Party: Its Composition, Aims and Influence, 1885–1914," *Historical Journal* 14 (1971):99–128.

82. The French expansion in the Senegambia in the nineteenth century can be followed in Georges Hardy, *La mise en valeur du Sénégal* (Paris, 1921); Leland C. Barrows, "General Faidherbe, the Maurel and Prom Company, and French Expansion in Senegal" (Ph.D. diss., University of California, Los Angeles, 1974). The push into the Western Sudan is detailed in William B. Cohen, "Imperial Mirage: The Western Sudan in French Thought and Action," *Journal of the Historical Society of Nigeria* 7 (December 1974):417–45. The contacts down the coast are treated in Bernard Schnapper, *La politique et le commerce français dans le golfe de Guinée de 1830 à 1871* (Paris, 1961).

Afterword

1. Typical are those expressed by the explorer (Claudius Madrolle, *En Guinée* [Paris, 1895], p. 70), the military (Dr. Binet, "Observations sur les Déhoméens," *BSAP* [July 5, 1900]:249), the administrator (Alexandre d'Albeca, *Les établissements français du golfe de Bénin* [Paris, 1889], pp. 21, 87), and the missionary (J. Sand, *L'enfant en Afrique* [Paris, n.d. (1890s)], pp. 5, 11).

2. Jean Bayol, *Les Dahoméens au champs de Mars, moeurs et coutumes, exposition d'ethnographie coloniale* (Paris, n.d. [1892]), p. 21; William Howard Schneider, "The Image of West Africa in Popular French Culture, 1870–1900," (Ph.D. diss., University of Pennsylvania, 1976), pp. 149–55.

3. Edmond Ferry, *La France en Afrique* (Paris, 1905), p. 223.

4. Roger Villamur and Léon Richard, *Notre colonie de la Côte d'Ivoire* (Paris, 1903), p. 253.

5. His popularizing works are conveniently collected and translated by F. Fligelman, *The Negroes in Africa, History and Culture* (Port Washington, N. Y., 1931; reissued 1968).

6. François Aupiais, "Aspirations religieuses des non-civilisés," *Les missions catholiques et l'oeuvre de civilisation-conférences données à l'Institut Catholique de Paris, 1927–1928* (Paris, 1929), p. 59.

7. Manuela Semidei, "De l'empire à la décolonisation à travers les manuels scolaires français," *Revue française de science politique* 16 (February 1966):63–64.

8. Léon Fanoudh-Siefer, *Le mythe du nègre et de l'Afrique noire dans la littérature française* (Paris, 1968), pp. 113–85. The most complete survey is Ada Martinkus-Zemp, *Le blanc et le noir: Essai d'une description de la vision du Noir par le blanc dans la littérature française de l'entre-deux guerres* (Paris, 1975). Pierre Leprohon, *L'Exotisme et le cinéma* (Paris, 1945), p. 208.

9. Clemenceau, cited in Shelby Cullom Davis, *Reservoirs of Men: A History of the Black Troops in French West Africa* (Geneva, 1934), p. 167.

10. Robert Goldwater, "L'expérience de l'art nègre," *1er Festival mondial des arts nègres, Dakar, 1–24 avril, 1966* (Paris, 1967), pp. 347–61; E. Okechukwu Odita, "African Art: The Concept in European Literature," *Journal of Black Studies* 8 (December 1977):189–204; Robert Pageard, *Littérature négro-africaine* (Paris, 1966), pp. 11, 16–17.

11. Q. in Roi Ottley, *No Green Pastures* (New York, 1951), p. 3.

12. Robert Delerm, "Immigration noire en France, perspectives, conséquences," *Hommes et migrations* (Paris, 1967), p. 75; Banine, *La France étrangère* (Paris, 1968).

13. Institut français d'opinion publique, *La Coopération entre la France et les états africains et malgache* (October-December 1962), p. 36; *Nouvel observateur* (November 1, 1967).

14. Ministère de la coopération, *Attitudes et opinions des français sur l'Afrique et la coopération franco-africaine, enquête clinique* (May-November 1962), pp. 3, 20.

15. Ottley, p. 71.

16. Some among the many incidents related in Jean Benoit, "On ne sert plus les noirs," *Le Monde* (January 6, 1972). Anne-Marguerite Nouillac, *La peur de l'autre* (Paris, 1972), pp. 148–50.

17. Wilmot Alfred Fraser, "Lettre de Paris," *L'Express* (January 23, 1964).

18. Jeannine Verdès-Leroux, "Les Nord africains dans l'opinion," in *Racisme et société*, ed. Patrice Comarmond and Claude Duchet (Paris, 1969), p. 94.

19. *Nouvel observateur* (November 1, 1967). A survey of white female attitudes toward sexual relations with blacks showed 70 percent favorable, 6 percent opposed, and 24 percent with no opinion. The survey was not based upon a stratified sample, and the responses may have been affected by the color of the interviewer, a young African student in sociology; Bengono Ewondo, *La blanche et le noir africain,* 1 (Paris, 1970), p. 25.

20. F. N. Bernardi et al., *Les dossiers noirs du racisme dans le midi de la France* (Paris, 1976).

21. Paul Lendvai, *Anti-Semitism without Jews: Communist Eastern Europe* (New York, 1971).

22. Jean Lacouture, "Les français sont-ils racistes?" *Le Monde* (March 20–22, 1970).

23. François Denantes, "Un problème mal posé: L'immigration," *Esprit* (December 1973):739–52.

24. Q. in Fraser.

25. That is the position on the issue that *Hommes et migrations* (1967) entitled "Approches du problème de la migration noire en France." It is implicit in the stress by the French press on what is called the "threshold of tolerance" or the maximum number of blacks who can be allowed into France without creating racial confrontation; Georges Valance, "Immigrés, les bons et les mauvais," *L'Express* (January 3–9, 1972):20; Pierre Viansson-Ponté, "Racistes, les français?" *Le Monde* (June 19, 1972).

26. Valance, p. 21.

Index

353

WILLIAM B. COHEN (1941–2002) was Professor and former Chair of the Department of History at Indiana University. His books include *Rulers of Empire: The French Colonial Service in Africa* and *Urban Government and the Rise of the French City: Five Municipalities in the Nineteenth Century.* At the time of his death he was preparing a book entitled "The Algerian War and French Memory, 1962–2002."

JAMES D. LE SUEUR is Associate Professor of History at the University of Nebraska–Lincoln. He is author of *Uncivil War: Intellectuals and Identity Politics during the Decolonization of Algeria* and editor of *The Decolonization Reader.* He and William B. Cohen co-edited a special issue of the journal *Historical Reflections* entitled "France and Algeria: From Colonial Conflict to Postcolonial Memory."